POLITICAL MAN

SEYMOUR MARTIN LIPSET, Professor of Sociology and Director of the Institute of International Studies at the University of California in Berkeley, received his B.S. from City College in New York and his Ph.D. from Columbia University. He has been a lecturer and visiting professor at various schools and institutions throughout the world. His books include *Agrarian Socialism; Class, Status and Power* (edited with Reinhard Bendix), *Union Democracy* (with Martin Trow and James S. Coleman, Anchor 296); *Social Mobility in Industrial Society* (with Reinhard Bendix). He has edited Harriet Martineau's *Society in America* (Anchor 302); *Culture and Social Character* (with Leo Lowenthal); *Sociology: The Progress of a Decade* (with Neil Smelser); and *Labor and Trade Unionism* (with Walter Galenson). He has recently completed a monographic essay, *The United States as a New Nation* which examines parallels in problems and reactions of the early United States and contemporary New States.

POLITICAL MAN

The Social Bases of Politics

BY

SEYMOUR MARTIN LIPSET

ANCHOR BOOKS
DOUBLEDAY & COMPANY, INC.
GARDEN CITY, NEW YORK

Political Man was originally published in a hardbound edition by Doubleday & Company, Inc. in 1960.

Anchor Books edition: 1963

To David, Daniel, and Carola,
that they may grow up in a more democratic
and, therefore, more peaceful world.

Aristotle on *Political Man* and the Conditions
of the Democratic Order

"Man is by nature a political animal." (1129)

"A social instinct is implanted in all men by nature, and yet he who first founded the state was the greatest of benefactors. For man, when perfected, is the best of animals, but when separated from law and justice, he is the worst of all; since armed injustice is the most dangerous, and he is equipped at birth with arms, meant to be used by intelligence and virtue, which he may use for the worst ends. Wherefore, if he have not virtue, he is the most unholy and the most savage of animals, and the most full of lust and gluttony. But justice is the bond of men in states, for the administration of justice, which is the determination of what is just, is the principle of order in political society." (1130)

"Now any member of the assembly, taken separately, is certainly inferior to the wise man. But the state is made up of many individuals. And as a feast to which all the guests contribute is better than a banquet furnished by a single man, so a multitude is a better judge of many things than any one individual. Again, the many are more incorruptible than the few; they are like the greater quantity of water which is less easily corrupted than a little." (1200)

"Thus it is manifest that the best political community is formed by citizens of the middle class, and that those states are likely to be well administered, in which the middle class is large. . . . Great then is the good fortune of a state in which the citizens have a moderate and sufficient property; for where some possess much, and the others nothing, there may arise an extreme democracy, or a pure oligarchy; or a tyranny may develop out of either extreme—either out of the most rampant democracy, or out of an oligarchy; but it is not so likely to arise out of the middle constitutions and those akin to them. . . . And democracies are safer and more permanent than oligarchies, because they have a middle class which is more numerous and has a greater share in government; for when there is no middle class, and the poor greatly exceed in number, troubles arise, and the state soon comes to an end." (1221–1222)

". . . in democracies which are subject to the law the best citizens hold the first place, and there are no demagogues; but where the laws are not supreme, there demogogues spring up. For the people become a monarch, and is many in one; and the many have the power in their hands, not as individuals, but collectively. . . . At all events this sort of democracy, which is now a monarch, and no longer under the control of law, seeks to exercise monarchical sway, and grows into a despot; the flatterer is held in high honor." (1212)

"The reason why there are many forms of government is that every state contains many elements. In the first place we see that all states are made up of families, and in the multitude of citizens there must be some rich and some poor, and some in a middle condition. . . . Of the common people, some are husbandmen, and some traders, and some artisans. There are also among the notables differences of wealth and property. . . . Besides differences of wealth there are also differences of rank and merit. . . . It is evident then that there must be many forms of government, differing in kind, since the parts of which they are composed differ from each other in kind. For a constitution is an organization of offices, which all the citizens distribute among themselves, according to the power which different classes possess, for example the rich or the poor, or according to some principle of equality which includes both." (1208)

"The universal and chief cause of . . . revolutionary feeling . . . [is] the desire of equality, when men think that they are equal to others who have more than themselves; or again the desire of inequality and superiority, when conceiving themselves to be superior they think that they have not more but the same or less than their inferiors. . . . Now in oligarchies the masses make revolution under the idea they are unjustly treated, because as I said before, they are equals, and have not an equal share, and in democracies the notables revolt, because they are not equals, and yet have only an equal share." (1236–1237)

Citations from "Politica" translated by Benjamin Jowett in *The Basic Works of Aristotle*, edited by Richard McKeon (New York: Random House, 1941).

Foreword

EVER SINCE the term sociology was first applied to the systematic study of social relationships, the analysis of political processes and institutions has been one of its most important concerns. No sociologist can conceive of a study of society that does not include the political system as a major part of the analysis. And many political scientists, particularly in recent years, have argued, sometimes with others in their own field, that it is impossible to study political processes except as special cases of more general sociological and psychological relationships. The increasing collaboration, as well as the acceptance of common concepts and methods, among those studying political behavior within the fields of political science, sociology, psychology, and anthropology (each of the latter three now having a recognized sub-discipline dealing with politics) is new evidence of the basic unity of the social sciences. The study of man in society cannot fruitfully be compartmentalized according to substantive concerns.

This book is intended for a number of audiences: people generally interested in politics, academic analysts, students, and practitioners. Some readers will be predominantly concerned with the causes and consequences of political behavior; others, with the theoretical and methodological problems of the academic discipline. I trust that both groups will be satisfied by the package presented here: some of the methodological discussions have been placed in appendixes to chapters (see Chapters 2 and 12), so that those less interested in such matters may skip them.

The main problem with which this book deals is democracy as a characteristic of social systems. The principal topics discussed are the conditions necessary for democracy in societies and organizations; the factors which affect men's participation in politics, particularly their behavior as voters; and the sources of support for values and movements which sustain or threaten democratic institutions.

These studies in the sociology of politics are not intended primarily as a collection of essays which happen to be written by the same person. Rather, I tried to select from my various articles those which best illustrate the contribution the sociologist can make to an understanding of democratic political systems. In so doing, it became clear that a book prepared solely from already existing articles would create difficulties for the reader because it would omit many problems and issues which should logically be discussed. I have attempted to remedy this deficiency by writing a number of essays especially for this volume and by extensively rewriting others. By these revisions, I have tried to create an integrated book.

Since the book illustrates my basic intellectual concerns and personal values more fully than my earlier publications, I think it appropriate to acknowledge here some of my major debts. These include above all three of my teachers and former colleagues at Columbia University, Paul Lazarsfeld, Robert Lynd, and Robert Merton. To Robert Lynd I owe, among many other things, sustained reinforcement of my belief that social science research must be socially significant. Robert Merton made me and many others understand the real power of sociological concepts as tools of analysis and the exciting intellectual frontiers of sociology. From Paul Lazarsfeld, the most brilliant logician in the social sciences, I learned the difference between analysis and illustration, a difference so basic and important that it would take many books to develop, books which he has fortunately been writing or stimulating. I would also like to mention others of my friends who at different times have played no less important roles in stimulating my concerns. I, perhaps, owe more intellectually to Juan Linz, with whom I have worked for a number of years, than to any other individual. Reinhard Bendix has given me sage advice on many topics, not the least of which has been how to put this book together. My colleague and former student Robert Alford helped greatly in revising the essays. Anne Freedgood of Doubleday has added much to their logic and style. Others to whom I am indebted include Daniel Bell, James S. Coleman, Robert Dahl, Nathan Glazer, Richard Hofstadter, Herbert Hyman, Alex Inkeles, William Kornhauser, Leo Lowenthal, Daniel Miller, Philip Selznick, Martin Trow, and David Truman.

Three chapters, 6, 7, and 8, deserve special mention, since they were originally written as part of a collaborative effort with Paul Lazarsfeld, Allen Barton, and Juan Linz of the Department of Sociology at Columbia University, co-authors with me of "The Psychology of Voting," in *Handbook of Social Psychology*, Gardner Lindzey, editor, Vol. II (Cambridge: Addison-Wesley, 1954). I have, however, made major changes in these materials, both deleting some sections and adding others. Since my co-authors were not involved in these decisions, I do not feel it proper to ask them to share the responsibility of decisions which reflect my interests and the needs of this book, and not their own. It is important to note, however, that most of the theoretical framework, as well as the gathering of data for these chapters, is a result of this collaboration.

Many of the empirical generalizations reported here are based on analysis of public opinion surveys made by research organizations in different countries. A number of such agencies have co-operated with my interests by making available to me duplicate sets of IBM cards from their studies, and by giving me tabulations of unpublished data from their files. I would like to gratefully acknowledge such assistance. Among the individuals and agencies which have co-operated are Professor Erik Allardt of the University of Helsinki and the Finnish Gallup Poll; Professor P. Luzzatto Fegiz and the Institute "DOXA" at Milan, Italy; Dr. Alain Girard and the French National Institute for the Study of Demography; Jean Stoetzel and Louis Angelby of the French Institute of Public Opinion Research; Roy Morgan of the Australian Public Opinion Polls; Dr. Erich Reigrotzki and UNESCO

Research Institute of Cologne, Germany; Dr. Stein Rokkan and the Institute of Social Research at the University of Oslo, Norway; Professor Ithiel de Sola Pool of the Center for International Studies at the Massachusetts Institute of Technology; and Dr. Jan Stapel of the Netherlands Institute of Public Opinion Research.

Only a small part of the available materials is reported here. Much more is contained in S. M. Lipset and Juan Linz, *The Social Bases of Diversity in Western Democracy* (Stanford: Center for Advanced Study in the Behavioral Sciences, 1956, mimeographed). A revised version of that manuscript will deal extensively with comparative political behavior.

Earlier drafts of much of the work presented here appeared in various journals and collections of essays. I am grateful to their publishers and editors for their permission to reprint or rework these articles for this book. The relevant articles are:

"Political Sociology," in *Sociology Today*, Robert K. Merton, Leonard Broom, and Leonard Cottrell, eds. (New York: Basic Books, 1959), pp. 81–114.

"Some Social Requisites of Democracy: Economic Development and Political Legitimacy," *American Political Science Review*, 53 (1959), pp. 69–105.

"American Intellectuals: Their Politics and Status," *Daedalus*, 88 (Summer 1959), pp. 460–86.

"Democracy and Working-Class Authoritarianism," *American Sociological Review*, 24 (1959), pp. 482–502.

"Socialism—Left and Right—East and West," *Confluence*, 7 (Summer 1958), pp. 173–92.

"The American Voter," *Encounter*, 7 (August 1956), pp. 55–62.

"The State of Democratic Politics," *Canadian Forum*, 35 (1955) 170–71.

(With Paul F. Lazarsfeld, Allen Barton, and Juan Linz) "The Psychology of Voting: An Analysis of Political Behavior," in *Handbook of Social Psychology*, G. Lindzey, ed., Vol. II (Cambridge: Addison-Wesley, 1954), pp. 1124–70.

"The Political Process in Trade Unions: A Theoretical Statement," in *Freedom and Control in Modern Society*,

Morroe Berger, Charles Page, and Theodore Abel, eds. (New York: D. Van Nostrand Co., 1954), pp. 82–124.

Two research organizations of which I have been a member have greatly facilitated my research work by providing research and clerical assistance, and a stimulating research environment: in the past, the Bureau of Applied Social Research of Columbia University, directed while I was at Columbia by Professor Charles Y. Glock (now director of the Survey Research Center of the University of California), and, more recently, the Institute of Industrial Relations of the University of California at Berkeley, administered by Professor Arthur Ross, director, and Dr. Margaret Gordon, associate director. The former organization has been particularly interested in the problem of codifying theory and method in the social sciences, and much of the work reported in Chapters 1, 6, 7, 8, and 9 was done under its aegis with the support of a grant from the Behavioral Sciences Division of the Ford Foundation for an inventory of research in the field of political behavior.[1] (This grant was made to an interdisciplinary group which included Richard Hofstadter, Herbert Hyman, and David Truman, with myself as chairman.)

The Berkeley Institute of Industrial Relations has been concerned with, among other things, the impact of industrialization and differing stratification systems on the state of the labor movement, class tensions, and the political behavior of occupational strata in different countries. Much of the work underlying the original form of publication of the remaining chapters was done with its sponsorship, and with the support of additional grants from the Behavioral Sciences Division of the Ford Foundation, and the Committee on Comparative Politics of the Social Science Research Council. The year which I spent as a Fellow of the Center for Advanced Study in the Behavioral Sciences in 1955–56, free from

[1] Besides my own writings, other publications of this inventory are Herbert Hyman, *Political Socialization* (Glencoe: The Free Press, 1959) and William Kornhauser, *The Politics of Mass Society* (Glencoe: The Free Press, 1959).

all responsibilities except my own concerns, must also be gratefully acknowledged.

Among those who have been my research assistants on projects, the results of which are partially reported in this book are Robert Blauner, Amitai Etzioni, Rena Katznelson, and Carlos Kruytbosch.

Seymour Martin Lipset

Berkeley, California
May 15, 1959

Contents

PART IV. THE POLITICS OF PRIVATE
GOVERNMENT: A CASE STUDY

A PERSONAL POSTSCRIPT

Introduction to the Anchor Edition

THE PROCESS of writing is inevitably one of selection. When writing, an author, consciously or not, has some audience in mind. And he does not want to bore his readers by stating facts or concepts that are obvious. The height of intellectual achievement is to be original. This is as true in the social sciences as in the arts or the natural sciences. The social scientist or the political analyst, however, has a special problem: what may be well known to many of his prospective readers will be unknown to others. And his writings are inevitably and necessarily subject to criticism for having ignored matters of which he is well aware, and on which he may, in fact, have written in other places.

This general problem, inherent in any work by an academic dealing with problems of interest to nonspecialists, is particularly great in a sociological work which addresses itself to contemporary political issues. In reviewing this book, a number of politically involved critics have taken me to task for my presumed conservatism.[1] The evidence for my alleged conservatism rests primarily, in the eyes of the leftist reviewers, in my failure to address myself to the analysis of economic power or the punitive character of inequality. A number of these analysts, particularly in Europe, chose to comment on *Political Man* as an example not only of my conservative bias, but of the way in which the basic theoretical orientation and methodology of American political

[1] However, William Henry Chamberlain writing in the *Wall Street Journal* and Samuel Lubell in his review in the *New York Times Book Review* noted my presumed liberal or New Deal leanings with regret.

sociology leads to conservative conclusions, "whatever is, is right"—in this case Western political democracy which is the principal subject of this book.

It may surprise such readers to learn that Talcott Parsons, America's foremost sociological theorist, in reviewing *Political Man*, described it as an example of a nondogmatic *Marxist* approach. I doubt that many avowed Marxists would be willing to count me among their numbers. The division of intellectual categories by politically active Marxists is very different from what it is within sociology. What Parsons believes, of course, is that sociological analysis may be divided between those who place a primary stress on values as the key source of action, and those who emphasize the significance of interests. The former orientation, stemming from Max Weber, is pitted against the latter, which flows from Karl Marx. As Parsons has put writing of sociology in general, "it is a striking fact that *general* orientations in this field have, in recent years, tended increasingly to polarize between a nondogmatic and nonpolitical 'Marxian' position and one which in the broadest sense may be called one or another version of the theory of action."[2]

Parsons is not unique in finding major Marxist influences in American sociology. Lewis Coser, the sociologist editor of the socialist magazine, *Dissent*, has written: "Marxian modes of analysis, certain strands of Marxist doctrine and of Marxist method, have become an enduring component of . . . American social science."[3] And Lewis Feuer has stated in his introduction to an anthology of the writings of Marx and Engels: "Most contemporary political sociology consists of glosses to Marx."[4] The fact that American scholars who know

[2] Talcott Parsons, "The Point of View of the Author," in Max Black, ed., *The Social Theories of Talcott Parsons* (Englewood Cliffs: Prentice-Hall, 1961), p. 362.

[3] Lewis A. Coser, "USA: Marxists at Bay," in Leopold Labenz, ed., *Revisionism: Essays on the History of Marxist Ideas* (New York: Frederick A. Praeger, 1962), p. 362.

[4] Lewis S. Feuer, "Introduction," Marx and Engels. *Basic Writings on Politics and Philosophy* (Garden City: Doubleday Anchor Books, 1959), p. xxi.

their Marx recognize major Marxist elements within American sociology, while many European and some American radicals see the same area of intellectual inquiry as reflecting the influence of pragmatism or idealism characteristic of a conservative bourgeois civilization, is but another indicator of the great differences political beliefs have on intellectual judgments. The same ideas, the same interpretations, the same "facts," if you will, mean different things to men who live under varying social conditions or adhere to different ideologies. In reading reviews of *Political Man*, I have been unable at times to believe that they were all about the same book, or to recognize views credited to me as my own. A recent review which discussed other critiques of the book pointed to the fact that "the reviews of *Political Man* in the American magazines of liberal opinion (such as the *New Republic* and the *Nation*) were generally favorable, and spoke approvingly of the way Lipset destroyed 'outworn slogans' and the 'myths' of liberalism. The British liberal [left socialist] reviewers in the *New Statesman* and the *Guardian* were—predictably—far more hostile, accusing the author in effect of complacency, indifference, an opposition to democracy, and a host of other sins normally imputed to 'bourgeois intellectuals.' "[5]

I should state at the outset that I consider myself a man of the left, but, I must add that I think of the United States as a nation in which *leftist values* predominate. And since readers have disagreed concerning the exact character of my politics, it may be worthwhile to describe my attitudes briefly. Essentially they consist of the belief that while a system of stratification (differences in the distribution of status, income, and power) is inherent in the nature of any complex

[5] James Q. Wilson, review of *Political Man*, *American Journal of Sociology*, 67 (March 1962), p. 589. It should be noted, however, that the *New Statesman* and *Guardian* reviews were written by left-wing socialist critics of Hugh Gaitskell, the leader of the Labor Party. The reviews which appeared in the pro-Gaitskell magazine *Socialist Commentary*, in the official Labor Party newspaper, the *Daily Herald*, in *Encounter* (by Gaitskell's friend, C. A. R. Crosland, Labor M.P.) in the *Spectator* (by Gary Runciman), and in *The Listener* (by Denis Brogan) were—predictably—extremely friendly.

social system, such inequality is basically punitive and discriminatory. The lower strata in all societies are punished psychically and often physically for being in an inferior position. They and their children have less of an opportunity to achieve the advantages available in the society than those of equal ability who enter the system at a higher class level. Stratification advantages or disadvantages cumulate in a self-supporting cycle. And since I feel that inequality though inevitable is *immoral*, I support all measures that would serve to reduce its extent, or that would bring the utopian goals of "equality of status and of opportunity" closer to reality.

My commitment to democracy as a political system does not rest solely on the belief that free debate and institutionalized conflict among opposing interest groups are the best way for society to progress intellectually as well as materially, but also on the assumption that only a politically democratic society can reduce the pressures endemic in social systems to increase the punitive and discriminatory aspects of stratification. I believe with Marx that all privileged classes seek to maintain and *enhance* their advantages against the desire of the underprivileged to reduce them. I agree with Plato that the family necessarily fosters inequality, that parents and others tied by the affective values basic to kinship must seek to give to their children and others to whom they are tied by familial sentiments all the possible advantages they can. And consequently, ruling strata under *all* economic and social systems will try to institutionalize their superiority so that their kin may inherit. This tendency is as true for the Soviet Union as it is for the United States, as strong in China as in France or Japan.

If it is true as I assume that pressures toward inequality and status ascription are basic to human society, then it follows that those who would reduce such reactions as much as possible must seek for institutionalized means of restraining them. And I know of no means to do so which are superior to or even approach the method of conflict. The only groups which have an "interest" to modify and reduce inequality are the underprivileged. But the underprivileged can impress their concerns on the social system only in a polity in which they are free to organize in unions, parties, co-operatives, and the like. *The only effective restraint on the power of the dominant class is counter-power.* The primary weapons of the lower strata, of the exploited classes, are the ability to organize, to strike, to demonstrate, and to vote rulers out of office. In any given society at any given time in history, the lower classes may not use these weapons effectively, they may not recognize their interests, but there is no other way. Hence a society which denies the masses such rights is not only un-democratic politically, it also fosters the increased privileges of the ruling groups. As Milovan Djilas and many others have demonstrated, Communist dictatorship has meant the creation of a "New Class" more exploitative than the ruling classes of Western capitalism. The distribution of rewards in the Soviet Union is much more unequal than it is in most other industrialized nations. And it is primarily the fear of the potentially revolutionary masses that has, since 1953, led the rulers of the Eastern European states to make concessions to alleviate the standard of living of the workers and peasants.

In Chapters 9 and 10 I elaborate on some of the implications of the fact that the dominant political ideology of the United States is a leftist one, that traditional conservatism has much less legitimacy as an appropriate political tradition in the United States than it does in Japan or Western Europe. This is a phenomenon that stems from the history of the United States as a former colony that made a success-ful revolution against its imperialist master. This revolution was a more thorough one than most foreigners realize. The values of liberty and equality became institutionalized within America to a greater extent than in other nations. Anyone reading the writings of foreign travelers to the United States will see how the phenomenon of equality has impressed itself on them.[6] This emphasis on equality does not mean, of course, severe limitations on income or power differentiation.

[6] For a detailed analysis of the foreign traveler writings as they related to problems of American values and national character see S. M. Lipset, "A Changing American Character?" in S. M. Lipset and Leo Lowenthal, eds., *Culture and Social Character* (New York: The Free Press, 1961), pp. 136–74.

Obviously, the variations between the wealthy in America and the poor are great, as are the differences in status or authority. And the American value system has never denied the existence of such inequalities. As Tocqueville and others have noted, Americans act as if they believed that such differences are accidental, not essential attributes of man; that among men of equal worth it is not good taste to insist on publicly emphasizing the accidental and perhaps temporary distinctions which divide them.

The concern with equality of status has fostered or supported the objective of equality of opportunity, of achievement for all. Though men may differ in their positions in the stratification structure, their children should not be deprived of the opportunity to secure the best the society offers by the inferior position of their parents. This goal of equal opportunity has been pressed in the American political arena since the beginning of the Republic. The first Workingmen's Parties in the world were founded in the United States in the 1820s. These organizations were greatly concerned with securing free education for all, with reducing the advantages of the children of the well-to-do. The Workingmen's Party of New York even proposed that *all* children be required to attend state boarding schools from the age of six on, so that the cultural advantages of the offspring of all classes be equalized. This desire to share opportunity played a major role in the extension of the American educational system, and continues to play a role today. Currently, about two thirds of all American youth graduate from high school (age eighteen), and over one third enter college. And these proportions are increasing steadily. Some years ago, a Presidential Commission on Higher Education stated as an attainable objective that two thirds of the population could and should receive a college education. The fact that this concern for opportunity and education is a basic value of America and not simply a reflection of the greater wealth of the country may be seen in the fact that the United States' two former colonies, the Philippines and Puerto Rico, are the second and third leading nations in proportions attending college. A larger ratio of their youth (12 to 14 per cent) are in insti-

tutions of higher learning than in any country in Asia or
Europe including the Soviet Union. In a sense, while the
European and Japanese left parties have concentrated on
protecting the underprivileged from insecurity through social security, state medicine, government ownership and
planning, the American left has emphasized increasing opportunity for access to economic and cultural opportunities
through the more equal spread of educational opportunities.
Since the 1930s, however, American liberals and leftists,
among whom I number myself, have sought to extend the
welfare and planning function of government in much the
same way as the democratic left has done in other countries.
And the domestic issues that divide the left from the right
in contemporary America are much the same as those that
differentiate politics abroad.

The image that exists abroad of the United States as a
conservative nation rests on the fact that this country has no
significant socialist movement, and that it is the wealthiest
capitalist nation. But perhaps the most interesting hypothesis
explaining the absence of socialism in America, that of the
socialist writer Leon Samson, suggests that the failure of
socialism in America results from the fact that *the values of
socialism and Americanism are similar*. Samson found that
when he took the writings and speeches of conservative
American politicians and leading capitalists such as Herbert
Hoover, Andrew Carnegie, John D. Rockefeller, and others,
and contrasted them with the writings of Marx, Engels, and
Lenin, they advocated the same set of social relations among
men, economic system apart. In his book *Towards a United
Front*, Samson presents these writings and shows that it is
almost impossible to tell which are by a Marxist and which
by a conservative American. Both see the ideal society as one
that emphasizes social equality, opportunity, and abundance
through hard work. He argues, in effect, that socialism has
appeared to Americans as what they already have, or what
their existing political parties take as a goal.[7] Neither I nor

[7] Leon Samson, *Towards a United Front* (New York: Farrar and
Rinehart, 1933), pp. 1–90.

Samson argues that America is socialist. His book, in fact, was an effort to suggest how one could build an effective socialist movement in America. What I am suggesting, however, is that many Americans still view themselves as an equalitarian democratic people, and they see the Soviet Union as a reactionary state, for reaction to them consists in re-creating the monolithic all-powerful imperialist state which their ancestors fought.

Americans are, of course, naïve about the relationship of economic to political power. They have been remarkably unsophisticated about the realities of economic imperialism. But anyone who seeks to understand American foreign policy must recognize that it has rested primarily on the commitment of the United States to extend democracy and to oppose political imperialism ever since the country overthrew its own colonial rulers. Even during World War II, the political leaders of the United States continued to view Churchill and Britain as imperialists whose machinations to preserve their empire had to be defeated. The United States sought to end Western rule in Asia and Africa, and, to a considerable extent, ignored the extension of Soviet power in Europe and Asia. America pressed the English to leave their colonies; it intervened against the Dutch in Indonesia; it backed the colonial uprisings against France. Much to Stalin's surprise it did little to help Chiang Kai-shek retain power on the mainland, since most Americans who dealt with him, including a number of conservatives, were convinced he was a reactionary and corrupt dictator. Stalin had been absolutely convinced that capitalist America would never allow the Communists to take over China. The fact that it did undoubtedly contributed to his willingness to unleash the Korean war, since it must have seemed obvious that a nation which would not fight for China in 1948–49 would hardly intervene for South Korea in 1950. Today, most Americans view the struggle against Communism primarily as a fight with a reactionary and oppressive tyranny which seeks to subjugate peoples to foreign imperialist domination, not as one in defense of capitalism. The alliance with right-wing regimes in different parts of the world is seen by most politically aware Americans as a regrettable lesser evil made necessary by the aggressive power of the Communist bloc, not as something which is good.

It is, of course, also true that American conservatives and businessmen oppose Communism and socialism because they see these as threats to their interests. And American business has had considerable power and influence in affecting government policy. But I would argue that such power would be ineffective were it not for the fact that Communism appears as an evil to the American left, unions, intellectuals, and others, because it is an expanding totalitarian imperialism. Today American policy toward Italy supports "the opening to the left," the admission of the Nenni Socialists to the governing coalition, even though this means that major Italian industries such as electric power will be nationalized. For the stability of Italian democracy is more important to those who hold office in the United States than the issue of who owns industry. America has given much more aid per capita to Yugoslavia or Poland than Russia has given China, but it has set fewer conditions on this aid than the Soviet Union has done in dealing with China. It was Stalin, not Truman, who insisted in 1948 that the nations of Eastern Europe be barred from participation in the Marshall Plan program. The United States strongly supports the growth of the European Community as an economic and political entity, though one consequence of the Community's success is to weaken the economic position of the United States.

It should never be forgotten that during the period in which the United States was the only power in the world that possessed atom bombs, it rejected the advice of those like Bertrand Russell and Winston Churchill, who urged that it use its bomb monopoly to force the Soviet Union to accept controls over its atomic potential. Russell, in fact, publicly stated in 1948 that the United States should threaten Russia with use of the bomb, that the alternative to such an American policy was Russia's becoming an atomic-bomb power which would then have the ability to carry out its objective of reducing Western Europe to the status of a Soviet colony. The refusal of the United States to force the Soviet Union to agree to a system of international control and inspection during the period of its bomb monopoly followed directly on its unwillingness during World War II to use its military superiority to prevent the Soviet Union from absorbing parts of Eastern Europe. Thus, the United States vetoed Churchill's demand that the Western Allies invade the Balkans, a plan that would have retained at least some parts of this area for the West. And Dwight Eisenhower, himself, made the decision to permit the Russians to occupy Berlin, though American troops could have reached there first. The left-wing British socialist, Richard Crossman, then on Eisenhower's staff, who urged a different policy, reports: "I was nearly dismissed from my job for challenging the wisdom of a Supreme Commander who was content to halt on the Elbe and see the Russians take Berlin, 'because they will treat the Germans toughly, as they deserve, whereas we should be soft to them.'"[8]

The underlying desire to avoid war, which characterizes democratic regimes and which contributed to the appeasement policies followed by the Western powers in dealing with Nazi Germany, continued to affect American policy even under the conservative administration of Eisenhower. During the East German uprising in June 1953, American policy was chiefly concerned with preventing any clash between the Communists and West Germans, rather than with finding ways to aid the East Germans. I was teaching at the Free University of Berlin at that time, and I witnessed American military police being stationed some blocks from the zonal borders *to hold West Berliners back*. The American military commandant in West Berlin ordered the Social Democratic party *not* to hold a mass meeting in solidarity with their brethren in the eastern part of the city. In Poland, during the revolt against the Stalinist regime in October 1956, American Embassy personnel devoted themselves to

[8] Richard Crossman, "The New American Liberalism," *Commentary*, 34 (July 1962), p. 4.

advising leaders of the movement, both inside and outside of the Communist party, that they could expect no help from the West, that they should endeavor to come to terms with the Russians. Last summer when I was in Poland, I was informed of such episodes by high-ranking officials of the Workers (Communist) party. One such leader told me that after the revolt was over, a top officer in our Embassy, who had advised him to be moderate, called to congratulate him on his role in restraining the uprising. And can anyone who sees the United States as a warmongering imperialist power explain why the United States joined with the Soviet Union in 1956 to force the French, British, and Israelis out of Egypt, at the same time that the United States did nothing to aid the government of Hungary against an invasion by the Russian Army? The big-business-supported Eisenhower regime helped the neutralist "socialist" Nasser against three of its best allies, while it refused to help the revolutionary democratic government of Hungary. In the first case, of course, there was no danger that American intervention would lead to war; in the second, as in East Germany and Poland, the State Department was concerned with avoiding the slightest possibility of giving the Soviet Union an excuse for starting an international conflict.

The relationship of the United States with Cuba may seem to belie the argument that Americans see themselves primarily in the role of democratic opponents to foreign rule and tyranny. But this is not so. True, the United States worked with Batista before he was overthrown, as did the Cuban Communist party. But Castro's rise was made possible by American help and sympathy. The *New York Times*, the paper with closest connections with the State Department, was the first to bring Castro's struggle to the attention of the American people and world public opinion in a highly sympathetic series of articles, published at a time when his armed supporters numbered in the few hundreds. Although the American military co-operated with Batista until his fall, Castro was able to secure arms from America, and the State Department clearly opposed Batista long before he left Cuba, and demanded he hold genuinely free elections and give up office. Right-wing senators and organs of opinion in the United States have, in fact, blamed State Department policy for Castro's rise to power. American officials, including then Vice-President Nixon, have reported that they sought to discuss financial aid to Castro during his first tour of the United States, but that he *refused*, a contention that has been confirmed by Castro's former finance minister and others of his entourage after they broke with him. And in 1962 the Kennedy administration offered economic assistance to the Marxist and pro-Communist regime in British Guiana, asking only that it remain formally neutral in international affairs and democratic in its electoral system.

The plans to assist Cuban refugees to overthrow Castro began only after he had indicated his sympathies with the Soviet Union, and many democratic leftist leaders of his revolution had defected and fled to the United States. And it should be noted that the disastrous "invasion" effort at the Bay of Pigs consisted of landing 1500 Cuban emigrés *without air support* or heavy equipment, much less aid, in fact, than Communist regimes have given to the Pathet Lao in Laos or the Viet Cong in Vietnam. In spite of its conviction that Cuba was in the hands of a Communist regime, the United States did not organize a foreign invasion, rather it assisted an extremely stupid and ill-planned effort by exiles to begin an uprising in their country. To place this event on a par with the Russian invasion of Hungary with many divisions of Soviet troops, the Chinese conquest of Tibet, or the suppression of the East German uprising by Russian forces in 1953 is equivalent to placing the Nazi murder of six million Jews on the same level with current anti-Semitic policies within the Soviet Union. The United States has not made a serious effort to overthrow Fidel Castro by force, to a considerable degree because the American political tradition finds such behavior so repugnant. It is, of course, true that certain groups in the military and the Central Intelligence Agency have engaged in secret operations which clearly violate these assumptions. But the very fact that these are done secretly pays tribute to the political morality of most Americans, and it should also be noted that, with the exception of Guatemala, accusations by foreign or domestic critics of such efforts have pointed to supposed American failures, as in Laos, rather than successes in affecting affairs abroad. "Secret" intervention is necessarily minimal and weak as compared to the open intervention by the Communist states.

The moralism that affects American foreign policy is not an unmixed blessing. It leads Americans to perceive other states as good or evil; and if a state is defined as an enemy and, therefore, the essence of evil, compromise with it is difficult, if not impossible. The World War II policies of demanding unconditional surrender, as well as the Morgenthau Plan designed to reduce Germany to an agrarian state, illustrate this well. And currently, popular attitudes toward Communism as a monolithic and unchanging evil inhibit the freedom of action of the administration to deal with Communist China, or to engage in unilateral initiatives which might serve both to show up the falsity of the Soviet claims to favor the resolution of international tensions, and to encourage those within the Communist leadership who support international comity. A Swiss journalist has recently argued that foreigners must understand the essential concern with morality which underlies American action abroad and stop treating the United States as if it were a cynical materialist power, if they are to avoid pressing it into an isolationist "fortress America" policy:

> Whoever interprets American foreign policy in terms of economic interest or imperial power does not understand that it springs from sincere convictions rooted in the Puritan inheritance. Anyone who takes the trouble to investigate will find that this is the view of most Americans and that, more or less consciously, it permeates all social classes. . . .
>
> The idealistic approach to foreign policy of a people who are assumed to be hard-headed businessmen is one

of the most important reasons for serious misunderstanding between Europe and America.[9]

Democracy and equality, then, are not simply ideological propoganda phrases for Americans. In this sense I must confess to being a typical American. Economic well-being for the masses is much more likely to flow from a concern with democracy and equality than *vice versa*. Consequently all interest in the conditions that foster and maintain democracy is a concern for the good society in all its aspects, economic, social, cultural, and political. Democracy, as I suggest in the final chapter of this book, is not simply a means to the end of the good society, it is the only society in which the social tendencies that press man to exploit man may be restrained. This does not mean that any democratic society is a good society. All of them retain enormous areas of behavior that men of good will must reject as evil. In the United States, discrimination against Negroes continues to make a mockery of all our claims to be egalitarian. In spite of America's great wealth, there is much poverty here. The state may provide more adequately for education than any other country in the world; it performs much less well in caring for the tribulations of its citizens which flow from illness and old age. Slums continue to exist in large numbers in all our large cities. According to the 1960 U.S. census, 25 per cent of all family units in the country had an income of *less* than $2500 a year.

There is much to be done in America. But, as in other free societies, men may and do struggle to end these and other ills. The Negro is able to fight to better his condition, and it does improve. Unions and the more liberal political groups seek to increase the amount of state intervention designed to reduce the insecurities flowing from the operation of the economy, the maldistribution of wealth, and illness and old age. This is a struggle which has its continuing victories as well as defeats. Currently, American right-wingers

[9] B. R. Iffmark, "The Surest Way to World War III," *Atlas*, 4 (July 1962), p. 58, reprinted from the *Neue Zürcher Zeitung*, May 2, 1962.

and businessmen feel themselves weak and isolated. Anyone who reads the conservative and business press in the United States will find that those writing for it see themselves as spokesmen for politically weak groups, not for those running the country. The right-wing leaders speak of "the liberal Establishment," that is, they see the ruling circles of the United States as the liberals, not the conservatives. A recent poll of 30,000 American businessmen reported that 86 per cent of them believed that the Kennedy administration was opposed to business.[10] Of course, businessmen are not persecuted in America; profits are still high even if their authority is subject to restriction by government and unions. But the fact that they see themselves as inferior attests to the reality of the American democratic process.

It is difficult to apply generalizations drawn from the experiences of one set of countries to others with sharply different conditions. But it is also possible to exaggerate the qualitative character of the differences. Thus, some European commentators on this book, who are themselves deeply committed to ideological politics, have questioned the discussion in the final chapter on "The End of Ideology?" and have, in fact, suggested that I reflect a typical American attitude in repudiating such beliefs and behavior. I trust it will be clear that I do not favor a decline in political interest or in reform movements, but rather that I have attempted to analyze the sources of an actual phenomenon. Agreement with this point of view has recently come from a surprising source, Richard Crossman of the *New Statesman*, who writes of Western Europe and America: "The truth is that *'we are all conservatives now,'* that liberalism and socialism, which even thirty years ago were still doctrines of social revolution, have become necessities for conserving national independence and personal freedom."[11]

This point of view may seem utopian or reactionary in the

---

[10] See *National Observer*, July 2, 1962, p. 4. Over half those polled, 52 per cent, thought the government was "strongly anti-business."

[11] Richard Crossman, *op. cit.*, p. 7. (Emphasis mine. SML)

context of the domestic politics of countries like France, Italy, or Japan, but one may hazard the prediction that another decade or two of political democracy and economic growth will find in these nations as well a "welfare democracy" in which the extremists of the right and the left will find little support. Such developments have their bad side as well as good, since all nations no matter how "affluent" retain many sources of human misery that men of good will should seek to eliminate. Stable nonideological welfare democracies face the problem that they may no longer possess the internal leftist dynamism to counter the forces endemic in all stratified societies to cumulate advantages for the "have" groups. The fact that the "satisfied" classes in these countries now include a majority in numerical terms, embracing the middle classes and the skilled and well organized trade-unionists, makes the tasks of further reform that much more difficult. Perhaps the one group sensitive to the injustices of stratification that retains weapons to activate opposition to them is the intellectuals. Since many of them remain motivated to be "political men" even after the "end of ideology," they bear a heavy responsibility to keep democracy representative as well as free.

It is ironic that many intellectuals who think of themselves as Marxists have such little knowledge of the history of socialism that they think a concern with political democracy must reflect naïveté about the realities of economic power and social change, that only "bourgeois intellectuals" are interested in such problems. A close reading of Marx and Engels as well as of almost all other major European Marxist figures will indicate that, from the 1860s down to the Russian Revolution, socialism had no meaning that did not involve the continuation or extension of political democracy. Thus, Friedrich Engels, Marx's great collaborator, wrote in 1891: "If one thing is certain it is that our Party and the working class can only come to power under the form of the democratic republic. This is even the specific form for the dictatorship of the proletariat."[12] And if anyone thinks that this is a

[12] Karl Marx and Friedrich Engels, *Correspondence 1846–1895* (New York: International Publishers, 1935), p. 486.

statement taken out of context, or made by Engels in his dotage, no less an authority than Stalin himself is available to testify that political democracy was an integral aspect of socialism, advocated by all Marxists, until Lenin *revised* and drastically changed the meaning of Marxism and socialism. In the famous *History of the Communist Party of the Soviet Union* written under the close supervision of Stalin and later directly attributed to him is the following:

> Before the Second Russian Revolution (February 1917), the Marxists of all countries assumed that the parliamentary democratic republic was the most suitable form of political organization in the period of the transition from capitalism to Socialism. . . . Engels' authoritative statement in his criticism of the draft of the Erfurt Program in 1891, namely, that "the democratic republic . . . is . . . the specific form for the dictatorship of the proletariat" left no doubt that the Marxists continued to regard the democratic republic as the political form for the dictatorship of the proletariat. . . .
>
> What would have happened to the Party, to our revolution, to Marxism, if Lenin had been overawed by the letter of Marxism and had not had the courage to replace one of the old propositions of Marxism . . . by the new proposition concerning the republic of Soviets. . . .[13]

When contemporary democratic socialists and other leftists and liberals reject various measures of state intervention because recent history in various totalitarian states suggests these policies are incompatible with the goal of freedom, they are acting in the direct tradition of the nineteenth-century democratic left in which Marx and Engels and most socialists played such a key role. Those men and those political parties that seek to extend democracy *and* to reduce the punitive aspects of stratification are the contemporary legitimate heirs of the democratic and socialist revolutionaries of the last century. Class privilege and minority rule are de-

[13] A Commission of the Central Committee of the C.P.S.U. (B.), *History of the Communist Party of the Soviet Union (Bolsheviks)* (New York: International Publishers, 1939), pp. 356–57.

fended or fostered today by the reactionaries of the right and the totalitarians of the left. The former would maintain the power and privilege of the old class, the latter would replace them with the even more intensive forms of exploitation and tyranny characteristic of the "New Class."

I have written this statement of some of my political beliefs for the Anchor edition of *Political Man* since in the body of the book itself I endeavor to deal as objectively as I can with the conditions of democratic politics, comparatively as well as in America. I am certain that, like all writers on such subjects, I have not been objective in any pure sense. However, an explicit statement such as this one may at least enable the reader or critic to locate the politics that accompany the analysis. But I trust that the fact that many of my readers will disagree with my politics will not lead them to reject the sociological tradition of political analysis which this work seeks to extend.[14]

Seymour Martin Lipset

July 1962

[14] I have recently extended the analyses presented in this book in monographic essay which seeks to demonstrate the parallels between the problems and reactions of contemporary New States with those of the first New State, the United States. In it, I attempt to show the way in which such reactions as a leftist national tradition, a neutralist (isolationist) foreign policy, reliance on the state for development and reform, an emphasis on education, and the alienation of the intellectuals, among others, are inherent in the situation of a nation which has made a genuine anti-imperialist revolution as the United States was the first to do. It is important that we recognize the extent to which this Revolutionary tradition remains the legitimate background of American institutions. Like India or Ghana, today, the United States separate existence is justified only if it continues to emphasize its egalitarian values.

See S. M. Lipset, *The United States as a New Nation* (d: Hoed: Research Group in Comparative Development, Institute of Industrial Relations, University of California, Berkeley, April 1962). This will also be printed in the *Transactions of the Fifth World Congress of Sociology*, 1962.

POLITICAL MAN

CHAPTER 1

The Sociology of Politics[1]

ONE OF political sociology's prime concerns is an analysis of the social conditions making for democracy. Surprising as it may sound, a stable democracy requires the manifestation of conflict or cleavage so that there will be struggle over ruling positions, challenges to parties in power, and shifts of parties in office; but without consensus—a political system allowing the peaceful "play" of power, the adherence by the "outs" to decisions made by the "ins," and the recognition by the "ins" of the rights of the "outs"—there can be no democracy. The study of the conditions encouraging democracy must therefore focus on the sources of both cleavage and consensus.

Cleavage—where it is legitimate—contributes to the integration of societies and organizations. Trade-unions, for example, help to integrate their members in the larger body politic and give them a basis for loyalty to the system. Marx's focus on unions and workers' parties as expediters of revolutionary tension was incorrect. As Chapters 2 and 3 make clear, it is precisely in those countries where workers have

[1] A number of bibliographic reports dealing with political sociology and political behavior research may be of interest. A few recent bibliographic reports dealing with politics are: R. Bendix and S. M. Lipset, "Political Sociology—A Trend Report and Bibliography," *Current Sociology*, 6 (1957), pp. 79–169; Joseph R. Gusfield, "The Sociology of Politics," in Joseph B. Gittler, ed., *Review of Sociology* (New York: John Wiley & Sons, 1957), pp. 520–30. Compendia of important research are: Robert E. Lane, *Political Life* (Glencoe: The Free Press, 1959) and Heinz Eulau, Samuel J. Eldersveld, and Morris Janowitz, eds., *Political Behavior* (Glencoe: The Free Press, 1956).

been able to form strong unions and obtain representation in politics that the disintegrative forms of political cleavage are least likely to be found. And various studies have suggested that those trade-unions which allow legitimate internal opposition retain more loyalty from their members than do the more dictatorial and seemingly more unified organizations. Consensus on the norms of tolerance which a society or organization accepts has often developed only as a result of basic conflict, and requires the continuation of conflict to sustain it.

This book seeks to contribute to an understanding of democratic political systems by discussing a number of areas: the social requirements for democratic systems and varying types of political conflict within the United States and other democratic societies, particularly electoral cleavage; some of the specific causes of antidemocratic tendencies; the sources of participation in politics; the social bases of party support in the United States and other countries; and finally, the conditions which determine the political life of trade-unions. To understand the sociological rationale underlying the study of these topics, it is necessary to look first at the evolution of ideas about modern society.

The Intellectual Background

The crises of the Reformation and the industrial revolution which heralded modern society also brought the sociology of politics into being. The breakdown of a traditional society exposed to general view for the first time the difference between society and the state. It also raised the problem: How can a society face continuous conflict among its members and groups and still maintain social cohesion and the legitimacy of state authority?

The cleavage between the absolutist rulers of the seventeenth century and the emergent bourgeoisie made the distinctions between man and citizen, society and state, clear. These distinctions were both a cause and a consequence of the crisis over the legitimacy of the state, which some men were beginning to question and some to deny completely. Bodin, in the seventeenth century, formulated for the first time the principle of the sovereignty of the state over other institutions within the boundaries of the nation in order to justify the primacy of the state, particularly in an age of religious conflict. A number of philosophers—Hobbes, Locke, and Rousseau among them—tried, each in his own way, to solve the basic problem: the need for secular consensus which could substitute for the religious solution of the Middle Ages and bridge the gap between society and state.

The nineteenth-century fathers of political sociology took sides in the argument. Men like Saint-Simon, Proudhon, and Marx were on the side of society: for them it was the fabric which had to be strengthened and reinforced, while the state had to be limited, controlled by society, or abolished. On the other side were Hegel and his followers, Lorenz von Stein and others, who believed that the solution lay in the subordination of society's disparate elements to the sovereignty of the state.

The sociology of politics appears to have outgrown this controversy and solved the basic problem. The solution to the dilemma, like the solution to so many others, seemed to be that the question was asked in the wrong way. The error lay in dealing with state and society as two independent organisms, and asking which was the more important or preferable. Political sociologists now argue that the state is just one of many political institutions, and that political institutions are only one of many clusters of social institutions; that the relationships among these institutions and clusters of institutions is the subject of sociology in general; and that the relationship between political and other institutions is the special province of a sociology of politics. In debating with political scientists about the credentials of political sociology, sociologists have held that the independent study of the state and other political institutions does not make theoretical sense. Talcott Parsons, for example, perhaps the major contemporary sociological theorist, has suggested that the study of politics cannot be "treated in terms of a specifically specialized conceptual scheme . . . precisely for the reason that the political problem of the social system is a focus for the integration of all of its analytically distinguished components, not of a specially differentiated class of these components."[2]

From the standpoint of sociology, the debate between the "supporters" of the state and those of society is closed. But although the subjects of the controversy are no longer referred to as "state" and "society," the underlying dilemma—the proper balance between conflict and consensus—continues. It is the central problem with which this book deals.

Sociologists until fairly recently have been much more involved in studying the conditions producing cleavage than in determining the requisites of political consensus. The implications become clearer if we consider the four great Europeans whose ideas are, more or less, the basis of political sociology: Marx, Tocqueville, Weber, and Michels.

Class Conflict and Consensus: Marx and Tocqueville

It was after the French Revolution that the problems of conflict versus consensus came into focus. The revolutionaries were naturally primarily concerned with furthering conflict, the conservatives with maintaining social stability. But for many years few men analyzed the conditions under which conflict and consensus were or could be kept in balance.

The most articulate spokesman for viewing conflict as the central interest in the study of politics was Karl Marx, and, as much of the later analysis in this book indicates, he had many fruitful insights into its causes. Alexis de Tocqueville, on the other hand, was the first major exponent of the idea that democracy involves a balance between the forces of conflict and consensus.

To Marx a complex society could be characterized either by constant conflict (even if suppressed) *or* by consensus, but not by a combination of the two. He saw conflict and consensus as alternatives rather than as divergent tendencies

[2] Talcott Parsons, *The Social System* (Glencoe: The Free Press, 1951), pp. 126–27.

that could be balanced. On the one hand, he projected consensus, harmony, and integration into the communist future (and to some degree into the communist past); on the other hand, he saw conflict and absolutism as the great fact of history in the epoch between ancient primitive communism and the coming success of the proletarian revolution.

Marx's conception of the harmonious future society had significant bearing on his sociological outlook. The political system which he projected was not institutionalized democracy, but anarchy. This meant in particular the end of the division of labor, for elimination of the differentiation of roles in the economic spheres of life would, according to Marx, eliminate the major source of social conflict:

> In communist society, where nobody has one exclusive sphere of activity but each can become accomplished in any branch he wishes, society regulates the general production and thus makes it possible for me to do one thing today and another tomorrow, to hunt in the morning, fish in the afternoon, rear cattle in the evening, criticize after dinner, just as I have a mind, without ever becoming hunter, fisherman, shepherd, or critic.[3]

This statement is not simply Marx's daydream about a utopian future. It describes one of the basic conditions of communist society, for communism "is the true solution of the antagonism between man and nature, [and] man and man. . . ."[4] It is the elimination of all social sources of differences, even the distinction between town and country.[5]

Since consensus is impossible in a stratified society dominated by an exploiting class, Marx could not conceive of the sources of solidarity in precommunist society. His primary in-

---

[3] Karl Marx, *The German Ideology* (New York: International Publishers, 1939), p. 22.

[4] Quoted from the French edition of *The Holy Family*, in G. Gurvitch, "La Sociologie du jeune Marx," *Cahiers internationaux de sociologie*, 4 (1948), p. 25.

[5] Karl Marx, *op. cit.*, p. 44.

terest was an analysis of the factors making for the strength
of the contending forces. He was, however, never really interested in understanding the psychological mechanisms
through which the interests of individuals are disciplined,
even for the purpose of increasing class strength. In an interesting passage, written when he was young, Marx did raise
the problem in Hegelian terms:

> How does it come about that personal interests con-
> tinually grow, despite the person, into class interests,
> into common interests which win an independent ex-
> istence over against the individual persons, in this in-
> dependence take on the shape of general interests, enter
> as such into opposition with the real individuals, and
> in this opposition, according to which they are defined
> as general interests, can be conceived by the conscious-
> ness as ideal, even as religious, sacred interests.[6]

But he never tried to answer the question.[7] He was basically unconcerned with society's need to maintain institutions
and values which facilitate stability and cohesion. To Marx,
social constraints did not fulfill socially necessary functions
but rather supported class rule.

Marx's theory has no place for democracy under communism. It has only two mutually exclusive social types: a society of conflict and a society of harmony. The first type,
according to Marx, is inherently destructive of human dignity
and must be destroyed. The second is freed of the sources
of conflict and, therefore, has no need for democratic institutions, such as safeguards against state power, the division of
powers, the protections of juridical guarantees, a constitution
or "bill of rights."[8] The history of the Russian Revolution

[6] K. Marx, "Ideology—'Saint Max,'" *Gesamtausgabe*, I, 5, p. 226,
quoted in *The German Ideology*, p. 203.
[7] The best Marxist discussion of the problem of the development
of class cohesion and the transcending of personal interests in favor
of class interests may be found in Georg Lukacs, *Geschichte und
Klassenbewusstsein* (Berlin: Malik, 1923).
[8] See his attack on the bill of rights of the Second French Republic as a sham in "The Eighteenth Brumaire of Louis Napoleon,"

has already demonstrated some of the dire consequences of operating with a theory which deals only with nonexistent ideal types—that is to say, with societies of complete harmony and societies of constant conflict.

At first glance, Tocqueville's theory seems to be similar to Marx's, since both men emphasized the solidarity of social units and the necessity for conflict among these units. (For Marx the units were classes; for Tocqueville they were local communities and voluntary organizations.) However, Tocqueville, unlike Marx, deliberately chose to emphasize those aspects of social units which could maintain political cleavage and political consensus at the same time. He did not project his harmonious society into the future and did not separate in time the sources of social integration and the sources of cleavage. The same units—for example, federal and state governments, Congress and the President—which function independently of each other and therefore necessarily in a state of tension, are also dependent on each other and are linked by political parties. Private associations which are sources of restrictions on the government also serve as major channels for involving people in politics. In short, they are the mechanisms for creating and maintaining the consensus necessary for a democratic society.

Tocqueville's concern for a pluralistic political system resulted from his interpretation of the trends of modern society. Industrialization, bureaucratization, and nationalism, which were bringing the lower classes into politics, were also undermining the smaller local centers of authority and concentrating power in the state leviathan. Tocqueville feared that social conflict would disappear because there would be only one center of power—the state—which no other group would be strong enough to oppose.[9] There would be no more

---

in V. Adoratsky, ed., *Selected Works of Karl Marx* (Moscow: Cooperative Publishing Society of Foreign Workers in the USSR, 1935), pp. 328–29.

[9] Alexis de Tocqueville, *Democracy in America*, Vol. I (New York: Vintage Books, 1954), pp. 9–11. The drift toward a mass society through the elimination of local groups and intermediate centers of

political competition because there would be no social bases to sustain it. He also feared that consensus as well would be undermined in the mass society. The atomized individual, left alone without membership in a politically significant social unit, would lack sufficient interest to participate in politics or even simply to accept the regime. Politics would be not only hopeless but meaningless. Apathy undermines consensus, and apathy was the attitude of the masses toward the state which Tocqueville saw as the outcome of an industrial bureaucratic society.

His study of America suggested to him two institutions which might combat the new leviathan: local self-government and voluntary associations. Involvement in such institutions seemed to him a condition for the stability of the democratic system. By disseminating ideas and creating consensus among their members, they become the basis for conflict between one organization and another. And, in the process of doing so, they also limit the central power, create new and autonomous centers of power to compete with it, and help to train potential opposition leaders in political skills.[10]

The approaches of Tocqueville and Marx did not result in contradictory analyses of the functions of various social institutions, although they did make for very different evaluations. Marx's statement that religion is the "opiate of the masses" is a recognition of its integrative function. Tocqueville also recognized the "opiative" quality of religion: "Religion, then, is simply another form of hope."[11] To Marx religion was a source of delusion for the lower strata, a mechanism to adjust them to their lot in life, and to prevent them from recognizing their true class interests. Tocqueville, conversely, saw that the need for religious belief grew in direct propor-

---

power between the individual and the national state has been analyzed by Robert Nisbet, *The Quest for Community* (New York: Oxford University Press, 1953).

[10] For an elaboration of these ideas see S. M. Lipset, M. Trow, and J. S. Coleman, *Union Democracy* (Glencoe: The Free Press, 1956).

[11] Tocqueville, *op. cit.*, p. 321.

tion to political liberty. The less coercive and dictatorial the political institutions of a society became, the more it needed a system of sacred belief to help restrict the actions of both the rulers and the ruled.

Bureaucracy and Democracy: Weber and Michels

If one abiding interest of political sociology—cleavage and consensus—has been linked to the names of Marx and Tocqueville, another—the study of bureaucracy—is identified with the work of Max Weber and Robert Michels. The two problems are, of course, closely related, since bureaucracy is one of the chief means of creating and maintaining consensus and at the same time one of the major sources of the forces disrupting integration.

The difference between Marx and Tocqueville, with their emphasis on consensus and class conflict, and Weber and Michels, with their concern for the fulfillment or betrayal of values through bureaucracy, represents an accommodation of social thought to the subsequent stages of the industrial revolution. Many nineteenth-century social philosophers were worried about the disruptive effects of the industrial revolution on society, and about the possibility of achieving democratic political structures. Like Marx, some believed or hoped that political and social stability were inherently impossible in an urban industrial society characterized by economic competition and concern with profit, and they looked for a new, more stable, more moral system. In contrast, a number of twentieth-century thinkers, of whom Weber and Michels are the most significant, have moved away from the problem of the relationship between the economic system (as defined in terms of ownership and control of the means of production) and other social institutions. For them the problem is no longer the changes needed to modify or destroy the institutions of capitalism, but the social and political conditions of a bureaucratized society. Since few people now believe it feasible to return to small producers' communes, the question becomes: What institutional arrangements are possible *within* bureaucratic society?

Many opponents of Marxism said long ago that socialism would not end many of the evils it attacked. Weber and Michels were among the first, however, to engage in research on the postulate that the problem of modern politics is not capitalism or socialism but the relationship between bureaucracy and democracy. Weber saw bureaucratization as an institutional form inherent in all modern societies.[12] To Michels, oligarchy—government by a small group of persons who co-opt their successors—was a process common to all large organizations. Both men tried to demonstrate that socialist organizations and societies were or would necessarily be as bureaucratic and oligarchic as capitalist ones.

Weber's interest in bureaucracy was not primarily political. His belief that the growth of bureaucratic institutions was a prerequisite for a highly industrial society led him to view bureaucratization as the single most important source of institutional change and hence a threat to existing forces of cohesion. As Parsons has pointed out, "Roughly, for Weber, bureaucracy plays the same part that the class struggle played for Marx and competition for Sombart."[13] However, Weber gave great importance to the integrative aspects of bureaucratization in a democratic society, such as the transfer to the entire society of the bureaucratic standards of equal treatment before the law and before authority, and the use of achievement criteria for selection and promotion.

[12] See Max Weber, "Zur Lage der bürgerlichen Demokratie in Russland," *Archiv für Sozialwissenschaft und Sozialpolitik*, 22 (1906), pp. 234–353; "Der Sozialismus," in *Gesammelte Aufsätze zur Soziologie und Sozialpolitik* (Tübingen: Mohr, 1924), pp. 492–518; Carlo Antoni, *From History to Sociology: The Transition in German Historical Thinking*, trans. by Hayden V. White (Detroit: Wayne State University Press, 1959), pp. 145–46.

[13] T. Parsons, *The Structure of Social Action* (New York: McGraw-Hill Book Co., 1937), p. 509. See also C. Wright Mills and Hans Gerth, "Introduction: The Man and His Work," in Max Weber, *Essays in Sociology* (New York: Oxford University Press, 1946), p. 49.

In analyzing the actual operation of a democratic society, Weber considered control over the execution of the laws the greatest problem faced by politicians who held the confidence of the electorate: "the day-to-day exercise of authority was in the hands of the bureaucracy and even success in the struggle for votes and in parliamentary debate and decision-making would come to naught unless it was translated into effective control over administrative implementation."[14] And he was rather pessimistic about the ultimate effects of growing bureaucratization on democracy and freedom. Like Tocqueville, he feared that the growth of the superstate would eventually lead to the downfall of due process and the rule of law. Socialism meant for him the extension of bureaucratic authority to the entire society, resulting in a "dictatorship of the bureaucrats" rather than of the proletariat. It would be a world "filled with nothing but those little cogs, little men clinging to little jobs and striving towards bigger ones. The great question is therefore not how we can promote and hasten it [a situation of bureaucratic domination] but what can we oppose to this machinery in order to keep a portion of mankind free from this parcelling-out of the soul, from this supreme mastery of the bureaucratic way of life."[15]

Michels, too, was interested in the factors which maintain or undermine democracy. In analyzing political parties and trade-unions, he noted those elements inherent in large-scale organizations which make control by their mass membership technically almost impossible.[16] He pointed to the advantages of control over organizations for the incumbent leaders, to the political incapacity of rank-and-file members, to the causes of their apathy, and to the pressures on leaders to perpetuate themselves in office. And he saw the pattern of oligarchy within bureaucratic socialist parties extended to

[14] Reinhard Bendix, *Max Weber: An Intellectual Portrait* (New York: Doubleday & Co., Inc., 1960), p. 433.

[15] Quoted in J. P. Mayer, *Max Weber and German Politics* (London: Faber & Faber, 1943), p. 128.

[16] Robert Michels, *Political Parties* (Glencoe: The Free Press, 1949). This book was first published in Germany in 1911 and in the United States in 1915.

the society governed by such parties. The discussion of the internal politics of trade-unions in Chapter 12 is essentially an attempt to systematize some of Michels' ideas.

The theories of Weber and Michels on bureaucracy and democracy, together with those of Marx and Tocqueville on conflict and consensus, established the basic concerns of modern political sociology. The second part of this chapter deals with some of the contemporary work inspired by these concerns.

Contemporary Research

VOTING

Voting is the key mechanism of consensus in democratic society. Election studies in this country and others, however, have rarely been designed as studies of consensus. For the most part, students of elections have been concerned with the relationship between one type of cleavage—political parties—and such other types as class, occupation, religion, ethnic group, and region, and have considered these factors primarily in their role as the social basis of political strife rather than of political consensus.

The study of the integrative aspects of electoral behavior suggested here fills important lacunae in our understanding of democracy as a system. For considered from this perspective such phenomena as the Tory worker or the middle-class socialist are not merely deviants from class patterns, but basic requirements for the maintenance of the political system.[17] A stable democracy requires a situation in which all the major political parties include supporters from many segments of the population. A system in which the support of different parties corresponds too closely to basic social divisions cannot continue on a democratic basis, for it reflects

[17] It is important to keep separate the analysis of different functional systems: society, structural groups, and personality. Voting Tory by a segment of the manual workers may be regarded as dysfunctional for a Labor party or class organization, functional or dysfunctional for the personality, and functional for the society.

a state of conflict so intense and clear-cut as to rule out compromise. Where parties are cut off from gaining support among a major stratum, they lose a major reason for compromise. It is also important that parties have leaders from diverse backgrounds, so as to represent symbolically their concern with many groups, even if they have little support from some of them. The fact that Republicans have nominated Negroes and Jews even though most members of these groups in recent years have voted Democratic has undoubtedly had an important unifying effect and reduced the chance that party division along racial or religious lines could become permanent. Similarly, the presence of a Harriman or a Dilworth among Democratic leaders, or a Cripps or a Shawcross among British Labor party leaders, may induce conservative upper classes to accept a government dominated by a lower-class-based party. (See Chapter 3.) Michels, discussing the pre-World War I Social Democrats in Germany, suggested that the absence of upper-class leaders in the party explained in part why most members of the middle class did not accept it as a legitimate opposition.[18]

The problem of agreement on issues across group lines and party cleavages is also worth study. Voting research, the results of which are analyzed in Chapter 7, has shown that cross-pressures resulting from multiple-group affiliations or loyalties account for much of the "deviation" from the dominant pattern of a given group. Individuals who are subject to pressures driving them in different political directions must either deviate or "escape into apathy." Multiple-group identification has the effect of reducing the emotion in political choices. Also, in the United States and Great Britain, manual workers who vote Republican or Conservative are less liberal on economic issues than workers who support the Democratic or Labor parties, but more liberal than middle-class supporters of their own party.[19] The fact that a significant segment

[18] R. Michels, *Sozialismus und Fascismus in Italien* (München: Meyer & Jessen, 1925), Vol. 1.

[19] Bernard Berelson, Paul F. Lazarsfeld, and William McPhee, *Voting* (Chicago: University of Chicago Press, 1954), p. 27; M. Ben-

of the voters of each major party identifies with values associated with other parties has forced the leaders of each party
to make concessions to the other party when they have been
in power, and has offered them hope for much needed support when they have been in opposition.

Similarly, the problem of political participation may be
viewed in different ways, depending upon whether one is
concerned with cleavage or consensus. The belief that a very
high level of participation is always good for democracy is not
valid.[20] As the events of the 1930s in Germany demonstrated
(see Chapter 5), an increase in the level of participation may
reflect the *decline* of social cohesion and the breakdown of
the democratic process; whereas a stable democracy may rest
on the general belief that the outcome of an election will not
make too great a difference in society. A principal problem
for a theory of democratic systems is: Under what conditions
can a society have "sufficient" participation to maintain the
democratic system without introducing sources of cleavage
which will undermine the cohesion?[21]

---

ney, A. P. Gray, and R. H. Pear, *How People Vote* (London: Routledge and Kegan Paul, 1956), p. 194.

[20] For a statement of the position that political apathy may reflect
the health of a democracy see Herbert Tingsten, *Political Behavior:
Studies in Election Statistics* (London: P. S. King & Son, 1937), pp.
225–26; and W. H. Morris Jones, "In Defense of Political Apathy,"
Political Studies, 2 (1954), pp. 25–37.

Data from various American studies show that nonvoters are much
more likely than voters to oppose democratic values, to desire strong
leadership, and to disagree with allowing civil liberties to radicals
and other political minorities. See Samuel A. Stouffer, *Communism,
Conformity, and Civil Liberties* (New York: Doubleday & Co., Inc.,
1955), pp. 83–86; H. H. Field, "The Non-Voter—Who He Is, What
He Thinks," *Public Opinion Quarterly,* 8 (1944), pp. 175–87; Robert E. Lane, "Political Personality and Electoral Choice," *American
Political Science Review,* 49 (1955), pp. 178–79; F. H. Sanford,
Authoritarianism and Leadership (Philadelphia: Stephenson Brothers,
1950), p. 168.

[21] The major attempt to link the voting studies with the general
problem of social cohesion may be found in Talcott Parsons' "Voting and the Equilibrium of the American Political System," in E. Burdick and A. Brodbeck, eds., *American Voting Behavior* (Glencoe:

At this point, I might suggest that the more cohesive and stable a democratic system is, the more likely it becomes that all segments of the population will react in the same direction to major stimuli; that is, if conditions facilitate the growth of leftist opinion, the socialists will gain votes among both the well-to-do and the workers, although they will remain relatively weaker in the upper strata. In the same way, during a period of right-wing ascendancy conservative votes will increase among the poorer groups. Conversely, an indicator of low consensus would be a situation in which a political tendency grows only among the groups to whom it primarily appeals—for example, the left gaining among the workers, while an opposite trend grows in other strata—i.e., the right gaining among the middle classes. This is precisely the situation which Marxists call revolutionary, and which, as is pointed out in Chapter 5, occurred in Germany before 1933 and in Moscow and Petrograd in 1917.[22] Researches on historical variations in the voting behavior of American states may be summed up in the epigram, "As your state goes, so goes the nation," and are demonstrations of the basic cohesion of American society.[23] It is possible to study the relative

---

The Free Press, 1959), pp. 80–120. This paper is full of suggestive hypotheses and interpretations concerning the American electoral system.

[22] In Germany between 1929 and 1933, as the Nazis grew from a small party to one which secured more than one third of the vote, most middle-class centrist parties declined sharply; the Communist vote also increased in this period while the Social Democratic percentage went down. A study of the elections which occurred in Russia between the February and October revolutions indicates clearly how a bifurcation of class support occurred in the two major cities, Petrograd and Moscow. The Bolsheviks who were a small group in February gained most of the working-class vote by October, as the Cadets did from the middle classes. See Oliver Radkey, *The Election to the Russian Constituent Assembly of 1917* (Cambridge: Harvard University Press, 1950).

[23] See Louis Bean, *Ballot Behavior: A Study of Presidential Elections* (Washington: Public Affairs Press, 1940); *How to Predict Elections* (New York: Alfred A. Knopf, 1948). An examination of the data from survey studies of various American elections since 1936 shows similar patterns among classes. A study of British elec-

degree of political cohesion in different countries, or in the same country, over a period of time by analyzing the extent to which changes in electoral behavior occur in the same direction among different strata and regions.

An important recent historical work dealing with consensus, Manning Dauer's *The Adams Federalists*,[24] is an ecological study of the decline of the Federalist party and the triumph of Jefferson in the elections around 1800. Although Dauer documents the lines of division among the parties at that time, they are not his central concern. Rather, he is interested in why the two-party system of the period failed. He suggests, as is elaborated in Chapter 9, that the Federalist party declined because Hamilton and the right wing of the party failed to understand the rules of the game of democratic politics—that to remain a major party they had to appeal to all strata. By too narrowly serving the needs of the urban merchants, the Federalists alienated their rural supporters and, in a basically agrarian country, necessarily ceased to be a major party.

In investigating the cleavages and social differences between Democratic and Republican voters in 1948, three Columbia University sociologists[25] noted the general agreement among voters of both parties on such matters as what the major issues were; positions on some of these issues, especially internationalism and civil rights; expectations of important events, such as war and depression; the legitimate criteria for judging candidates; the importance of the election itself; and the rules of the game which guide the democratic process.[26]

---

tions also shows that an increase in Tory votes means more Conservatives among workers as well as the middle class, while a general Labor party increase occurs in the upper classes as well as in strong labor areas. See John Bonham, *The Middle Class Vote* (London: Faber & Faber, 1954).

[24] Manning Dauer, *The Adams Federalists* (Baltimore: The Johns Hopkins Press, 1953).

[25] Bernard Berelson, Paul F. Lazarsfeld, and William McPhee, *op. cit.*

[26] A study by Janowitz and Marvick dealing with the general issue of consensus and elections is an analysis of the 1952 presidential elec-

POLITICAL MOVEMENTS

The study of reform and extremist movements consitutes the second largest substantive area in American political sociology, and Chapters 4 and 5 report on our knowledge of some of these groups. It may seem odd, but American as well as European social scientists have been much more interested in reform and extremist movements than in conventional and conservative parties.[27] There are many more entries in library catalogues under "British Labor Party"

---

tion which focused on "evaluating the election process in terms of the requirements for maintaining a democratic society . . . [and asked] To what degree did the elections represent a process of consent?" They set up a number of conditions to be fulfilled if an election is to produce a "process of consent" and analyzed the available survey data to see whether the 1952 election met the requirements derived from theory. Their finding that "the election of 1952 could be judged as a process of consent" is less important than the example that the survey interview data can be fruitfully employed to deal with some of the most complex problems of political analysis. Morris Janowitz and Dwaine Marvick, *Competitive Pressure and Democratic Consent*, Michigan Governmental Studies, No. 32 (Ann Arbor: University of Michigan Press, 1956), p. 96.

Robert A. Dahl has raised many important points on a theoretical level about the conditions for a democratic electoral system. Many of his conclusions are formulated as empirically testable propositions. His book is particularly important for directing the attention of researchers to the general problem of the relationship of intensity of feeling to the stability of the system, particularly when the minority feels much more intensely than the majority. See Robert A. Dahl, *A Preface to Democratic Theory* (Chicago: University of Chicago Press, 1956), esp. Chap. 4, pp. 90–123. The recent work of the political scientist David Easton is also of sociological interest. David Easton, "An Approach to the Analysis of Political Systems," *World Politics*, 9 (1957), pp. 383–400.

[27] S. M. Lipset, "Political Sociology, 1945–1955," in H. Zetterberg, ed., *Sociology in the United States of America* (Paris: UNESCO, 1956), pp. 43–55. This comment applies to my own work as much as to any other social scientist. For a discussion of the ideological assumptions underlying concern with conflict (radical) or consensus (conservative) see Bendix and Lipset, *op. cit.* It is worth noting that Rudolf Heberle subtitles his book on social movements, *An Introduction to Political Sociology*.

than under "Conservative Party." Many Americans have studied labor parties in various parts of the British Commonwealth; few have written books or articles about the Conservatives. The Social Democratic party and the co-operatives of Sweden and other parts of Scandinavia have proved of great interest to American scholars: few, if any, have touched on the nonsocialist parties. Conservative movements and forces, conservative political philosophers like Burke, Bonald, and De Maistre, and the problems of integration and cohesion have been virtually neglected until fairly recently.

Similarly, most of the studies of fascist and communist movements stress the factors which create and sustain extremism rather than those which curtail them in stable democracies. In America we have studies of the sources of threats to civil liberties, of the social roots of McCarthyism, of symbols and appeals used by fascist groups in the thirties and by McCarthy in the fifties, and of the dangers to "due process" inherent in populist ideology.[28] Hardly any attention has been directed toward locating the sources of American resistance to extremes of right and left during the Depression, which probably affected the nation more, relative to its previous economic situation, than any other Western country except Germany. Some of the materials presented in Parts I and III of this book deal with these issues in detail.

THE POLITICS OF BUREAUCRACY

Weber's focus on bureaucracy and power as elements of large-scale formal structures and his systematization of the basic traits inherent in bureaucratic organization have been followed up in a large number of studies.[29] But political

[28] See Samuel A. Stouffer, *op. cit.*; Daniel Bell, ed., *The New American Right* (New York: Criterion Books, 1955); Leo Lowenthal and Norbert Guterman, *Prophets of Deceit: A Study of the Techniques of the American Agitator* (New York: Harper & Bros., 1949); and Edward Shils, *The Torment of Secrecy* (Glencoe: The Free Press, 1956).

[29] For an analysis and summary of various American studies which have developed out of this tradition, see Peter Blau, *Bureaucracy in Modern Society* (New York: Random House, 1956).

sociology has paid little heed to his analysis of the relationship between the growth of centralized bureaucratic state power and the decline of democracy. Few of his basic writings on bureaucracy and democracy have even been translated. Scholars following Weber's hypotheses, explicitly or implicitly, have separated the study of bureaucracy from the study of political organization in the specific sense of the term, and have included all kinds of other organizations: hospitals, business offices, factories, churches, and labor unions. These investigations have shown, as Weber himself recognized, that there are constant, systematically determined tensions and conflicts within bureaucratic organizations that result in deviations from the bureaucratic ideals of "rational efficiency," "hierarchy," and "neutrality." In other words, the tension between power needs and bureaucratization exists not only in the relationship between political organization and society but within *all* organizations *per se*. Examples of such tensions are innumerable: the clash between physicians and hospital administrators, journalists and newspaper editors, professors and university administrators, staff and line in industry and government. Conflicts over goals and procedures are in fact an integral part of all organizations, whether the State Department, the Red Cross, the Communist party of the Soviet Union, or the sales department of a corporation.

Weber's analysis of bureaucratic political neutrality, i.e., the norm that a member of a bureaucracy is an impartial expert rather than an interested party, has been elaborated from the perspective of the requisites of a democratic political system. This norm makes possible the continuity of democratic government during a turnover in political offices. By permitting a separation between the personnel of the government and the personalities and policies of politicians temporarily in office, bureaucracy in government decreases the strains of party strife. Inherent in bureaucratic structures is a tendency to reduce conflicts from the political to the administrative arena. Constant emphasis on the need for objective criteria as the bases for settling conflicts enables bureaucratic

institutions to play major mediating roles.[30] Thus in many
ways the pressures to extend bureaucratic norms and practices strengthen democratic consensus.[31]

THE INTERNAL GOVERNMENT
OF VOLUNTARY ORGANIZATIONS

Michels, unlike Weber, has inspired few later studies. For
the most part, his ideas have been used for descriptive purposes or for polemics denouncing organizations as undemocratic. No American sociologist has thought it worth while to
examine the general validity of his theory of oligarchy in the
light of, say, the differences between German socialist party
life, as he described it in *Political Parties*, and that of the
two major American parties. It is clear that constant factionalism, fairly rapid turnover in leadership, and the absence of
a central power structure characterize American parties in

[30] A recent work in political sociology which has dealt with the
role of bureaucracy in social cohesion is Philip Selznick's *TVA and
the Grass Roots* (Berkeley: University of California Press, 1949).
Selznick does not ignore conflict—he shows how the very processes
which result in co-operation between some groups lead to alienation
and conflict with others. But he is primarily concerned with the
mechanisms which bring together organizations and groups with
different objectives, and he stresses the role of ideology and self-
recruitment of collaborators in serving this objective. In *Leadership
in Administration* (Evanston: Row, Peterson and Co., 1957) Selznick has formalized many of the ideas developed in the study of the
TVA and laid down a thorough sociological framework for dealing
with the relationship between conflict and integration within organizations by focusing on the meaning and process of institutionalization,
the "rules of the game" of organizational life. His propositions about
the development of values and procedures which increase the com-
petency of given organizations might also be used in the study of
larger systems.

[31] The human relations school of industrial sociology has been
concerned with cohesion and consensus within bureaucracies. However, these writers view conflict as always abnormal and dysfunctional for specific organizations and the society as a whole. A bibliography of the work of this school and of some of the many critical
discussions may be found in Louis Kriesberg, "Industrial Sociology,
1945–1955," in H. Zetterberg, ed., *op. cit.*, pp. 71–77.

contrast to the Social Democratic party of pre-World War I Germany. In America only interest organizations like labor unions or professional societies have internal structures resembling those described by Michels as necessary in political parties.[32]

The existence of oligarchy in large-scale organizations raises the problem: To what extent does the fact that various voluntary associations are or are not democratic make a difference in their effectiveness as instruments of social and political cohesion? Tocqueville wrote of the contribution of various oligarchically organized associations to the maintenance of democratic tensions and consensus, and some later writers have argued that the absence of internal democracy does not matter, since voluntary organizations are constrained to fulfill an essentially representative function in order to survive. It has been pointed out, for example, that John L. Lewis, the head of the United Mine Workers Union, although a dictator in his organization and a Republican in politics, led the union in strike tactics and collective-bargaining policies as militant as those pursued by leftist labor leaders in other parts of the world. On the other hand, there is much evidence that members of private associations often do little to oppose policies which they detest. This has been true in communist-controlled labor unions and in the British Medical Association, a poll of whose members in 1944 found that the majority favored various aspects of socialized medicine to which their leaders strongly objected.[33]

The principal justifications given for oligarchic rule in voluntary organizations are (1) that it better enables the organizations to fulfill their particular combat roles in the general social conflict with other groups, or to gain concessions

[32] See Chap. 12 of this book for an attempt to develop the theory of oligarchy in the context of analysis of the American labor movement.

[33] Harry H. Eckstein, "The Politics of the British Medical Association," *The Political Quarterly*, 26 (1955), pp. 345–59; see also Oliver Garceau, *The Political Life of the American Medical Association* (Cambridge: Harvard University Press, 1941) for an analysis of the problem of oligarchy and representation in the AMA.

from government; and (2) that there is no structural basis for conflict within them (as in the case of labor unions representing a single interest group). However, a recent study of trade-unions suggests that democracy and conflict within organizations may, like democracy and conflict in the larger society, contribute to cohesion and solidarity,[34] since in a one-party system, in either civil society or a trade-union, abhorrence of the politics of the administration often results in rejection of the whole system, because it becomes difficult to distinguish between the permanent rulers and the organization itself. Conversely, in a democratic system which has a turnover of its officers, members and citizens can blame any particular evil on the incumbents and remain completely loyal to the organization. Thus more loyalty and less treason will be found in a union or a state with a legitimate multiparty system than in a dictatorial one.

INTEGRATIVE INSTITUTIONS

If the study of democracy as a form of social system is one key task of political sociology, there are clearly many other topics which need further elaboration and investigation. Perhaps the most important of these is the legitimacy of a political system—the degree to which it is generally accepted by its citizens—discussed in Chapter 3. Most sociologists would agree that stable authority is power plus legitimacy. Yet little work has been done using the concept of legitimacy in the analysis of political systems.

Even such a basic relation as that between religion and national consensus is usually assumed rather than verified. Tocqueville stated more than a century ago that America was a more religious country than most European countries and suggested that there was a causal relationship between its religiosity and its democratic institutions. Today many American intellectuals, at the end of a long period of adherence to secularism, are rediscovering religion's strength. Some are now

[34] S. M. Lipset, M. Trow, and J. S. Coleman, *op. cit.*

ready to accept the assumption that it is a major source of stability and democracy. This tendency to applaud uncritically religion's social functions is, however, potentially as unfruitful for the understanding of its role as was the previous antagonism. There is evidence (see Chapter 4) that religion, particularly in the form of sects, has served as a functional alternative to political extremism. During the Depression, when organized radicalism made little headway in this country, small religious sects grew rapidly.[35] On the other hand, more recent data indicate that those who are highly religious tend to be among the most intolerant politically.[36] Clearly there is room for much more research on the relationship of religion to the relative strength of democratic institutions, as well as for a continuation of the more conventional analysis of religion as a source of cleavage in public controversies.

The question arises whether social institutions may be ranked and analyzed according to their integrative and non-integrative character.[37] If we look at the major institutions, it is clear that economic ones, although a prime source of social integration since "the processes of production . . . require the 'co-operation' or integration of a variety of different agencies,"[38] are also the most disruptive and centrifugal.

It is obvious that the distribution of wealth is the most important source of interest-conflict in complex societies. At the opposite pole is the institution of the family: the integrator par excellence. The second most powerful integrating force, as has been indicated, is often considered to be religion, which presumably ameliorates the strains arising out of the stratification system by diverting attention from it and adjusting men to their lot in life. However, religion has also been the source of considerable tension in many societies.

[35] See Elmer T. Clark, *The Small Sects in America* (New York: Abingdon Press, 1949).

[36] Samuel A. Stouffer, *op. cit.*, pp. 140–49.

[37] However, no institution is ever purely one or the other. Implicit in any institutional arrangement are integrative and disintegrative elements. Even such extremely disruptive patterns as crime, as Durkheim noted, contribute indirectly to social integration.

[38] T. Parsons, *The Social System, op. cit.*, p. 139.

Institutions which are organized along class lines contribute to both cleavage and integration. In general, the system of stratification creates discontent among those who are lowly placed, and is hence a source of cleavage, but it is also the principal means for placing people in different positions and motivating them to fulfill their roles. The organization of working-class groups into trade-unions or a labor party, for example, creates a mechanism for the expression of conflict but, perhaps even more important, integrates the workers into the body politic by giving them a legitimate means of obtaining their wants.

Research is also needed on the changing function of the intellectual in political life, especially on his relation to other elites and power groups, and on his role as the definer of issues.[39] Professors, professionals, and creative artists have too long deprecated their role in the political sphere, a judgment which is not shared by various congressional committees and many business leaders. The values held by a nation's teachers and intellectuals constitute an important political resource, as I have tried to indicate in Chapter 10.

Essentially this book suggests that the sociology of politics return to the problem posed by Tocqueville: the social requisites and consequences of democracy. And I think it shows that any attempt to deal adequately with such a problem forces us to the method he employed so successfully: comparative analysis.

[39] See especially Theodore Geiger, *Aufgaben und Stellung der Intelligenz in der Gesellschaft* (Stuttgart: F. Enke, 1949); Karl Mannheim, *Ideology and Utopia* (New York: Harcourt, Brace & Co., 1936), esp. pp. 136–46; Joseph Schumpeter, *Capitalism, Socialism and Democracy* (New York: Harper & Bros., 1947), pp. 145–55.

PART I

THE CONDITIONS OF
THE DEMOCRATIC ORDER

CHAPTER 2

Economic Development and Democracy

DEMOCRACY in a complex society may be defined as a political system which supplies regular constitutional opportunities for changing the governing officials, and a social mechanism which permits the largest possible part of the population to influence major decisions by choosing among contenders for political office.

This definition, abstracted largely from the work of Joseph Schumpeter and Max Weber,[1] implies a number of specific conditions: (1) a "political formula" or body of beliefs specifying which institutions—political parties, a free press, and so forth—are legitimate (accepted as proper by all); (2) one set of political leaders in office; and (3) one or more sets of recognized leaders attempting to gain office.

The need for these conditions is clear. *First,* if a political system is not characterized by a value system allowing the peaceful "play" of power, democracy becomes chaotic. This has been the problem faced by many Latin-American states. *Second,* if the outcome of the political game is not the periodic awarding of effective authority to one group, unstable and irresponsible government rather than democracy will result. This state of affairs existed in pre-Fascist Italy, and through much, though not all, of the history of the Third and Fourth

[1] Joseph Schumpeter, *Capitalism, Socialism and Democracy* (New York: Harper & Bros., 1947), pp. 232–302, esp. 269; Max Weber, *Essays in Sociology* (New York: Oxford University Press, 1946), p. 226; see also the brilliant discussion of the meaning of democracy by John Plamenatz in his chapter in Richard McKean, ed., *Democracy in a World of Tensions* (Chicago: University of Chicago Press, 1951), pp. 302–327.

French Republics, which were characterized by weak coalition governments, often formed among parties having major interest and value conflicts with each other. *Third,* if the conditions for perpetuating an effective opposition do not exist, the authority of the officials in power will steadily increase, and popular influence on policy will be at a minimum. This is the situation in all one-party states, and by general agreement, at least in the West, these are dictatorships.

This and the following chapter will consider two characteristics of a society which bear heavily on the problem of stable democracy: economic development and legitimacy, or the degree to which institutions are valued for themselves and considered right and proper. Since most countries which lack an enduring tradition of political democracy lie in the underdeveloped sections of the world, Weber may have been right when he suggested that modern democracy in its clearest form can occur only under capitalist industrialization.[2] However, an extremely high correlation between such things as income, education, and religion, on the one hand, and democracy, on the other, in any given society should not be anticipated even on theoretical grounds because, to the extent that the political subsystem of the society operates autonomously, a political form may persist under conditions normally adverse to the *emergence* of that form. Or a political form may develop because of a syndrome of unique historical factors even though the society's major characteristics favor another form. Germany is an example of a nation where growing industrialization, urbanization, wealth, and education favored the establishment of a democratic system, but in which a series of adverse historical events prevented democracy from securing legitimacy and thus weakened its ability to withstand crisis.

Key historical events may account for *either* the persistence *or* the failure of democracy in any particular society by starting a process which increases (or decreases) the likelihood

[2] See Max Weber, "Zur Lage der bürgerlichen Demokratie in Russland," *Archiv für Sozialwissenschaft und Sozialpolitik,* 22 (1906), pp. 346 ff.

that at the next critical point in the country's history democracy will win out again. Once established, a democratic political system "gathers momentum" and creates social supports (institutions) to ensure its continued existence.[3] Thus a "premature" democracy which survives will do so by (among other things) facilitating the growth of other conditions conducive to democracy, such as universal literacy, or autonomous private organizations.[4] In this chapter I am primarily concerned with the social conditions like education which serve to *support* democratic political systems, and I will not deal in detail with the internal mechanisms like the specific rules of the political game which serve to *maintain* them.[5]

A comparative study of complex social systems must necessarily deal rather summarily with the particular historical features of any one society.[6] However, the deviation of a given nation from a particular aspect of democracy is not too important, as long as the definitions used cover the great

[3] See S. M. Lipset, "A Sociologist Looks at History," *Pacific Sociological Review*, 1 (1958), pp. 13–17.

[4] Walter Galenson points out that democracy may also endanger economic development by allowing public pressure for consumption to divert resources from investment. The resultant conflict between the intense commitment to industrialization and the popular demand for immediate social services in turn undermines the democratic state. Thus, even if democracy is achieved by an underdeveloped nation, it is under constant pressure from the inherent conflicts in the developmental process. See Walter Galenson, ed., *Labor and Economic Development* (New York: John Wiley & Sons, 1959), pp. 16 ff.

[5] See Morris Janowitz and Dwaine Marvick, *Competitive Pressure and Democratic Consent*, Michigan Governmental Studies, No. 32 (Ann Arbor: University of Michigan Press, 1956); and Robert A. Dahl, *A Preface to Democratic Theory* (Chicago: University of Chicago Press, 1956), esp. Chap. 4, pp. 90–123, for recent systematic efforts to specify some of the internal mechanisms of democracy. See David Easton, "An Approach to the Analysis of Political Systems," *World Politics*, 9 (1957), pp. 383–400, for discussion of problems of internal analysis of political systems.

[6] No detailed examination of the political history of individual countries will be undertaken, since the relative degree or social content of democracy in different countries is not the real problem of this chapter.

majority of nations which are considered democratic or undemocratic. The precise dividing line between "more democratic" and "less democratic" is also not basic, since presumably democracy is not a unitary quality of a social system,
but a complex of characteristics which may be ranked in
many different ways. For this reason I have divided the countries under consideration into general categories, rather than
attempting to rank them from highest to lowest, although
even here such countries as Mexico pose problems.

Efforts to classify all countries raised a number of problems. To reduce some of the complications introduced by
the sharp variations in political practices in different parts
of the earth I have concentrated on differences among countries within the same political culture areas. The two best
areas for such internal comparison are Latin America, and
Europe and the English-speaking countries. More limited
comparisons can also be made among the Asian states and
among the Arab countries.

The main criteria used to define European democracies
are the uninterrupted continuation of political democracy
since World War I *and* the absence over the past twenty-five
years of a major political movement opposed to the democratic "rules of the game."[7] The somewhat less stringent criterion for Latin America is whether a given country has had
a history of more or less free elections for most of the post-
World War I period.[8] Where in Europe we look for stable

[7] The latter requirement means that no totalitarian movement,
either fascist or communist received 20 per cent of the vote during
this time. Actually all the European nations falling on the democratic
side of the continuum had totalitarian movements which secured
less than 7 per cent of the vote.

[8] The historian Arthur P. Whitaker has summarized the judgments of experts on Latin America to be that "the countries which
have approximated most closely to the democratic ideal have been
. . . Argentina, Brazil, Chile, Colombia, Costa Rica, and Uruguay."
See "The Pathology of Democracy in Latin America: A Historian's
Point of View," *American Political Science Review,* 44 (1950), pp.
101–18. To this group I have added Mexico. Mexico has allowed
freedom of the press, of assembly, and of organization to opposition
parties, although there is good evidence that it does not allow them

democracies, in South America we look for countries which have not had fairly constant dictatorial rule (See Table I).

Economic Development in Europe and the Americas

Perhaps the most common generalization linking political systems to other aspects of society has been that democracy is related to the state of economic development. The more well-to-do a nation, the greater the chances that it will sustain democracy. From Aristotle down to the present, men have argued that only in a wealthy society in which relatively few citizens lived at the level of real poverty could there be a situation in which the mass of the population intelligently participate in politics and develop the self-restraint necessary to avoid succumbing to the appeals of irresponsible demagogues. A society divided between a large impoverished mass and a small favored elite results either in oligarchy (dictatorial rule of the small upper stratum) or in tyranny (popular-based dictatorship). To give these two political forms modern labels, tyranny's face today is communism or Peronism; while oligarchy appears in the traditionalist dictatorships found in parts of Latin America, Thailand, Spain, or Portugal.

To test this hypothesis concretely, I have used various indices of economic development—wealth, industrialization, urbanization, and education—and computed averages (means)

---

the opportunity to win elections since ballots are counted by the incumbents. The existence of opposition groups, contested elections, and adjustments among the various factions of the governing *Partido Revolucionario Institucional* does introduce a considerable element of popular influence in the system.

The interesting effort of Russell Fitzgibbon to secure a "statistical evaluation of Latin American democracy" based on the opinion of various experts is not useful for the purposes of this paper. The judges were not only asked to rank countries as democratic on the basis of purely political criteria, but also considered the "standard of living" and "educational level." These latter factors may be conditions for democracy, but they are not an aspect of democracy as such. See Russell H. Fitzgibbon, "A Statistical Evaluation of Latin American Democracy," *Western Political Quarterly*, 9 (1956), pp. 607–19.

TABLE I

CLASSIFICATION OF EUROPEAN, ENGLISH-SPEAKING, AND LATIN-AMERICAN NATIONS BY DEGREE OF STABLE DEMOCRACY

European and English-speaking Nations		Latin-American Nations	
Stable Democracies	*Unstable Democracies and Dictatorships*	*Democracies and Unstable Dictatorships*	*Stable Dictatorships*
Australia	Albania	Argentina	Bolivia
Belgium	Austria	Brazil	Cuba
Canada	Bulgaria	Chile	Dominican Republic
Denmark	Czechoslovakia	Colombia	Ecuador
Ireland	Finland	Costa Rica	El Salvador
Luxembourg	France	Mexico	Guatemala
Netherlands	Germany	Uruguay	Haiti
New Zealand	Greece		Honduras
Norway	Hungary		Nicaragua
Sweden	Iceland		Panama
Switzerland	Italy		Paraguay
United Kingdom	Poland		Peru
United States	Portugal		Venezuela
	Rumania		
	Spain		
	U.S.S.R.		
	Yugoslavia		

for the countries which have been classified as more or less democratic in the Anglo-Saxon world and Europe, and in Latin America.

In each case, the average wealth, degree of industrialization and urbanization, and level of education is much higher for the more democratic countries, as the data in Table II indicate. If I had combined Latin America and Europe in one table, the differences would have been even greater.[9]

The main indices of *wealth* used are per capita income, number of persons per motor vehicle and thousands of persons per physician, and the number of radios, telephones, and newspapers per thousand persons. The differences are striking on every score (See Table II). In the more democratic European countries, there are 17 persons per motor vehicle compared to 143 for the less democratic. In the less dictatorial Latin-American countries there are 99 persons per motor vehicle versus 274 for the more dictatorial.[10] Income differ-

[9] Lyle W. Shannon has correlated indices of economic development with whether a country is self-governing or not, and his conclusions are substantially the same. Since Shannon does not give details on the countries categorized as self-governing and nonself-governing, there is no direct measure of the relation between "democratic" and "self-governing" countries. All the countries examined in this chapter, however, were chosen on the assumption that a characterization as "democratic" is meaningless for a nonself-governing country, and therefore, presumably, all of them, whether democratic or dictatorial, would fall within Shannon's "self-governing" category. Shannon shows that underdevelopment is related to lack of self-government; my data indicate that once self-government is attained, development is still related to the character of the political system. See the book edited by Shannon, *Underdeveloped Areas* (New York: Harper & Bros., 1957), and also his article, "Is Level of Development Related to Capacity for Self-Government?" *American Journal of Economics and Sociology*, 17 (1958), pp. 367–82. In the latter paper Shannon constructs a composite index of development, using some of the same indices, such as inhabitants per physician, and derived from the same United Nations sources, as appear in the tables to follow. Shannon's work did not come to my attention until after this chapter was first prepared, so that the two analyses can be considered as separate tests of comparable hypotheses.

[10] It must be remembered that these figures are means, compiled from census figures for the various countries. The data vary widely in

ences for the groups are also sharp, dropping from an average per capita income of $695 for the more democratic countries of Europe to $308 for the less democratic; the corresponding difference for Latin America is from $171 to $119. The ranges are equally consistent, with the lowest per capita income in each group falling in the "less democratic" category, and the highest in the "more democratic."

Industrialization, to which indices of wealth are of course clearly related, is measured by the percentage of employed males in agriculture and the per capita commercially produced "energy" being used in the country (measured in terms of tons of coal per person per year). Both of these show equally consistent results. The average percentage of employed males working in agriculture and related occupations was 21 in the "more democratic" European countries and 41 in the "less democratic"; 52 in the "less dictatorial" Latin-American countries and 67 in the "more dictatorial." The differences in per capita energy employed are equally large.

The degree of *urbanization* is also related to the existence of democracy.[11] Three different indices of urbanization are available from data compiled by International Urban Research (Berkeley, California): the percentage of the population in communities of 20,000 and over, the percentage in

---

accuracy, and there is no way of measuring the validity of compound calculated figures such as those presented here. The consistent direction of all these differences, and their large magnitude, is the main indication of validity.

[11] Urbanization has often been linked to democracy by political theorists. Harold J. Laski asserted that "organized democracy is the product of urban life," and that it was natural therefore that it should have "made its first effective appearance" in the Greek city states, limited as was their definition of "citizen." See his article "Democracy" in the *Encyclopedia of the Social Sciences* (New York: Macmillan, 1937), Vol. V, pp. 76–85. Max Weber held that the city, as a certain type of political community, is a peculiarly Western phenomenon, and traced the emergence of the notion of "citizenship" from social developments closely related to urbanization. For a partial statement of his point of view, see the chapter on "Citizenship" in *General Economic History* (Glencoe: The Free Press, 1950), pp. 315–38.

TABLE II*

A COMPARISON OF EUROPEAN, ENGLISH-SPEAKING, AND LATIN-AMERICAN COUNTRIES, DIVIDED INTO TWO GROUPS, "MORE DEMOCRATIC" AND "LESS DEMOCRATIC," BY INDICES OF WEALTH, INDUSTRIALIZATION, EDUCATION, AND URBANIZATION[1]

A. Indices of Wealth

Means	Per Capita Income[2]	Thousands of Persons per Doctor[3]	Persons per Motor Vehicle[4]
European and English-speaking Stable Democracies	U.S.$ 695	.86	17
European and English-speaking Unstable Democracies and Dictatorships	308	1.4	143
Latin-American Democracies and Unstable Dictatorships	171	2.1	99
Latin-American Stable Dictatorships	119	4.4	274
Ranges			
European Stable Democracies	420–1,453	.7–1.2	3–62
European Dictatorships	128–482	.6–4	10–538
Latin-American Democracies	112–346	.8–3.3	31–174
Latin-American Stable Dictatorships	40–331	1.0–10.8	38–428

Means	Telephones per 1,000 Persons[5]	Radios per 1,000 Persons[6]	Newspaper Copies per 1,000 Persons[7]
European and English-speaking Stable Democracies	205	350	341
European and English-speaking Unstable Democracies and Dictatorships	58	160	167

* Notes 1 to 16 at end of chapter.

Means	Telephones per 1,000 Persons	Radios per 1,000 Persons	Newspaper Copies per 1,000 Persons
Latin-American Democracies and Unstable Dictatorships	25	85	102
Latin-American Stable Dictatorships	10	43	43
Ranges			
European Stable Democracies	43–400	160–995	242–570
European Dictatorships	7–196	42–307	46–390
Latin-American Democracies	12–58	38–148	51–233
Latin-American Stable Dictatorships	1–24	4–154	4–111

B. Indices of Industrialization

Means	Percentage of Males in Agriculture[8]	Per Capita Energy Consumed[9]
European Stable Democracies	21	3.6
European Dictatorships	41	1.4
Latin-American Democracies	52	.6
Latin-American Stable Dictatorships	67	.25
Ranges		
European Stable Democracies	6–46	1.4–7.8
European Dictatorships	16–60	.27–3.2
Latin-American Democracies	30–63	.30–0.9
Latin-American Stable Dictatorships	46–87	.02–1.27

C. Indices of Education

Means	Percentage Literate[10]	Primary Education Enrollment per 1,000 Persons[11]	Post-Primary Enrollment per 1,000 Persons[12]	Higher Education Enrollment per 1,000 Persons[13]
European Stable Democracies	96	134	44	4.2
European Dictatorships	85	121	22	3.5
Latin-American Democracies	74	101	13	2.0
Latin-American Dictatorships	46	72	8	1.3
Ranges				
European Stable Democracies	95–100	96–179	19–83	1.7–17.83
European Dictatorships	55–98	61–165	8–37	1.6–6.1
Latin-American Democracies	48–87	75–137	7–27	.7–4.6
Latin-American Dictatorships	11–76	11–149	3–24	.2–3.1

D. Indices of Urbanization

Means	Per Cent in Cities over 20,000[14]	Per Cent in Cities over 100,000[15]	Per Cent in Metropolitan Areas[16]
European Stable Democracies	43	28	38
European Dictatorships	24	16	23
Latin-American Democracies	28	22	26
Latin-American Stable Dictatorships	17	12	15

	Per Cent in Cities over 20,000	Per Cent in Cities over 100,000	Per Cent in Metropolitan Areas
Ranges			
European Stable Democracies	28–54	17–51	22–56
European Dictatorships	12–44	6–33	7–49
Latin-American Democracies	11–48	13–37	17–44
Latin-American Stable Dictatorships	5–36	4–22	7–26

communities of 100,000 and over, and the percentage residing in standard metropolitan areas. On all three of these indices the more democratic countries score higher than the less democratic for both of the areas under investigation.

Many people have suggested that the higher the *education* level of a nation's population, the better the chances for democracy, and the comparative data available support this proposition. The "more democratic" countries of Europe are almost entirely literate: the lowest has a rate of 96 per cent; while the "less democratic" nations have an average rate of 85 per cent. In Latin America the difference is between an average rate of 74 per cent for the "less dictatorial" countries and 46 per cent for the "more dictatorial."[12] The educational enrollment per thousand total population at three different levels—primary, post-primary, and higher educational—is equally consistently related to the degree of democ-

[12] The pattern indicated by a comparison of the averages for each group of countries is sustained by the ranges (the high and low extremes) for each index. Most of the ranges overlap; that is, some countries which are in the "less democratic" category are higher on any given index than some which are "more democratic." It is noteworthy that in both Europe and Latin America, the nations which are lowest on any of the indices presented in the table are also in the "less democratic" category. Conversely, almost all countries which rank at the top of any of the indices are in the "more democratic" class.

racy. The tremendous disparity is shown by the extreme cases of Haiti and the United States. Haiti has fewer children (11 per thousand) attending school in the primary grades than the United States has attending colleges (almost 18 per thousand).

The relationship between education and democracy is worth more extensive treatment since an entire philosophy of government has seen increased education as the basic requirement of democracy.[13] As James Bryce wrote, with special reference to South America, "education, if it does not make men good citizens, makes it at least easier for them to become so."[14] Education presumably broadens man's outlook, enables him to understand the need for norms of tolerance, restrains him from adhering to extremist doctrines, and increases his capacity to make rational electoral choices.

The evidence on the contribution of education to democracy is even more direct and strong on the level of individual behavior *within* countries than it is in cross-national correlations. Data gathered by public opinion research agencies which have questioned people in different countries about their beliefs on tolerance for the opposition, their attitudes toward ethnic

[13] See John Dewey, *Democracy and Education* (New York: Macmillan, 1916).

[14] James Bryce, *South America: Observations and Impressions* (New York: Macmillan, 1912), p. 546. Bryce considered several classes of conditions in South America which affected the chances for democracy, some of which are substantially the same as those presented here. The physical conditions of a country determined the ease of communications between areas, and thus the ease of formation of a "common public opinion." By "racial" conditions Bryce really meant whether there was ethnic homogeneity or not, with the existence of different ethnic or language groups preventing that "homogeneity and solidarity of the community which are almost indispensable conditions to the success of democratic government." Economic and social conditions included economic development, widespread political participation, and literacy. Bryce also detailed the specific historical factors which, over and above these "general" factors, operated in each South American country. See James Bryce, *op. cit.*, pp. 527–33 and 580 ff. See also Karl Mannheim, *Freedom, Power and Democratic Planning* (New York: Oxford University Press, 1950).

or racial minorities, and their feelings for multi-party as against one-party systems have showed that the most important single factor differentiating those giving democratic responses from the others has been education. The higher one's education, the more likely one is to believe in democratic values and support democratic practices.[15] All the relevant studies indicate that education is more significant than either income or occupation.

These findings should lead us to anticipate a far higher correlation between national levels of education and political practice than we in fact find. Germany and France have been among the best educated nations of Europe, but this by itself did not stabilize their democracies.[16] It may be, however, that their educational level has served to inhibit other anti-democratic forces.

If we cannot say that a "high" level of education is a *sufficient* condition for democracy, the available evidence suggests that it comes close to being a *necessary* one. In Latin America, where widespread illiteracy still exists, only one of all the nations in which more than half the population is

[15] See G. H. Smith, "Liberalism and Level of Information," *Journal of Educational Psychology*, 39 (1948), pp. 65–82; Martin A. Trow, *Right Wing Radicalism and Political Intolerance* (Ph.D. thesis, Department of Sociology, Columbia University, 1957), p. 17; Samuel A. Stouffer, *Communism, Conformity, and Civil Liberties* (New York: Doubleday & Co., Inc., 1955); Kotaro Kido and Masataka Sugi, "A Report of Research on Social Stratification and Mobility in Tokyo" (III), *Japanese Sociological Review*, 4 (1954), pp. 74–100. This point is also discussed in Chap. 4.

[16] Dewey has suggested that the character of the educational system will influence its effect on democracy, and this may shed some light on the sources of instability in Germany. The purpose of German education, according to Dewey, writing in 1916, was one of "disciplinary training rather than of personal development." The main aim was to produce "absorption of the aims and meaning of existing institutions," and "thoroughgoing subordination" to them. This point raises issues which cannot be entered into here, but indicates the complex character of the relationship between democracy and closely related factors, such as education. See John Dewey, *op. cit.*, pp. 108–10.

illiterate—Brazil—can be included in the "more democratic" group.

Lebanon, the one member of the Arab League which has maintained democratic institutions since World War II, is also by far the best educated (over 80 per cent literacy). East of the Arab world, only two states, the Philippines and Japan, have since 1945 maintained democratic regimes without the presence of large antidemocratic parties. And these two countries, although lower than most European states in per capita income, are among the world's leaders in educational attainment. The Philippines actually rank second to the United States in the proportion of people attending high schools and universities, and Japan has a higher educational level than any European nation.[17]

Although the evidence has been presented separately, all the various aspects of economic development—industrialization, urbanization, wealth, and education—are so closely interrelated as to form one major factor which has the political correlate of democracy.[18] A recent study of the Middle East further substantiates this. In 1951–52, a survey of Turkey, Lebanon, Egypt, Syria, Jordan, and Iran, conducted by Daniel Lerner and the Bureau of Applied Social Research, found a close connection between urbanization, literacy, voting rates, media consumption and production, and educa-

---

[17] Ceylon, which shares the distinction with the Philippines and Japan of being the only democratic countries in South and Far East Asia in which the communists are unimportant electorally, also shares with them the distinction of being the only countries in this area in which a *majority* of the population is literate. It should be noted, however, that Ceylon does have a fairly large Trotskyist party, now the official opposition, and while its educational level is high for Asia, it is much lower than either Japan or the Philippines.

[18] This statement is a "statistical" statement, which necessarily means that there will be many exceptions to the correlation. Thus we know that poorer people are more likely to vote for the Democratic or Labor parties in the U.S. and England. The fact that a large minority of the lower strata vote for the more conservative party in these countries does not challenge the proposition that stratification position is a main determinant of party choice.

tion.[19] Simple and multiple correlations between the four basic variables were computed for all countries for which United Nations statistics were available (in this case 54) with the following results:[20]

Dependent Variable	Multiple Correlation Coefficient
Urbanization	.61
Literacy	.91
Media Participation	.84
Political Participation	.82

In the Middle East, Turkey and Lebanon score higher on most of these indices than do the other four countries analyzed, and Daniel Lerner, in reporting on the study, points out that the "great post-war events in Egypt, Syria, Jordan and Iran have been the violent struggles for the control of power—struggles notably absent in Turkey and Lebanon [until very recently] where the control of power has been decided by elections."[21]

Lerner further points out the effect of disproportionate development, in one area or another, for over-all stability, and the need for co-ordinated changes in all of these variables. Comparing urbanization and literacy in Egypt and Turkey,

[19] The study is reported in Daniel Lerner's *The Passing of Traditional Society* (Glencoe: The Free Press, 1958). These correlations are derived from census data; the main sections of the survey dealt with reactions to and opinions about the mass media, with inferences as to the personality types appropriate to modern and to traditional society.

[20] *Ibid.*, p. 63. The index of political participation was the per cent voting in the last five elections. These results cannot be considered as independent verification of the relationships presented in this paper, since the data and variables are basically the same (as they are also in the work by Lyle Shannon, *op. cit.*), but the identical results using three entirely different methods, the phi coefficient, multiple correlations, and means and ranges, show decisively that the relationships cannot be attributed to artifacts of the computations. It should also be noted that the three analyses were made without knowledge of each other.

[21] *Ibid.*, pp. 84–85.

he concludes that although Egypt is far more urbanized than Turkey, it is not really "modernized," and does not even have an adequate base for modernization, because literacy has not kept pace. In Turkey, all of the several indices of modernization have kept pace with each other, with rising voting participation (36 per cent in 1950), balanced by rising literacy, urbanization, etc. In Egypt, the cities are full of "homeless illiterates," who provide a ready audience for political mobilization in support of extremist ideologies. On Lerner's scale, Egypt should be twice as literate as Turkey, since it is twice as urbanized. The fact that it is only half as literate explains, for Lerner, the "imbalances" which "tend to become circular and to accelerate social disorganization," political as well as economic.[22]

Lerner introduces one important theoretical addition—the suggestion that these key variables in the modernization process may be viewed as historical phases, with democracy part of later developments, the "crowning institution of the participant society" (one of his terms for a modern industrial society). His view on the relations between these variables, seen as stages, is worth quoting at some length:

> The secular evolution of a participant society appears to involve a regular sequence of three phases. Urbanization comes first, for cities alone have devel-

[22] *Ibid.*, pp. 87–89. Other theories of underdeveloped areas have also stressed the circular character of the forces sustaining a given level of economic and social development, and in a sense this paper may be regarded as an effort to extend the analysis of the complex of institutions constituting a "modernized" society to the political sphere. Leo Schnore's forthcoming monograph, *Economic Development and Urbanization: An Ecological Approach*, relates technological, demographic, and organizational (including literacy and per capita income) variables as an interdependent complex. Harvey Leibenstein's recent volume, *Economic Backwardness and Economic Growth* (New York: John Wiley & Sons, 1957), views "underdevelopment" within the framework of a "quasi-equilibrium" economic theory, as a complex of associated and mutually supportive aspects of a society, and includes cultural and political characteristics—illiteracy, the lack of a middle class, a crude communications system—as part of the complex. (See pp. 39–41.)

oped the complex of skills and resources which characterize the modern industrial economy. Within this urban matrix develop both of the attributes which distinguish the next two phases—literacy and media growth. There is a close reciprocal relationship between these, for the literate develop the media which in turn spread literacy. But, literacy performs the key function in the second phase. The capacity to read, at first acquired by relatively few people, equips them to perform the varied tasks required in the modernizing society. Not until the third phase, when the elaborate technology of industrial development is fairly well advanced, does a society begin to produce newspapers, radio networks, and motion pictures on a massive scale. This, in turn, accelerates the spread of literacy. Out of this interaction develop those institutions of participation (e.g., voting) which we find in all advanced modern societies.[23]

Lerner's thesis, that these elements of modernization are functionally interdependent, is by no means established by his data. But the material presented in this chapter offers

[23] Lerner, *op. cit.*, p. 60. Lerner also focuses upon certain personality requirements of a "modern" society which may also be related to the personality requirements of democracy. According to him, the physical and social mobility of modern society requires a mobile personality, capable of adaption to rapid change. Development of a "mobile sensibility so adaptive to change that rearrangement of the self-system is its distinctive mode" has been the work of the twentieth century. Its main feature is *empathy*, denoting the "general capacity to see oneself in the other fellow's situation, whether favorably or unfavorably." (See pp. 49 ff.)

Whether this psychological characteristic results in a predisposition toward democracy (implying a willingness to accept the viewpoint of others) or is rather associated with the antidemocratic tendencies of a "mass society" type of personality (implying the lack of any solid personal values rooted in rewarding participation) is an open question. Possibly empathy (a more or less "cosmopolitan" outlook) is a general personality characteristic of modern societies, with other special conditions determining whether or not it has the social consequence of tolerance and democratic attitudes, or rootlessness and anomie.

an opportunity for research along these lines. Deviant cases, such as Egypt, where "lagging" literacy is associated with serious strains and potential upheaval, may also be found in Europe and Latin America, and their analysis—a task not attempted here—will further clarify the basic dynamics of modernization and the problem of social stability in the midst of institutional change.

Economic Development and the Class Struggle

Economic development, producing increased income, greater economic security, and widespread higher education, largely determines the form of the "class struggle," by permitting those in the lower strata to develop longer time perspectives and more complex and gradualist views of politics. A belief in secular reformist gradualism can be the ideology of only a relatively well-to-do lower class. Striking evidence for this thesis may be found in the relationship between the patterns of working-class political action in different countries and the national income, a correlation that is almost startling in view of the many other cultural, historical, and juridical factors which affect the political life of nations.

In the two wealthiest countries, the United States and Canada, not only are communist parties almost nonexistent but socialist parties have never been able to establish themselves as major forces. Among the eight next wealthiest countries—New Zealand, Switzerland, Sweden, United Kingdom, Denmark, Australia, Norway, Belgium, Luxembourg and Netherlands—all of whom had a per capita income of over $500 a year in 1949 (the last year for which standardized United Nations statistics exist), moderate socialism predominates as the form of leftist politics. In none of these countries did the Communists secure more than 7 per cent of the vote, and the actual Communist party average among them has been about 4 per cent. In the eight European countries which were below the $500 per capita income mark in 1949—France, Iceland, Czechoslovakia, Finland, West Germany, Hungary, Italy, and Austria—and which have had at

least one postwar democratic election in which both communist and noncommunist parties could compete, the Communist party has had more than 16 per cent of the vote in
six, and an over-all average of more than 20 per cent in the
eight countries as a group. The two low-income countries in
which the Communists are weak—Germany and Austria—
have both had direct experience with Soviet occupation.[24]

Leftist extremism has also dominated working-class politics in two other European nations which belong to the
under $500 per capita income group—Spain and Greece. In
Spain before Franco, anarchism and left socialism were much
stronger than moderate socialism; while in Greece, whose per
capita income in 1949 was only $128, the Communists have
always been much stronger than the socialists, and fellow-
traveling parties have secured a large vote in recent years.[25]

The inverse relationship between national economic development as reflected by per capita income and the strength
of Communists and other extremist groups among Western
nations is seemingly stronger than the correlations between
other national variables like ethnic or religious factors.[26] Two

---

[24] It should be noted that before 1933–34, Germany had one of
the largest Communist parties in Europe; while the Socialist party
of Austria was the most left-wing and Marxist European party in the
Socialist International.

[25] Greece, economically the poorest political democracy in Europe, "is now the only country in Europe where there is no
socialist party. The Socialist party (ELD), established in 1945 by
individuals who collaborated with the Communists during the Occupation, dissolved itself in August 1953, a victim of its fickle and
pro-Communist policy. The whole field was then surrendered to the
Communists with the justification that conditions were not mature
enough for the development of a socialist movement!" Manolis
Korakas, "Grecian Apathy," *Socialist Commentary*, May 1957, p.
21; in the elections of May 11, 1958, the "Communist directed"
Union of the Democratic Left won 78 out of 300 parliamentary
seats and is now the second largest party in the country. See *New York
Times*, May 16, 1958, p. 3, col. 4.

[26] The relationship expressed above can be presented in another
way. The seven European countries in which Communist or fellow-
traveling parties have secured large votes in free elections had an
average per capita income in 1949 of $330. The ten European coun-

of the poorer nations with large Communist movements—Iceland and Finland—are Scandinavian and Lutheran. Among the Catholic nations of Europe, all the poor ones except Austria have large Communist or anarchist movements. The two wealthiest Catholic democracies—Belgium and Luxembourg—have few Communists. Though the French and Italian cantons of Switzerland are strongly affected by the cultural life of France and Italy, there are almost no Communists among the workers in these cantons, living in the wealthiest country in Europe.

The relation between low per capita wealth and the precipitation of sufficient discontent to provide the social basis for political extremism is supported by a recent comparative polling survey of the attitudes of citizens of nine countries. Among these countries, feelings of personal security correlated with per capita income (.45) and with per capita food supply (.55). If satisfaction with one's country, as measured by responses to the question, "Which country in the world gives you the best chance of living the kind of life you would like to live?" is used as an index of the amount of discontent in a nation, then the relationship with economic wealth is even higher. The study reports a rank order correlation of .74 between per capita income and the degree of satisfaction with one's own country.[27]

This does not mean that economic hardship or poverty *per se* is the main cause of radicalism. There is much evidence to sustain the argument that stable poverty in a situation in which individuals are not exposed to the possibilities of change breeds, if anything, conservatism.[28] Individuals whose experience limits their significant communications and interaction to others on the same level as themselves will,

---

tries in which the Communists have been a failure electorally had an average per capita income of $585.

[27] William Buchanan and Hadley Cantril, *How Nations See Each Other* (Urbana: University of Illinois Press, 1953), p. 35.

[28] See Emile Durkheim, *Suicide: A Study in Sociology* (Glencoe: The Free Press, 1951), pp. 253–54; see also Daniel Bell, "The Theory of Mass Society," *Commentary*, 22 (1956), p. 80.

other conditions being equal, be more conservative than people who may be better off but who have been exposed to the possibilities of securing a better way of life.[29] The dynamic in the situation would seem to be exposure to the possibility of a better way of life rather than poverty as such. As Karl Marx put it in a perceptive passage: "A house may be large or small; as long as the surrounding houses are equally small it satisfies all social demands for a dwelling. But if a palace arises beside the little house, the little house shrinks into a hut."[30]

With the growth of modern means of communication and transportation both within and among countries, it seems increasingly likely that the groups in the population that are poverty-stricken but are isolated from knowledge of better ways of life or unaware of the possibilities for improvement in their condition are becoming rarer and rarer, particularly in the urban areas of the Western world. One may expect to find such stable poverty only in tradition-dominated societies.

Since position in a stratification system is always relative and gratification or deprivation is experienced in terms of being better or worse off than other people, it is not surprising that the lower classes in all countries, regardless of the wealth of the country, show various signs of resentment against the existing distribution of rewards by supporting political parties and other organizations which advocate some form of redistribution.[31] The fact that the form which these

[29] There is also a considerable body of evidence which indicates that those occupations which are economically vulnerable and those workers who have experienced unemployment are prone to be more leftist in their outlook. See Chap. 7, pp. 242–49.

[30] Karl Marx, "Wage-Labor and Capital," in *Selected Works,* Vol. I (New York: International Publishers, 1933), pp. 268–69. "Social tensions are an expression of unfulfilled expectations," Daniel Bell, *op. cit.,* p. 80.

[31] A summary of the findings of election studies in many countries shows that, with few exceptions, there is a strong relationship between lower social position and support of "leftist" politics. There are, of course, many other characteristics which are also related to left voting, some of which are found among relatively well paid but socially isolated groups. Among the population as a whole, men are much

political parties take in poorer countries is more extremist and radical than it is in wealthier ones is probably more related to the greater degree of inequality in such countries than to the fact that their poor are actually poorer in absolute terms. A comparative study of wealth distribution by the United Nations "suggest[s] that the richest fraction of the population (the richest 10th, 5th, etc.) generally receive[s] a greater proportion of the total income in the less developed than in the more developed countries."[32] The gap between the income of professional and semiprofessional personnel on the one hand and ordinary workers on the other is much wider in the poorer than in the wealthier countries. Among manual workers, "there seems to be a greater wage discrepancy between skilled and unskilled workers in the less developed countries. In contrast the leveling process, in several of the developed countries at least, has been facilitated by the over-all increase of national income . . . not so much by reduction of the income of the relatively rich as by the faster growth of the incomes of the relatively poor."[33]

---

more likely to vote for the left than women, while members of minority religious and ethnic groups also display a leftist tendency. (See Chaps. 7 and 8.)

[32] *United Nations Preliminary Report on the World Social Situation* (New York: 1952), pp. 132–33. Gunnar Myrdal, the Swedish economist, has recently pointed out: "It is, indeed, a regular occurrence endowed almost with the dignity of an economic law that the poorer the country, the greater the difference between poor and rich." *An International Economy* (New York: Harper & Bros., 1956), p. 133.

[33] *United Nations Preliminary Report . . . , ibid.* (See also Table II.) A recently completed comparison of income distribution in the United States and a number of western European countries concludes that "there has not been any great difference" in patterns of income distribution among these countries. These findings of Robert Solow appear to contradict those reported above from the U.N. Statistics Office, although the latter are dealing primarily with differences between industrialized and underdeveloped nations. In any case, it should be noted that Solow agrees that the relative position of the lower strata in a poor as compared with a wealthy country is quite different. As he states, "in comparing Europe and America, one may ask whether it makes sense to talk about relative income in-

The distribution of consumption goods also tends to become more equitable as the size of national income increases. The wealthier a country, the larger the proportion of its population which owns automobiles, telephones, bathtubs, refrigerating equipment, and so forth. Where there is a dearth of goods, the sharing of such goods must inevitably be less equitable than in a country in which there is relative abundance. For example, the number of people who can afford automobiles, washing machines, decent housing, telephones, good clothes, or have their children complete high school or go to college still represents only a small minority of the population in many European countries. The great national wealth of the United States or Canada, or even to a lesser extent the Australasian Dominions or Sweden, means that there is relatively little difference between the standards of living of adjacent social classes, and that even classes which are far apart in the social structure will enjoy more nearly similar consumption patterns than will comparable classes in Southern Europe. To a Southern European, and to an even greater extent to the inhabitant of one of the "underdeveloped" countries, social stratification is characterized by a much greater distinction in ways of life, with little overlap in the goods the various strata own or can afford to purchase. It may be suggested, therefore, that the wealthier a country, the less is status inferiority experienced as a major source of deprivation.

Increased wealth and education also serve democracy by increasing the lower classes' exposure to cross-pressures which reduce their commitment to given ideologies and make them less receptive to extremist ones. The operation of this process will be discussed in more detail in the next chapter, but it

---

equality independently of the absolute level of income. An income four times another income has different content according as the lower income means malnutrition on the one hand or provides some surplus on the other." Robert M. Solow, A *Survey of Income Inequality Since the War* (Stanford: Center for Advanced Study in the Behavioral Sciences, 1958, mimeographed), pp. 41–44, 78.

means involving those strata in an integrated national culture as distinct from an isolated lower-class one.

Marx believed that the proletariat was a revolutionary force because it had nothing to lose but its chains and could win the whole world. But Tocqueville, analyzing the reasons why the lower strata in America supported the system, paraphrased and transposed Marx before Marx ever made his analysis by pointing out that "only those who have nothing to lose ever revolt."[34]

Increased wealth also affects the political role of the middle class by changing the shape of the stratification structure from an elongated pyramid, with a large lower-class base, to a diamond with a growing middle class. A large middle class tempers conflict by rewarding moderate and democratic parties and penalizing extremist groups.

The political values and style of the upper class, too, are related to national income. The poorer a country and the lower the absolute standard of living of the lower classes, the greater the pressure on the upper strata to treat the lower as vulgar, innately inferior, a lower caste beyond the pale of human society. The sharp difference in the style of living between those at the top and those at the bottom makes this psychologically necessary. Consequently, the upper strata in such a situation tend to regard political rights for the lower strata, particularly the right to share power, as essentially absurd and immoral. The upper strata not only resist democracy themselves; their often arrogant political behavior serves to intensify extremist reactions on the part of the lower classes.

The general income level of a nation also affects its receptivity to democratic norms. If there is enough wealth in the country so that it does not make too much difference whether some redistribution takes place, it is easier to accept the idea that it does not matter greatly which side is in power. But if loss of office means serious losses for major power groups, they will seek to retain or secure office by any means available.

[34] Alexis de Tocqueville, *Democracy in America*, Vol. I (New York: Alfred A. Knopf, Vintage ed., 1945), p. 258.

A certain amount of national wealth is likewise necessary to ensure a competent civil service. The poorer the country, the greater the emphasis on nepotism—support of kin and friends. And this in turn reduces the opportunity to develop the efficient bureaucracy which a modern democratic state requires.[35]

Intermediary organizations which act as sources of countervailing power seem to be similarly associated with national wealth. Tocqueville and other exponents of what has come to be known as the theory of the "mass society"[36] have argued that a country without a multitude of organizations relatively independent of the central state power has a high dictatorial as well as revolutionary potential. Such organizations serve a number of functions: they inhibit the state or any single source of private power from dominating all political resources; they are a source of new opinions; they can be the means of communicating ideas, particularly opposition ideas, to a large section of the citizenry; they train men in political skills and so help to increase the level of interest and participation in politics. Although there are no reliable data on the relationship between national patterns of voluntary organization and national political systems, evidence from studies of individual behavior demonstrates that, regardless of other factors, men who belong to associations are more likely than others to give the democratic answer to questions concerning

[35] For a discussion of this problem in a new state, see David Apter, *The Gold Coast in Transition* (Princeton: Princeton University Press, 1955), esp. Chaps. 9 and 13. Apter shows the importance of efficient bureaucracy, and the acceptance of bureaucratic values and behavior patterns for the existence of a democratic political order.

[36] See Emil Lederer, *The State of the Masses* (New York: Norton, 1940); Hannah Arendt, *Origins of Totalitarianism* (New York: Harcourt, Brace & Co., 1951); Max Horkheimer, *Eclipse of Reason* (New York: Oxford University Press, 1947); Karl Mannheim, *Man and Society in an Age of Reconstruction* (New York: Harcourt, Brace & Co., 1940); Philip Selznick, *The Organizational Weapon* (New York: McGraw-Hill Book Co., 1952); José Ortega y Gasset, *The Revolt of the Masses* (New York: Norton, 1932); William Kornhauser, *The Politics of Mass Society* (Glencoe: The Free Press, 1959).

tolerance and party systems, to vote, or to participate actively in politics. Since the more well-to-do and better educated a man is, the more likely he is to belong to voluntary organizations, the propensity to form such groups seems to be a function of level of income and opportunities for leisure within given nations.[37]

The Politics of Rapid Economic Development

The association between economic development and democracy has led many Western statesmen and political com-

[37] See Edward Banfield, *The Moral Basis of a Backward Society* (Glencoe: The Free Press, 1958), for an excellent description of the way in which abysmal poverty serves to reduce community organization in southern Italy. The data which do exist from polling surveys conducted in the United States, Germany, France, Great Britain, and Sweden show that somewhere between 40 and 50 per cent of the adults in these countries belong to voluntary associations, without lower rates of membership for the less stable democracies, France and Germany, than among the more stable ones, the United States, Great Britain, and Sweden. These results seemingly challenge the general proposition, although no definite conclusion can be made, since most of the studies employed noncomparable categories. This point bears further research in many countries. For the data on these countries see the following studies.

For France, see Arnold Rose, *Theory and Method in the Social Sciences* (Minneapolis, University of Minnesota Press, 1954), p. 74 and O. R. Gallagher, "Voluntary Associations in France," *Social Forces*, 36 (1957), pp. 154–56; for Germany see Erich Reigrotzki, *Soziale Verflechtungen in der Bundesrepublik* (Tübingen: J. D. B. Mohr, 1956), p. 164; for the U.S. see Charles L. Wright and Herbert H. Hyman, "Voluntary Association Memberships of American Adults: Evidence from National Sample Surveys," *American Sociological Review*, 23 (1958), p. 287, J. C. Scott, Jr., "Membership and Participation in Voluntary Associations," *American Sociological Review*, 22 (1957), pp. 315–26 and Herbert Maccoby, "The Differential Political Activity of Participants in a Voluntary Association," *American Sociological Review*, 23 (1958), pp. 524–33; for Great Britain see Mass Observation, *Puzzled People* (London: Victor Gollancz, 1947), p. 119 and Thomas Bottomore, "Social Stratification in Voluntary Organizations," in David Glass, ed., *Social Mobility in Britain* (Glencoe: The Free Press, 1954), p. 354; for Sweden see Gunnar Heckscher, "Pluralist Democracy: The Swedish Experience," *Social Research*, 15 (1948), pp. 417–61.

mentators to conclude that the basic political problem of our day is produced by the pressure for rapid industrialization. If only the underdeveloped nations can be successfully started on the road to high productivity, the assumption runs, we can defeat the major threat to newly established democracies, their domestic Communists. In a curious way, this view marks the victory of economic determinism or vulgar Marxism within democratic political thought. Unfortunately for this theory, political extremism based on the lower classes, communism in particular, is not to be found only in low-income countries but also in newly industrializing nations. This correlation is not, of course, a recent phenomenon. In 1884, Engels noted that explicitly socialist labor movements had developed in Europe during periods of rapid industrial growth, and that these movements declined sharply during later periods of slower change.

The pattern of leftist politics in northern Europe in the first half of the twentieth century in countries whose socialist and trade-union movements are now relatively moderate and conservative illustrates this point. Wherever industrialization occurred *rapidly*, introducing sharp *discontinuities* between the pre-industrial and industrial situation, more rather than less extremist working-class movements emerged. In Scandinavia, for example, the variations among the socialist movements of Denmark, Sweden, and Norway can be accounted for in large measure by the different timing and pace of industrialization, as the economist Walter Galenson has pointed out.[38] The Danish Social Democratic movement and trade-unions have always been in the reformist, moderate, and relatively non-Marxist wing of the international labor movement. In Denmark, industrialization developed as a slow and gradual process. The rate of urban growth was also moderate, which had a good effect on urban working-class housing conditions. The slow growth of industry meant that a large

[38] See Walter Galenson, *The Danish System of Labor Relations* (Cambridge: Harvard University Press, 1952); see also Galenson, "Scandinavia," in Galenson, ed., *Comparative Labor Movements* (New York: Prentice-Hall, 1952), esp. pp. 105–20.

proportion of Danish workers all during the period of industrialization were men who had been employed in industry for a long time, and, consequently, newcomers who had been pulled up from rural areas and who might have supplied the basis for extremist factions were always in a minority. The left-wing groups which gained some support in Denmark were based on the rapidly expanding industries.

In Sweden, on the other hand, manufacturing industry grew very rapidly from 1900 to 1914. This caused a sudden growth in the number of unskilled workers, largely recruited from rural areas, and the expansion of industrial rather than craft unions. Paralleling these developments in industry, a left-wing movement arose within the trade-unions and the Social Democratic party which opposed the moderate policies that both had developed before the great industrial expansion. A strong anarcho-syndicalist movement also emerged in this period. Here again, these aggressive left-wing movements were based on the rapidly expanding industries.[39]

Norway, the last of the three Scandinavian countries to industrialize, had an even more rapid rate of growth. As a result of the emergence of hydroelectric power, the growth of an electrochemical industry, and the need for continued construction, Norway's industrial workers doubled between 1905 and 1920. And as in Sweden, this increase in the labor force meant that the traditional moderate craft-union movement was swamped by unskilled and semiskilled workers, most of whom were young migrants from rural areas. A left wing emerged within the Federation of Labor and the Labor party, capturing control of both in the latter stages of World War I. It should be noted that Norway was the only Western European country which was still in its phase of rapid industrialization when the Comintern was founded, and its Labor party was the only one which went over almost intact to the Communists.

In Germany before World War I, a revolutionary Marxist

[39] See Rudolf Heberle, *Zur Geschichte der Arbeiterbewegung in Schweden*, Vol. 39 of *Probleme der Weltwirtschaft* (Jena: Gustav Fischer, 1925).

left wing, in large measure derived from workers in the rapidly growing industries, retained considerable support within the Social Democratic party, while the more moderate sections of the party were based on the more stable established industries.[40]

The most significant illustration of the relationship between rapid industrialization and working-class extremism is the Russian Revolution. In Czarist Russia, the industrial population jumped from 16 million in 1897 to 26 million in 1913.[41] Trotsky in his *History of the Russian Revolution* has shown how an increase in the strike rate and in union militancy paralleled the growth of industry. It is probably not coincidental that two nations in Europe in which the revolutionary left gained control of the dominant section of the labor movement before 1920—Russia and Norway—were also countries in which the processes of rapid capital accumulation and basic industrialization were still going on.[42]

The revolutionary socialist movements which arise in response to strains created by rapid industrialization decline, as Engels put it, wherever "the transition to large-scale industry is more or less completed . . . [and] the conditions in which the proletariat is placed become stable."[43] Such

[40] See Ossip Flechtheim, *Die KPD in der Weimarer Republik* (Offenbach am Main: Bollwerk-Verlag Karl Drott, 1948), pp. 213–14; see also Rose Laub Coser, *An Analysis of the Early German Socialist Movement* (unpublished M.A. thesis, Department of Sociology, Columbia University, 1951).

[41] Colin Clark, *The Conditions of Economic Progress* (London: Macmillan, 1951), p. 421.

[42] The Communists also controlled the Greek trade-unions and Socialist Labor party. The Greek case while fitting this pattern is not completely comparable, since no real pre-Communist labor movement existed and a pro-Bolshevik movement arose from a combination of the discontents of workers in the war-created new industry and the enthusiasm occasioned by the Russian Revolution.

[43] Friedrich Engels, "Letter to Karl Kautsky," Nov. 8, 1884, in Karl Marx and Friedrich Engels, *Correspondence 1846–1895* (New York: International Publishers, 1946), p. 422; see also Val R. Lorwin, "Working-class Politics and Economic Development in Western Europe," *American Historical Review*, 63 (1958), pp. 338–51; for an excellent discussion of the effects of rapid industrialization on politics,

countries are, of course, precisely the industrialized nations where Marxism and revolutionary socialism exist today only as sectarian dogmas. In those nations of Europe where industrialization never occurred, or where it failed to build an economy of efficient large-scale industry with a high level of productivity and a constant increase in mass-consumption patterns, the conditions for the creation or perpetuation of extremist labor politics also exist.

A different type of extremism, based on the small entrepreneurial classes (both urban and rural), has emerged in the less developed and often culturally backward sectors of more industrialized societies. The social base of classic fascism seems to arise from the ever present vulnerability of part of the middle class, particularly small businessmen and farm owners, to large-scale capitalism and a powerful labor movement. Chapter 5 analyzes this reaction in detail as it is manifest in a number of countries.

It is obvious that the conditions related to stable democracy discussed here are most readily found in the countries of northwest Europe and their English-speaking offspring in America and Australasia; and it has been suggested, by Weber among others, that a historically unique concatenation of elements produced both democracy and capitalism in this area. Capitalist economic development, the basic argument runs, had its greatest opportunity in a Protestant society and created the burgher class whose existence was both a catalyst and a necessary condition for democracy. Protestantism's emphasis on individual responsibility furthered the emergence of democratic values in these countries and resulted in an alignment between the burghers and the throne which preserved the monarchy and extended the acceptance of democracy among the conservative strata. Men may question whether any aspect of this interrelated cluster of economic development, Protestantism, monarchy, gradual political change, le-

see also Reinhold Niebuhr, *The Irony of American History* (New York: Charles Scribner's Sons, 1952), pp. 112–18.

gitimacy, and democracy is primary, but the fact remains that the cluster does hang together.[44]

I want to turn in the next chapter to an examination of some of the requisites of democracy which are derived from specifically historical elements, particularly those which relate to the needs of a democratic political system for legitimacy and for mechanisms which reduce the intensity of political conflict. These requisites, although related to economic development, are distinct from it since they are elements within the political system, and not attributes of the total society.

Methodological Appendix

The approach in this chapter is implicitly different from some other studies which have attempted to handle social phenomena on a total societal level, and it may be useful to make explicit some of the methodological postulates underlying this presentation.

Complex characteristics of a social system, such as democracy, the degree of bureaucratization, the type of stratification system, have usually been handled by either a reductionist or an "ideal-type" approach. The former dismisses the possibility of considering these characteristics as system-attributes

---

[44] In introducing historical events as part of the analysis of factors *external* to the political system, which are part of the causal nexus in which democracy is involved, I am following in good sociological and even functionalist tradition. As Radcliffe-Brown has well put it: ". . . one 'explanation' of a social system will be its history, where we know it—the detailed account of how it came to be what it is and where it is. Another 'explanation' of the same system is obtained by showing . . . that it is a special exemplification of laws of social psychology or social functioning. The two kinds of explanation do not conflict but supplement one another." A. R. Radcliffe-Brown, "On the Concept of Function in Social Science," *American Anthropologist*, New Series, 37 (1935), p. 401; see also Max Weber, *The Methodology of the Social Sciences* (Glencoe: The Free Press, 1949), pp. 164–88, for a detailed discussion of the role of historical analysis in sociological research.

as such, and maintains that the qualities of individual actions are the sum and substance of sociological categories. For this school of thought, the extent of democratic attitudes, or of bureaucratic behavior, or the numbers and types of prestige or power rankings, constitute the essence of the meaning of the attributes of democracy, bureaucracy, or class.

The "ideal-type" approach starts from a similar assumption, but reaches an opposite conclusion. The similar assumption is that societies are a complex order of phenomena, exhibiting such a degree of internal contradiction that generalizations about them as a whole must necessarily constitute a constructed representation of selected elements, stemming from the particular concerns and perspectives of the scientist. The opposite conclusion is that abstractions of the order of "democracy" or "bureaucracy" have no necessary connection with states or qualities of complex social systems which actually exist, but comprise collections of attributes which are logically interrelated but characteristic in their entirety of no existing society.[45] An example is Weber's concept of "bureaucracy," comprising a set of offices which are not "owned" by the officeholder, continuously maintained files of records, functionally specified duties, etc.; so is the common definition of democracy in political science, which postulates individual political decisions based on rational knowledge of one's own ends and of the factual political situation.

Criticism of such categories or ideal-types solely on the basis that they do not correspond to reality is irrelevant, because they are not intended to describe reality, but to provide a basis for comparing different aspects of reality with the consistently logical case. Often this approach is quite fruitful, and there is no intention here of substituting another in its place, but merely of presenting another possible way of conceptualizing complex characteristics of social systems, stemming from the multi-variate analysis pioneered by Paul

[45] Max Weber's essay on " 'Objectivity' in Social Science and Social Policy," in his *Methodology of the Social Sciences, op. cit.*, pp. 72–93.

Lazarsfeld and his colleagues on a quite different level of analysis.[46]

The point at which this approach differs is on the issue of whether generalized theoretical categories can be considered to have a valid relationship to characteristics of total social systems. The implication of the statistical data presented in this chapter on democracy, and the relations between democracy, economic development, and political legitimacy, is that there are aspects of total social systems which exist, can be stated in theoretical terms, can be compared with similar aspects of other systems, and, at the same time, are derivable from empirical data which can be checked (or questioned) by other researchers. This does not mean that situations contradicting the general relationship may not exist, or that at lower levels of social organization quite different characteristics may not be evident. For example, a country like the United States may be characterized as "democratic" on the national level, even though most secondary organizations within the country may not be democratic. On another level, a church may be characterized as an "unbureaucratic" organization compared to a corporation, even though important segments of the church organization may be as bureaucratized as the most bureaucratic parts of the corporation. On yet another level, it may be quite legitimate, for purposes of psychological evaluation of the total personality, to consider a certain individual "schizophrenic," even though under certain conditions he may not act schizophrenically. The point is that when comparisons are being made on a certain level of generalization, referring to the functioning of a total sys-

[46] The methodological presuppositions of this approach on the level of the multi-variate correlations and interactions of individual behavior with various social characteristics have been presented in Paul F. Lazarsfeld, "Interpretation of Statistical Relations as a Research Operation," in P. F. Lazarsfeld and M. Rosenberg, eds., *The Language of Social Research* (Glencoe: The Free Press, 1955), pp. 115–25; and in H. Hyman, *Survey Design and Analysis* (Glencoe: The Free Press, 1955), Chaps. 6 and 7. See also the methodological appendixes to Lipset, *et al., Union Democracy* (Glencoe: The Free Press, 1956), pp. 419–32; and to Chap. 12 of this book.

tem (whether on a personality, group, organization, or society level), generalizations applicable to a total society have the same kind and degree of validity that those applicable to other systems have, and are subject to the same empirical tests. The lack of systematic and comparative study of several societies has obscured this point.

This approach also stresses the view that complex characteristics of a total system have multi-variate causation and consequences, in so far as the characteristic has some degree of autonomy within the system. Bureaucracy and urbanization, as well as democracy, have many causes and consequences, in this sense.[47]

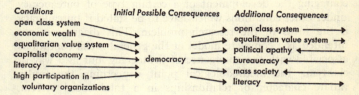

From this point of view, it would be difficult to identify any *one* factor crucially associated with, or "causing," any complex social characteristic. Rather, all such characteristics (and this is a methodological assumption to guide research, and not a substantive point) are considered to have multi-variate causation, and consequences. The point may be clarified by a diagram of some of the possible connections between democracy, the initial conditions associated with its emergence, and the consequences of an existent democratic system.

The appearance of a factor on both sides of "democracy"

[47] This approach differs from Weber's attempt to trace the origins of modern capitalism. Weber sought to establish that *one* antecedent factor, a certain religious ethic, was crucially significant in the syndrome of economic, political, and cultural conditions leading up to the development of Western capitalism. Our concern is not to establish the causal necessity of any one factor, but rather the syndrome of conditions which most frequently distinguish nations which may be empirically categorized as "more democratic" or "less democratic," without implying any absolute qualities to the definition.

implies that it is both an initial condition of democracy, and that democracy, once established, sustains that characteristic of the society—an open class system, for example. On the other hand, some of the initial consequences of democracy, such as bureaucracy, may have the effect of *undermining* democracy, as the reversing arrows indicate. Appearance of a factor to the right of democracy does not mean that democracy "causes" its appearance, but merely that democracy is an initial condition which favors its development. Similarly, the hypothesis that bureaucracy is one of the consequences of democracy does not imply that democracy is the sole cause, but rather that a democratic system has the effect of encouraging the development of a certain type of bureaucracy under other conditions which have to be stated if bureaucracy is the focus of the research problem. This diagram is not intended as a complete model of the general social conditions associated with the emergence of democracy, but as a way of clarifying the methodological point concerning the multivariate character of relationships in a total social system.

Thus, in a multi-variate system, the focus may be upon any element, and its conditions and consequences may be stated without the implication that we have arrived at a complete theory of the necessary and sufficient conditions of its emergence. This chapter does not attempt a *new* theory of democracy, but only the formalizing and empirical testing of certain sets of relationships implied by traditional theories of democracy.

NOTES TO TABLE II

1. A large part of this table has been compiled from data furnished by International Urban Research, University of California, Berkeley, California. Not all the countries in each category were used for each calculation, as uniform data were not available for them all. For instance, the data available on Albania and East Germany are very sparse. The U.S.S.R. was left out because a large part of it is in Asia.

2. United Nations, Statistical Office, *National and Per Capita Income in Seventy Countries*, 1949, Statistical Papers, Series E, No. 1, New York, 1950, pp. 14–16.

3. United Nations, *A Preliminary Report on the World Social Situation*, 1952, Table 11, pp. 46–48.

4. United Nations, *Statistical Yearbook*, 1956, Table 139, pp. 333–38.

5. *Ibid.*, Table 149, p. 387.

6. *Ibid.*, Table 189, p. 641. The population bases for these figures are for different years than those reporting the numbers of telephones and radios, but for purposes of group comparisons, the differences are not important.

7. United Nations, *A Preliminary Report . . .* , *op. cit.*, Appendix B, pp. 86–89.

8. United Nations, *Demographic Yearbook*, 1956, Table 12, pp. 350–70.

9. United Nations, *Statistical Yearbook*, 1956, *op. cit.*, Table 127, pp. 308–10. Figures refer to commercially produced energy, in equivalent numbers of metric tons of coal.

10. United Nations, *A Preliminary Report . . .* , *op. cit.*, Appendix A, pp. 79–86. A number of countries are listed as more than 95 per cent literate.

11. United Nations, *A Preliminary Report . . .* , *op. cit.*, pp. 86–100. Figures refer to persons enrolled at the earlier year of the primary range, per 1,000 total population, for years ranging from 1946 to 1950. The first primary year varies from five to eight in various countries. The less developed countries have more persons in that age range per 1,000 population than the more developed countries, but this biases the figures presented in the direction of increasing the percentage of the total population in school for the less developed countries, although fewer of the children in that age group attend school. The bias from this source thus reinforces the positive relationship between education and democracy.

12. *Ibid.*, pp. 86–100.

13. UNESCO. *World Survey of Education*, Paris, 1955. Figures are the enrollment in higher education per 1,000 population. The years to which the figures apply vary between 1949 and 1952, and the definition of higher education varies for different countries.

14. Obtained from International Urban Research, University of California, Berkeley, California.

15. *Ibid.*

16. *Ibid.*

CHAPTER 3

Social Conflict, Legitimacy, and Democracy

Legitimacy and Effectiveness

THE STABILITY of any given democracy depends not only on economic development but also upon the effectiveness and the legitimacy of its political system. Effectiveness means actual performance, the extent to which the system satisfies the basic functions of government as most of the population and such powerful groups within it as big business or the armed forces see them. Legitimacy involves the capacity of the system to engender and maintain the belief that the existing political institutions are the most appropriate ones for the society. The extent to which contemporary democratic political systems are legitimate depends in large measure upon the ways in which the key issues which have historically divided the society have been resolved.

While effectiveness is primarily instrumental, legitimacy is evaluative. Groups regard a political system as legitimate or illegitimate according to the way in which its values fit with theirs. Important segments of the German Army, civil service, and aristocratic classes rejected the Weimar Republic, not because it was ineffective, but because its symbolism and basic values negated their own. Legitimacy, in and of itself, may be associated with many forms of political organization, including oppressive ones. Feudal societies, before the advent of industrialism, undoubtedly enjoyed the basic loyalty of most of their members. Crises of legitimacy are primarily a recent historical phenomenon, following the rise of sharp cleavages among groups which are able, because of mass communication, to organize around different values than those previously considered to be the only acceptable ones.

A crisis of legitimacy is a crisis of change. Therefore, its roots must be sought in the character of change in modern society. Crises of legitimacy occur during a transition to a new social structure, if (1) the *status* of major conservative institutions is threatened during the period of structural change; (2) all the major groups in the society do not have access to the political system in the transitional period, or at least as soon as they develop political demands. After a new social structure is established, if the new system is unable to sustain the expectations of major groups (on the grounds of "effectiveness") for a long enough period to develop legitimacy upon the new basis, a new crisis may develop.

Tocqueville gives a graphic description of the first general type of loss of legitimacy, referring mainly to countries which moved from aristocratic monarchies to democratic republics: ". . . epochs sometimes occur in the life of a nation when the old customs of a people are changed, public morality is destroyed, religious belief shaken, and the spell of tradition broken . . ." The citizens then have "neither the instinctive patriotism of a monarchy nor the reflecting patriotism of a republic; . . . they have stopped between the two in the midst of confusion and distress."[1]

If, however, the status of major conservative groups and symbols is not threatened during this transitional period, even though they lose most of their power, democracy seems to be much more secure. And thus we have the absurd fact that ten out of the twelve stable European and English-speaking democracies are monarchies.[2] Great Britain, Sweden, Norway, Denmark, the Netherlands, Belgium, Luxembourg, Australia, Canada, and New Zealand are kingdoms, or do-

[1] Alexis de Tocqueville, *Democracy in America*, Vol. I (New York: Alfred A. Knopf, Vintage ed., 1945), pp. 251-52.

[2] Walter Lippman in referring to the seemingly greater capacity of the constitutional monarchies than the republics of Europe to "preserve order with freedom" suggests that this may be because "in a republic the governing power, being wholly secularized, loses

minions of a monarch, while the only republics which meet the conditions of stable democratic procedures are the United States and Switzerland, plus Uruguay in Latin America.

The preservation of the monarchy has apparently retained for these nations the loyalty of the aristocratic, traditionalist, and clerical sectors of the population which resented increased democratization and equalitarianism. And by accepting the lower strata and not resisting to the point where revolution might be necessary, the conservative orders won or retained the loyalty of the new "citizens." In countries where monarchy was overthrown by revolution, and orderly succession was broken, forces aligned with the throne have sometimes continued to refuse legitimacy to republican successors down to the fifth generation or more.

The one constitutional monarchy which became a fascist dictatorship, Italy, was, like the French Republic, considered illegitimate by major groups in the society. The House of Savoy alienated the Catholics by destroying the temporal power of the Popes, and was also not a legitimate successor in the old Kingdom of the Two Sicilies. Catholics were, in fact, forbidden by the church to participate in Italian politics until almost World War I, and the church finally rescinded its position only because of its fear of the Socialists. French Catholics took a similar attitude to the Third Republic during the same period. Both the Italian and French democracies have had to operate for much of their histories without loyal support from important groups in their societies, on both the left and the right. Thus one main source of legitimacy lies in the continuity of important traditional integrative institutions during a transitional period in which new institutions are emerging.

The second general type of loss of legitimacy is related to the ways in which different societies handle the "entry into politics" crisis—the decision as to when new social groups shall obtain access to the political process. In the nineteenth century these new groups were primarily industrial workers;

---

much of its prestige; it is stripped, if one prefers, of all the illusions of intrinsic majesty." See his *The Public Philosophy* (New York: Mentor Books, 1956), p. 50.

in the twentieth, colonial elites and peasant peoples. Whenever new groups become politically active (e.g., when the workers first seek access to economic and political power through economic organization and the suffrage, when the *bourgeoisie* demand access to and participation in government, when colonial elites insist on control over their own system), easy access to the *legitimate* political institutions tends to win the loyalty of the new groups to the system, and they in turn can permit the old dominating strata to maintain their own status. In nations like Germany where access was denied for prolonged periods, first to the *bourgeoisie* and later to the workers, and where force was used to restrict access, the lower strata were alienated from the system and adopted extremist ideologies which, in turn, kept the more established groups from accepting the workers' political movement as a legitimate alternative.

Political systems which deny new strata access to power except by revolution also inhibit the growth of legitimacy by introducing millennial hopes into the political arena. Groups which have to push their way into the body politic by force are apt to overexaggerate the possibilities which political participation affords. Consequently, democratic regimes born under such stress not only face the difficulty of being regarded as illegitimate by groups loyal to the *ancien régime* but may also be rejected by those whose millennial hopes are not fulfilled by the change. France, where right-wing clericalists have viewed the Republic as illegitimate and sections of the lower strata have found their expectations far from satisfied, is an example. And today many of the newly independent nations of Asia and Africa face the thorny problem of winning the loyalties of the masses to democratic states which can do little to meet the utopian objectives set by nationalist movements during the period of colonialism and the transitional struggle to independence.

In general, even when the political system is reasonably effective, if at any time the status of major conservative groups is threatened, or if access to politics is denied to emerging groups at crucial periods, the system's legitimacy will remain in question. On the other hand, a breakdown of effectiveness, repeatedly or for a long period, will endanger even a legitimate system's stability.

A major test of legitimacy is the extent to which given nations have developed a common "secular political culture," mainly national rituals and holidays.[3] The United States has developed a common homogeneous culture in the veneration accorded the Founding Fathers, Abraham Lincoln, Theodore Roosevelt, and their principles. These common elements, to which all American politicians appeal, are not present in all democratic societies. In some European countries, the left and the right have a different set of symbols and different historical heroes. France offers the clearest example of such a nation. Here battles involving the use of different symbols which started in 1789 are, as Herbert Luethy points out, "still in progress, and the issue is still open; every one of these dates [of major political controversy] still divides left and right, clerical and anti-clerical, progressive and reactionary, in all their historically determined constellations."[4]

Knowledge concerning the relative degree of legitimacy of a nation's political institutions is of key importance in any attempt to analyze the stability of these institutions when faced with a crisis of effectiveness. The relationship between different degrees of legitimacy and effectiveness in specific political systems may be presented in the form of a fourfold table, with examples of countries characterized by the various possible combinations:

	Effectiveness	
	+	−
Legitimacy +	A	B
−	C	D

---

[3] See Gabriel Almond, "Comparative Political Systems," *Journal of Politics*, 18 (1956), pp. 391–409.

[4] Herbert Luethy, *The State of France* (London: Secker and Warburg, 1955), p. 29.

Societies which fall in box A, which are, that is, high on the scales of both legitimacy and effectiveness, have stable political systems, like the United States, Sweden, and Britain.[5] Ineffective and illegitimate regimes, which fall in box D, are by definition unstable and break down, unless they are dictatorships maintaining themselves by force, like the governments of Hungary and eastern Germany today.

The political experiences of different countries in the early 1930s illustrate the effect of other combinations. In the late 1920s, neither the German nor the Austrian republic was held legitimate by large and powerful segments of its population. Nevertheless, both remained reasonably effective.[6] In terms of the table, they fell in box C. When the effectiveness of various governments broke down in the 1930s, those societies which were high on the scale of legitimacy remained democratic, while such countries as Germany, Austria, and Spain lost their freedom, and France narrowly escaped a similar fate. Or to put the changes in terms of the table, countries which shifted from A to B remained democratic, while those which shifted from C to D broke down. The military defeat of 1940 underlined French democracy's low position on the scale of legitimacy. It was the sole defeated democracy which furnished large-scale support for a Quisling regime.[7]

[5] The race problem in the American South does constitute one basic challenge to the legitimacy of the system, and at one time did cause a breakdown of the national order. This conflict has reduced the commitment of many white southerners to the democratic game down to the present. Great Britain had a comparable problem as long as Catholic Ireland remained part of the United Kingdom. Effective government could not satisfy Ireland. Political practices by both sides in Northern Ireland, Ulster, also illustrate the problem of a regime which is not legitimate to a major segment of its population.

[6] For an excellent analysis of the permanent crisis of the Austrian republic which flowed from the fact that it was viewed as an illegitimate regime by the Catholics and conservatives, see Charles Gulick, *Austria from Hapsburg to Hitler* (Berkeley: University of California Press, 1948).

[7] The French legitimacy problem is well described by Katherine Munro. "The Right wing parties never quite forgot the possibility

Situations like these demonstrate the usefulness of this type of analysis. From a short-range point of view, a highly effective but illegitimate system, such as a well-governed colony, is more unstable than regimes which are relatively low in effectiveness and high in legitimacy. The social stability of a nation like Thailand, despite its periodic *coups d'état*, stands out in sharp contrast to the situation in neighboring former colonial nations. On the other hand, prolonged effectiveness over a number of generations may give legitimacy to a political system. In the modern world, such effectiveness means primarily constant economic development. Those nations which have adapted more successfully to the requirements of an industrial system have the fewest internal political strains, and have either preserved their traditional legitimacy or developed strong new symbols.

The social and economic structure which Latin America inherited from the Iberian peninsula prevented it from following the lead of the former English colonies, and its republics never developed the symbols and aura of legitimacy. In large measure, the survival of the new political democracies of Asia and Africa will depend on their ability to meet the needs of their populations over a prolonged period, which will probably mean their ability to cope with industrialization.

Legitimacy and Conflict

Inherent in all democratic systems is the constant threat that the group conflicts which are democracy's life-blood may

---

of a counter revolution while the Left wing parties revived the Revolution militant in their Marxism or Communism; each side suspected the other of using the Republic to achieve its own ends and of being legal only so far as it suited it. This suspicion threatened time and time again to make the Republic unworkable, since it led to obstruction in both the political and the economic sphere, and difficulties of government in turn undermined confidence in the regime and its rulers." Quoted in Charles Micaud, "French Political Parties: Ideological Myths and Social Realities," in Sigmund Neumann, ed., *Modern Political Parties* (Chicago: University of Chicago Press, 1956), p. 108.

solidify to the point where they threaten to disintegrate the society. Hence conditions which serve to moderate the intensity of partisan battle are among the key requisites of democratic government.

Since the existence of a moderate state of conflict is in fact another way of defining a legitimate democracy, it is not surprising that the principal factors determining such an optimum state are closely related to those which produce legitimacy viewed in terms of continuities of symbols and statuses. The character and content of the major cleavages affecting the political stability of a society are largely determined by historical factors which have affected the way in which major issues dividing society have been solved or left unresolved over time.

In modern times, three major issues have emerged in Western nations: first, the place of the church and/or various religions within the nation; second, the admission of the lower strata, particularly the workers, to full political and economic "citizenship" through universal suffrage and the right to bargain collectively; and third, the continuing struggle over the distribution of the national income.

The significant question here is: Were these issues dealt with one by one, with each more or less solved before the next arose; or did the problems accumulate, so that traditional sources of cleavage mixed with newer ones? Resolving tensions one at a time contributes to a stable political system; carrying over issues from one historical period to another makes for a political atmosphere characterized by bitterness and frustration rather than tolerance and compromise. Men and parties come to differ with each other, not simply on ways of settling current problems, but on fundamental and opposed outlooks. This means that they see the political victory of their opponents as a major moral threat, and the whole system, as a result, lacks effective value-integration.

The place of the church in society was fought through and solved in most of the Protestant nations in the eighteenth and nineteenth centuries. In some, the United States, for example, the church was disestablished and accepted the fact. In others, like Britain, Scandinavia, and Switzerland, religion is still state-supported, but the state churches, like constitutional monarchs, have ceased to be major sources of controversy. It remains for the Catholic countries of Europe to provide us with examples of situations in which the historic controversy between clerical and anticlerical forces has continued to divide men politically down to the present day. In such countries as France, Italy, Spain, and Austria, being Catholic has meant being allied with rightist or conservative groups in politics, while being anticlerical, or a member of a minority religion, has most often meant alliance with the left. In a number of these countries, newer issues have been superimposed on the religious question. For conservative Catholics the fight against socialism has been not simply an economic struggle, or a controversy over social institutions, but a deep-rooted conflict between God and Satan.[8] For many secular intellectuals in contemporary Italy,

---

[8] The linkage between democratic instability and Catholicism may also be accounted for by elements inherent in Catholicism as a religious system. Democracy requires a universalistic political belief system in the sense that it accepts various different ideologies as legitimate. And it might be assumed that religious value systems which are more universalistic, in the sense of placing less stress on being the only true church, will be more compatible with democracy than those which assume that they are the only truth. The latter belief, which is held much more strongly by the Catholic than by most other Christian churches, makes it difficult for the religious value system to help legitimate a political system which requires as part of its basic value system the belief that "good" is served best through conflict among opposing beliefs.

Kingsley Davis has argued that a Catholic state church tends to be irreconcilable with democracy since "Catholicism attempts to control so many aspects of life, to encourage so much fixity of status and submission to authority, and to remain so independent of secular authority that it invariably clashes with the liberalism, individualism, freedom, mobility and sovereignty of the democratic nation." See "Political Ambivalence in Latin America," *Journal of Legal and Political Sociology*, 1 (1943), reprinted in A. N. Christensen, *The Evolution of Latin American Government* (New York: Henry Holt, 1951), p. 240.

opposition to the church legitimizes alliance with the Communists. And as long as religious ties reinforce secular political alignments, the chances for compromise and democratic give-and-take are weak.

The "citizenship" issue has also been resolved in various ways. The United States and Britain gave the workers suffrage in the nineteenth century. In countries like Sweden, which resisted until the first part of the twentieth century, the struggle for citizenship became combined with socialism as a *political* movement, thereby producing a revolutionary socialism. Or, to put it in other terms, where the workers were denied both economic and political rights, their struggle for redistribution of income and status was superimposed on a revolutionary ideology. Where the economic and status struggle developed outside of this context, the ideology with which it was linked tended to be that of gradualist reform. The workers in Prussia, for example, were denied free and equal suffrage until the revolution of 1918, and thereby clung to revolutionary Marxism. In southern Germany, where full citizenship rights were granted in the late nineteenth century, reformist, democratic, and nonrevolutionary socialism was dominant. However, the national Social Democratic party continued to embrace revolutionary dogmas. These served to give ultra-leftists a voice in party leadership, enabled the Communists to win strength after the military defeat, and, perhaps even more important historically, frightened large sections of the German middle class who feared that a socialist victory would end all their privileges and status.

In France, the workers won the suffrage but were refused basic economic rights until after World War II. Large numbers of French employers refused to recognize French trade-unions and sought to weaken or destroy them after every union victory. The instability of the French unions, and their constant need to preserve militancy in order to survive, made the workers susceptible to the appeals of extremist political groups. Communist domination of the French labor movement can in large part be traced to the tactics of the French business classes.

These examples do not explain why different countries varied in the way they handled basic national cleavages. They should suffice, however, to illustrate the way in which the conditions for stable democratic government are related to the bases of diversity. Where a number of historic cleavages intermix and create the basis for ideological politics, democracy will be unstable and weak, for by definition such politics does not include the concept of tolerance.

Parties with such total ideologies attempt to create what the German-American political scientist Sigmund Neumann has called an "integrated" environment, in which the lives of the members are encased within ideologically linked activities. These actions are based on the party's assumption that it is important to isolate its followers from the "falsehoods" expressed by nonbelievers. Neumann has suggested the need for a basic analytic distinction between parties of representation, which strengthen democracy, and parties of integration, which weaken it.[9] The former are typified by most parties in the English-speaking democracies and Scandinavia, plus most centrist and conservative parties other than religious ones. These parties view their function as primarily one of securing votes around election time. The parties of integration, on the other hand, are concerned with making the world conform to their basic philosophy. They do not see themselves as contestants in a give-and-take game of pressure politics, but as partisans in a mighty struggle between divine or historic truth on one side and fundamental error on the other. Given this conception of the world, it becomes necessary to prevent their followers from being ex-

[9] See Sigmund Neumann, *Die Deutschen Parteien: Wesen und Wandel nach dem Kriege* (Berlin: Junker und Dünnhaupt Verlag, 1932) for exposition of the distinction between parties of integration and parties of representation. Neumann has further distinguished between parties of "democratic integration" (the Catholic and Social Democratic parties) and those of "total integration" (fascist and Communist parties) in his more recent chapter, "Toward a Comparative Study of Political Parties," in the volume which he edited: *Modern Political Parties, op. cit.*, pp. 403–5.

posed to the cross-pressures flowing from contact with outsiders which will reduce their faith.

The two major nontotalitarian groups which have followed such procedures have been the Catholics and the Socialists. In much of Europe before 1939 the Catholics and Socialists attempted to increase intra-religious or intra-class communications by creating a network of social and economic organizations within which their followers could live their entire lives. Austria offers perhaps the best example of a situation in which two groups, the Social Catholics and the Social Democrats, dividing over all three historic issues and carrying on most of their social activities in party or church-linked organizations, managed to split the country into two hostile camps.[10] Totalitarian organizations, fascist and Communist alike, expand the integrationist character of political life to the furthest limit possible by defining the world completely in terms of struggle.

Efforts, even by democratic parties, to isolate their social base from cross-pressures clearly undermine stable democracy, which requires shifts from one election to another and the resolving of issues between parties over long periods of time. Isolation may intensify loyalty to a party or church, but it will also prevent the party from reaching new groups. The Austrian situation illustrates the way in which the electoral process is frustrated when most of the electorate is confined within parties of integration. The necessary rules of democratic politics assume that conversion both ways, into and out of a party, is possible and proper, and parties which hope to gain a majority by democratic methods must ultimately give up their integrationist emphasis. As the working class has gained complete citizenship in the political and economic spheres in different countries, the socialist parties of Europe have dropped their integrationist emphasis. The only nontotalitarian parties which now maintain such policies are religious parties like the Catholic parties or the Calvinist Anti-Revolutionary party of Holland. Clearly the Catholic and

[10] See Charles Gulick, *op. cit.*

Dutch Calvinist churches are not "democratic" in the sphere of religion. They insist there is but one truth, as the Communists and fascists do in politics. Catholics may accept the assumptions of political democracy, but never those of religious tolerance. And where the political conflict between religion and irreligion is viewed as salient by Catholics or other believers in one true church, then a real dilemma exists for the democratic process. Many political issues which might easily be compromised are reinforced by the religious issue and cannot be settled.

Wherever the social structure operates so as to isolate *naturally* individuals or groups with the same political outlook from contact with those who hold different views, the isolated individuals or groups tend to back political extremists. It has been repeatedly noted, for example, that workers in so-called "isolated" industries—miners, sailors, fishermen, lumbermen, sheepshearers, and longshoremen—who live in communities predominately inhabited by others in the same occupation usually give overwhelming support to the more left-wing platforms.[11] Such districts tend to vote Communist or socialist by large majorities, sometimes to the point of having what is essentially a "one-party" system. The political intolerance of farm-based groups in times of crisis may be another illustration of this same pattern, since farmers, like workers in isolated industries, have a more homogeneous political environment than do those employed in most urban occupations.[12]

[11] See Chap. 7 of this book, pp. 244–47, 263.

[12] This tendency obviously varies with relation to urban communities, type of rural stratification, and so forth. For a discussion of the role of vocational homogeneity and political communication among farmers, see S. M. Lipset, *Agrarian Socialism* (Berkeley: University of California Press, 1950), Chap. 10, "Social Structure and Political Activity." For evidence on the undemocratic propensities of rural populations see Samuel A. Stouffer, *Communism, Conformity, and Civil Liberties* (New York: Doubleday & Co., Inc., 1955), pp. 138–39. National Public Opinion Institute of Japan, Report No. 26, *A Survey Concerning the Protection of Civil Liberties* (Tokyo, 1951) reports that the farmers were the occupational group by far the least concerned with civil liberties. Carl Friedrich, in accounting for the

These conclusions are confirmed by studies of individual voting behavior which indicate that individuals under cross-pressures—those who belong to groups predisposing them in different directions, or who have friends supporting different parties, or who are regularly exposed to the propaganda of different groups—are less likely to be strongly committed politically.[13]

Multiple and politically inconsistent affiliations, loyalties, and stimuli reduce the emotion and aggressiveness involved in political choice. For example, in contemporary Germany, a working-class Catholic, pulled in two directions, will most probably vote Christian-Democratic, but is much more tolerant of the Social Democrats than the average middle-class Catholic.[14] Where a man belongs to a variety of groups that all predispose him toward the same political choice, he is in the situation of the isolated worker and is much less likely to be tolerant of other opinions.

The available evidence suggests that the chances for stable democracy are enhanced to the extent that groups and individuals have a number of crosscutting, politically relevant affiliations. To the degree that a significant proportion of the

---

strength of nationalism and Nazism among German farmers, suggests similar factors to the ones discussed here; that "the rural population is more homogeneous, that it contains a smaller number of outsiders and foreigners, that it has much less contact with foreign countries and peoples, and finally that its mobility is much more limited." Carl J. Friedrich, "The Agricultural Basis of Emotional Nationalism," Public Opinion Quarterly, 1 (1937), pp. 50–51.

[13] Perhaps the first general statement of the consequences of "cross-pressures" on individual and group behavior may be found in a work written over fifty years ago by Georg Simmel, Conflict and the Web of Group Affiliations (Glencoe: The Free Press, 1956), pp. 126–95. It is an interesting example of discontinuity in social research that the concept of cross-pressures was used by Simmel, but had to be independently rediscovered in voting research. For a detailed application of the effect of multiple-group affiliations on the political process in general, see David Truman, The Governmental Process (New York: Alfred A. Knopf, 1951).

[14] See Juan Linz, The Social Bases of German Politics (unpublished Ph.D. thesis, Department of Sociology, Columbia University, 1958).

population is pulled among conflicting forces, its members have an interest in reducing the intensity of political conflict.[15] As Robert Dahl and Talcott Parsons have pointed out, such groups and individuals also have an interest in protecting the rights of political minorities.[16]

A stable democracy requires relatively moderate tension

[15] See Bernard Berelson, Paul F. Lazarsfeld, and William McPhee, *Voting* (Chicago: University of Chicago Press, 1954), for an exposition of the usefulness of cross-pressure as an explanatory concept. Also, see Chap. 6 for an attempt to specify the consequences of different group memberships for voting behavior, and a review of the literature.

[16] As Dahl puts it, "If most individuals in the society identify with more than one group, then there is some positive probability that any majority contains individuals who identify for certain purposes with the threatened minority. Members of the threatened minority who strongly prefer their alternative will make their feelings known to those members of the tentative majority who also, at some psychological level, identify with the minority. Some of these sympathizers will shift their support away from the majority alternative and the majority will crumble." See Robert A. Dahl, *A Preface to Democratic Theory* (Chicago: University of Chicago Press, 1956), pp. 104–5. Parsons suggests that "pushing the implications of political difference too far activates the solidarities between adherents of the two parties which exist on other, nonpolitical bases so that members of the political majority come to defend those who share other of their interests who differ from them politically." See Parsons' essay "Voting and the Equilibrium of the American Political System," in E. Burdick and A. Brodbeck, eds., *American Voting Behavior* (Glencoe: The Free Press, 1959), p. 93. A recent discussion of this problem in a Norwegian context points up "the integrative functions of cross-cutting conflict . . . [when] the conflict lines between the voter groups cut across the divisions between readers of newspapers of different political tendencies and this places a considerable proportion of the electorate in a situation of cross-pressure . . . In the Norwegian situation there is an interesting two way process of mutual restraints: on the one hand a majority of the Socialist voters are regularly exposed to newspaper messages from the opposition parties, on the other hand the non-Socialist papers, just because they in so many cases dominate their community and address themselves to a variety of politically heterogeneous groups, are found to exercise a great deal of restraint in the expression of conflicting opinions." Stein Rokkan and Per Torsvik, "The Voter, the Reader and the Party Press" (Mimeographed, Oslo: 1959).

among its contending political forces. And political moderation is facilitated by the system's capacity to resolve key dividing issues before new ones arise. If the issues of religion, citizenship, and "collective bargaining" are allowed to accumulate, they reinforce each other, and the more reinforced and correlated the sources of cleavage, the less likelihood for political tolerance. Similarly, the greater the isolation from heterogeneous political stimuli, the more the background factors "pile up" in one direction, the greater the chances that the group or individual will have an extremist perspective. These two relationships, one on the level of partisan issues, the other on the level of party support, are joined by the fact that parties reflecting accumulated unresolved issues will further seek to isolate their followers from conflicting stimuli. The best conditions for political cosmopolitanism are again those of economic development—the growth of urbanization, education, communications media, and increased wealth. Most of the obviously isolated occupations—mining, lumbering, agriculture—are precisely those whose relative share of the labor force declines sharply with industrialization.[17]

Thus the factors involved in modernization or economic development are linked to those which establish legitimacy and tolerance. But it should always be remembered that correlations are only statements about relative degrees of congruence, and that another condition for political action is that the correlation never be so clear-cut that men feel they cannot change the direction of affairs by their actions. And this lack of high correlation also means that for analytic purposes the variables should be kept distinct even if they intercorrelate. For example, the analysis of cleavage presented here suggests specific ways in which different electoral and constitutional arrangements may affect the chances for democracy. These are discussed in the following section.

[17] Colin Clark, *The Conditions of Economic Progress* (New York: Macmillan, 1940).

Systems of Government

If crosscutting bases of cleavage make a more vital democracy, it follows that, all other factors being constant, two-party systems are better than multi-party systems, that the election of officials on a territorial basis is preferable to proportional representation, and federalism is superior to a unitary state. Of course there have been and are stable democracies with multi-party systems, proportional representation, and a unitary state. In fact, I would argue that such variations in systems of government are much less important than those derived from the basic differences in social structure discussed in the previous sections. Nevertheless, they may contribute to over-all stability or unstability.

The argument for the two-party system rests on the assumption that in a complex society parties must necessarily be broad coalitions which do not serve the interests of one major group, and that they must not be parties of integration but must seek to win support among groups which are preponderantly allied to the opposition party. The British Conservative or American Republican parties, for instance, must not basically antagonize the manual workers, since a large part of their votes must come from them. The Democratic and Labor parties are faced with a similar problem vis-à-vis the middle classes. Parties which are never oriented toward gaining a majority seek to win the greatest possible electoral support from a limited base—a "workers" party will accentuate working-class interests, and a party appealing primarily to small businessmen will do the same for its group. For these splinter parties, elections, instead of being occasions for seeking the broadest possible base of support by convincing divergent groups of their common interests, become events in which they stress the cleavages separating their supporters from other segments of the society.

The proposition that proportional representation weakens rather than strengthens democracy rests on an analysis of the differences between multi-party and majority party situations.

If it is true, as suggested above, that the existence of many parties accentuates differences and reduces consensus, then any electoral system which increases the chance for more rather than fewer parties serves democracy badly.

Besides, as the German sociologist Georg Simmel has pointed out, the system of electing members of parliament to represent territorial constituencies rather than groups (as proportional representation encourages), forces the various groups to secure their ends within an electoral framework that involves concern with many interests and the need for compromise.[18]

Federalism increases the opportunity for multiple sources of cleavage by adding regional interests and values to the others which crosscut the social structure. A major exception to this generalization occurs when federalism divides a country across the lines of basic cleavage, e.g., between different ethnic, religious, or linguistic areas, as it does in India and Canada. Democracy needs cleavage within linguistic or religious groups, not between them. But where such divisions do not exist, federalism seems to serve democracy well. Besides creating a further source of crosscutting cleavage, it provides the various functions which Tocqueville noted it shared with strong voluntary associations—resistance to centralization of power, the training of new political leaders, and a means of giving the out party a stake in the system as a whole, since both national parties usually continue to control some units of the system.

I might emphasize again that I do not consider these aspects of the political structure essential for democratic systems. If the underlying social conditions facilitate democracy, as they seem to in, say, Sweden, then the combination of many parties, proportional representation, and a unitary state

---

[18] Georg Simmel, *op. cit.*, pp. 191–94. Talcott Parsons has recently made a similar point that one of the mechanisms for preventing a "progressively deepening rift in the electorate" is the "involvement of voting with the ramified solidarity structure of the society in such a way, that, though there is a correlation, there is no *exact* correspondence between political polarization and other bases of differentiation." Talcott Parsons, *op. cit.*, pp. 92–93.

does not seriously weaken it. At most it permits irresponsible minorities to gain a foothold in parliament. On the other hand, in countries like Weimar Germany and France, where a low level of effectiveness and legitimacy weakens the foundations of democracy, constitutional factors encouraging the growth of many parties further reduce the chances that the system will survive.

Contemporary Challenges: Communism and Nationalism

The characteristic pattern of stable Western democracies in the mid-twentieth century is that they are in a "post-politics" phase—that is, there is relatively little difference between the democratic left and right, the socialists are moderates, and the conservatives accept the welfare state. In large measure this situation reflects the fact that in these countries the workers have won their fight for full citizenship.

Representatives of the lower strata are now part of the governing groups, members of the club. The basic political issue of the industrial revolution, the incorporation of the workers into the legitimate body politic, has been settled.[19] The key domestic issue today is collective bargaining over differences in the division of the total product within the framework of a Keynesian welfare state, and such issues do not require or precipitate extremism on either side. However, even though the working class of the Western democracies is incorporated into the society, it still possesses authoritarian predispositions which, under certain conditions, appear in

---

[19] T. H. Marshall has analyzed the gradual process of incorporation of the working class into the body politic in the nineteenth century, and has seen that process as the achievement of a "basic human equality, associated with full community membership, which is not inconsistent with a superstructure of economic inequality." See his brief but brilliant book *Citizenship and Social Class* (London: Cambridge University Press, 1950), p. 77. Even though universal citizenship opens the way for the challenging of remaining social inequalities, it also provides a basis for believing that the process of social change toward equality will remain within the boundaries of allowable conflict in a democratic system.

support of extremist political and religious movements. The sources of these predispositions are dealt with in Chapter 4.

In most of Latin and Eastern Europe, the struggle for working-class integration into the body politic was not settled before the Communists appeared on the scene, and this fact drastically changed the political game. Communists could not be absorbed in the system in the way that the socialists have been. Communist workers, their parties and trade-unions, cannot possibly be accorded the right of access to actual political power by a democratic society. The Communists' self-image, and more particularly their ties to the Soviet Union, lead them to accept the self-fulfilling prophecy that they cannot secure their ends by democratic means. This belief prevents them from being allowed access, which in turn reinforces the Communist workers' sense of alienation from the government. The more conservative strata in turn are strengthened in their belief that giving increased rights to the workers or their representatives threatens all that is good in life. Thus the presence of Communists precludes an easy prediction that economic development will stabilize democracy in these European countries.

In the newly independent nations of Asia and Negro Africa the situation is somewhat different. In Europe the workers were faced with the problem of winning citizenship from the dominant aristocratic and business strata. In Asia and Africa the long-term presence of colonial rulers has identified conservative ideology and the more well-to-do classes with subservience to colonialism, while leftist ideologies, usually of a Marxist variety, have been identified with nationalism. The trade-unions and workers' parties of Asia and Africa have been a legitimate part of the political process from the beginning of the democratic system. Conceivably such a situation could mean a stable democracy, except for the fact that these political rights predate the development of a stable economy with a large middle class and an industrial society.

The whole system is standing on its head. The left wing in the stable European democracies grew gradually during a fight for more democracy and gave expression to the discontents created by the early stages of industrialization, while the right retained the support of traditionalist elements in the society, until eventually the system came into an easy balance with modifications on both sides. In Asia the left wing is now in power during a period of population explosion and early industrialization, and will have to accept responsibility for all the consequent miseries. And, as in the poorer areas of Europe, the Communists, who capitalize on all these discontents in a completely irresponsible fashion, are currently a major party—the second largest in most Asian states.

Given the existence of poverty-stricken masses, low levels of education, an elongated-pyramid class structure, and the "premature" triumph of the democratic left, the prognosis for political democracy in Asia and Africa is bleak. The nations with the best prospects—Israel, Japan, Lebanon, the Philippines, and Turkey—tend to resemble Europe in one or more major factors: high educational level (all except Turkey), a substantial and growing middle class, the retention of political legitimacy by conservative groups. The others are committed more deeply to a certain tempo of economic development and to national independence, under whatever political form, than they are to the pattern of party politics and free elections which exemplify our model of democracy. It seems likely that in countries which avoid Communist or military dictatorship, political developments will follow the pattern developing in countries such as Ghana, Guinea, Tunisia, or Mexico, with an educated minority using a mass movement and leftist slogans to exercise effective control, and holding elections as a gesture toward ultimate democratic objectives and as a means of estimating public opinion rather than as effective instruments for a legitimate turnover in office.[20] With the pressure for rapid industrialization and the imme-

[20] See David Apter, *The Gold Coast in Transition* (Princeton: Princeton University Press, 1955), for a discussion of the evolving political patterns of Ghana. For an interesting brief analysis of the Mexican "one-party" system see L. V. Padgett, "Mexico's One-Party System, a Re-evaluation," *American Political Science Review,* 51 (1957), pp. 995–1008.

diate solution of chronic problems of poverty and famine, it
is unlikely that many of the new governments of Asia and
Africa will be able to support an open party system representing basically different class positions and values.[21]

Latin America, economically underdeveloped like Asia, is
politically more nearly like Europe in the early nineteenth
century. Most Latin-American countries became independent
states before the rise of industrialism and Marxist ideologies
and so contain strongholds of traditional conservatism. The
countryside is often apolitical or traditional, and the leftist
movements secure support primarily from the industrial
proletariat. Latin-American Communists, for example, have
chosen the European Marxist path of organizing urban
workers, rather than the "Yenan way" of Mao, seeking a
peasant base.[22] If Latin America is allowed to develop on
its own and is able to increase its productivity, there is a
good chance that many Latin-American countries will follow
in the European direction. Recent developments, including
the overthrow of a number of dictatorships, reflect the effects
of a growing middle class and increased wealth and educa-

[21] As this chapter was being edited for publication, political crises
in several poor and illiterate countries occurred, which underline
again the instability of democratic government in underdeveloped
areas. The government of Pakistan was overthrown peacefully on
October 7, 1958, and the new self-appointed president announced
that "Western-type democracy cannot function here under present
conditions. We have only 16 per cent literacy. In America you have
98 per cent." (Associated Press release, October 9, 1958.) The new
government proceeded to abolish parliament and all political parties.
Similar crises have occurred, almost simultaneously, in Tunisia,
Ghana, and even in Burma, since World War II considered one
of the more stable governments in Southeast Asia, under Premier
U Nu. Guinea has begun political life as a one-party state.

It is possible that the open emergence of military semi-dictatorships
without much of a democratic "front" may reflect the weakening
of democratic symbols in these areas under the impact of Soviet
ideology, which equates "democracy" with rapid, efficient accomplish-
ment of the "will of the people" by an educated elite, not with
particular political forms and methods.

[22] Robert J. Alexander, *Communism in Latin America* (New
Brunswick: Rutgers University Press, 1957).

tion. There is, however, the great danger that these countries may yet follow in the French and Italian direction rather than that of northern Europe, that the Communists will seize the leadership of the workers, and that the middle class will be alienated from democracy. Once a politically active middle class is in existence, the key distinction between "left" and "right" political tendencies no longer suffices as a means of differentiation between supporters and opponents of democracy. As Chapter 5 shows, the further distinction between left, right, and center, each with a characteristic ideology and social base, and each with a democratic and an extremist tendency, clarifies the problem of "authoritarianism," and its relationship to the stage of economic development.

The next two chapters continue the discussion of the conditions of the democratic order. They seek to elaborate further on the theses presented here by examining in some detail the factors underlying the appeal of extremist movements and authoritarian values to the diverse strata of industrial society.

CHAPTER 4

Working-class Authoritarianism[1]

THE GRADUAL realization that extremist and intolerant movements in modern society are more likely to be based on the
lower classes than on the middle and upper classes has posed
a tragic dilemma for those intellectuals of the democratic
left who once believed the proletariat necessarily to be a force
for liberty, racial equality, and social progress. The Socialist
Italian novelist Ignazio Silone has asserted that "the myth of
the liberating power of the proletariat has dissolved along
with that other myth of progress. The recent examples of the
Nazi labor unions, like those of Salazar and Peron . . . have
at last convinced of this even those who were reluctant to
admit it on the sole grounds of the totalitarian degeneration
of Communism."[2]

Dramatic demonstrations of this point have been given
recently by the southern workers' support of White Citizens'
Councils and segregation in the United States and by the
active participation of many British workers in the 1958 race
riots in England. A "Short Talk with a Fascist Beast" (an
eighteen-year-old casual laborer who took part in the beating
of Negroes in London), which appeared in the left socialist
New Statesman, portrays graphically the ideological syndrome

[1] An early version of this chapter was written for a conference on
"The Future of Liberty" sponsored by the Congress for Cultural
Freedom in Milan, Italy, in September 1955.

[2] "The Choice of Comrades," *Encounter,* 3 (December 1954),
p. 25. Arnold A. Rogow writing in the Socialist magazine *Dissent*
even suggests that "the liberal and radical approach has always
lacked a popular base, that in essence, the liberal tradition has been
a confined minority, perhaps elitist, tradition." "The Revolt Against
Social Equality," *Dissent,* 4 (1957), p. 370.

which sometimes culminates in such behavior. "Len's" perspective is offered in detail as a prelude to an analytical survey of the authoritarian elements of the lower-class situation in modern society.

'That's why I'm with the Fascists,' he says. 'They're against the blacks. That Salmon, he's a Communist. The Labour Party is Communist too. Like the unions.' His mother and father, he says, are strict Labour supporters. Is he against the Labour Party? 'Nah, I'm for them. They're for y'know—us. I'm for the unions too.' Even though they were dominated by Communists? 'Sure,' he says. 'I like the Communist Party. It's powerful, like.' How can he be for the Communists when the fascists hate them?

Len says, 'Well, y'know, I'm for the fascists when they're against the nigs. But the fascists is really for the rich people y'know, like the Tories. All for the guv'nors, people like that. But the Communists are very powerful.' I told him the Communist Party of Britain was quite small.

'But,' he says, 'they got Russia behind them.' His voice was full of marvel. 'I admire Russia. Y'know, the people. They're peaceful. They're strong. When they say they'll do a thing, they do it. Not like us. Makes you think: they got a weapon over there can wipe us all out, with one wave of a general's arm. Destroy us completely and totally. Honest, those Russians. When they say they'll do a thing, they do it. Like in Hungary. I pity those people, the Hungarians. But did you see the Russians went in and stopped them. Tanks. Not like us in Cyprus. Our soldiers got shot in the back and what do we do? The Communists is for the small man.'[3]

Such strikingly visible demonstrations of working-class ethnic prejudice and support for totalitarian political movements have been paralleled in studies of public opinion, religion,

[3] Clancy Sigal in the *New Statesman*, October 4, 1958, p. 440.

family patterns, and personality structure. Many of these studies suggest that the lower-class way of life produces individuals with rigid and intolerant approaches to politics.

At first glance the facts of political history may seem to contradict this. Since their beginnings in the nineteenth century, workers' organizations and parties have been a major force in extending political democracy, and in waging progressive political and economic battles. Before 1914, the classic division between the working-class left parties and the economically privileged right was not based solely upon such issues as redistribution of income, status, and educational opportunities, but also rested upon civil liberties and international policy. The workers, judged by the policies of their parties, were often the backbone of the fight for greater political democracy, religious freedom, minority rights, and international peace, while the parties backed by the conservative middle and upper classes in much of Europe tended to favor more extremist political forms, to resist the extension of the suffrage, to back the established church, and to support jingoistic foreign policies.

Events since 1914 have gradually eroded these patterns. In some nations working-class groups have proved to be the most nationalistic sector of the population. In some they have been in the forefront of the struggle against equal rights for minority groups, and have sought to limit immigration or to impose racial standards in countries with open immigration. The conclusion of the anti-fascist era and the emergence of the cold war have shown that the struggle for freedom is not a simple variant of the economic class struggle. The threat to freedom posed by the Communist movement is as great as that once posed by Fascism and Nazism, and Communism, in all countries where it is strong, is supported mainly by the lower levels of the working class, or the rural population.[4] No other party has been as thoroughly and completely the party of the working class and the poor.

[4] The sources of variation in Communist strength from country to country have already been discussed in Chap. 2, in relation to the level and speed of economic development.

Socialist parties, past and present, secured much more support from the middle classes than the Communists have.

Some socialists and liberals have suggested that this proves nothing about authoritarian tendencies in the working class, since the Communist party often masquerades as a party seeking to fulfill the classic Western-democratic ideals of liberty, equality, and fraternity. They argue that most Communist supporters, particularly the less educated, are deceived into thinking that the Communists are simply more militant and efficient socialists. I would suggest, however, the alternative hypothesis that, rather than being a source of strain, the intransigent and intolerant aspects of Communist ideology attract members from that large stratum with low incomes, low-status occupations, and low education, which in modern industrial societies has meant largely, though not exclusively, the working class.

The social situation of the lower strata, particularly in poorer countries with low levels of education, predisposes them to view politics as black and white, good and evil. Consequently, other things being equal, they should be more likely than other strata to prefer extremist movements which suggest easy and quick solutions to social problems and have a rigid outlook.

The "authoritarianism" of any social stratum or class is highly relative, of course, and often modified by organizational commitments to democracy and by individual cross-pressures. The lower class in any given country may be more authoritarian than the upper classes, but on an "absolute" scale all the classes in that country may be less authoritarian than any class in another country. In a country like Britain, where norms of tolerance are well developed and widespread in every social stratum, even the lowest class may be less authoritarian and more "sophisticated" than the most highly educated stratum in an underdeveloped country, where immediate problems and crises impinge on every class and short-term solutions may be sought by all groups.[5]

[5] See Richard Hoggart, *The Uses of Literacy* (London: Chatto and Windus, 1957), pp. 78–79 and 146–48, for a discussion of the acceptance of norms of tolerance by the British working class. E. T.

Commitments to democratic procedures and ideals by the principal organizations to which low-status individuals belong may also influence these individuals' actual political behavior more than their underlying personal values, no matter how authoritarian.[6] A working class which has developed an early (prior to the Communists) loyalty to democratic political and trade-union movements which have successfully fought for social and economic rights will not easily change its allegiance.

Commitments to other values or institutions by individuals (cross-pressures) may also override the most established predispositions. For example, a French, Italian, or German Catholic worker who is strongly anticapitalist may still vote for a relatively conservative party in France, Italy, or Germany, because his ties to Catholicism are stronger than his resentments about his class status; a worker strongly inclined toward authoritarian ideas may defend democratic institutions against fascist attack because of his links to anti-fascist working-class parties and unions. Conversely, those who are not inclined toward extremist politics may back an extremist party because of certain aspects of its program and political role. Many persons supported the Communists in 1936 and 1943 as an anti-fascist internationalist party.

The specific propensity of given social strata to support either extremist or democratic political parties, then, cannot be predicted from a knowledge of their psychological pre-

---

Prothro and Levon Melikian, in "The California Public Opinion Scale in an Authoritarian Culture," *Public Opinion Quarterly*, 17 (1953), pp. 353–63, have shown, in a study of 130 students at the American University in Lebanon, that they exhibited the same association between authoritarianism and economic radicalism as is found among workers in America. A survey in 1951–52 of 1,800 Puerto Rican adults, representative of the entire rural population, found that 84 per cent were "somewhat authoritarian," as compared to 46 per cent for a comparable U.S. population. See Henry Wells, "Ideology and Leadership in Puerto Rican Politics," *American Political Science Review*, 49 (1955), pp. 22–40.

[6] The southern Democrats were the most staunch opponents of McCarthy and his tactics, not because of any deep opposition to undemocratic methods, but rather because of an organizational commitment to the Democratic party.

dispositions or from attitudes inferred from survey data.[7]
Both evidence and theory suggest, however, that the lower
strata are relatively more authoritarian, that (again, other
things being equal) they will be more attracted to an extremist movement than to a moderate and democratic one,
and that, once recruited, they will not be alienated by its
lack of democracy, while more educated or sophisticated supporters will tend to drop away.[8]

Democracy and the Lower Classes

The poorer strata everywhere are more liberal or leftist on
economic issues; they favor more welfare state measures,
higher wages, graduated income taxes, support of trade-
unions, and so forth. But when liberalism is defined in noneconomic terms—as support of civil liberties, internationalism, etc.—the correlation is reversed. The more well-to-do are
more liberal, the poorer are more intolerant.[9]

Public opinion data from a number of countries indicate
that the lower classes are much less committed to democracy
as a political system than are the urban middle and upper
classes. In Germany, for example, a study conducted by the
UNESCO Institute at Cologne in 1953 asked a systematic
sample of 3,000 Germans: "Do you think that it would be

---

[7] For a detailed discussion of the fallacy of attempting to suggest
that political behavior is a necessary function of political attitudes or
psychological traits, see Nathan Glazer and S. M. Lipset, "The Polls
on Communism and Conformity," in Daniel Bell, ed., *The New
American Right* (New York: Criterion Books, 1955), pp. 141–66.

[8] The term "extremist" is used to refer to movements, parties,
and ideologies. "Authoritarian" refers to the attitudes and predispositions of individuals (or of groups, where a statistical aggregate
of *individual* attitudes, and not group characteristics as such, are of
concern). The term "authoritarian" has too many associations with
studies of attitudes to be safely used to refer also to types of social
organizations.

[9] See two articles by G. H. Smith, "Liberalism and Level of Information," *Journal of Educational Psychology*, 39 (1948), pp. 65–
82; and "The Relation of 'Enlightenment' to Liberal-Conservative
Opinions," *Journal of Social Psychology*, 28 (1948), pp. 3–17.

better if there were one party, several parties, or no party?" The results analyzed according to occupational status indicate that the lower strata of the working class and the rural population were less likely to support a multi-party system (a reasonable index of democratic attitudes in Westernized countries) than the middle and upper strata. (See Table I.)

TABLE I

RESPONSES OF DIFFERENT GERMAN OCCUPATIONAL GROUPS TO PREFERRED PARTY SYSTEM IN PERCENTAGES* (MALES ONLY)

Occupational Group	Several Parties	One Party	No Party	No Opinion	Total Number of Persons
Civil Servants	88	6	3	3	111
Upper White-collar	77	13	2	8	58
Free Professionals	69	13	8	10	38
Skilled Workers	65	22	5	8	277
Artisans	64	16	9	11	124
Lower White-collar	62	19	7	12	221
Businessmen (small)	60	15	12	13	156
Farmers	56	22	6	16	241
Semiskilled Workers	49	28	7	16	301
Unskilled Workers	40	27	11	22	172

* Computed from IBM cards supplied to author by the UNESCO Institute at Cologne.

Comparable results were obtained in 1958 when a similar question was asked of national or regional samples in Austria, Japan, Brazil, Canada, Mexico, West Germany, the Netherlands, Belgium, Italy, and France. Although the proportion favoring a multi-party system varied from country to country, the lower classes within each nation were least likely to favor it.[10]

[10] Based on as yet unpublished data in the files of the World Poll, an organization established by International Research Associates which sponsors comparable surveys in a number of countries. The question asked in this survey was: "Suppose there was a political party here which corresponds to your own opinions—one you would more or less consider 'your' party. Would you wish this to be the only party in our country with no other parties besides, or would

Surveys in Japan, Great Britain, and the United States designed to secure general reactions to problems of civil liberties, or the rights of various minorities, have produced similar results. In Japan, the workers and the rural population were more authoritarian and less concerned with civil liberties than the middle and upper classes.[11]

In England, the psychologist H. J. Eysenck found comparable differences between people who were "tough-minded" and those who were "tender-minded" in their general social outlook. The first group tended to be intolerant of deviations from the standard moral or religious codes, to be anti-Negro, anti-Semitic, and xenophobic, while the "tender-minded" were tolerant of deviation, unprejudiced, and internationalist.[12] Summing up his findings, based on attitude scales given to supporters of different British parties, Eysenck reported that "middle-class Conservatives are more tender-minded than working-class Conservatives; middle-class Liberals are more tender-minded than working-class Liberals; middle-class Socialists are more tender-minded than working-class Socialists; and even middle-class Communists are more tender-minded than working-class Communists."[13]

The evidence from various American studies is also clear and consistent—the lower strata are the least tolerant.[14] In

you be against such a one-party system?" Similar correlations were found between low status and belief in the value of a strong leader.

[11] See Kotaro Kido and Masataka Sugi, "A Report of Research on Social Stratification and Mobility in Tokyo" (III), *Japanese Sociological Review*, 4 (1954), pp. 74–100; and National Public Opinion Institute of Japan, Report No. 26, *A Survey Concerning the Protection of Civil Liberties* (Tokyo, 1951).

[12] See H. J. Eysenck, *The Psychology of Politics* (London: Routledge and Kegan Paul, 1954), p. 127.

[13] *Ibid.*, p. 137: for a critique of the methodology of this study which raises serious questions about its procedures see Richard Christie, "Eysenck's Treatment of the Personality of Communists," *Psychological Bulletin*, 53 (1956), pp. 411–30.

[14] See Arnold W. Rose, *Studies in Reduction of Prejudice* (Chicago: American Council on Race Relations, 1948), for a review of the literature bearing on this point prior to 1948. Several studies have shown the key importance of education and the independent

the most systematic of these, based on a national sample of nearly 5,000 Americans, Samuel A. Stouffer divided his respondents into three categories, "less tolerant, in-between, and more tolerant," by using a scale based on responses to questions about such civil liberties as the right of free speech for Communists, critics of religion, or advocates of nationalization of industry, and the like. As the data presented in Table II demonstrate, tolerance increases with moves up the social ladder. Only 30 per cent of those in manual occupations are in the "most tolerant" category, as contrasted with 66 per cent of the professionals, and 51 per cent of the proprietors, managers, and officials. As in Germany and Japan, farmers are low in tolerance.

TABLE II

PROPORTION OF MALE RESPONDENTS WHO ARE "MORE TOLERANT" WITH RESPECT TO CIVIL LIBERTIES ISSUES*

Professional and Semiprofessional	66%	(159)
Proprietors, Managers, and Officials	51	(223)
Clerical and Sales	49	(200)
Manual Workers	30	(685)
Farmers or Farm Workers	20	(202)

* Samuel A. Stouffer, *Communism, Conformity and Civil Liberties* (New York: Doubleday & Co., 1955), p. 139. The figures for manual and farm workers were calculated from IBM cards kindly supplied by Professor Stouffer.

The findings of public opinion surveys in thirteen different countries that the lower strata are less committed to demo-

effect of economic status, both basic components of low status. See Daniel J. Levinson and R. Nevitt Sanford, "A Scale for the Measurement of Anti-Semitism," *Journal of Psychology*, 17 (1944), pp. 339–70, and H. H. Harlan, "Some Factors Affecting Attitudes toward Jews," *American Sociological Review*, 7 (1942), pp. 816–27, for data on attitudes toward one ethnic group. See also James G. Martin and Frank R. Westie, "The Tolerant Personality," *American Sociological Review*, 24 (1959), pp. 521–28. For a digest of recent research in the field of race relations in the U.S.A., see Melvin M. Tumin, *Segregation and Desegregation* (New York: Anti-Defamation League of B'nai B'rith, 1957).

cratic norms than the middle classes are reaffirmed by the research of more psychologically oriented investigators, who have studied the social correlates of the "authoritarian personality."[15] Many studies in this area, summarized recently, show a consistent association between authoritarianism and lower-class status.[16] One survey of 460 Los Angeles adults reported that "the working class contains a higher proportion of authoritarians than either the middle or the upper class," and that among workers, those who explicitly identified themselves as "working class" rather than "middle class" were more authoritarian.[17]

Recent research further suggests the possibility of a *negative* correlation between authoritarianism and neuroticism within the lower classes. In general, those who deviate from the standards of their group are more likely to be neurotic than those who conform, so if we assume that authoritarian traits are more or less standard among low-status people, then the more liberal members of this group should also be the more neurotic.[18] As two psychologists, Anthony Davids and Charles Eriksen, point out, where the "standard of reference on authoritarianism is quite high," people may be well adjusted *and* authoritarian.[19] And the fact that this is often

[15] See Theodore Adorno, *et al.*, *The Authoritarian Personality* (New York: Harper & Bros., 1950). This, the original study, has less consistent results on this point than the many follow-up studies. The authors themselves (p. 178) point to the inadequacy of their sample.

[16] Richard Christie and Peggy Cook, "A Guide to Published Literature Relating to the Authoritarian Personality," *Journal of Psychology*, 45 (1958), pp. 171–99.

[17] W. J. McKinnon and R. Centers, "Authoritarianism and Urban Stratification," *American Journal of Sociology*, 61 (1956), p. 618.

[18] Too much of contemporary psychological knowledge in this area has been gained from populations most convenient for the academic investigator to reach—university students. It is often forgotten that personality and attitude syndromes may be far different for this highly select group than for other segments of the total population.

[19] See Anthony Davids and Charles W. Eriksen, "Some Social and Cultural Factors Determining Relations Between Authoritarianism and Measures of Neuroticism," *Journal of Consulting Psychology*,

the case in lower-class groups fits the hypothesis that authoritarian attitudes are "normal" and expected in such groups.[20]

Extremist Religions and the Lower Classes

Many observers have called attention to a connection between low social status and fundamentalist or chiliastic religion. This suggests that extremist religion is a product of the same social forces that sustain authoritarian political attitudes. The liberal Protestant churches, on the other hand, have been predominantly middle class in membership. In the United States, this has created a dilemma for the liberal Protestant clergy, who have tended to be liberal in their politics as well as their religion and, hence, have often wanted to spread their social and religious gospel among the lower strata. But they have found that these classes want ministers who will preach of hell-fire and salvation rather than modern Protestant theology.[21]

In the early period of the Socialist movement, Engels observed that early Christianity and the revolutionary workers' movement had "notable points of resemblance," particularly in their millennial appeals and lower-class base.[22] Recently, Elmer Clark, a student of small sects in contemporary America, has noted that such sects, like early Christianity, "originate mainly among the religiously neglected poor." He writes

---

21 (1957), pp. 155–59. This article contains many references to the relevant literature.

20 The greater compatibility of the demands of Communist party membership and working-class background as indicated by Almond's finding that twice as many of the middle-class party members as of the working-class group in his sample of Communists had neurotic problems hints again at the normality and congruence of extremist politics with a working-class background. Gabriel Almond, *The Appeals of Communism* (Princeton: Princeton University Press, 1954), pp. 245–46.

21 See Liston Pope, *Millhands and Preachers* (New Haven: Yale University Press, 1942), pp. 105–16.

22 See Friedrich Engels, "On the Early History of Christianity," in K. Marx and F. Engels, *On Religion* (Moscow: Foreign Languages Publishing House, 1957), pp. 312–20.

that when "the revolts of the poor have been tinged with religion, which was nearly always the case until recent times, millennial ideas have appeared, and . . . these notions are prominent in most of the small sects which follow the evangelical tradition. Premillenarianism is essentially a defense mechanism of the disinherited; despairing of obtaining substantial blessings through social processes, they turn on the world which has withheld its benefits and look to its destruction in a cosmic cataclysm which will exalt them and cast down the rich and powerful."[23]

Ernst Troeltsch, the major historian of sectarian religion, has characterized the psychological appeal of fundamentalist religious sects in a way that might as appropriately be applied to extremist politics: "It is the lower classes which do the really creative work, forming communities on a genuine religious basis. They alone unite imagination and simplicity of feeling with a nonreflective habit of mind, a primitive energy, and an urgent sense of need. On such a foundation alone is it possible to build up an unconditional authoritative faith in a Divine Revelation with simplicity of surrender and unshaken certainty. Only within a fellowship of this kind is there room for those who have a sense of spiritual need, and who have not acquired the habit of intellectual reasoning, which always regards everything from a relative point of view."[24]

Jehovah's Witnesses, whose membership in the United States runs into the hundreds of thousands, is an excellent example of a rapidly growing sect which "continues to attract,

---

[23] Elmer T. Clark, *The Small Sects in America* (New York: Abingdon Press, 1949), pp. 16, 218–19. According to Bryan Wilson, "insecurity, differential status, anxiety, cultural neglect, prompt a need for readjustment which sects may, for some, provide. The maladjusted may be communities, or occupational groups, or dispersed individuals in similar marginal positions." See "An Analysis of Sect Development," *American Sociological Review*, 24 (1959), p. 8, and the same author's *Minority Religious Movements in Modern Britain* (London: Heinemann, 1960).

[24] Ernst Troeltsch, *The Social Teaching of the Christian Churches* (London: George Allen and Unwin, 1930), Vol. 1, p. 44.

as in the past, the underprivileged strata."[25] The Witnesses' principal teaching is that the Kingdom of Heaven is at hand: "The end of the age is near. Armageddon is just around the corner, when the wicked will be destroyed, and the theocracy, or rule of God, will be set up upon the earth."[26] And like the Communists, their organization is "hierarchical and highly authoritarian. There is little democratic participation in the management or in the formation of policies of the movement as a whole."[27]

Direct connections between the social roots of political and of religious extremism have been observed in a number of countries. In Czarist Russia, the young Trotsky recognized the relationship and successfully recruited the first working-class members of the South Russian Workers' Union (a revolutionary Marxist organization of the late 1890s) from adherents to religious sects.[28] In Holland and Sweden, recent studies show that the Communists are strongest in regions which were once centers of fundamentalist religious revivalism. In Finland, Communism and revivalist Christianity often are strong in the same areas. In the poor eastern parts of Finland, the Communists have been very careful not to offend people's religious feelings. It is reported that many Communist meetings actually begin with religious hymns.[29]

---

[25] See Charles S. Braden, *These Also Believe. A Study of Modern American Cults and Minority Religious Movement* (New York: Macmillan, 1949), p. 384.

[26] *Ibid.*, p. 370.

[27] *Ibid.*, p. 363. It may be suggested that, as in authoritarian political movements, the intolerant character of most of the sects is an attractive feature and not a source of strain for their lower-class members. Although no systematic evidence is available, this assumption would help account for the lack of tolerance for factionalism within these sects, and for the endless schisms, with the new groups as intolerant as the old, since the splits usually occur over the issue of *whose* intolerant views and methods shall prevail.

[28] See Isaac Deutscher, *The Prophet Armed, Trotsky, 1879–1921* (London: Oxford University Press, 1954), pp. 30–31.

[29] See Sven Rydenfelt, *Kommunismen i Sverige. En Samhallsvetenskaplig Studie.* (Kund: Gleerupska Universitetsbokhandeln, 1954), pp. 296, 336–37; Wiardi Beckman Institute, *Verkiezingen in Neder-*

This is not to imply that religious sects supported by lower-class elements necessarily or usually become centers of political protest. In fact, such sects often drain off the discontent and frustration which would otherwise flow into channels of political extremism. The point here is that rigid fundamentalism and dogmatism are linked to the same underlying characteristics, attitudes, and predispositions which find another outlet in allegiance to extremist political movements.

In his excellent study of the sources of Swedish Communism, Sven Rydenfelt analyzed the differences between two socially and economically comparable northern counties of Sweden—Vasterbotten and Norrbotten—in an attempt to explain the relatively low Communist vote in the former (2 per cent) and the much larger one in the latter (21 per cent). The Liberal party, which in Sweden gives much more support than any other party to religious extremism, was strong in Vasterbotten (30 per cent) and weak in Norrbotten (9 per cent). Since the total extremist vote in both was almost identical—30 and 32 per cent—he concluded that a general predisposition toward radicalism existed in both counties, containing some of the poorest, most socially isolated, and rootless groups in Sweden, but that its expression differed, taking a religious form in one county, and a Communist in the other: "The Communists and the religious radicals, as for instance, the Pentecostal sects, seem to be competing for the allegiance of the same groups."[30]

The Social Situation of the Lower Classes

A number of elements contribute to authoritarian predispositions in lower-class individuals. Low education, low par-

---

land (Amsterdam, 1951, mimeographed), pp. 15, 93–94; Jaako Novsiainen, *Kommunism Kuopion lää nisssä* (Helsinki: Joensuu, 1956).

[30] See W. Phillips Davison's extensive review of Sven Rydenfelt, *op. cit.*, which appeared in the *Public Opinion Quarterly*, 18 (1954–55), pp. 375–88. Quote is on p. 382.

ticipation in political or voluntary organizations of any type, little reading, isolated occupations, economic insecurity, and authoritarian family patterns are some of the most important. These elements are interrelated, but they are by no means identical.

There is consistent evidence that degree of formal education, itself closely correlated with social and economic status, is also highly correlated with undemocratic attitudes. Data from the American sociologist Samuel Stouffer's study of attitudes toward civil liberties in America and from the UNESCO Research Institute's survey of German opinion on a multi-party system (Tables III and IV) reveal this clearly.

These tables indicate that although higher occupational status within each educational level seems to make for greater tolerance, the increases in tolerance associated with higher educational level are greater than those related to higher

TABLE III

THE RELATIONSHIP BETWEEN OCCUPATION, EDUCATION, AND POLITICAL TOLERANCE IN THE UNITED STATES, 1955*

Percentage in the Two "Most Tolerant" Categories

Occupation

Education	Low Manual		High Manual		Low White Collar		High White Collar	
Grade School	13	(228)	21	(178)	23	(47)	26	(100)
Some High School	32	(99)	33	(124)	29	(56)	46	(68)
High School Grad	40	(64)	48	(127)	47	(102)	56	(108)
Some College	—	(14)	64	(36)	64	(80)	65	(37)
College Grad	—	(3)	—	(11)	74	(147)	83	(21)

* Computed from IBM cards kindly supplied by Samuel A. Stouffer from his study, *Communism, Conformity and Civil Liberties* (New York: Doubleday & Co., Inc., 1955).

occupational level, other factors being constant.[31] Inferior education and low occupational position are of course closely connected, and both are part of the complex making up low status, which is associated with a lack of tolerance.[32]

Low-status groups are also less apt to participate in formal organizations, read fewer magazines and books regularly, possess less information on public affairs, vote less, and, in gen-

TABLE IV

THE RELATIONSHIP BETWEEN OCCUPATION, EDUCATION, AND SUPPORT OF A DEMOCRATIC PARTY SYSTEM IN GERMANY—1953*

Per Cent Favoring the Existence of Several Parties

Educational Level

Occupation	Elementary School	High School or Higher
Farm Laborers	29 (59)	—
Manual Workers	43 (1439)	52 (29)
Farmers	43 (381)	67 (9)
Lower White Collar	50 (273)	68 (107)
Self-employed Business	53 (365)	65 (75)
Upper White Collar	58 (86)	69 (58)
Officials (Govt.)	59 (158)	78 (99)
Professions	56 (18)	68 (38)

* Same source as Table I, p. 93.

[31] A study based on a national sample of Americans reported that education made no difference in the extent of authoritarian responses on an "authoritarian personality" scale among workers, but that higher educational attainment reduced such responses among the middle class. The well-educated upper-middle class were least "authoritarian." Morris Janowitz and Dwaine Marvick, "Authoritarianism and Political Behavior," *Public Opinion Quarterly*, 17 (1953), pp. 195–96.

[32] The independent effect of education even when other social factors are least favorable has special long-range significance in view of the rising educational level of the population. Kornhauser and his associates found that auto workers with an eighth-grade education were more authoritarian than those with more education. See A. Kornhauser, A. L. Sheppard, and A. J. Mayer, *When Labor Votes* (New York: University Books, 1956), for further data on variations in authoritarianism *within* a working-class sample.

eral, take less interest in politics.[33] The available evidence suggests that each of these attributes is related to attitudes toward democracy. The 1953 UNESCO analysis of German data found that, at every occupational level, those who belonged to voluntary associations were more likely to favor a multi-party system than a one-party one.[34] American findings, too, indicate that authoritarians "do not join many community groups" as compared with nonauthoritarians.[35] And it has been discovered that people poorly informed on public issues are more likely to be both *more liberal* on economic issues and *less liberal* on noneconomic ones.[36] Nonvoters and those less interested in political matters are much more intolerant and xenophobic than those who vote and have political interests.[37]

The "hard core" of "chronic know-nothings" comes disproportionately from the less literate, lower socioeconomic groups, according to a study by two American social psychologists, Herbert Hyman and Paul Sheatsley. These people are not only uninformed, but "harder to reach, no matter what the level or nature of the information." Here is another hint of the complex character of the relationship between education, liberalism, and status. Noneconomic liberalism is not a simple matter of acquiring education and information; it is at least in part a basic attitude which is actively discouraged by the social situation of lower-status persons.[38] As

[33] The research showing the social factors such as education, status and income (themselves components of an over-all class or status index) associated with political participation is summarized in Chap. 6 of this book.

[34] Data computed for this study.

[35] F. H. Sanford, *Authoritarianism and Leadership* (Philadelphia: Stevenson Brothers, 1950), p. 168. See also Mirra Komarovsky, "The Voluntary Associations of Urban Dwellers," *American Sociological Review*, 11 (1946), p. 688.

[36] G. H. Smith, *op. cit.*, p. 71.

[37] G. M. Connelly and H. H. Field, "The Non-Voter, Who He Is, and What He Thinks," *Public Opinion Quarterly*, 8 (1944), p. 179; Samuel A. Stouffer, *op. cit.*, *passim*, and F. H. Sanford, *op. cit.*, p. 168. M. Janowitz and D. Marvick, *op. cit.*, p. 200.

[38] See Herbert Hyman and Paul B. Sheatsley, "Some Reasons Why Information Campaigns Fail," *Public Opinion Quarterly*, 11 (1947),

Genevieve Knupfer, an American psychiatrist, has pointed out in her revealing "Portrait of the Underdog," "economic underprivilege is psychological underprivilege: habits of submission, little access to sources of information, lack of verbal facility . . . appear to produce a lack of self-confidence which increases the unwillingness of the low-status person to participate in many phases of our predominantly middle-class culture . . ."[39]

These characteristics also reflect the extent to which the lower strata are *isolated* from the activities, controversies, and organizations of democratic society—an isolation which prevents them from acquiring the sophisticated and complex view of the political structure which makes understandable and necessary the norms of tolerance.

In this connection it is instructive to examine once again, as extreme cases, those occupations which are most isolated, in every sense, from contact with the world outside their own group. Manual workers in "isolated occupations" which require them to live in one-industry towns or areas—miners, maritime workers, forestry workers, fishermen, and sheepshearers—exhibit high rates of Communist support in most countries.[40]

---

p. 413. A recent survey of material on voluntary association memberships is contained in Charles L. Wright and Herbert Hyman, "Voluntary Association Memberships of American Adults: Evidence from National Sample Surveys," *American Sociological Review*, 23 (1958), pp. 284–94.

[39] Genevieve Knupfer, "Portrait of the Underdog," *Public Opinion Quarterly*, 11 (1947), p. 114.

[40] The greatest amount of comparative material is available on the miners. For Britain, see Herbert G. Nicholas, *British General Election of 1950* (London: Macmillan, 1951), pp. 318, 342, 361. For the United States, see Paul F. Brissenden, *The IWW: A Study of American Syndicalism* (New York: Columbia University Press, 1920), p. 74, and Harold F. Gosnell, *Grass Roots Politics* (Washington, D.C.: American Council on Public Affairs, 1942), pp. 31–32. For France see François Goguel, "Geographie des élections sociales de 1950–51," *Revue française de science politique*, 3 (1953), pp. 246–71. For Germany, see Ossip K. Flechtheim, *Die Kommunistische Partei Deutschlands in der Weimarer Republik* (Offenbach am Main:

Similarly, as all public opinion surveys show, the rural population, both farmers and laborers, tends to oppose civil liberties and multi-party systems more than any other occupational group. Election surveys indicate that farm owners have been among the strongest supporters of fascist parties, while farm workers, poor farmers, and share-croppers have given even stronger backing to the Communists than has the rest of labor in countries like Italy, France, and India.[41]

The same social conditions are associated with middleclass authoritarianism. The groups which have been most prone to support fascist and other middle-class extremist ideologies have been, in addition to farmers and peasants, the small businessmen of the smaller provincial communities—groups which are also isolated from "cosmopolitan" culture and are far lower than any other nonmanual-labor group in educational attainment.[42]

Bollwerk-Verlag Karl Drott, 1948), p. 211. Data are also available for Australia, Scandinavia, Spain, and Chile.

Isolation has also been linked with the differential propensity to strike of different industries. Violent strikes having the character of a mass grievance against society as a whole occur most often in isolated industries, and probably have their origins in the same social situations as those which produce extremism. See Clark Kerr and Abraham Siegel, "The Interindustry Propensity to Strike: An International Comparison," in *Industrial Conflict*, eds., A. Kornhauser, R. Dubin, and A. M. Ross (New York: McGraw-Hill Book Co., 1954), pp. 189–212.

[41] According to Carl Friedrich, agricultural groups are more emotionally nationalistic and potentially authoritarian politically because of the fact that they are more isolated from meeting people who are different than are urban dwellers. See "The Agricultural Basis of Emotional Nationalism," *Public Opinion Quarterly*, 1 (1937), pp. 50–51. See also Rudolf Heberle, *From Democracy to Nazism: A Regional Case Study on Political Parties in Germany* (Baton Rouge, Louisiana: Louisiana State University Press, 1945), pp. 32 ff., for a discussion of the appeal of Nazism to the German rural population, and K. Kido and M. Sugi, *op. cit.*, for similar survey findings in Japan.

[42] Statistical data indicate that German and Austrian Nazism, French Poujadism, and American McCarthyism have all drawn their heaviest nonrural support from the small businessmen of provincial small communities, particularly those with little education. See Chap. 5.

A second and no less important factor predisposing the lower classes toward authoritarianism is a relative lack of economic and psychological security. The lower one goes on the socioeconomic ladder, the greater economic uncertainty one finds. White-collar workers, even those who are not paid more than skilled manual workers, are less likely to suffer the tensions created by fear of loss of income. Studies of marital instability indicate that this is related to lower income and income insecurity. Such insecurity will of course affect the individual's politics and attitudes.[43] High states of tension require immediate alleviation, and this is frequently found in the venting of hostility against a scapegoat and the search for a short-term solution by support of extremist groups. Research indicates that the unemployed are less tolerant toward minorities than the employed, and more likely to be Communists if they are workers, or fascists if they are middle class. Industries which have a high rate of Communists in their ranks also have high economic instability.

The lower classes' insecurities and tensions which flow from economic instability are reinforced by their particular patterns of family life. There is a great deal of direct frustra-

---

[43] In addition to the insecurity which is normally attendant upon lower-class existence, special conditions which uproot people from a stable community life and upset the social supports of their traditional values make them receptive to extremist chiliastic ideologies which help to redefine their world. I have already discussed some of the evidence linking the *discontinuities* and rootlessness flowing from rapid industrialization and urbanization on the politics of workers in different countries in Chap. 2. Rydenfelt in his study of Swedish Communism suggests that "rootlessness" is a characteristic of individuals and occupations with high Communist voting records. See W. Phillips Davison, *op. cit.*, p. 378. Engels also called attention in the 1890s to the fact that chiliastic religions and social movements, including the revolutionary socialist one, attracted all the deviants or those without a place in society: "all the elements which had been set free, i.e., at a loose end, by the dissolution of the old world came one after the other into the orbit of [early] Christianity . . . [as today] all throng to the working-class parties in all countries." F. Engels, *op. cit.*, pp. 319–20. See also G. Almond, *op. cit.*, p. 236, and Hadley Cantril, *The Psychology of Social Movements* (New York: John Wiley & Sons, 1941), Chaps. 8 and 9.

tion and aggression in the day-to-day lives of members of the lower classes, both children and adults. A comprehensive review of the many studies of child-rearing patterns in the United States completed in the past twenty-five years reports that their "most consistent finding" is the "more frequent use of physical punishment by working-class parents. The middle class, in contrast, resorts to reasoning, isolation, and . . . 'love-oriented' techniques of discipline. . . . Such parents are more likely to overlook offenses, and when they do punish they are less likely to ridicule or inflict physical pain."[44] A further link between such child-rearing practices and adult hostility and authoritarianism is suggested by the finding of two investigations in Boston and Detroit that physical punishments for aggression, characteristic of the working class, tend to increase rather than decrease aggressive behavior.[45]

[44] See Urie Bronfenbrenner, "Socialization and Social Class Through Time and Space," in E. E. Maccoby, T. M. Newcomb, and E. L. Hartley eds., *Readings in Social Psychology* (New York: Henry Holt, 1958), p. 419. The sociologist Allison Davis has summarized in a similar vein research findings relating to intra-family relations in different classes: "The lower classes not uncommonly teach their children and adolescents to strike out with fists or knife and to be certain to hit first. Both girls and boys at adolescence may curse their father to his face or even attack him with fists, sticks, or axes in free-for-all family encounters. Husbands and wives sometimes stage pitched battles in the home; wives have their husbands arrested, and husbands try to break in or burn down their own homes when locked out. Such fights with fists or weapons, and the whipping of wives occur sooner or later in many lower-class families. They may not appear today, nor tomorrow, but they *will* appear if the observer remains long enough to see them." Allison Davis, "Socialization and Adolescent Personality," in Guy E. Swanson, *et al.*, eds., *Readings in Social Psychology* (New York: Henry Holt, 1954), p. 528. (Emphasis in original.)

[45] Some hint of the complex of psychological factors underlying lower-class authoritarianism is given in one study which reports a relationship between overt hostility and authoritarianism. See Saul M. Siegel, "The Relationship of Hostility to Authoritarianism," *Journal of Abnormal and Social Psychology*, 52 (1956), pp. 368–72.

Lower-class Perspectives

Acceptance of the norms of democracy requires a high level of sophistication and ego security. The less sophisticated and stable an individual, the more likely he is to favor a simplified view of politics, to fail to understand the rationale underlying tolerance of those with whom he disagrees, and to find difficulty in grasping or tolerating a gradualist image of political change.

Several studies focusing on various aspects of working-class life and culture have emphasized different components of an unsophisticated perspective. Greater suggestibility, absence of a sense of past and future (lack of a prolonged time perspective), inability to take a complex view, greater difficulty in abstracting from concrete experience, and lack of imagination (inner "reworking" of experience), each has been singled out by numerous students of quite different problems as characteristic of low status. All of these qualities are part of the complex psychological basis of authoritarianism.

The psychologist Hadley Cantril considered suggestibility to be a major psychological explanation for participation in extremist movements.[46] The two conditions for suggestibility are both typical of low-status persons: either the lack of an adequate frame of reference or general perspective, or a fixed, rigid one. A poorly developed frame of reference reflects a limited education, a paucity of the rich associations on a general level which provide a basis for evaluating experience. A fixed or rigid one—in a sense the opposite side of the same coin—reflects the tendency to elevate whatever general principles are learned to absolutes which even experience may fail to qualify and correct.

The stimulating book by the British journalist Richard Hoggart, *The Uses of Literacy*, makes the same point in another way. Low-status persons without rich and flexible perspectives are likely to lack a developed sense of the past

[46] See Hadley Cantril, *op. cit.*, p. 65.

and the future. "Their education is unlikely to have left them with any historical panorama or with any idea of a continuing tradition. . . . A great many people, though they may possess a considerable amount of disconnected information, have little idea of an historical or ideological pattern or process. . . . With little intellectual or cultural furniture, with little training in the testing of opposing views against reason and existing judgments, judgments are usually made according to the promptings of those group apothegms which come first to mind. . . . Similarly, there can be little real sense of the future. . . . Such a mind is, I think, particularly accessible to the temptation to live in a constant present."[47]

This concern with the present leads to a concentration on daily activities, without much inner reflection, imaginative planning of one's future, or abstract thinking unrelated to one's daily activities. One of the few studies of lower-class children which used projective techniques found that "these young people are making an adjustment which is orientated toward the outside world rather than one which rests on a developing acquaintance with their own impulses and the handling of these impulses by fantasy and introspection. . . . They do not have a rich inner life, indeed their imaginative activity is meagre and limited. . . . When faced with a new situation, the subjects tend to react rapidly, and they do not alter their original impressions of the situation which is seen as a crude whole with little intellectual discrimination of components."[48]

Working-class life as a whole emphasizes the concrete and

[47] Richard Hoggart, *op. cit.*, pp. 158–59.
[48] B. M. Spinley, *The Deprived and the Privileged* (London: Routledge and Kegan Paul, 1953), pp. 115–16. These conclusions were based on Rorschach tests given to 60 slum-area children. The last point is related to that made by another British scholar, that working-class people are not as likely as those with middle-class backgrounds to perceive the *structure* of an object, which involves thought on a more abstract level of relationships, but have an action-oriented reaction to the *content* of an object. For more discussion of this point, see B. Bernstein, "Some Sociological Determinants of Perception," *The British Journal of Sociology*, 9 (1958), pp. 160 ff.

immediate. As Hoggart puts it, "if we want to capture something of the essence of working-class life . . . we must say that it is the 'dense and concrete' life, a life whose main stress is on the intimate, the sensory, the detailed and the personal. This would no doubt be true of working-class groups anywhere in the world."[49] Hoggart sees the concreteness of working-class perceptions as the main difference between them and middle-class people, who more easily meet abstract and general questions. The sharp British working-class distinction between "Us" and "Them," he notes, is "part of a more general characteristic of the outlook of most working-class people. To come to terms with the world of 'Them' involves, in the end, all kinds of political and social questions, and leads eventually beyond politics and social philosophy to metaphysics. The question of how we face 'Them' (whoever 'They' are) is, at last, the question of how we stand in relation to anything not visibly and intimately part of our local universe. The working-class splitting of the world into 'Us' and 'Them' is on this side a symptom of their difficulty in meeting abstract or general questions."[50] Hoggart is careful to emphasize that probably most persons in *any* social class are uninterested in general ideas, but still "training in the handling of ideas or in analysis" is far more characteristic of the demands of middle-class parents and occupations.[51]

[49] Richard Hoggart, *op. cit.*, p. 88. This kind of life, like other social characteristics of human beings, has different consequences for different areas of society and social existence. It may be argued, though I personally doubt it, that this capacity to establish personal relationships, to live in the present, may be more "healthy" (in a strictly medical, mental-health sense) than a middle-class concern with status distinctions, one's own personal impact on one's life situation, and a preoccupation with the uncertain future. But on the political level of consequences, the problem of concern here, this same action-oriented, nonintellectualistic aspect of working-class life seems to prevent the realities of long-term social and economic trends from entering working-class consciousness, simply because such reality can enter only through the medium of abstractions and generalizations.

[50] *Ibid.*, p. 86.

[51] *Loc. cit.*

A recent analysis by the British sociologist Basil Bernstein of how differences in ways of perceiving and thinking in the different classes lead to variations in social mobility also underlines the manner in which different family patterns affect authoritarianism. The middle-class parent stresses "an awareness of the importance between means and long-term ends, cognitively and affectually regarded . . . [and has] the ability to adopt appropriate measures to implement the attainment of distant ends by a purposeful means-end chain. . . . The child in the middle classes and associative levels grows up in an environment which is finely and extensively controlled; the space, time and social relationships are explicitly regulated within and outside the family group."[52] The situation in the working-class family is quite different:

> The working-class family structure is less formally organized than the middle-class in relation to the development of the child. Although the authority within the family is explicit, the values which it expresses do not give rise to the carefully ordered universe spatially and temporally of the middle-class child. The exercise of authority will not be related to a stable system of rewards and punishments but may often appear arbitrary. The specific character of long-term goals tends to be replaced by more general notions of the future, in which chance, a friend or a relative plays a greater part than the rigorous working out of connections. Thus present, or near-present, activities have greater value than the relation of the present activity to the attainment of a distant goal. The system of expectancies, or the timespan of anticipation, is shortened and this creates different sets of preferences, goals, and dissatisfactions. The environment limits the perception of the developing child of and in time. Present gratifications or present deprivations become absolute gratifications or absolute deprivations, for there exists no developed time continuum upon which present activity can be ranged. Rela-

[52] B. Bernstein, *op. cit.*, pp. 161, 165.

tive to the middle-classes, the postponement of present pleasure for future gratifications will be found difficult. By implication *a more volatile patterning of affectual and expressive behavior will be found in the working-classes.*[53]

This emphasis on the immediately perceivable and concern with the personal and concrete is part and parcel of the short time perspective and the inability to perceive the complex possibilities and consequences of actions which often result in a general readiness to support extremist political and religious movements, and a generally lower level of liberalism on noneconomic questions.[54]

Even within extremist movements these differences in the perceptions and perspectives of working-class as against middle-class persons affect their experiences, readiness to join a "cause," and reasons for defecting. The American political scientist Gabriel Almond's study of 221 ex-Communists in four countries provides data on this point. He distinguishes between the "exoteric" (simple, for mass consumption) and "esoteric" (complex, for the inner circle) doctrines of the party. In contrast to middle-class members "relatively few working-class respondents had been exposed to the esoteric doctrine of the party before joining, and . . . they tended to remain unindoctrinated while in the party."[55] The middle-

[53] *Ibid.*, p. 168 (my emphasis).

[54] This hypothesis has suggestive implications for a theory of trade-union democracy, and possible strains within trade-union organizational life. Working-class union members may not be at all as concerned with dictatorial union leadership as are middle-class critics who assume that the rank and file would actively form factions, and critically evaluate union policies if not constrained by a monolithic structure imposed by the top leadership. On the other hand, the more educated, articulate staff members (on a union newspaper, for example) may want to include more literate and complex discussions of issues facing the union but feel constrained by the need to present simple, easily understood propagandistic slogans for rank-and-file consumption. The "house organ" type of union newspaper may not be due entirely to internal political necessities.

[55] G. Almond, *op. cit.*, p. 244.

class recruits "tended to come to the party with more complex value patterns and expectations which were more likely to obstruct assimilation into the party. . . . The working-class member, on the other hand, is relatively untroubled by doctrinal apparatus, less exposed to the media of communication, and his imagination and logical powers are relatively undeveloped."[56]

One aspect of the lower classes' lack of sophistication and education is their anti-intellectualism (a phenomenon Engels long ago noted as a problem faced by working-class movements). While the complex esoteric ideology of Communism may have been one of the principal features attracting middle-class people to it, the fundamental anti-intellectualism which it shares with other extremist movements has been a source of strain for the "genuine" intellectuals within it. Thus it has been the working-class rank and file which has been least disturbed by Communism's ideological shifts, and least likely to defect.[57] Their commitment, once established, cannot usually be shaken by a sudden realization that the party, after all, does not conform to liberal and humanistic values.

This helps to explain why socialist parties have been led by a high proportion of intellectuals, in spite of an original ideological emphasis on maintaining a working-class orientation, while the Communists have alienated their intellectual leaders and are led preponderantly by those with working-class occupations.[58] Almond's study concluded that ". . . while the party is open to all comers, working-class party members have better prospects of success in the party than

[56] *Ibid.*, p. 177.

[57] *Ibid.*, pp. 313 ff., 392.

[58] For French data from 1936 to 1956 see Mattei Dogan. "Les Candidats et les élus," in L'Association française de science politique, *Les Elections du 2 janvier* (Paris: Librairie Armand Colin, 1956), p. 462, and Dogan, "L'origine sociale du personnel parlementaire français," in *Parties politiques et classes sociales en France*, edited by Maurice Duverger (Paris: Librairie Armand Colin, 1955), pp. 291–329. For a comparison of German Social Democratic and Communist parliamentary leadership before Hitler see Viktor Engelhardt, "Die Zusammensatzung des Reichstage nach Alter, Beruf, und Religionsbekenntnis," *Die Arbeit*, 8 (1931), p. 34.

middle-class recruits. This is probably due both to party policy, which has always manifested greater confidence in the reliability of working-class recruits, and to the difficulties of assimilation into the party generally experienced by middle-class party members."[59]

Making of an Authoritarian

To sum up, the lower-class individual is likely to have been exposed to punishment, lack of love, and a general atmosphere of tension and aggression since early childhood—all experiences which tend to produce deep-rooted hostilities expressed by ethnic prejudice, political authoritarianism, and chiliastic transvaluational religion. His educational attainment is less than that of men with higher socioeconomic status, and his association as a child with others of similar background not only fails to stimulate his intellectual interests but also creates an atmosphere which prevents his educational experience from increasing his general social sophistication and his understanding of different groups and ideas. Leaving school relatively early, he is surrounded on the job by others with a similarly restricted cultural, educational, and family background. Little external influence impinges on his limited environment. From early childhood, he has sought immediate gratifications, rather than engaged in activities which might have long-term rewards. The logic of both his adult employment and his family situation reinforces this limited time perspective. As the sociologist C. C. North has put it, isolation from heterogeneous environments, characteristic of low status, operates to "limit the source of information, to retard the development of efficiency in judgment and reasoning abilities, and to confine the attention to more trivial interests in life."[60]

[59] G. Almond, *op. cit.*, p. 190. This statement was supported by analysis of the biographies of 123 Central Committee leaders of the Party in three countries, as well as by interviews with 221 ex-Communists (both leaders and rank-and-file members) in four countries, France, Italy, Great Britain, and the United States.

[60] C. C. North, *Social Differentiation* (Chapel Hill: University of North Carolina Press, 1926), p. 247.

All of these characteristics produce a tendency to view politics and personal relationships in black-and-white terms, a desire for immediate action, an impatience with talk and discussion, a lack of interest in organizations which have a long-range perspective, and a readiness to follow leaders who offer a demonological interpretation of the evil forces (either religious or political) which are conspiring against him.[61]

It is interesting that Lenin saw the character of the lower classes, and the tasks of those who would lead them, in somewhat these terms. He specified as the chief task of the Communist parties the leadership of the broad masses, who are "slumbering, apathetic, hidebound, inert, and dormant." These masses, said Lenin, must be aligned for the "final and decisive battle" (a term reminiscent of Armageddon) by the party which alone can present an uncompromising and unified view of the world, and an immediate program for drastic change. In contrast to "effective" Communist leadership, Lenin pointed to the democratic parties and their leadership as "vacillating, wavering, unstable" elements—a characterization that is probably valid for any political group lacking ultimate certainty in its program and willing to grant legitimacy to opposition groups.[62]

The political outcome of these predispositions, however, is not determined by the multiplicity of factors involved.

[61] Most of these characteristics have been mentioned by child psychologists as typical of adolescent attitudes and perspectives. Werner Cohn, in an article on Jehovah's Witnesses, considers youth movements as a prototype of all such "proletarian" movements. Both "adolescence fixation and anomie are causal conditions" of their development (p. 297), and all such organizations have an "aura of social estrangement" (p. 282). See Werner Cohn, "Jehovah's Witnesses as a Proletarian Movement," *The American Scholar*, 24 (1955), pp. 281–99.

[62] The quotes from Lenin are in his *Left Wing Communism: An Infantile Disorder* (New York: International Publishers, 1940), pp. 74–75. Lenin's point, made in another context, in his pamphlet, *What Is to Be Done?* that workers left to themselves would never develop socialist or class consciousness, and that they would remain on the level of economic "day to day" consciousness, unless an organized group of revolutionary intellectuals brought them a broader vision, is similar to the generalizations presented here concerning the inherent limited time perspective of the lower strata.

Isolation, a punishing childhood, economic and occupational insecurities, and a lack of sophistication are conducive to withdrawal, or even apathy, and to strong mobilization of hostility. The same underlying factors which predispose individuals toward support of extremist movements under certain conditions may result in total withdrawal from political activity and concern under other conditions. In "normal" periods, apathy is most frequent among such individuals, but they can be activated by a crisis, especially if it is accompanied by strong millennial appeals.[63]

Extremism as an Alternative: A Test of a Hypothesis

The proposition that the lack of a rich, complex frame of reference is the vital variable which connects low status and a predisposition toward extremism does not necessarily suggest that the lower strata will be authoritarian; it implies that, other things being equal, they will choose the least complex alternative. Thus in situations in which extremism represents the more complex rather than the less complex form of politics, low status should be associated with *opposition* to such movements and parties.

This is in fact the case wherever the Communist party is a small party competing against a large reformist party, as in England, the United States, Sweden, Norway, and

[63] Various American studies indicate that those lower-class individuals who are nonvoters, and who have little political interest, tend to reject the democratic norms of tolerance. See Samuel A. Stouffer, *op. cit.*, and G. M. Connelly and H. H. Field, *op. cit.*, p. 182. Studies of the behavior of the unemployed in countries in which extremist movements were weak, such as the United States and Britain, indicate that apathy was their characteristic political response. See E. W. Bakke, *Citizens Without Work* (New Haven: Yale University Press, 1940), pp. 46–70. On the other hand, German data suggest a high correlation between working-class unemployment and support of Communists, and middle-class unemployment and support of Nazis. In France, Italy, and Finland today, those who have been unemployed tend to back the large Communist parties of those countries. See Chap. 7 and Erik Allardt, *Social Struktur och Politisk Aktivitet* (Helsingfors: Söderstrom Förlagsaktiebolag, 1956), pp. 84–85.

other countries. Where the party is small and weak, it cannot hold out the promise of immediate changes in the situation of the most deprived. Rather, such small extremist parties usually present the fairly complex intellectual argument that in the long run they will be strengthened by tendencies inherent in the social and economic system.[64] For the poorer worker, support of the Swedish Social Democrats, the British Labor party, or the American New Deal is a simpler and more easily understood way of securing redress of grievances or improvement of social conditions than supporting an electorally insignificant Communist party.

The available evidence from Denmark, Norway, Sweden, Canada, Brazil, and Great Britain supports this point. In these countries, where the Communist party is small and a Labor or Socialist party is much larger, Communist support is stronger among the better paid and more skilled workers than it is among the less skilled and poorer strata.[65] In Italy, France, and Finland, where the Communists are the largest party on the left, the lower the income level of workers, the

[64] Recent research on the early sources of support for the Nazi party challenges the hypothesis that it was the apathetic who came to its support prior to 1930, when it still represented a complex, long-range alternative. A negative rank-order correlation was found between the per cent increase in the Nazi vote and the increase in the proportion voting in the German election districts between 1928 and 1930. Only after it had become a relatively large party did it recruit the previously apathetic, who now could see its immediate potential. For a report of this research, see Chapter 5.

[65] For Denmark, see E. Høgh, *Vaelgeradfaerdi Danmark* (Ph.D. thesis, Sociology Institute, University of Copenhagen, 1959), Tables 6 and 9. For Norway, see Allen Barton, *Sociological and Psychological Implications of Economic Planning in Norway* (Ph.D. thesis, Department of Sociology, Columbia University, 1957); and several surveys of voting behavior in Norway conducted by Norwegian poll organizations including the 1949 FAKTA Survey, and the February 1954 and April 1956, NGI Survey, the results of which are as yet unpublished. Data from the files of the Canadian Gallup Poll for 1945, 1949, and 1953 indicate that the Labor-Progressive (Communist) party drew more support from the skilled than the unskilled sections of the working class. For Brazil, see A. Simao, "O voto operario en São Paulo," *Revista Brasilieras estudos politicos*, 1 (1956), p. 130–41.

higher their Communist vote.[66] A comparison of the differences in the relative income position of workers who vote Social Democratic and those who back the Communists in two neighboring Scandinavian countries of Finland and Sweden shows these alternative patterns clearly (Table V). In

TABLE V

THE INCOME COMPOSITION OF THE WORKING-CLASS SUPPORT OF THE SOCIAL DEMOCRATIC AND COMMUNIST PARTIES IN FINLAND AND SWEDEN*

Finland—1956

Income Class in Markkaa	Social Democrats	Communists
Under 100	8%	13%
100–400	49	50
400–600	22	29
600+	21	8
(N)	(173)	(119)

Sweden—1946

Income Class in Kroner	Social Democrats	Communists
Under 2,000	14%	9%
2,001–4,000	43	40
4,001–6,000	34	35
6,001+	9	15
(N)	(4832)	(819)

* The Finnish data were secured from a special run made for this study by the Finnish Gallup Poll. The Swedish statistics were recomputed from data presented in Elis Hastad, *et al.*, eds., *"Gallup" och den Svenska Valjarkaren* (Uppsala: Hugo Gebers Forlag, 1950), pp. 175–76. Both studies include rural and urban workers.

[66] For a table giving precise statistics for Italy and France, see Chap. 7. See also Hadley Cantril, *The Politics of Despair* (New York: Basic Books, 1958), pp. 3–10. In pre-Hitler Germany, where the Communists were a large party, they also secured their electoral strength much more from the less skilled sections of the workers than from the more skilled. See Samuel Pratt, *The Social Basis of Nazism and Communism in Urban Germany* (M.A. thesis, Department of Sociology, Michigan State College, 1948), pp. 156 ff.

An as yet unpublished study by Dr. Pertti Pesonen, of the Institute

Finland, where the Communists are very strong, their support is drawn disproportionately from the poorer workers, while in Sweden, where the Communists are a minor party, they have considerably more success with the better paid and more skilled workers than they do with the unskilled and lowly paid.[67]

This holds true in all countries for which data exist.[68] One other country, India, offers even better evidence. In India, the Communists are a major party, constituting the government or the major opposition (with 25 per cent or

---

of Political Science of the University of Helsinki, of voting in the industrial city of Tampere reports that the Communist voters were more well to do than the Social Democrats. On the other hand, Communists were much more likely to have experienced unemployment during the past year (21 per cent) or in their entire work history (46 per cent) than Social Democrats (10 per cent and 23 per cent). This study suggests that the experience of recent unemployment in the family is the most important determinant of a Communist vote in Tampere.

[67] Or to present the same data in another way, in Finland, 41 per cent of all workers earning less than 100 markkaa a month vote Communist, as compared with only 12 per cent among those earning over 600 markkaa. In Sweden, 7 per cent of the workers earning less than 2,000 kroner a year vote Communist, as compared with 25 per cent among those earning over 8,000.

[68] It may be noted, parenthetically, that where the Socialist party is small and/or new, it also represents a complex alternative, and attracts more middle-class support proportionately than when it is a well-established mass party which can offer immediate reforms. On the other hand, when a small transvaluational group does *not* offer an intellectually complex alternative, it should draw disproportionate support from the lower strata. Such groups are the sectarian religions whose millennial appeals have no developed rationale. Some extremely slight evidence on this point in a political contest is available from a recent Norwegian poll which shows the composition of the support for various parties. Only eleven persons supporting the Christian party, a party which appeals to the more fundamentalist Lutherans who are comparable to those discussed earlier in Sweden, were included in the total sample, but 82 per cent of these came from lower-income groups (less than 10,000 kroner per year). In comparison 57 per cent of the 264 Labor Party supporters, and 39 per cent of the 21 Communist supporters earned less than 10,000 kroner. Thus the small Communist party as the most complex transvalua-

more of the votes) in two states, Kerala and Andhra. While they have substantial strength in some other states, they are much weaker in the rest of India. If the proposition is valid that Communist appeal should be substantially for the lower and uneducated strata where the Party is powerful, and for the relatively higher and better educated ones where it is weak, the characteristics of Party voters should vary greatly in different parts of India, and this is in fact precisely what Table VI below shows.[69]

TABLE VI

COMMUNIST AND SOCIALIST PREFERENCES IN INDIA, BY CLASS AND EDUCATION*

Communist Party Preferences in Kerala and Andhra	Rest of India	Preferences for Socialist Parties in All-India
Class		
Middle	7%	27%	23%
Lower-middle	19	30	36
Working	74	43	41
Education		
Illiterate	52%	43%	31%
Under-matric.	39	37	43
Matric. plus	9	20	26
(N)	(113)	(68)	(88)

* These figures have been computed from tables presented in the *Indian Institute of Public Opinion, Monthly Public Opinion Surveys,* Vol. 2, Nos. 4, 5, 6, 7 (Combined Issue), New Delhi, January–April, 1957, pp. 9–14. This was a pre-election poll, not a report of the actual voting results. The total sample was 2,868 persons. The Socialist party and the Praja-Socialist party figures are combined here, since they share essentially the same moderate program. The support given to them in Andhra and Kerala was too small to be presented separately.

tional alternative drew its backing from relatively high strata, while the fundamentalist Christians had the economically poorest social base of any party in the country. See the February 1954 NGI Survey, issued in December 1956 in preliminary mimeographed form.

[69] These data were located after the hypothesis was formulated, and thus can be considered an independent replication.

Where the Indian Communist party is small, its support, like that of the two small moderate socialist parties, comes from relatively well-to-do and better educated strata. The picture shifts sharply in Kerala and Andhra, where the Communists are strong. The middle class provides only 7 per cent of Communist support there, with the working class supplying 74 per cent.[70] Educational differences among party supporters show a similar pattern.

Historical Patterns and Democratic Action

Despite the profoundly antidemocratic tendencies in lower-class groups, workers' political organizations and movements in the more industrialized democratic countries have supported *both* economic and political liberalism.[71] Workers'

[70] The hypothesis presented here does not attempt to explain the growth of small parties. Adaptations to major crisis situations, particularly depressions and wars, are probably the key factors initially increasing the support for a small "complex" party. For an analysis of the change in electoral support of a Socialist party as it moved up to major party status see S. M. Lipset, *Agrarian Socialism* (Berkeley: University of California Press, 1950), esp. pp. 159–78.

[71] There have been many exceptions to this. The Australian Labor party has been the foremost supporter of a "white Australia." Similarly, in the United States until the advent of the ideological New Deal in the 1930s, the lower-class-based Democratic party has always been the more anti-Negro of the two parties. The American labor movement has opposed nonwhite immigration, and much of it maintains barriers against Negro members. When the American Socialist party was a mass movement before World War I, its largest circulation newspapers, such as the Milwaukee *Social Democratic Herald* and the *Appeal to Reason* opposed racial integration. The latter stated explicitly, "Socialism will separate the races." See David A. Shannon, *The Socialist Party of America* (New York: Macmillan, 1955), pp. 49–52. Even the Marxist Socialist movement of Western Europe was not immune to the virus of anti-Semitism. Thus, before World War I there were a number of anti-Semitic incidents in which Socialists were involved, some avowedly anti-Semitic leaders connected with different socialist parties, and strong resistance to committing the socialist organizations to opposition to anti-Semitism. See E. Silberner, "The Anti-Semitic Tradition in Modern Socialism," *Scripta Hierosolymitana*, III (1956), pp. 378–96. In an article on the recent British race riots, Michael

organizations, trade-unions and political parties played a major role in extending political democracy in the nineteenth and early twentieth centuries. However, these struggles for political freedom by the workers, like those of the middle class before them, took place in the context of a fight for economic rights.[72] Freedom of organization and of speech,

---

Rumney points out the working-class base of the anti-Negro sentiment and goes so far as to predict that "the Labour party will become the enemy of the Negro as time goes on." He reports that "while the Conservative party has been able to stand behind the police and take any means it feels necessary to preserve the peace, the Labour party has been strangely silent. If it speaks it will either antagonize the men who riot against West Indians, or forfeit its claim to being the party of equal rights." See "Left Mythology and British Race Riots," *The New Leader* (September 22, 1958), pp. 10–11.

British Gallup Poll surveys document these judgments. Thus in a survey completed in July 1959, the poll asked whether Jews "have more or less power than they should really have," and found, when respondents were compared according to party choice, that the anti-Semitic response of "more power" was given by 38 per cent of the Labor voters, 30 per cent of the Tories, and 27 per cent of the Liberals. Seven per cent of the Laborites, 8 per cent of the Conservatives, and 9 per cent of the Liberals thought that Jews have too little power. The same organization has reported a 1958 survey in which fewer Laborites and lower class people said that they would vote for a Jew if their party nominated one than did upper class and Conservative voters. But in all fairness it must also be noted that almost every Jew in the House of Commons represents the Labor party, and that almost all of the approximately two dozen Jews represent overwhelmingly non-Jewish constituencies.

[72] Actually there are some striking similarities between the behavior of various middle-class strata when they constituted the lower strata within a predominantly aristocratic and feudal society, and the working class in newly industrialized societies who have not yet won a place in society. The affinities of both for religious and economic "radicalism," in the same sense, are striking. Calvin's doctrine of predestination, as Tawney points out, performed the same function for the eighteenth-century *bourgeoisie* as did Marx's theory of the inevitability of socialism for the proletariat in the nineteenth. Both "set their virtue at their best in sharp antithesis with the vices of the established order at its worst, taught them to feel that they were a chosen people, made them conscious of their great destiny in the Providential and resolute to realize it." The Communist party, as did the Puritans, insists on "personal responsibility,

together with universal suffrage, were necessary weapons in the battle for a better standard of living, social security, shorter hours, and the like. The upper classes resisted the extension of political freedom as part of their defense of economic and social privilege.

Few groups in history have ever voluntarily espoused civil liberties and freedom for those who advocate measures they consider despicable or dangerous. Religious freedom emerged in the Western world only because the contending powers each found themselves unable to destroy the other without destroying the entire society, and because in the course of the struggle itself many men lost faith and interest in religion, and consequently the desire to suppress dissent. Similarly, universal suffrage and freedom of organization and opposition developed in many countries either as concessions to the established strength of the lower classes, or as means of controlling them—a tactic advocated and used by such sophisticated conservatives as Disraeli and Bismarck.

Once in existence, however, and although originating in a conflict of interests, democratic norms became part of the institutional system. Thus the Western labor and socialist movement has incorporated these values into its general ideology. But the fact that the movement's ideology is democratic does not mean that its supporters actually understand the implications. The evidence seems to indicate that understanding of and adherence to these norms are highest among leaders and lowest among followers. The general opinions or predispositions of the rank and file are relatively unimportant in predicting behavior as long as the organization to which they are loyal continues to act democratically. In spite of the workers' greater authoritarian propensity, their organizations which are anti-Communist still function as better

---

discipline and asceticism," and although the historical contents differ, they may have the same sociological roots: in isolated, status-deprived occupational groups. See R. H. Tawney, *Religion and the Rise of Capitalism* (New York: Penquin Books, 1947), pp. 9, 99. For a similar point see Donald G. MacRae, "The Bolshevik Ideology," *The Cambridge Journal*, 3 (1950), pp. 164–77.

defenders and carriers of democratic values than parties based on the middle class. In Germany, the United States, Great Britain, and Japan, individuals who support the democratic left party are more likely to support civil liberties and democratic values than people *within* each occupational stratum who back the conservative parties. Organized social democracy not only defends civil liberties but influences its supporters in the same direction.[73]

Conservatism is especially vulnerable in a political democracy since, as Abraham Lincoln said, there are always more poor people than well-to-do ones, and promises to redistribute wealth are difficult to rebut. Consequently, conservatives have traditionally feared a thoroughgoing political democracy and have endeavored in most countries—by restricting the franchise or by manipulating the governmental structure through second chambers or overrepresentation of rural districts and small towns (traditional conservative strongholds)—to prevent a popular majority from controlling the government. The ideology of conservatism has frequently been based on elitist values which reject the idea that there is wisdom in the voice of the electorate. Other values often defended by conservatives, like militarism or nationalism, probably also have an attraction for individuals with authoritarian predispositions.[74]

[73] A striking case in point occurred in Australia in 1950. During a period of much agitation about the dangers of the Communist party, a Gallup Poll survey reported that 80 per cent of the electorate favored outlawing the Communists. Shortly after this survey, the Conservative government submitted a proposal to outlaw the party to referendum. During the referendum electoral campaign, the Labor party and the trade-unions came out vigorously against the proposal. Considerable shifting took place after this, to the point that the measure to outlaw the Communists was actually defeated by a small majority, and Catholic workers who had overwhelmingly favored the outlaw measure when first questioned by the Gallup Poll eventually followed the advice of their party and unions and voted against it. See Leicester Webb, *Communism and Democracy in Australia: A Survey of the 1951 Referendum* (New York: Frederick A. Praeger, 1955).

[74] A study of the 1952 elections in the United States revealed that at every educational level (grammar school, high school, and college) individuals who scored high on an "authoritarian personality" scale

It would be a mistake to conclude from the data presented here that the authoritarian predispositions of the lower classes necessarily constitute a threat to a democratic social system; nor should similar conclusions be drawn about the antidemocratic aspects of conservatism. Whether or not a given class supports restrictions on freedom depends on a wide constellation of factors of which those discussed here are only a part.

The instability of the democratic process in general and the strength of the Communists in particular, as we have seen, are closely related to national levels of economic development, including national levels of educational attainment. The Communists represent a mass movement in the poorer countries of Europe and elsewhere, but are weak where economic development and educational attainment are high. The lower classes of the less developed countries are poorer, more insecure, less educated, and relatively more underprivileged in terms of possession of status symbols than are the lower strata of the more well-to-do nations. In the more developed, stable democracies of Western Europe, North America, and Australasia the lower classes are "in the society" as well as "of it"—that is, their isolation from the rest of the culture is much less than the social isolation of the poorer groups in other countries, who are cut off by abysmally low incomes and very low educational levels, if not by widespread illiteracy. This incorporation of the workers into the body politic in the industrialized Western world has reduced their authoritarian tendencies greatly, although in the United States, for example, McCarthy demonstrated that an irresponsible demagogue who combines a nationalist and antielitist appeal can still secure considerable support from the less educated.[75]

---

were much more likely to vote for Eisenhower rather than Stevenson. Robert Lane, "Political Personality and Electoral Choice," *American Political Science Review*, 49 (1955), pp. 173–90. In Britain, a study of working-class anti-Semitism found that the small group of Conservatives in the sample were much more anti-Semitic than the Liberals and the Laborites. See James H. Robb, *Working-class Anti-Semite* (London: Tavistock Publications, 1954), pp. 93–94.

[75] "The history of the masses, however, has been a history of the most consistently anti-intellectual force in society . . . It was the

While the evidence as to the effects of rising national standards of living and education permits us to be hopeful about working-class politics and behavior in those countries in which extremism is weak, it does suggest pessimistic conclusions with regard to the less economically developed, unstable democracies. Where an extremist party has secured the support of the lower classes—often by stressing equality and economic security at the expense of liberty—it is problematic whether this support can be taken away from it by democratic methods. The Communists, in particular, combine the two types of a chiliastic view of the world. Whether democratic working-class parties, able to demonstrate convincingly their ability to defend economic and class interests, can be built up in the less stable democracies is a moot question. But the threat to democracy does not come solely from the lower strata. And in the next chapter we will turn from working-class authoritarianism to an examination of the different varieties of fascism, which is usually identified with the middle class.

American lower classes, not the upper, who gave their overwhelming support to the attacks in recent years on civil liberties. It is among the working people that one finds dominant those sects and churches most hostile to the free spirit." Lewis S. Feuer, Introduction to *Marx and Engels, Basic Writings on Politics and Philosophy* (New York: Doubleday Anchor Books, 1959), pp. xv–xvi. And in another wealthy country white South Africa, Herbert Tingsten points out that "industrialization and commercialization . . . have formed that social class now constituting the stronghold of Boer nationalism: workers, shop assistants, clerks, lower grades of civil servants. Here, as in the United States, these 'poor whites'—more correctly, whites threatened by poverty—are the leading guardians of prejudice and white supremacy." *The Problem of South Africa* (London: Victor Gollancz, Ltd., 1955), p. 23.

CHAPTER 5

"Fascism"—Left, Right, and Center

THE RETURN of De Gaulle to power in France in 1958 following a military *coup d'état* was accompanied by dire predictions of the revival of fascism as a major ideological movement, and raised anew the issue of the character of different kinds of extremist movements. Much of the discussion between Marxist and non-Marxist scholars before 1945 was devoted to an analysis of fascism in power and focused on whether the Nazis or other fascist parties were actually strengthening the economic institutions of capitalism or creating a new post-capitalist social order similar to Soviet bureaucratic totalitarianism.

While an analysis of the actual behavior of parties in office is crucial to an understanding of their functional significance, the social base and ideology of any movement must also be analyzed if it is to be truly understood. A study of the social bases of different modern mass movements suggests that each major social stratum has both democratic and extremist political expressions. The extremist movements of the left, right, and center (Communism and Peronism, traditional authoritarianism, and fascism) are based primarily on the working, upper, and middle classes, respectively. The term "fascism" has been applied at one time or another to all of these varieties of extremism, but an analytical examination of the social base and ideology of each reveals their different characters.

The political and sociological analysis of modern society in terms of left, center, and right goes back to the days of the first French Republic when the delegates were seated, according to their political coloration, in a continuous semicircle from the most radical and egalitarian on the left to the most moderate and aristocratic on the right. The identification of the left with advocacy of social reform and egalitarianism; the right, with aristocracy and conservatism, deepened as politics became defined as the clash between classes. Nineteenth-century conservatives and Marxists alike joined in the assumption that the socioeconomic cleavage is the most basic in modern society. Since democracy has become institutionalized and the conservatives' fears that universal suffrage would mean the end of private property have declined, many people have begun to argue that the analysis of politics in terms of left and right and class conflict oversimplifies and distorts reality. However, the tradition of political discourse, as well as political reality, has forced most scholars to retain these basic concepts, although other dimensions, like religious differences or regional conflicts, account for political behavior which does not follow class lines.[1]

Before 1917 extremist political movements were usually thought of as a rightist phenomenon. Those who would eliminate democracy generally sought to restore monarchy or the rule of the aristocrats. After 1917 politicians and scholars alike began to refer to both left and right extremism, i.e., Communism and fascism. In this view, extremists at either end of the political continuum develop into advocates of dictatorship, while the moderates of the center remain the defenders of democracy. This chapter will attempt to show that this is an error—that extremist ideologies and groups can be classified and analyzed in the same terms as democratic groups, i.e., right, left, and *center*. The three positions resemble their democratic parallels in both the compositions of their social bases and the contents of their appeals. While

[1] In spite of the complexities of French politics, the foremost students of elections in that country find that they must classify parties and alternatives along the left-right dimension. See F. Goguel, *Géographie des élections françaises de 1870 à 1951, Cahiers de la fondation nationale des sciences politiques*, No. 27 (Paris: Librairie Armand Colin, 1951).

comparisons of all three positions on the democratic and extremist continuum are of intrinsic interest, this chapter concentrates on the politics of the center, the most neglected type of political extremism, and that form of "left" extremism sometimes called "fascism"—Peronism—as manifested in Argentina and Brazil.

The center position among the democratic tendencies is usually called liberalism. In Europe where it is represented by various parties like the French Radicals, the Dutch and Belgian Liberals, and others, the liberal position means: in economics—a commitment to *laissez-faire* ideology, a belief in the vitality of small business, and opposition to strong trade-unions; in politics—a demand for minimal government intervention and regulation; in social ideology—support of equal opportunity for achievement, opposition to aristocracy, and opposition to enforced equality of income; in culture—anticlericalism and antitraditionalism.

If we look at the supporters of the three major positions in most democratic countries, we find a fairly logical relationship between ideology and social base. The Socialist left derives its strength from manual workers and the poorer rural strata; the conservative right is backed by the rather well-to-do elements—owners of large industry and farms, the managerial and free professional strata—and those segments of the less privileged groups who have remained involved in traditionalist institutions, particularly the Church. The democratic center is backed by the middle classes, especially small businessmen, white-collar workers, and the anticlerical sections of the professional classes.

The different extremist groups have ideologies which correspond to those of their democratic counterparts. The classic fascist movements have represented the extremism of the center. Fascist ideology, though antiliberal in its glorification of the state, has been similar to liberalism in its opposition to big business, trade-unions, and the socialist state. It has also resembled liberalism in its distaste for religion and other forms of traditionalism. And, as we shall see later, the social characteristics of Nazi voters in pre-Hitler Germany and Austria resembled those of the liberals much more than they did those of the conservatives.

The largest group of left extremists are the Communists, whose appeal has already been discussed in some detail and who will not concern us much in this chapter. The Communists are clearly revolutionary, opposed to the dominant strata, and based on the lower classes. There is, however, another form of left extremism which, like right extremism, is often classified under the heading of fascism. This form, Peronism, largely found in poorer underdeveloped countries, appeals to the lower strata against the middle and upper classes. It differs from Communism in being nationalistic, and has usually been the creation of nationalist army officers seeking to create a more vital society by destroying the corrupt privileged strata which they believe have kept the masses in poverty, the economy underdeveloped, and the army demoralized and underpaid.

Conservative or rightist extremist movements have arisen at different periods in modern history, ranging from the Horthyites in Hungary, the Christian Social party of Dollfuss in Austria, the Stahlhelm and other nationalists in pre-Hitler Germany, and Salazar in Portugal, to the pre-1958 Gaullist movements and the monarchists in contemporary France and Italy. The right extremists are conservative, not revolutionary. They seek to change political institutions in order to preserve or restore cultural and economic ones, while extremists of the center and left seek to use political means for cultural and social revolution. The ideal of the right extremist is not a totalitarian ruler, but a monarch, or a traditionalist who acts like one. Many such movements—in Spain, Austria, Hungary, Germany, and Italy—have been explicitly monarchist, and De Gaulle returned monarchical rights and privileges to the French presidency. Not surprisingly, the supporters of these movements differ from those of the centrists; they tend to be wealthier, and—more important in terms of mass support—more religious.

"Fascism" and the Middle Class

The thesis that fascism is basically a middle-class movement representing a protest against both capitalism *and* socialism, big business *and* big unions, is far from original. Many analysts have suggested it ever since fascism and Nazism first appeared on the scene. Nearly twenty-five years ago, the economist David Saposs stated it well:

Fascism . . . [is] the extreme expression of middle-classism or populism. . . . The basic ideology of the middle class is populism. . . . Their ideal was an independent small property-owning class consisting of merchants, mechanics, and farmers. This element . . . now designated as middle class, sponsored a system of private property, profit, and competition on an entirely different basis from that conceived by capitalism. . . . From its very inception it opposed "big business" or what has now become known as capitalism.

Since the war the death knell of liberalism and individualism has been vociferously, albeit justly sounded. But since liberalism and individualism are of middle-class origin, it has been taken for granted that this class has also been eliminated as an effective social force. As a matter of fact, populism is now as formidable a force as it has ever been. And the middle class is more vigorously assertive than ever. . . .[2]

2 David J. Saposs, "The Role of the Middle Class in Social Development: Fascism, Populism, Communism, Socialism," in *Economic Essays in Honor of Wesley Clair Mitchell* (New York: Columbia University Press, 1935), pp. 395, 397, 400. An even earlier analysis by André Siegfried, based on a detailed ecological study of voting patterns in part of France from 1871 to 1912, suggested that the petty bourgeoisie who had been considered the classic source of French democratic ideology were becoming the principal recruiting grounds for extremist movements. Siegfried pointed out that though they are "by nature egalitarian, democratic, and envious . . . they are fearful above all of new economic conditions which threatened to eliminate them, crushed between the aggressive

And although some have attributed the lower middle-class support for Nazism to the specific economic difficulties of the 1930s, the political scientist, Harold Lasswell, writing in the depths of the Depression, suggested that middle-class extremism flowed from trends inherent in capitalist industrial society which would continue to affect the middle class even if its economic position improved.

> Insofar as Hitlerism is a desperation reaction of the lower middle classes, it continues a movement which began during the closing years of the nineteenth century. Materially speaking, it is not necessary to assume that the small shopkeepers, teachers, preachers, lawyers, doctors, farmers and craftsmen were worse off at the end than they had been in the middle of the century. Psychologically speaking, however, the lower middle class was increasingly overshadowed by the workers and the upper bourgeoisie, whose unions, cartels and parties took the center of the stage. The psychological impoverishment of the lower middle class precipitated emotional insecurities within the personalities of its members, thus fertilizing the ground for the various movements of mass protest through which the middle classes might revenge themselves.[3]

As the relative position of the middle class declined and its resentments against on-going social and economic treads continued, its "liberal" ideology—the support of individual rights against large-scale power—changed from that of a revolution-

---

capitalism of the great companies and the increasing rise of the working people. They place great hopes in the Republic, and they do not cease being republican or egalitarian. But they are in that state of discontent, from which the Boulangisms marshal their forces, in which reactionary demagogues see the best ground in which to agitate, and in which is born passionate resistance to certain democratic reforms." André Siegfried, *Tableau politique de la France de l'ouest sous la troisième république* (Paris: Librairie Armand Colin, 1913), p. 413.

[3] Harold Lasswell, "The Psychology of Hitlerism," *The Political Quarterly*, 4 (1933), p. 374.

ary class to that of a reactionary class. Once liberal doctrines had supported the *bourgeoisie* in their fight against the remnants of the feudal and monarchical order, and against the limitations demanded by mercantilist rulers and the Church. A liberal ideology opposed to Throne and Altar and favoring a limited state emerged. This ideology was not only revolutionary in political terms; it fulfilled some of the functional requirements for efficient industrialization. As Max Weber pointed out, the development of the capitalist system (which in his analysis coincides with industrialization) necessitated the abolition of artificial internal boundaries, the creation of an open international market, the establishment of law and order, and relative international peace.[4]

But the aspirations and ideology which underlay eighteenth- and nineteenth-century liberalism and populism have a different meaning and serve a different function in the advanced industrial societies of the twentieth century. Resisting large-scale organizations and the growth of state authority challenges some of the fundamental characteristics of our present society, since large industry and a strong and legitimate labor movement are necessary for a stable, modernized social structure, and government regulation and heavy taxes seem an inevitable concomitant. To be against business bureaucracies, trade-unions, and state regulation is both unrealistic and to some degree irrational. As Talcott Parsons has put it, the "new negative orientation to certain primary aspects of the maturing modern social order has above all centered in the symbol of 'capitalism'. . . . The reaction against the 'ideology' of the rationalization of society is the principal aspect at least of the ideology of fascism."[5]

[4] See also Karl Polanyi, *The Great Transformation* (New York: Farrar and Rinehart, 1944).

[5] Talcott Parsons, "Some Sociological Aspects of the Fascist Movement," in his *Essays in Sociological Theory* (Glencoe: The Free Press, 1954), pp. 133–34. Marx himself pointed out that "the small manufacturer, the small merchant, the artisan, the peasant, all fight against the [big] bourgeois, in order to protect their position as a middle class from being destroyed. They are, however, not revolutionary, but conservative. Even more, they are reactionary, they look

While continuing conflict between management and labor is an integral part of large-scale industrialism, the small businessman's desire to retain an important place for himself and his social values is "reactionary"—not in the Marxist sense of slowing down the wheels of revolution, but from the perspective of the inherent trends of a modern industrial society. Sometimes the efforts of the small business stratum to resist or reverse the process take the form of democratic liberal movements, like the British Liberal party, the French Radicals, or the American Taft Republicans. Such movements have failed to stop the trends which their adherents oppose, and as another sociologist, Martin Trow, recently noted: "The tendencies which small businessmen fear—of concentration and centralization—proceed without interruption in depression, war and prosperity, and irrespective of what party is in power; thus they are *always* disaffected. . . ."[6] It is not surprising, therefore, that under certain conditions small businessmen turn to extremist political movements, either fascism or antiparliamentary populism, which in one way or another express contempt for parliamentary democracy. These movements answer some of the same needs as the more conventional liberal parties; they are an outlet for the stratification strains of the middle class in a mature industrial order. But while liberalism attempts to cope with the problems by legitimate social changes and "reforms" ("reforms" which would, to be sure, reverse the modernization process), fascism and populism propose to solve the problems by taking over the state and running it in a way which will restore the old middle classes' economic security and high standing in society, and at the same time reduce the power and status of big capital and big labor.

The appeal of extremist movements may also be a response

for a way to reverse the path of history," quoted in S. S. Nilson, "Wahlsoziologische Probleme des Nationalsozialismus," *Zeitschrift für die Gesamte Staatswissenchaft*, 110 (1954), p. 295.

[6] Martin A. Trow, "Small Businessmen, Political Tolerance, and Support for McCarthy," *American Journal of Sociology*, 64 (1958), pp. 279–80.

by different strata of the population to the social effects of industrialization at different stages of its development. These variations are set in sharp relief by a comparison of the organized threats to the democratic process in societies at various stages of industrialization. As I have already shown, working-class extremism, whether Communist, anarchist, revolutionary socialist, or Peronist, is most commonly found in societies undergoing rapid industrialization, or in those where the process of industrialization did not result in a predominantly industrial society, like the Latin countries of southern Europe. Middle-class extremism occurs in countries characterized by both large-scale capitalism and a powerful labor movement. Right-wing extremism is most common in less developed economies, in which the traditional conservative forces linked to Throne and Altar remain strong. Since some countries, like France, Italy, or Weimar Germany, have possessed strata in all three sets of circumstances, all three types of extremist politics sometimes exist in the same country. Only the well-to-do, highly industrialized and urbanized nations seem immune to the virus, but even in the United States and Canada there is evidence that the self-employed are somewhat disaffected.

The different political reactions of similar strata at different points in the industrialization process are clearly delineated by a comparison of the politics of certain Latin-American countries with those of Western Europe. The more well-to-do Latin-American countries today resemble Europe in the nineteenth century; they are experiencing industrial growth while their working classes are still relatively unorganized into trade-unions and political parties, and reservoirs of traditional conservatism still exist in their rural populations. The growing middle class in these countries, like its nineteenth-century European counterpart, supports a democratic society by attempting to reduce the influence of the anticapitalist traditionalists and the arbitrary power of the military.[7] To the

[7] For an analysis of the political role of the rapidly growing Latin-American middle classes see John J. Johnson, *Political Change in*

extent that there is a social base at this stage of economic development for extremist politics, it lies not in the middle classes but in the growing, still unorganized working classes who are suffering from the tensions inherent in rapid industrialization. These workers have provided the primary base of support for the only large-scale "fascist" movements in Latin America—those of Peron in the Argentine and Vargas in Brazil. These movements, like the Communist ones with which they have sometimes been allied, appeal to the "displaced masses" of newly industrializing countries.

The real question to answer is: which strata are most "displaced" in each country? In some, it is the new working class, or the working class which was never integrated in the total society, economically or politically; in others, it is the small businessmen and other relatively independent entrepreneurs (small farm owners, provincial lawyers) who feel oppressed by the growing power and status of unionized workers and by large-scale corporative and governmental bureaucracies. In still others, it is the conservative and traditionalist elements who seek to preserve the old society from the values of socialism and liberalism. Fascist ideology in Italy, for example, arose out of an opportunistic movement which sought at various times to appeal to all three groups, and remained sufficiently amorphous to permit appeals to widely different strata, depending on national varia-

---

Latin America—the Emergence of the Middle Sectors (Stanford: Stanford University Press, 1958). The different political propensities of a social group at successive stages of industrialization are indicated by James Bryce's comment in 1912 that "the absence of that class of small landowners which is the soundest and most stable element in the United States and in Switzerland and is equally stable, if less politically trained, in France and parts of Germany, is a grave misfortune for South and Central America." This may have been true in an early period, before the impact of large-scale organization of the farms meant economic competition for small farmers and added them to the rank of the potential supporters of fascism, as the data on Germany and other countries discussed here show. See James Bryce, *South America: Observations and Impressions* (New York: Macmillan, 1912), p. 533.

tions as to who were most "displaced."[8] Since fascist politicians have been extremely opportunistic in their efforts to secure support, such movements have often encompassed groups with conflicting interests and values, even when they primarily expressed the needs of one stratum. Hitler, a centrist extremist, won backing from conservatives who hoped to use the Nazis against the Marxist left. And conservative extremists like Franco have often been able to retain centrists among their followers without giving them control of the movement.

In the previous chapter on working-class authoritarianism I tried to specify some of the other conditions which dispose different groups and individuals to accept more readily an extremist and demonological view of the world.[9] The thesis presented there suggested that a low level of sophistication and a high degree of insecurity predispose an individual toward an extremist view of politics. Lack of sophistication is largely a product of little education and isolation from varied experiences. On these grounds, the most authoritarian segments of the middle strata should be found among the small entrepreneurs who live in small communities or on farms. These people receive relatively little formal education as compared with those in other middle-class positions; and living in rural areas or small towns usually means isolation from heterogeneous values and groups. By the same token, one would expect more middle-class extremism among the self-employed, whether rural or urban, than among white-collar workers, executives, and professionals.

The following sections bring together available data for different countries which indicate the sharp difference between the social roots of classic fascism and populism and those of right-wing movements.

[8] A comparison of the European middle class and the Argentine working class, which argues that each is most "displaced" in its respective environment, is contained in Gino Germani, *Integracion politica de las masas y la totalitarismo* (Buenos Aires: Colegio Libre de Estudios Superiores, 1956). See also his *Estructura social de la Argentina* (Buenos Aires: Raigal, 1955).

[9] See pp. 108–14 of Chap. 4.

Germany

The classic example of a revolutionary fascist party is, of course, the National Socialist Workers' party led by Adolf Hitler. For Marxian analysts, this party represented the last stage of capitalism, winning power in order to maintain capitalism's tottering institutions. Since the Nazis came to power before the days of public opinion polls, we have to rely on records of the total votes to locate their social base. If classic fascism appeals largely to the same elements as those which back liberalism, then the previous supporters of liberalism should have provided the backing for the Nazis. A look at the gross election statistics for the German Reich between 1928 and 1933 would seem to verify this (Table I).

Although a table like this conceals changes by individuals which go against the general statistical trend, some reasonable inferences may be made. As the Nazis grew, the liberal bourgeois center parties, based on the less traditionalist elements of German society—primarily small business and white-collar workers—completely collapsed. Between 1928 and 1932 these parties lost almost 80 per cent of their vote, and their proportion of the total vote dropped from a quarter to less than 3 per cent. The only center party which maintained its proportionate support was the Catholic Center party whose support was reinforced by religious allegiance. The Marxist parties, the socialists and the Communists, lost about a tenth of their percentage support, although their total vote dropped only slightly. The proportionate support of the conservatives dropped about 40 per cent, much less than that of the more liberal middle-class parties.

An inspection of the shifts among the non-Marxist and non-Catholic parties suggests that the Nazis gained most heavily among the liberal middle-class parties, the former bulwarks of the Weimar Republic. Among these parties, the one which lost most heavily was the *Wirtschaftspartei*, which represented primarily small businessmen and artisans.[10] The

[10] Karl D. Bracher, *Die Auflösung der Weimarer Republik* (Stuttgart und Düsseldorf: Ring Verlag, 1954), p. 94. The parliamentary

TABLE I

PERCENTAGES OF TOTAL VOTE RECEIVED BY VARIOUS GERMAN
PARTIES, 1928–1933, AND THE PERCENTAGE OF THE 1928 VOTE
RETAINED IN THE LAST FREE ELECTION 1932*

Party	Percentage of Total Vote					Ratio of 1928 to Second 1932 Election Expressed as Percentage
Conservative Party	1928	1930	1932	1932	1933	
DNVP	14.2	7.0	5.9	8.5	8.0	60
Middle-class Parties						
DVP (right liberals)	8.7	4.85	1.2	1.8	1.1	21
DDP (left liberals)	4.8	3.45	1.0	.95	.8	20
Wirtschaftspartei (small business)	4.5	3.9	0.4	0.3	†	7
Others	9.5	10.1	2.6	2.8	.6	29
Total proportion of middle-class vote maintained:						21
Center (Catholic)	15.4	17.6	16.7	16.2	15.0	105
Workers' Parties						
SPD (Socialist)	29.8	24.5	21.6	20.4	18.3	69
KPD (Communist)	10.6	13.1	14.3	16.85	12.3	159
Total proportion of working-class vote maintained:						92
Fascist Party						
NSDAP	2.6	18.3	37.3	33.1	43.9	1277
Total proportion of increase in Fascist party vote:						1277

* The basic data are presented in Samuel Pratt, *The Social Basis
of Nazism and Communism in Urban Germany* (M.A. thesis, Dept.
of Sociology, Michigan State University, 1948), pp. 29, 30. The
same data are presented and analyzed in Karl D. Bracher, *Die
Auflösung der Weimarer Republik* (Stuttgart und Düsseldorf: Ring
Verlag, 1954), pp. 86–106. The 1933 election was held after Hitler
had been chancellor for more than a month.

† The *Wirtschaftspartei* did not run any candidates in the 1933
elections.

---

delegation of this party was almost exclusively composed of businessmen who were active in the interest group associations of
small business. See Sigmund Neumann, "Germany: Changing Patterns and Lasting Problems" in S. Neumann, ed., *Modern Political
Parties* (Chicago: University of Chicago Press, 1956), p. 364.

right-wing nationalist opponent of Weimar, the German National People's party (DNVP), was the only one of the non-Marxist and non-Catholic parties to retain over half of its 1928 proportion of the total vote.

The largest drop-off in the conservative vote lay mainly in the election districts on the eastern border of Germany. The proportion of the vote obtained by the German National People's party declined by 50 per cent or more between 1928 and 1932 in ten of the thirty-five election districts in Germany. Seven of these ten were border areas, including every region which fronted on the Polish corridor, and Schleswig-Holstein, fronting on the northern border. Since the party was both the most conservative and the most nationalist pre-Nazi opponent of the Versailles Treaty, these data suggest that the Nazis most severely weakened the conservatives in those areas where nationalism was their greatest source of strength, while the conservatives retained most of their voters in regions which had not suffered as directly from the annexations imposed by Versailles and in which, it may be argued, the party's basic appeal was more conservative than nationalist. The German-American sociologist Rudolf Heberle has demonstrated in a detailed study of voting patterns in Schleswig-Holstein that the conservatives lost the backing of the small property owners, both urban and rural, whose counterparts in nonborder areas were most commonly liberals, while they retained the backing of the upper-strata conservatives.[11]

Some further indirect evidence that the Nazis did not appeal to the same sources as the traditional German right may be found in the data on the voting of men and women. In the 1920s and 1930s the more conservative or religious a party, the higher, in general, its feminine support. The German National People's party had more female backing than any party except the Catholic Center party. The Nazis, together with the more liberal middle-class parties and Marxist parties, received disproportionate support from men.[12]

[11] Rudolf Heberle, *From Democracy to Nazism* (Baton Rouge: Louisiana State University Press, 1945).
[12] The most comprehensive set of German election data presenting party vote in different elections by sex may be found in Maurice

More direct evidence for the thesis is given in Heberle's study of Schleswig-Holstein, the state in which the Nazis were strongest. In 1932 *the Conservatives were weakest where the Nazis were strongest and the Nazis were relatively weak where the Conservatives were strong.* The correlation in 18 predominantly rural election districts between percentages of votes obtained by the NSDAP [Nazis] and by the DNVP [Conservatives] is negative (minus .89). . . . It appears that the Nazis had in 1932 really succeeded the former liberal parties, like the *Landespartei* and Democratic party, as the preferred party among the small farmers . . . while the landlords and big farmers were more reluctant to cast their vote for Hitler."[13]

A more recent analysis by a German political scientist, Günther Franz, identifying voting trends in another state in which the Nazis were very strong—Lower Saxony—reported similar patterns. Franz concluded:

> The majority of the National Socialist voters came from the bourgeois center parties. The DNVP [conservatives] had also lost votes, but in 1932, they held the votes which they received in 1930, and increased their total vote in the next two elections. They were (except for the Catholic Center) the only bourgeois party, which had not simply collapsed before the NSDAP. . . .[14]

This situation in Schleswig-Holstein and Lower Saxony also existed in Germany as a whole. Among the thirty-five elec-

---

Duverger, *La Participation des femmes à la vie politique* (Paris: UNESCO, 1955), pp. 56–63; and Gabriele Bremme, *Die politische Rolle der Frau in Deutschland* (Göttingen: Vandenhoeck and Ruprecht, 1956), pp. 74–77, 111, 243–52; see also Heinrich Striefler, *Deutsche Wahlen in Bildern und Zahlen* (Düsseldorf: Wilhelm Hagemann, 1946), pp. 20–22; Günther Franz, *Die politischen Wahlen in Niedersachsen 1867 bis 1949* (Bremen-Horn: Walter Dorn Verlag, 1957), pp. 28–32; Karl D. Bracher, *op. cit.*, p. 476; Herbert Tingsten, *Political Behavior: Studies in Election Statistics* (London: P. S. King & Son, 1937), pp. 37–65.

[13] Rudolf Heberle, *op. cit.*, pp. 113, 114, 119 (emphasis supplied).
[14] Günther Franz, *op. cit.*, p. 62.

toral districts, the rank-order correlation of the proportionate Nazi gain with the liberal parties' loss was greater (.48) than with the conservatives' loss (.25).[15]

Besides the liberal parties, there was one other group of German parties, based on the *Mittel-stand*, whose supporters seem to have gone over almost en masse to the Nazis— the so-called "federalist" or regional autonomy parties.[16] These parties objected either to the unification of Germany or to the specific annexation of various provinces like Hesse, Lower Saxony, and Schleswig-Holstein to Prussia. In large measure they gave voice to the objections felt by the rural and urban middle classes of provincial areas to the increasing

[15] The six eastern border districts in which Nazi gain and conservative loss were both high account for the small positive correlation between the two. Without these six districts, the correlation is actually negative.

[16] In Schleswig-Holstein, the regionalist *Landespartei* was strong in 1919 and 1921 in the same districts in which the liberal Democratic party secured its greatest vote. These were the same areas which went most heavily Nazi in the 1930s. See R. Heberle, *op. cit.*, pp. 98–100; in Lower Saxony, an examination of the vote suggests that the supporters of the *Welfen*, the Hanoverian regionalists, who were a major party in the state until 1932, went over to the Nazis. Those "middle-class and rural voting districts . . . in which the Welfen secured their largest vote, became the earliest and strongest centers of Nazism." See G. Franz, *op. cit.*, pp. 53–54, also p. 62. In Bavaria, a somewhat comparable party, the *Bayerischer Bauern und Mittelstandsbund*, dropped from 11.1 per cent in 1928 to 3.3 per cent in 1932. And a study of Bavarian voting patterns suggests that it, like the other regionalist parties, lost its voters predominantly to the Nazis. See Meinrad Hagman, *Der Weg ins Verhängnis, Reichstagswahlergebnisse 1919 bis 1933 besonders aus Bayern* (München; Michael Beckstein Verlag, 1946), pp. 27–28. A sympathetic analysis of the way in which an agrarian regionalist movement paved the way for Nazi electoral victory in Hesse is Eugen Schmahl, *Entwicklung der völkischen Bewegung* (Giessen: Emil Roth Verlag, 1933). This book contains an appendix which analyzes electoral shifts from 1930 to 1932 by a Nazi, Wilhelm Seipel, "Entwicklung der nationalsozialistischen Bauern-bewegung in Hessen," pp. 135–67. In the elections for the provincial assembly in 1931, the Hessen Landbund's representation dropped from 14 per cent to 3 per cent, and the organization shortly thereafter withdrew as a political party, and made an agreement with the Nazis. *Ibid.*, pp. 163–65.

bureaucratization of modern industrial society and sought to turn the clock back by decentralizing government authority. At first glance, the decentralist aspirations of the regional autonomy parties and the glorification of the state inherent in fascism or Nazism seem to reflect totally dissimilar needs and sentiments. But in fact both the "state's rights" ideology of the regionalists and the Nazis' ideological antagonism to the "big" forces of industrial society appealed to those who felt uprooted or challenged. In their economic ideology, the regional parties expressed sentiments similar to those voiced by the Nazis before the latter were strong. Thus the *Schleswig-Holsteinische Landespartei*, which demanded "regional and cultural autonomy for Schleswig-Holstein within Germany," wrote in an early program:

> The craftsman [artisan] has to be protected on the one hand against capitalism, which crushes him by means of its factories, and on the other hand against socialism, which aims at making him a proletarian wage-laborer. At the same time the merchant has to be protected against capitalism in the form of the great department stores, and the whole retail trade against the danger of socialism.[17]

The link between regionalism as an ideology protesting bigness and centralization, and the direct expression of the economic self-interest of the small businessmen may be seen in the joining of the two largest of the regional parties, the Lower Saxon *Deutsch-Hanoverischen Partei* and the Bavarian *Bauern und Mittelstandsbund*, into one parliamentary faction with the *Wirtschaftspartei*, the party which explicitly defined itself as representing the small entrepreneurs. In the 1924 elections the Bavarian regionalists and the small businessmen's party actually presented a joint electoral ticket.[18] As

[17] Cited in R. Heberle, *op. cit.*, p. 47. The *Hessische Volksbund* expressed similar sentiments in Hesse. *Ibid.*, p. 52.

[18] F. A. Hermens, *Demokratie und Wahlrecht* (Paderborn: Verlag Ferdinand Schöningh, 1933), pp. 125–26; and Günther Franz, *op. cit.*, p. 53.

Heberle points out about these parties: "The criticism of Prussian policy . . . the demand for native civil servants, the refusal to accept Berlin as the general center of culture, were all outlets for a disposition which had been formed a long time before the war. . . . At bottom the criticism against Prussia was merely an expression of a general antipathy against the social system of industrial capitalism. . . ."[19]

The appeal of the Nazis to those elements in German society which resented the power and culture of the large cities is also reflected in the Nazis' success in small communities. A detailed ecological analysis of voting in German cities with 25,000 or more population, in 1932, indicates that *the larger the city, the smaller the Nazi vote*. The Nazis secured less of their total vote in cities over 25,000 in size than did any of the other five major parties, including the Catholic Center and the conservative DNVP.[20] And Berlin, the great metropolis, was the only predominantly Protestant election district in which the Nazis received under 25 per cent of the vote in July 1932.[21] These facts sharply challenge the various interpretations of Nazism as the product of the growth of anomie and the general rootlessness of modern urban industrial society.

Examination of the shifts in patterns of German voting between 1928 and 1932 among the non-Marxist and non-Catholic parties indicates, as we have seen, that the Nazis gained disproportionately from the ranks of the center and

[19] R. Heberle, *op. cit.*, p. 49.

[20] Samuel A. Pratt, *op. cit.*, pp. 63, 261–66; Heberle also reports that within Schleswig-Holstein, "An analysis of election returns by communities showed a rather strong inverse correlation between the size of the community and the percentage of votes obtained by the NSDAP." R. Heberle, *op. cit.*, p. 89; Bracher, differentiating the 35 large election districts into those which were high or low in voting Nazis, found that the high Nazi districts were more rural than the low ones. This parallels Pratt's findings. See Karl A. Bracher, *op. cit.*, pp. 647–48.

[21] All the studies agree that religion affected support of the Nazis *more* than any other factor. The Nazis were weak in Catholic regions and cities, and secured majorities in many Protestant small communities.

liberal parties rather than from the conservatives, thus validating one aspect of the thesis that classic fascism appeals to the same strata as liberalism. The second part of the argument, that fascism appeals predominantly to the self-employed among the middle strata, has been supported by three separate ecological studies of German voting between 1928 and 1932. Two American sociologists, Charles Loomis and J. Allen Beegle, correlated the percentage of the Nazi vote in 1932 in communities under 10,000 in population in three states with the percentage of the labor force in specific socioeconomic classes and found that "areas in which the middle classes prevailed [as indicated by the proportion of proprietors in the population and the ratio of proprietors to laborers and salaried employees] gave increasingly larger votes to the Nazis as the economic and social crises settled on Germany."

This high correlation between Nazi vote and proprietorship holds for farm owners as well as owners of small business and industry in Schleswig-Holstein and Hanover, but not in Bavaria, a strongly Catholic area where the Nazis were relatively weak.[22] Heberle's study of Schleswig-Holstein, which analyzed all of the elections under Weimar, concluded that "the classes particularly susceptible to Nazism were neither the rural nobility and the big farmers nor the rural proletariat, but rather the small farm proprietors, very much the rural equivalent of the lower middle class or petty bourgeoisie (*Kleinbuergertum*) which formed the backbone of the NSDAP in the cities."[23]

[22] Charles P. Loomis and J. Allen Beegle, "The Spread of German Nazism in Rural Areas," *American Sociological Review*, 11 (1946), pp. 729, 730. Catholic affiliation constantly overrides class or other allegiances as a major determinant of party support in practically all election data for Germany, in both the Weimar and Bonn republics. The Nazis' largest support in Bavaria and other Catholic areas came from Protestant enclaves, a fact which makes ecological analysis that does not hold religious affiliation constant relatively useless in such regions.

[23] R. Heberle, *op. cit.*, p. 112; Franz also reports that in Lower Saxony, "It was the bourgeois middle-class in the cities, and the farm-owners on the land who supported the NSDAP." Günther Franz, *op. cit.*, p. 62.

The sociologist Samuel Pratt's excellent study of urban voting prior to the Nazi victory related the Nazi vote in July 1932 to the proportion of the population in the "upper middle class," defined as "proprietors of small and large establishments and executives," and to the proportion in the "lower middle class," composed of "civil servants and white-collar employees." The Nazi vote correlated highly with the proportion in both middle-class groups in different-size cities and in different areas of the country, but the correlations with the "lower middle class" were not as consistently high and positive as those with the "upper middle." As Pratt put it: "Of the two elements of the middle class, the upper seemed to be the more thoroughly pro-Nazi."[24] The so-called upper class, however, was predominantly composed of small businessmen, so that the correlation reported is largely that of self-employed economic status with Nazi voting.[25] This interpretation is enhanced by Pratt's finding that the Nazi vote also correlated ($+.6$) with the proportion of business establishments with only one employee—in other words, self-employment. "This would be expected, for plants of one employee are another measure of the proprietorship class which was used in measuring the upper middle class."[26]

The occupational distribution of the membership of the Nazi party in 1933 indicates that it was largely drawn from the various urban middle-class strata, with the self-employed again being the most overrepresented (Table II). The second most overrepresented category—domestic servants and nonagricultural family helpers—also bears witness to the party's appeal to small business, since this category is primarily composed of helpers in family-owned small businesses.

The relation of German big business to the Nazis has been a matter of considerable controversy, particularly since various

[24] See Samuel A. Pratt, *op. cit.*, p. 148.

[25] Examination of the German census for 1933 reveals that over 90 per cent of the "upper middle-class" category used by Pratt is filled by "proprietors," with only a small proportion coming from employed groups.

[26] Samuel A. Pratt, *op. cit.*, p. 171.

Marxists have attempted to demonstrate that the movement was from the outset "fostered, nourished, maintained and subsidized by the big *bourgeoisie*, by the big landlords, financiers, and industrialists."[27] The most recent studies suggest that the opposite is true. With the exception of a few isolated individuals, German big business gave Nazism little financial support or other encouragement *until* it had risen to the status of a major party. The Nazis did begin to pick up financial backing in 1932, but in large part this backing was a result of many businesses' policy of giving money to

TABLE II

THE RATIO OF THE PERCENTAGE OF MEN IN THE NAZI PARTY TO THE PERCENTAGE IN THE GENERAL POPULATION FROM VARIOUS OCCUPATIONS, 1933*

Occupational Category	1933
Manual Workers	68%
White-collar Workers	169
Independents†	187
Officials (civil servants)	146
Peasants	60
Domestic servants, and nonagricultural family helpers	178

* Computed from a table in Hans Gerth, "The Nazi Party: Its Leadership and Composition," in Robert K. Merton, *et al.*, eds., *Reader in Bureaucracy* (Glencoe: The Free Press, 1952), p. 106.
† Includes self-employed businessmen, artisans, and free professionals.

all major parties except the Communists in order to be in their good graces. Some German industrialists probably hoped to tame the Nazis by giving them funds. On the whole, however, this group remained loyal to the conservative parties, and many gave no money to the Nazis until after the party won power.[28]

[27] R. Palme Dutt, *Fascism and Social Revolution* (New York: International Publishers, 1934), p. 80.
[28] See F. Thyssen, *I Paid Hitler* (New York: Farrar and Rinehart, 1941), p. 102; Walter Gorlitz and Herbert Quint, *Hitler. Eine Biographie* (Stuttgart: Steingrubben Verlag, 1952), pp. 284, 286;

The ideal-typical Nazi voter in 1932 was a middle-class self-employed Protestant who lived either on a farm or in a small community, and who had previously voted for a centrist or regionalist political party strongly opposed to the power and influence of big business and big labor. This does not mean that most Nazi voters did not have other characteristics. Like all parties looking for an electoral majority, the Nazis tried to appeal to some degree to every large group of voters.[29] They clearly had a great deal of success with other middle-class groups, particularly the unemployed.[30] And at the low point of the Great Depression, which affected Germany more than any other industrial nation, discontent with the "system" was widespread throughout the society. However, as a movement, Nazism was most attractive to those with the characteristics summarized above.

A NOTE ON THE GERMAN NONVOTER

Perhaps the most important argument against the thesis that Nazism developed pre-eminently as a movement of the liberal petty bourgeoisie has been the suggestion that the major source of the first great gain in Nazi strength (between

---

Edward Norman Peterson, *Hjalmar Schacht for and against Hitler* (Boston: The Christopher Publishing House, 1954), pp. 112–17; for general discussion and documentation see also August Heinrichsbauer, *Schwerindustrie und Politik* (Essen: Verlag Glückauf, 1948); Arild Halland, *Nazismen i Tyskland* (Bergen: John Griegs Forlag, 1955); and Louis P. Lochner, *Tycoons and Tyrants, German Industry from Hitler to Adenauer* (Chicago: Henry Regnery Co., 1954).

[29] An analysis of the sources of the vote for the Social Democratic party in 1930 estimated that 40 per cent of the SPD voters were not manual workers, that the party was backed in that year by 25 per cent of the white-collar workers, 33 per cent of the lower civil servants, and 25 per cent of the self-employed in artisan shops and retail business. But the core of the SPD support was employed, skilled manual workers, while the core of the Nazi strength was small owners, both urban and rural. See Hans Neisser, "Sozialstatistischen Analyse des Wahlergebnisses," *Die Arbeit*, 10 (1930), pp. 657–58.

[30] Pratt reports a high positive correlation between white-collar unemployment and the Nazi vote in the cities. See S. Pratt, *op. cit.*, Chap. 8.

1928 when they secured 2.6 per cent of the vote and 1930 when they captured 18.3 per cent of the electorate) was previous nonvoters. Between these two elections, nonvoting dropped sharply from 24.4 per cent to 18 per cent of the eligible electorate—a fact which has led to the conclusion that the Nazis' great gain came from the traditionally apathetic and from young first voters.[31] The most comprehensive critique of the class analysis has been that of the American sociologist Reinhard Bendix, who suggested a process of growth in which the middle class *followed* the new voters into support of Nazism:

> The importance of the newly eligible voters and of the politically apathetic casts doubt on the conception of fascism as a middle-class movement. This is not to deny that the economic insecurity of middle-class groups was important for the conquest of power as a secondary response. It is to assert rather that the radicalization of the electorate originated among the previous nonparticipants in party politics, who probably came from various social groups, and that the significant support of the totalitarian movement by members of the middle class and of other social groups occurred subsequently in the hope of relief from economic distress and in the desire to gain from backing the victorious movement.[32]

This thesis challenges the class analysis of Nazism and contradicts the generalizations about the growth of new social movements which were presented in the discussion of work-

[31] See an early statement of this view in Theodore Geiger, *Die Soziale Schichtung des Deutschen Volkes* (Stuttgart: Enke Verlag, 1932), p. 112; Heinrich Striefler, *op. cit.*, pp. 23–28; Reinhard Bendix, "Social Stratification and Political Power," in R. Bendix and S. M. Lipset, eds., *Class, Status and Power* (Glencoe: The Free Press, 1956), p. 605; Günther Franz, *op. cit.*, pp. 61–62.

[32] Reinhard Bendix, *op. cit.*, p. 605. Bendix has since modified his position. See R. Bendix and S. M. Lipset, "On the Social Structure of Western Societies: Some Reflections on Comparative Analysis," *Berkeley Journal of Sociology*, 5 (1959), pp. 1–15.

ing-class authoritarianism in the previous chapter. This analysis suggested that the most outcast and apathetic sections of
the population can be won to political action by extremist and
authoritarian parties only *after* such parties have become major movements, not while they are in their period of early
rise. To support a new and small movement requires a
relatively complex, long-term view of the political process,
which insecure, ignorant, and apathetic persons cannot sustain. This logic should apply to the Nazis as well, and a
statistical analysis of the relationship between the decline in
nonvoting and the growth of Nazism indicates that in fact
it does.

Geiger, Bendix, and others who concluded that the Nazis
derived their early backing from traditional nonvoters based
this opinion on the over-all election figures which showed an
enormous increase of Nazi votes simultaneous with the sudden participation of over four million previous nonvoters. But
when the changes in the rates of nonvoting and of the Nazi
vote are broken down by districts, we actually find a small
negative rank order correlation of −.2 between the per cent
increase in the Nazi vote and the increase in the proportion
of the eligible electorate voting. More vividly stated, in only
five of the electoral districts where the Nazi gain between
1928 and 1930 exceeded their *average* gain for all of Germany
was the increase in the size of the electorate also disproportionately high. In twenty-two of the thirty-five national
districts, there is a negative relationship; either the voting
gain is low and the Nazi gain is high, or vice versa. The
evidence on the decline in nonvoting between 1928 and 1930
thus does not challenge the class analysis of Nazism.[33]

[33] These findings are sustained by the analysis of Loomis and
Beegle. They report that in 1932, in the 59 election districts in
rural Hanover, the correlation between the proportion of nonvoters
and the Nazi percentage of the vote was .43. This correlation also
challenges the thesis that the Nazis appealed primarily to the non-
voter. See Charles P. Loomis and J. Allen Beegle, *op. cit.*, p. 733.
Both this study and an earlier one by James K. Pollock have been
ignored by most of the literature in the field. Pollock pointed out that
"In studying another aspect of German electoral behavior, we find

It is true that there are reasons other than a simple inspection of changes in votes which suggest that the Nazis recruited heavily from the apathetic sector of the population. As I pointed out in the preceding chapter, those sections of the population that are normally apathetic tend to have authoritarian attitudes and values.[34] The political interests of the apathetic, however, can be awakened only by a *mass* movement which presents a *simple* extremist view of politics. The Nazis did not fit this category from 1928 to 1930; they did, however, after 1930. Those analysts who concentrated on the Nazis' presumed 1930 gain among the apathetic ignored a growth which, in fact, happened later. The largest single drop in nonvoting in Germany actually occurred in the last election of March 1933, which was held after Hitler took office as head of a coalition government. Nonvoting dropped from 19 per cent in 1932 to 11 per cent in 1933, a drop of 8 percentage points, while the Nazi vote increased from 33 per cent to 43 per cent. And if we again correlate the growth in the Nazi vote with the increase in the electorate, we find, precisely as the hypothesis demands, that the two trends show a high positive relationship (.6).

To present the result by district, in twenty-eight out of the thirty-five districts the Nazi vote gain was higher or lower than the national average gain when the increase in the voting electorate was congruently higher or lower than the national average. As a mass authoritarian party whose leader was already chancellor, the Nazi party received additional support (bringing it for the first time above the 40 per cent mark) from the ranks of the antipolitical apathetics, thus paralleling

little relationship between the size of the vote cast in these elections [1930–33] and the nature of the political result. . . . In these critical years in Germany, many of the urban industrial areas showed a greater electoral interest than did the agricultural areas. At the same time, this increased popular vote in the large cities as a rule was cast against Hitler, while the agricultural areas regularly showed a strong interest in him." James K. Pollock, "An Areal Study of the German Electorate, 1930–1933," *American Political Science Review*, 38 (1944), pp. 93–94.

[34] See pp. 102–4.

the pattern of growth of leftist extremists who also recruit from the most outcast strata as they reach the status of a contender for power.

Austria

Voting patterns in Austria during the first Republic are similar to Germany's, although the sharply different political scene prevents precise comparisons. The Austrian electorate was divided into three main groups before 1930: the Socialist party, securing about 40 per cent of the vote; the conservative clerical Christian Social party, supported by about 45 per cent of the electorate; and the much smaller liberal pan-German parties (largely the *grossdeutsche Volkspartei*), with between 10 and 15 per cent of the vote. The *Volkspartei* is the one which chiefly interests us here since it represented the liberal anticlerical policies also pursued by the German liberal center parties. To these it added a strong pro-German orientation, which was linked after 1918 to the liberal traditions in Germany. Its support up to and including 1930 came largely from a sizable anticlerical segment of the urban middle classes, plus the Protestant and Jewish minorities. Throughout the 1920s, the *Volkspartei* was included in an anti-Marxist government coalition with the Christian Social party. It broke with that party in 1930 largely because of its opposition to the seemingly antiparliamentary measures pursued by the Christian Social leaders and the *Heimwehr*, their private army. In order to preserve democratic procedures against attack from clerical authoritarians, Dr. Schober, the leader of the *Volkspartei*, formed a coalition with another pan-German anticlerical rural group, the *Landbund* which "stood for . . . law and order, and for . . . parliamentary government."[35] The new coalition polled 12 per cent of the vote nationally. In the 1930 elections this

[35] Walter B. Simon, *The Political Parties of Austria* (Ph.D. thesis, Department of Sociology, Columbia University, 1957, Microfilm 57–2894 University Microfilms, Ann Arbor, Michigan), pp. 28, 71.

pan-German alliance was probably the closest to the expression of a democratic anticlerical liberal ideology. But within two years most of those who had supported it backed the Nazi party. The American sociologist Walter Simon, who analyzed the electoral data of that era in detail, reports the events of these two years succinctly and vividly:

It is highly significant that in November 1930 Dr. Schober's fusion ticket of "liberal" Germanism, the *"Nationaler Wirtschaftsblock und Landbund, Führung Dr. Schober,"* received its votes from an electorate that consisted largely of voters who were to go over to the Hitler movement within less than a year and a half as well as of voters who belonged to the Jewish middle-class. With this Dr. Schober had succeeded to rally for the last time in one camp the Jewish Liberal and anti-Marxist middle class and the German-oriented anticlerical middle class. Both groups still continued to cherish the traditions of the 1848 revolution in which their great-grandfathers had fought side by side against the forces of autocratic government and for constitutional government. . . . Nearly all of the non-Jewish voters of the party had gone over to vote for the Nazis by 1932. Dr. Schober himself died in the summer of 1932, and the urban wing of his ticket, constituted as *"gross-deutsche Volkspartei"* affiliated with the Nazis in May 15th, 1933 under the terms of the so-called *"Kampfbündnis"* or fighting alliance.[36]

The shift to the Nazis by the supporters of the *gross-deutsche Volkspartei* cannot be explained as the pro-German Austrians' accommodation to the governing tendency in Germany. The Nazis captured the support of the non-Jewish sector of the anticlerical Austrian middle class over a year before they took power in Germany and replaced the *Volks-*

[36] *Ibid.*, pp. 322–23. The statements concerning the sources of the vote and the shifts to the Nazis are documented by Simon in a careful and elaborate examination of electoral statistics.

partei as the major third party in various provincial elections held throughout Austria in 1931 and 1932.[37]

The Austrian political scene also illustrates the distinctive character of conservative or right-wing "fascism." The Christian Social party never accepted the legitimacy of democratic institutions in the first Austrian Republic; many of its leaders and followers could not conceive of allowing the Marxist atheists of the Social Democratic party a place in the government, and in 1934 Austrian clerical conservatism imposed a dictatorship. It was a conservative dictatorship; no group was punitively injured unless it remained an organized opposition to the regime. The socialists and the trade-unions were suppressed, but were able to maintain a powerful underground. In 1938, when the Nazis took over Austria, the difference between the two dictatorships became obvious: the totalitarian Nazis actively sought to control the entire society, quickly destroyed the socialist and trade-union underground, and began active persecution of Jews and all opponents of Nazi ideas, regardless of whether or not they were politically active.[38]

France

Before the Algerian revolt of May 1958, postwar France had witnessed the growth of two relatively large movements, each of which has been labeled fascist by its opponents—the Gaullist *Rassamblement du Peuple Française* (RPF) and

[37] Although anti-Semitism had characterized part of the pan-German movement before 1918, the *grossdeutsche Volkspartei*, whose supporters went Nazi in 1931–32, and which united with the Austrian Nazis in 1933, had been liberal on the religious question. During the twenties the party was charged with "being overly sympathetic towards the Jews," and its electoral ticket was strongly supported in 1930 by the *Neue Freie Presse*, "the organ of the liberal Jewish middle and upper class." Walter Simon, *op. cit.*, p. 328.

[38] For an excellent description of the political events which led to the destruction of the Austrian Republic, see Charles A. Gulick, *Austria from Hapsburg to Hitler* (Berkeley: University of California Press, 1948).

the *L'Union de Défense des Commerçants et Artisans* (UDCA), most generally known as the Poujadist movement. When the Poujadists secured a large vote (around 10 per cent) in the 1956 elections and temporarily replaced the Gaullists as the principal "rightist" foes of the Republic, this suggested to some analysts that Poujade had inherited the support which De Gaulle had given up when he dissolved the RPF and retired to Colombey-les-deux Églises to await his recall by the French people.

The ideologies of the two leaders and their movements are sharply divergent, however. De Gaulle is a classic conservative, a man who believes in the traditional verities of the French right. He has sought in various ways to give France a stable conservative regime with a strong president. In advocating a strong executive he follows in a tradition which in France has been largely identified with monarchism and the Church. In his appeal to rebuild France, De Gaulle never set the interests of one class against another; neither he nor his movement ever sought to win the backing of the middle classes by suggesting that their interests were threatened by big business and the banks or by the trade-unions. Rather, De Gaulle identified himself with all that advanced France as a nation: the growth of efficient large industry, the nationalizations which had occurred under his regime before 1946, and the strengthening of state power. He also ostentatiously maintained his identification with the Catholic Church. De Gaulle falls directly in the tradition of strong men of the conservative right. He has sought to change political institutions in order to conserve traditionalist values.

The materials available on Gaullist support bear out the contention that the RPF recruited its strength from the classic sources of conservatism. Survey data indicate that the RPF won more votes at its height before 1948 from those who previously had voted for the PRL—the party of liberty, or the *"modères,"* the French conservatives—than from backers of any other party. In 1947, 70 per cent of those who said they had previously been for the PRL said they intended to vote Gaullist. The other large source of Gaullist converts was the Catholic MRP which, though leftist on a number of economic issues, had secured the votes of many traditional conservatives for some time after the war because of its explicit Catholicism. Fifty-four per cent of the former MRP supporters were Gaullists in 1947. This support from the parties linked to Catholicism and conservatism compares with 26 per cent Gaullist support among those who had previously backed the Radical party, the traditional liberal and middle-class anticlerical party of France.[39]

Even more direct evidence of the basically conservative character of Gaullist support is the survey results from the period following De Gaulle's temporary retirement from politics and the dissolution of the RPF. In 1955 about half (52 per cent) of those who reported having voted Gaullist in 1951 said they would vote for the dissident Gaullist party (URAS), but four out of five who had changed to another party intended to vote for the conservative moderates.[40]

A variety of survey data compiled by *Sondages*, the French Gallup Poll, shows that the RPF secured its heaviest support from those who normally back the more conservative parties in European countries: the more well to do, the more religious, the older, and the women. RPF voters were better educated than the backers of any other French party (38 per cent of them had more than a higher elementary education); more of their supporters were over 65; they were stronger than any other party among industrial executives, engineers, and businessmen; and, as with other Catholic parties, the majority of their voters were women. Only 12 per cent of the RPF supporters reported no religious observance, as contrasted with 40 per cent of the Radicals.[41] *Sondages* reported in 1952 that "the RPF is the most feminine of all the parties. . . . The [occupational] categories which are predominant

[39] *Sondages*, February 16, 1948, p. 47.

[40] Jean Stoetzel, "Voting Behavior in France," *British Journal of Sociology*, 6 (1955), p. 105.

[41] These data are reported in English in J. Stoetzel, *op. cit.*, pp. 116–19 and in Philip Williams, *Politics in Post-War France* (London: Longmans, Green & Co., 1954), p. 446.

and are represented more than their proportion in the population are the white-collar workers, the businessmen, industrial managers and engineers."

Survey findings not only demonstrate the conservative character of De Gaulle's supporters but also indicate that they were more likely to distrust parliamentary institutions and favor strong-man government than the electorate of any other major party except the Communists. The Gaullists were second only to Communists in the proportion of their members who believed that their party should, in some circumstances, take power by force, and who favored progress by means of revolution. A larger proportion of Gaullist voters than that of any other party including the Communists believed that "some party or parties should be banned," that only a minority of "cabinet ministers are honest men," that the "leadership" of a political party is more important than doctrine or program, and had "full confidence" in their party leader.[42]

In the election of 1956, much to the surprise of many political observers, the Poujadist movement rose to important proportions. Some saw Poujadism as the latest response of the more authoritarian antirepublican elements on the French right to an opportunity to vote against democracy and the Republic.[43]

In fact, Poujadism, like Nazism in Austria and Germany, was essentially an extremist movement appealing to and based on the same social strata as the movements which support the "liberal center." While it is impossible to know whether in power it would have resembled Nazism, its ideology was like that of the Nazis and other middle-class extremist populist movements. Poujadism appealed to the petty bourgeoisie,

[42] *Sondages*, 14 (1952, No. 3), presents a detailed report on the social characteristics and opinions of the supporters of the various major parties, from which the data in the above two paragraphs are taken. For a later report of the same survey, see Philip Williams, *Politics in Post-War France* (London: Longmans, Green & Co., 1958, 2d ed.), pp. 452–54.

[43] See Georges Lavau, "Les Classes moyennes et la politique," in Maurice Duverger, ed., *Partis politiques et classes sociales en France* (Paris: Librairie Armand Colin, 1955), pp. 60, 76.

the artisans, merchants, and peasants, inveighing against the dire effects of a modern industrial society on them. It opposed big business, the trusts, the Marxist parties, the trade-unions, department stores and banks, and such state control over business as social security and other welfare state measures which raised the taxes of the little man. But while Poujadism explicitly attacked both the left and right, it strongly linked itself with the revolutionary republican tradition. Appealing to populist sentiments—the idea that the people rather than parties should control the government—Poujade praised the French revolutionaries who did not "hesitate to guillotine a king," and demanded the revival of various revolutionary institutions like the *Estates-General,* to which would be presented lists of grievances submitted by local bodies of citizens in the fashion of 1789.[44] Combined with its attacks on big business, left parties, and unions, were attacks on the Jews and a nationalist defense of colonialism.[45]

The relationship of Poujadist ideology to the anticlerical liberal rather than the right tradition in France has been well summed up by the British writer Peter Campbell:

> In its various forms the traditional anti-democratic Right has held that the Republic has betrayed France: according to Poujadism it is the politicians and the administrators who have betrayed the Republic and the honest folk it ought to protect. The task of the Poujadists is to reconquer the Republic in the spirit of the Revolution of 1789–1793. The Poujadists demand a new States-General with new *cahiers* of the people's grievances and instructions. . . . The Poujadists have preferred the motto of the Republic to the various trinities of the

[44] See Jean Meynaud, "Un essai d'interpretation du mouvement Poujade," *Revue de l'institute de sociologie* (1956, No. 1), p. 27, for discussion of republican populist symbols in Poujadism; for further documentation on Poujadist ideology see other sections of this article, pp. 5–38; S. Hoffman, *Le mouvement Poujade* (Paris: Librairie Armand Colin, 1956); M. Duverger, *et al.,* eds., *Les élections du 2 janvier 1956* (Paris: Librairie Armand Colin, 1957), esp. pp. 61–64.

[45] Poujade publicly even gave money to support a major strike at Saint-Nazaire. See J. Meynaud, *op. cit.,* p. 26.

extreme Right (such as Marshal Pétain's "Work, Family, and Fatherland") but they have stressed their own special interpretations of "liberty, equality, and fraternity."

Its attachment to the Republic and to the principles and symbols of the Revolution place Poujadism in the democratic tradition. . . . Nevertheless, its psychology is very near to that of Fascism, or rather, that of the rank and file's fascism in contrast to that of the social elite's fascism. In Poujadism there is the same fear of being merged into the proletariat (a fear associated with hostility to both the organized workers below and the social ranks above the threatened lower-middle class), desire for scapegoats (domestic and foreign), and hostility towards culture, intellectuals, and non-conformists.[46]

The ideological differences between Gaullism and Poujadism do not necessarily demonstrate that these two movements represented different strata of the population. Many have argued that "the essential core of Poujadism was its 'opposition to the [democratic] regime,' so that it could absorb the Gaullism of 1951."[47] But a look at a map of France upon which is superimposed the Gaullist vote of 1951 and the Poujadist vote of 1956 quickly challenges this theory. Poujadist strength lay largely in areas of France, principally the south, where the Gaullists had been weak, while the Gaullists were strong in areas which resisted Poujadist inroads. Although Poujade received fewer votes in the country as a whole than De Gaulle—2,500,000 as against 3,400,000—the 1956 Poujadist ticket was far stronger than the 1951 Gaullist one in many southern districts.[48] Gaullist strength centered in the more well-to-do, industrialized, and econom-

[46] Peter Campbell, "Le Mouvement Poujade," *Parliamentary Affairs*, 10 (1957), pp. 363–65.

[47] See S. Hoffman, *op. cit.*, pp. 190 ff., for a disscussion of the various hypotheses which have been advanced to account for the growth of the Poujadists.

[48] *Ibid.*, p. 193; for a detailed analysis of the ecological sources of the Poujadist vote, see François Goguel, "Géographie des élections du 2 janvier," in M. Duverger, *et al.*, eds., *op. cit.*, esp. pp. 477–82.

ically expanding regions of France, while the geographical core of Poujadism was in the poorer, relatively underdeveloped, and economically stagnant departments.

In addition to the ecological evidence, a considerable amount of more direct survey or voting data demonstrates that Poujadism drew its backing from the traditional social base of liberalism—the anticlerical middle classes—and that it was a revolutionary movement, not a conservative one. A survey of a national sample of the electorate conducted by the French National Institute for Population Study in 1956 found that about half of the Poujadist voters were self-employed.[49] These national findings were reiterated in a survey conducted by the French Institute of Public Opinion Research in the first sector of Paris, which found that 67 per cent of the Poujadist vote in this district came from small businessmen or artisans.[50] While sample surveys of the Gaullist electorate had shown them to be the best educated of any party's supporters, the Parisian Poujadists had less education than the supporters of any other party with the exception of the Communists. Their economic status, judged by the ranking given respondents by interviewers, was also considerably less than that of the Gaullists.[51]

[49] This is the same survey which is reported in Table I in Chap. 7. These data were computed from the IBM cards of the study which were kindly supplied by Alain Girard of the Institute.

[50] Jean Stoetzel and Pierre Hassner point out that the Poujadist success meant the "entry into the National Assembly of a large group of representatives of professions up to now poorly represented: the list of Poujade elected deputies published in Le Monde gives 26 out of the 52 Poujadists as in commercial occupations (10 food sellers, 10 diverse tradesmen, and 6 wholesale merchants); the other 26 are either artisans, or owners of rather small or medium sized enterprises, plus a school director and two 'students.' " Thus, the official representatives of Poujadism, as well as its social base, were lower middle class. See Stoetzel and Hassner, "Resultats d'un sondage dans le prèmier secteur de la Seine," in M. Duverger, et al., eds., op. cit., p. 190.

[51] These data are derived from tables reported in Jean Stoetzel and Pierre Hassner, op. cit., esp. pp. 236–42. This article reflects the vote in Paris, with its diversified occupational structure, and its large middle class, both independent and salaried. Other articles in

These data are consistent with the interpretation suggested by ecological analysis—that Poujadism was largely a movement of the self-employed lower middle class and the petty bourgeoisie in declining provincial areas, and thus differed greatly from Gaullism, backed in 1951 by that section of the middle class which was either well to do or lived in the more economically developed regions of France.[52]

These data, however, still do not demonstrate that Poujadism's basic appeal was to traditional "liberals."[53] For such evidence, we must turn to two sources—the religious beliefs and behavior of the movement's supporters and their opinions on questions which are linked to acceptance or rejection of traditional French family values. As the data reported in Table VII in Chapter 7 indicate, the parties which draw their support disproportionately from practicing Catholics have been the Catholic MRP, the conservative Independents, and the Gaullists, while the Communists, Socialists, Radicals, and Poujadists are overrepresented among the nonpracticing Catholics, and among those with no religion.[54] The

this volume analyze election results in other departments, and indicate that Poujade was supported by tradesmen, artisans, and in some districts peasants. See pp. 316, 322–52, 369–95, in particular.

[52] Gaullism, of course, also drew heavily from strata to whom Poujade had limited access, particularly the bureaucracy of large industry, managers, engineers, and white-collar workers. "In the few economically progressive departments in which Poujadism gained some success (e.g., Isere), careful study has revealed that this success came principally in the backward cantons within the department." Maurice Duverger, *The French Political System* (Chicago: University of Chicago Press, 1958), p. 97.

[53] Maurice Duverger points out that the traditional supporters of the Radicals were "almost the same social groups which today support Poujade, that is, small shopkeepers and artisans." *Ibid.*, p. 98.

[54] Various data indicate that the Poujadists are disproportionately male as compared with the Independents, MRP, and Gaullists. For data from actual voting returns see Claude Lelau, "La géographie des partis dans l'Isere," in M. Duverger, *et al.*, eds., *op. cit.*, p. 394; see also Jean Stoetzel and Pierre Hassner, *op. cit.*, p. 236; see *Sondages*, December 1, 1948, p. 223, January 16, 1949, pp. 16–18 and August 1949, p. 126, and 1952, n. 3, p. 24, for data on the sex composition of the Gaullist backers.

conservative Independents and the Gaullists drew about two thirds of their vote in 1956 (according to the survey already cited) from practicing Catholics, while only 35 per cent of the Poujadists and 29 per cent of the Radicals were regular churchgoers.

Previously published data from this same survey dealing with attitudes toward family size and birth control, matters which in France are closely linked to religion and politics, also confirm the thesis that Poujadists are more likely to resemble anticlerical leftists in their opinions than right-wing conservatives. (See Table III.) Thus when the respondents were divided according to party affiliation, the sentiments among the Poujadist voters were similar to those among the left parties, while voters who backed the Social Republicans

TABLE III

RELATIONSHIP BETWEEN PARTY VOTE AND ATTITUDES TOWARD BIRTH CONTROL IN FRANCE*

Attitudes	Party Affiliation						
			Soc. Rep. (Soustelle)	UDCA (Poujade)	Radical		
	Indep.	MRP				Soc.	Com.
The number of births in France is:							
Too great	27%	21%	26%	48%	42%	43%	42%
As it should be	56	59	48	39	43	43	39
Not enough	10	14	19	11	8	6	8
Approve birth-control information	29	24	29	42	51	60	68
Disapprove giving birth-control information	59	65	64	46	37	30	19

* Alain Girard and Raul Samuel, "Une enquête sur l'opinion publique à l'égard de la limitation des naissances," *Population*, 11 (1956), p. 500. The total sample was 2,432.

(the Gaullist rump group led by Jacques Soustelle, which remained loyal to De Gaulle after he withdrew from politics) had social attitudes close to those of the MRP and the Independents.

In 1958 following the military *coup d'état* which returned De Gaulle to the presidency of France yet another large political party which denigrated the traditions of parliamentary democracy, the Union for a New Republic (UNR), was formed. The UNR contested the first elections of the Fifth Republic, claiming with some justice to be the Gaullist party *par excellence*, since it was led by many men who had taken part in previous Gaullist movements, such as Jacques Soustelle and Michel Debré. The party secured about 20 per cent of the vote, less than the support which had rallied around the RPF in 1947–51, but much more than Soustelle had secured in 1956 for the pro-De Gaulle URAS. Although there have been no published studies of the 1958 elections, polling results made available by the French Institute of Public Opinion Research from a survey conducted in February 1959 indicate that the Gaullism of 1958 was based on the same relatively well-to-do and conservative strata as that of the earlier RPF and URAS, and bears little similarity to the support of the populist extremist, Poujade. As the data contained in Table IV indicate, less than one quarter of the self-employed businessmen backed the UNR, considerably less than the proportion which had voted for Poujade two and a half years earlier. Conversely, the UNR drew considerable backing from those in "upper-class" occupations and from the white-collar workers. And as in the case of the earlier Gaullist groups, the majority of the voters for the new party were women, and 54 per cent had more than a primary-school education. In fact, the UNR's voters were much better educated on the average than the supporters of any other major party, as contrasted with the Poujadists of 1956, who had less schooling than the backers of any other non-Communist party. Unfortunately, there are as yet no reliable data concerning the way in which those who backed Poujade in 1956 voted in 1958. A panel survey by Georges

TABLE IV

THE PARTY CHOICES OF VOTERS IN DIFFERENT OCCUPATIONAL CATEGORIES IN THE FIRST ELECTIONS OF THE FIFTH FRENCH REPUBLIC*

	Occupation					
Party	Industrialists, Executives, Professionals	Self-Employed	White-Collar	Workers	Peasants	Retired and Rentiers
Communist	0%	2%	10%	26%	6%	6%
Socialist	5	13	16	25	12	22
UFD (Mendes)	7	5	9	6	6	4
Radical	2	12	6	5	9	9
RFD (left Gaullist)	3	4	1	**	2	**
MRP (liberal Catholic)	5	9	9	10	14	13
UNR	40	23	30	17	13	21
Christian Democrat (Bedault Gaullist)	8	8	6	3	3	9
Independent and Peasant (conservative)	28	18	11	7	35	15
Poujadist	2	5	1	**	1	**
Nationalist (fascist)	0	2	**	**	**	0
(N)	(60)	(129)	(282)	(416)	(317)	(217)

* This table and other references in the text to the 1958 elections are from data kindly supplied by Professor Jean Stoetzel and Louis Angelby of the French Institute of Public Opinion Research from a national survey of the French electorate made from February 17 to February 26, 1959. An earlier survey by the Institute which provides much data about the attitudes of the French population during the birth of the Fifth Republic is reported in *Sondages*, (1958, n. 4), pp. 3–62.

** Less than 1 per cent.

Dupeux of the University of Bordeaux which sought to answer this question during the election campaign itself was unable to obtain replies from over half of those interviewed, but of the few who admitted having been Poujade supporters, only two out of eleven voted for the UNR.

The ideological characters of Gaullism and Poujadism and the social attributes of their supporters indicate that the distinction between conservative (right) authoritarianism and liberal (centrist) authoritarianism which helps to account for the social roots of Nazism is also useful in interpreting postwar French politics. Both the conservative and the liberal strata gave birth to large social movements which were critical of the parliamentary regime of the Fourth Republic, and which were anti-Marxist and extremely nationalistic. But one has been basically conservative, the other revolutionary in the populist sense.

Italy

It is difficult to analyze Italian political history in terms of the three types of antidemocratic politics, because of the special manner in which Italian Fascism originally came to power. As a movement, it began as a neo-socialist party, more perhaps in the later Peronist tradition than the others, but, led by a thorough opportunist, it took every chance offered it to win support from diverse strata. Its ideology for a long time seemed directed mainly at the anticlerical middle classes, but after 1929 it came to terms with the Vatican and signed the first concordat in the history of unified Italy. For much of its period in power, Italian Fascism represented a coalition between antidemocratic traditionalism and middle-class populist authoritarianism directed against the leftist revolutionary sectors of the urban and rural populations.

Many analysts of Italian Fascism have seen its origins in middle-class areas and ideological appeal. According to the *Encyclopedia of the Social Sciences*, the valley of the Po, inhabited chiefly by "small property owners and tenant farmers essentially middle-class in their material interests as well as in their intellectual and moral outlook" was even "commemorated by Mussolini himself as the cradle of the Fascist movement." Much Fascist legislation was "designed to increase the number of small land-holders," and Mussolini's initial syndicalist program, appealing to very heterogeneous groups, was dropped when he "carried his agitation successfully to the urban and rural middle classes, who gradually attached themselves to the original inner nucleus of shock troops."[55]

The two partners in the Fascist coalition split during the war when the more conservative segment made peace with the Western powers and the more genuinely fascist part led by Mussolini set up the Italian Social Republic to fight on as an ally of the Nazis. Since the end of the war, two basically antidemocratic non-Marxist movements have continued in Italian politics. The Monarchists represent the traditionalist elements who seek to defend Throne and Altar, while the neo-Fascists, the Movimento Sociale Italiano (MSI), attempt to continue the revolutionary fascist tradition. Though many of the social conditions, ideologies, and programs are different, in the Monarchists and MSI we find again versions of right-wing and centrist extremism. The images which both present to the Italian public are clearly colored by the Mussolini experience, and the voters are probably reacting to that even more than to the programs of the moment. This fact makes it difficult to expect any close analogy between these groups and those we have discussed in other countries. The limited survey data available do suggest, however, that in some ways these parties differ from each other in ways comparable to the differences between the Gaullists and the Poujadists, or the German right and the Nazis. The monarchists are more well to do, older, religious, and predominantly female. The MSI supporters come from the less well to do and are comparatively young, predominantly masculine, and irreligious or anticlerical.

Poll data locate the greatest concentration of neo-Fascist

[55] See Erwin von Beckerath, "Fascism," *Encyclopedia of the Social Sciences*, Vol. VI (New York: Macmillan, 1937), p. 135.

voters in small communities.[56] And ecological studies show that the MSI, like Poujadism in France, has been strongest in the less developed and less urbanized regions of the country.[57] Mavio Rossi, an American student of Italian politics, has reported that "the neo-Fascist movement is spreading most rapidly in the backward southern provinces, . . . that most of the neo-Fascists [attending party meetings] are teen-age students or young men in their thirties, . . . [and that] the older neo-Fascists are for the most part veterans of the last war."[58] The evidence bearing on the class composition of the neo-Fascist supporters is, however, not consistent with the over-all hypothesis that neo-Fascism as a centrist movement should be pre-eminently a movement of the self-employed. The data from the 1953 International Public Opinion Research survey reported in Table II in Chapter 7 indicate that small farm owners and artisans are the only occupational categories to give the party disproportionate support (15 per cent) as compared with its vote in the total sample (12 per cent). Other more recent surveys conducted in 1956 and 1958 by DOXA, an Italian survey organization, found, in 1956, little difference in the amount of support given to the MSI by the self-employed (8 per cent) as com-

[56] See data in the files of the World Poll. See also P. L. Fegiz, *Il Volto Sconosciuto dell'Italia* (Milano: Dott. A. Giuffrè, 1956), pp. 501–26.

[57] Francesco Compagna and Vittorio de Caprariis, *Geografia dell' elezioni italiane dal 1946 al 1953* (Bologna: Il Mulino, no date), pp. 25, 34.

[58] Mavio Rossi, "Neo-Fascism in Italy," *Virginia Quarterly Review*, 29 (1953), pp. 506–7. A detailed ecological study of Italian elections from 1946 on by the French sociologist Mattei Dogan unfortunately treats Monarchists and neo-Fascists as one group. He reports they are strongest in southern Italy, but also that their strength increases with the size of community, being particularly high in southern cities such as Naples and Bari, but also in Rome and Trieste. He accounts for "Right-wing" strength in Rome by the presence of civil servants and retired civil servants "who remember the Fascist regime nostalgically," and in Trieste by the fact that there "nationalism has been exacerbated by the conflict with Yugoslavia." "Le Comportement politique des Italiens," *Revue française de science politique*, 9 (1959), pp. 398–402.

pared with manual workers (9 per cent), and in 1958 that the neo-Fascists received about the same percentage (6 per cent) among self-employed artisans as they did among manual workers.[59]

It should be noted, however, that most sample surveys of the Italian electorate indicate that the Monarchists are much more well to do than are the neo-Fascist supporters. Thus a 1957 survey conducted by International Research Associates found that 12 per cent of the well to do are Monarchist voters, as contrasted with only 2 per cent for the Fascists. The main Fascist strength reported in this and most other studies lies in the middle strata, as does that of the Christian Democrats and the right-wing socialists and the Republicans, while the Nenni left-wing socialists and the Communists have the bulk of their strength among the poorer classes.[60]

The disparity between Italian neo-Fascism and the other movements may reflect its character as a Fascist movement after Fascism has already been in power. The electorate may be reacting more to their memory of Mussolini in office than to the current program of the party. The relative weakness of the party among the self-employed may be a product of the fact that the Fascist regime did not help the self-employed strata, but came to terms with big business, large landlords, and the Church. Also, in its last year, 1944–45, as the Italian Social Republic, it tried to win the support of the working class of northern Italy by nationalization of industry, workers' councils, and a general radical socialist appeal.

[59] These statistics are based on a secondary analysis of the data of these studies made from IBM cards kindly supplied by Dr. P. Luzzatto Fegiz, director of DOXA.

[60] The statistics are from a 1957 survey, the results of which have not been published. In all, six different Italian surveys conducted by three different research organizations have been inspected, or reanalyzed. Given the fact that we are concerned with the support of a party that has less than 5 per cent of the electorate behind it, it is only natural that there should be considerable variation in results from one sample survey to another. The conclusions cited above represent the best estimate that can be made of the sources of neo-Fascist and Monarchist support from all the surveys.

The United States: McCarthyism as Populist Extremism

The tradition of a strong liberal movement designed to protect the social and economic position of the small independent farmer or urban merchant, historically a part of the democratic left, has also existed in the United States. As many historians have pointed out, the Populist and Progressive movements of the late nineteenth and early twentieth centuries took this classic form. In this period of rising industrial capitalism and the growth of trusts, large sections of the farm and urban petty bourgeoisie responded to an appeal to control big business, the trusts, the railroads, and the banks. These movements contained a strong element of anti-Semitism and generalized xenophobia directed against any emerging power and influence of immigrants.[61] On the political level they showed a strong distrust of parliamentary or constitutional democracy and were particularly antagonistic to the concept of party. They preferred to break down the sources of partisan strength and create as much direct democracy as possible through the introduction of initiative and referendum, and through easy recall elections. Parties, politicians, big business, bankers, and foreigners were bad; only the people acting for themselves were good.

The Populist movement lost much of its direct political influence with the rapid growth of large industries and large cities. To some extent the Ku Klux Klan of the 1920s was a latter-day expression of provincial Populism appealing to farmers and the small businessmen in towns and villages against the domination by metropolitan centers. In the 1930s outright fascist movements sought to win strength by appealing directly to the economic interests of farmers and small merchants, attacking democratic institutions, and placing the blame for social and economic difficulties on international financiers and Jews.[62]

[61] See Richard Hofstadter, *The Age of Reform* (New York: Alfred A. Knopf, 1955), for a detailed exposition of this thesis.
[62] See Victor C. Ferkiss, "Populist Influence in American Fascism," *Western Political Quarterly*, 10 (1957), pp. 350–73.

There is no accurate measure of the actual strength of the various American extremist populist movements in the 1930s. Some place their support in the many millions. Whatever their strength, they were unable to convert it into partisan victories or become a major third party. Perhaps the most successful neo-populist extremist of the thirties, Huey Long, Governor and Senator from Louisiana, is a clear example of populist continuity. In the South and for a short time on the national scene, he attacked "the Bourbons and absentee corporation interests," promised to destroy large fortunes through heavy taxation and to sustain the middle class and redistribute the wealth to the poor. How successful Long would have been on the national scene we shall never know, since an assassin's bullet removed him in 1935. But that he represented a strong link with the populism of the nineties is clear not only from an examination of his ideology but also from the fact that there is a high correlation between the vote he obtained in elections in Louisiana in the 1920s and 1930s and that secured by the Populists in 1896.[63] Whether Longism on the national scene would have meant dictatorship is unknown, but Longism in power in Louisiana meant a severe attack on the freedom of opposition and a free press, and contempt for juridical and constitutional processes.

One recent expression of populist extremism in America was McCarthyism. McCarthy had no party, not even an organization, but for a few years he ranged the American political scene denouncing the forces of the left—the New Deal Democrats—as traitors or the accomplices of traitors, and at the same time insisted that the bulk of the traitors were nurtured by the traditional enemy of populism, the Eastern upper class.[64]

That McCarthy appealed to the same social groups as did "left-wing" populism can be verified by data from opinion

[63] Perry H. Howard, *Political Tendencies in Louisiana, 1812–1952* (Baton Rouge: Louisiana State University Press, 1957), p. 128.

[64] For an analysis of the twin components of McCarthyite ideology, see the essays in Daniel Bell, ed., *The New American Right* (New York: Criterion Books, 1956).

surveys. A study by the sociologist Martin Trow attempted to locate McCarthy's social support by dividing respondents from a small New England city into four political categories: (1) labor-liberals—those who were favorable to trade-unions and hostile to large corporations; (2) nineteenth-century liberals—those who were opposed to trade-unions and to large corporations; (3) moderate conservatives—those who supported trade-unions and were also favorable to large business; and (4) right-wing conservatives—those who were hostile to unions and favorable to big business. In terms of this typology, those in category 2, the "nineteenth-century liberals," correspond to the liberals of Europe, and, as Trow shows, their ideology is preponderantly that of the small businessman. [65] And when we examine the way in which the supporters of each of these four political positions reacted to McCarthy, we find that it was the nineteenth-century liberals—not the moderate or extreme conservatives—who were most likely to support him (Table V).

TABLE V

McCARTHY'S SUPPORT BY POLITICAL ORIENTATION*

Per cent favor his methods

Labor Liberals	37	(191)
Nineteenth-century Liberals	60	(142)
Moderate Conservatives	35	(190)
Right-wing Conservatives	38	(140)

* Computed by Martin A. Trow, *op. cit.*, p. 276.

The support for McCarthy among the nineteenth-century liberals was almost twice as great as among those holding other political positions. As Trow points out, this is the one political tradition in America which currently has "no institutionalized place on the political scene, little representation or leadership in the major parties, [and] which sought that voice and place through McCarthy. And he expressed for them their fear and mistrust of bigness, and the slick and

[65] See Martin A. Trow, *op. cit.*, pp. 277–78.

subversive ideas that come out of the cities and the big institutions to erode old ways and faiths."[66] Like Poujadism, McCarthyism and nineteenth-century liberalism are primarily the reactions of the small businessmen. Though small businessmen comprised only one fifth of the men in Trow's sample, "they contributed a third of the nineteenth-century liberals." And the small businessmen among the nineteenth-century liberals were even more likely to be McCarthyites than those in other occupations. As in the case of Poujadism, the highest proportion of McCarthy supporters was "found among the poorly educated small businessmen holding these nineteenth-century liberal attitudes: almost three out of four of these men were McCarthy supporters." But while McCarthy was drawing the traditional supporters of American populism behind him, the chief defenders of the established order ultimately joined together to defeat him. As I have tried to show elsewhere, American conservatism and big business resisted McCarthy.[67]

In discussing McCarthyism and Poujadism in the same section as Italian Fascism and German and Austrian Nazism, I do not intend to suggest that these movements would have resulted in dictatorships if their leaders had attained power. What I do suggest is that they, like other movements appealing to the self-employed urban and rural middle classes, were in large part products of the insoluble frustrations of those who feel cut off from the main trends of modern society. Not only were these five national movements disproportionately backed by the small independents, but in each country they secured much more support from those living on farms or in provincial small towns and cities. Here are the declining "liberal" classes living in declining areas. The petty bourgeoisie of these sections not only suffer deprivation because

---

[66] *Ibid.*, p. 276. A less comprehensive study based, however, on a national sample also reported that small businessmen were more likely to be McCarthy supporters than any other occupational stratum. See Immanuel Wallerstein, *McCarthyism and the Conservative* (M.A. thesis, Department of Sociology, Columbia University, 1954).

[67] S. M. Lipset, "The Sources of the Radical Right," in Daniel Bell, ed., *op. cit.*, pp. 216–17, 232–33.

of the relative decline of their class, they are also citizens of communities whose status and influence within the larger society is rapidly declining. From time to time, depending on various specific historical factors, their discontent leads them to accept diverse irrational protest ideologies—regionalism, racism, supernationalism, anticosmopolitanism, Mc-Carthyism, fascism.

Peronism—the "Fascism" of the Lower Class

The third type of social movement which has often been described as fascist is Peronism, the movement and ideology which formed around Juan Peron, President of the Argentine from 1946 to 1955. Unlike right-wing antidemocratic tendencies based on the more well-to-do and traditionalist strata and those tendencies I prefer to call "true" fascism—centrist authoritarianism, based on the liberal middle classes, primarily the self-employed—Peronism, much like Marxist parties, has been oriented toward the poorer classes, primarily urban workers but also the more impoverished rural population. Peronism has a strong-state ideology quite similar to that advocated by Mussolini.[68] It also has a strong antiparliamentary populist content, stressing that the power of the party and the leader is derived directly from the people, and that parliamentarianism results in government by incompetent and corrupt politicians. It shares with right-wing and centrist authoritarianism a strong nationalist bent, blaming many of the difficulties faced by the country on outsiders—international financiers and so forth. And like the other two forms of extremism, it glorifies the position of the armed forces.

Peronism differs from the other movements, however, in its positive orientation toward the workers, the trade-unions, and the class struggle. Peron came to power in 1946 in a revolutionary coup backed by the army and the working class which

[68] It should be noted that Peron sometimes accepted the linkage with fascism and praised Hitler and Mussolini.

followed the overthrow of a Conservative party regime. But Peron and his party remained in power in reasonably honest elections, winning overwhelming majorities. In the 1946 elections, the working-class-based Socialists failed to elect even one member of the Chamber of Deputies for the first time in forty years. According to the expert on Latin America, Robert Alexander, "Even in the city of Buenos Aires, which had been overwhelmingly Radical and Socialist, the Peronistas came in first with about a quarter of a million votes, the [middle-class] Radicals were second with 150,000, and the Socialists polled third with little over a hundred thousand."[69]

In these elections class lines were drawn more sharply than in any previous election. Peron was supported by the lower strata and opposed by the middle and upper classes.[70] The Argentine sociologist Gino Germani has explained the receptivity of the Argentine working class to Peron's revolutionary appeal as a typical phenomenon of a period of rapid industrialization and urbanization much like the pattern in Europe discussed in Chapter 2.[71]

In power Peron enacted a great deal of legislation which increased the standard of living, pay, rewards, leisure, and social security of the workers. He also passed laws known as the Statute of the Peon to benefit farm laborers and tenants against the landlords. These laws dealt with days off, housing, minimum pay, medical aid, and unwarranted discharges. His administration organized a plan to give land to farm laborers. Perhaps the principal institutional base of Peronist power

[69] Robert J. Alexander, *The Peron Era* (New York: Columbia University Press, 1951), p. 51.

[70] The continued working-class appeal of Peronism has been shown by the fact that in the elections of 1957, about one quarter of all voters cast a blank so-called "white" ballot indicating their support for the Peronista party, which was not allowed on the ballot. A survey conducted by Gino Germani indicates that most of the "white" voters were workers. For a detailed analysis of the vote in various elections which correlates the support of different parties with occupational categories, see G. Germani, *Estructura social de la Argentina, op. cit.,* Chap. XVI.

[71] See pp. 53–57.

was the trade-unions, which were completely dominated by his followers, grew to great size, and functioned as real agencies of collective bargaining backed by the state.

All of these measures, which sound like the program of a fairly radical labor party, were combined with extreme nationalism, strong emphasis on the dominant role of the "leader," corporatist ideology, populist demagogy, and lack of respect for constitutionalism and tradition. Not surprisingly, Peron won the enthusiastic support of the lower strata, both rural and urban, and the strong opposition of the middle classes, big business, and the landlords. For much of his rule he was backed by the armed forces from whose officer corps he had come.[72] In some measure his regime was a coalition between the nationalist officers of an underdeveloped country and its lower classes oriented against foreign imperialists and local bourgeois "renegades." Ultimately the regime was brought down by the officers and the church who were alienated by Peron's extremism, lack of responsibility, and continued antagonism to strata with which they were aligned. Even in exile, exposed as a corrupt politician and as a man who used his position for immoral purposes, Peron has remained the leader of the Argentine workers, and Peronist leaders have remained powerful in the trade-unions.

The phenomenon known as Peronism—anticapitalist populist nationalism which appeals to the lower strata in alignment with the army—is, of course, not unique to the Argentine. In Brazil, Getulio Vargas successfully developed the same theme a decade earlier, was also identified with fascism, and continued to retain the support of the workers after he

[72] But even within the armed services it has been suggested that Peron's power rested more with the enlisted men than the officer corps. "There is also a division between officers and enlisted men; this was widened under Peron, who was more successful to Peronizing the latter than the former, as evidenced by the abortive revolt of 1951, which was largely the work of some of the officer group and was defeated partly by the loyalty of the enlisted men to Peron." Arthur P. Whitaker, *Argentine Upheaval* (New York: Frederick A. Praeger, 1956), p. 67.

left power.[73] "Getulisme," like Peronism, was characterized by a practical program of social reforms designed to benefit the urban industrial workers. The main opposition came from "the landed aristocracy, the old families, who were attached to the old social structure of Brazil."[74] Vargas' Labor party is a major force in Brazilian politics, sometimes allied with the Communists who, as has been noted, also supported Peron during much of his administration.[75] If Peronism is considered a variant of fascism, then it is a fascism of the left because it is based on the social strata who would otherwise turn to socialism or Communism as an outlet for their frustrations.

The Social Bases of Fascism

The analysis of modern totalitarian movements has reflected the old concepts of left, right, and center. Politicians and scholars alike have seen these movements as representing the extremes of the political spectrum, hence they speak of Communism as the extreme left and Fascism as the extreme

---

[73] "Of all the decisions made by Vargas, probably none had greater political implications than his determination to bring the working groups into the political arena. . . . By 1938 . . . as a consequence of labor's support when he was consolidating his dictatorship under the neo-Fascist *Estado Novo* (New State), Vargas came to appreciate the political potential of the workers. He retained their approval through elaborate welfare programs and by imposing restrictions and obligations on business management." John J. Johnson, *op. cit.*, pp. 167–68.

[74] Jacques Lambert, *Le Brésil: Structure sociale et institutions politiques* (Paris: Librairie Armand Colin, 1953), pp. 146–47.

[75] Leslie Lipson describes the Brazilian Labor party, Getulio Vargas' postwar creation, as "nationalistic, friendly to industrialism, and sympathetic to urban labor." See his article "Government in Contemporary Brazil," *Canadian Journal of Economics and Political Science*, 22 (1956), pp. 192–93, and also Theodore Wyckoff, "Brazilian Political Parties," *South Atlantic Quarterly*, 56 (1957), pp. 281–98, for a discussion of the principal Brazilian parties and their social base. A recent ecological study which analyzes the working-class support of the Brazilian Labor party and the Communists is A. Simao, "O voto operario en São Paulo," *Revista brasilieras estudos politicos*, 1 (1956), pp. 130–41.

right. But antidemocratic ideologies as well as antidemocratic groups can be more fruitfully classified and analyzed if it is recognized that "left," "right," and "center" refer to ideologies, each of which has a moderate and an extremist version, the one parliamentary and the other extra-parliamentary in its orientation. It is also necessary to recognize that a left extremist movement that is working-class based and oriented also may be militaristic, nationalistic, and anti-Marxist.[76]

While all the varieties of antidemocratic mass movements are of equal interest, I have tried here to establish the usefulness of the tripartite distinction by examining the social bases of different political movements. Data from a number of countries demonstrate that classic fascism is a movement of the propertied middle classes, who for the most part normally support liberalism, and that it is opposed by the conservative strata, who have, however, at different times backed conservative antiparliamentary regimes. The conservative regimes are, in contrast to centrist ones, nonrevolutionary and nontotalitarian. In a conservative dictatorship, one is not expected to give total loyalty to the regime, to join a party or other institutions, but simply to keep out of politics. Though the dictatorship of the Austrian clerical conservatives has been described as fascist, the differences between it and its Nazi successor are abundantly clear. Similarly, although Franco is backed by the Spanish fascists—the Falange—his regime has been dominated by conservative authoritarians. The party has never been allowed to dominate the society; most institutions remain independent of the state and the

---

[76] Some have found it difficult to accept the fact that a leader and movement whose ideology, symbolism, and methods resembled Fascism and Nazism could in fact not be rightist. Thus a book written before Peron consolidated his power suggested that he represented the interests of the *estancieros*, the large landlords who had controlled the Conservative party and ruled the Argentine for much of its history. See Felix J. Weil, *Argentine Riddle* (New York: John Day, 1944). Even *Time* magazine wrote in 1951 "as though it were not news to anybody, that 'Peron operates a state essentially modeled on the classic Nazi-Fascist pattern.' " *Time*, May 21, 1951, p. 43, cited in George I. Blankstein, *Peron's Argentina* (Chicago: University of Chicago Press, 1953), p. 277.

party, and the opposition is not asked to conform or join, only to abstain from organized opposition.

Although a distinction may be made among these movements analytically, in any given country there is considerable overlap, as in the case of the Spanish Nationalists. Basically revolutionary movements like Nazism did secure some support from conservatives who agreed with its nationalistic and anti-Marxist aspects. Italian Fascism represented a coalition of both centrist and conservative extremism led by a pure opportunist. It would be a mistake, however, to conclude from the absence of movements which are purely one or the other variety that the analytic distinction is of merely speculative interest. Recent political movements—Poujadism, McCarthyism, Gaullism—all exhibit particular characteristics associated with the nature of their social base. If we want to preserve and extend parliamentary democracy, we must understand the source of threats to it, and threats from conservatives are as different from those originating in the middle-class center as these are from Communism.

Extremist movements have much in common. They appeal to the disgruntled and the psychologically homeless, to the personal failures, the socially isolated, the economically insecure, the uneducated, unsophisticated, and authoritarian persons at every level of the society. As Heberle puts it, such movements are supported by "those who for some reason or other had failed to make a success in their business or occupation, and those who had lost their social status or were in danger of losing it. . . . The masses of the organized [Nazi] party members consisted therefore before 1933 largely of people who were outsiders in their own class, black sheep in their family, thwarted in their ambitions. . . ."[77] As far back as the 1890s, Engels described those who "throng to the working-class parties in all countries" as "those who have nothing to look forward to from the official world or have come to the end of their tether with it—opponents of inoculation, supporters of abstemiousness, vegetarians, antivivi-

[77] R. Heberle, *op. cit.*, p. 10.

sectionists, nature-healers, free-community preachers whose communities have fallen to pieces, authors of new theories on the origin of the universe, unsuccessful or unfortunate inventors, victims of real or imaginary injustice . . . honest fools and dishonest swindlers."[78] It is often men from precisely such origins who give the fanatical and extremist character to these movements and form the core of believers.[79] But the various extremist movements, like their democratic alternatives, wax or wane depending on whether they can win and retain the support of the strata whom they are trying to represent and lead. It is impossible to understand the role and varying success of extremist movements unless we distinguish them and identify their distinctive social bases and ideologies much as we do democratic parties and movements.[80]

In the next section we turn from the social characteristics of the supporters of antidemocratic tendencies back to the conditions of effective democracy in action. Part II seeks to locate the persistent patterns associated with varying rates and types of participation in the electoral struggle in various democratic countries.

[78] Friedrich Engels, "On the History of Early Christianity," in K. Marx and F. Engels, *On Religion* (Moscow: Foreign Languages Publishing House, 1957), p. 319.

[79] See G. Almond, *The Appeals of Communism* (Princeton: Princeton University Press, 1954), Chaps. 9 and 10, esp. pp. 258–61.

[80] In emphasizing the consistencies in the type of extremist politics associated with various social groupings, I do not mean to assert that such findings permit a high order of political prediction. As Reinhard Bendix has pointed out: "The point is not that certain types of farmers in relatively industrialized countries are potential fascists *or* communists, but that they have a certain propensity to radicalization under conditions of acute distress. When such radicalization will eventuate and which way it will turn, the analyst of social stratification is not in a position to predict. His knowledge does enable him to estimate the relative chances for such a development, but only in the sense that certain types of farmers are more likely to be affected than others. Obviously, local conditions, historical antecedents, the acuteness of the crisis, and the intensity of the organizational drive on the part of a totalitarian movement will play a role and can be judged only in specific cases. R. Bendix, *op. cit.*, p. 602.

PART II

VOTING IN WESTERN DEMOCRACIES

CHAPTER 6

Elections: Who Votes and Who Doesn't?

PARTICIPATION by the members of an organization or the citizens of a society in political affairs is neither a necessary nor a sufficient condition for rank-and-file influence on organizational or government policy. On the one hand, members may show a low level of political participation in an organization or society, but still affect policy by their ability to withdraw or contribute election support to one or another of the different bureaucracies competing for power. On the other hand, a membership or citizenry may regularly attend meetings, belong in large numbers to various political organizations, and even have a high rate of voting turnout, and yet have little or no influence on policy.

The latter is the situation in totalitarian states and in some one-party trade-unions. The totalitarian leader wants his followers to attend meetings, read political literature, listen to broadcasts, and engage in other similar activities, since these are means of reaching them with his point of view and indoctrinating them. If the members or citizens are not "politically" active, they are removed from the influence of the controlling power. Some totalitarian states have undertaken large-scale literacy drives with the explicit purpose of increasing the probability that the citizenry will absorb the prescribed ideology. Similarly some trade-unions, especially those under Communist control, have made strenuous efforts—including compulsory attendance at meetings—to increase participation by their members. It is fairly obvious that Communist labor leaders are not anxious to encourage and deepen internal democracy in their unions, but rather recognize that by multiplying the controlled activities of the members they are increasing their own chances to reach and indoctrinate them.

As a general hypothesis, I suggest that the greater the changes in the structure of the society or organization that a governing group is attempting to introduce, the more likely the leadership is to desire and even require a high level of participation by its citizens or members. The radical changes that accompany social revolution (or, on a smaller scale, the transformation of a trade-union into a political weapon) put severe strains on group loyalties and create the potential for strong membership hostility toward the leadership. A high level of controlled and manipulated rank-and-file participation is perhaps the only effective way, given the leadership's purposes, of draining off or redirecting the discontent which violent or sudden changes in traditional patterns and relationships engender.

Nevertheless, a situation which results in high participation by members of a group normally has higher potential for democracy—that is, for the maintenance of an effective opposition—than one where few people show interest or participate in the political process. An opposition faced with the problem of communicating with and activating an uninterested, passive citizenry is under great handicaps compared to the incumbents.[1] And conversely, a society in which a large proportion of the population is outside the political arena is potentially more explosive than one in which most citizens are *regularly* involved in activities which give them some sense of participation in decisions which affect their lives.

Although participation in politics includes leadership in national affairs, local leadership, activity as an organization member, and informal "opinion leadership" among one's associates, this chapter is primarily concerned with voting and nonvoting, although of course the act of voting is usually

[1] Contributing greatly to the existence of one-party oligarchy in the trade-union movement is the fact that few members normally show any interest in the political process of the union. The factors which are conducive to apathy in trade-unions are part of the general cluster with which Chap. 12 deals.

only the final stage in a process of paying attention to politics —reading, talking, and thinking. Chapters 7 and 8 will be devoted to the group memberships and experiences regularly associated with left or right (liberal or conservative) voting.[2]

The percentage of the potential electorate voting in national American elections is now considerably below what it was in 1896, when 80 per cent of those eligible went to the polls. From a low in 1920 of 49 per cent, in more recent elections the figure has oscillated around 60 per cent. As the political scientist V. O. Key, Jr., points out, this is considerably lower than the participation in other major democracies like Great Britain, Holland, and Norway.[3]

What does this lack of participation reflect? An unhealthy apathy and the weakening of democracy, some liberal rhetoricians suggest. Although the kinds and causes of apathy and nonvoting vary for different historical periods and for different sections of the population, it is possible that nonvoting is now, at least in the Western democracies, a reflection of the stability of the system, a response to the decline of major social conflicts, and an increase in cross-pressures, particularly those affecting the working class. But clearly there are different sources of nonvoting which have varying consequences for a democratic state.

[2] I do not wish to consider here the effects of legal and technical restrictions like residence requirements, poll taxes and property qualifications, literacy tests (often used as a cover for racial discrimination) and burdensome registration requirements (often maintained by political machines to hold down the vote). These factors can be of great practical importance, but the main problem for analysis here is *voluntary* nonvoting.

[3] See V. O. Key, Jr., *Politics, Parties, and Pressure Groups*, 4th ed. (New York: Crowell, 1958), p. 625. Voting in America may be particularly low when compared with European countries because of a peculiar feature of our voting system: *two* decisions are often required, one to register and another to vote, and the first decision must be made when political issues and activity are at a low point. This factor in itself may account for many of the differences between America and those European countries where a person is automatically registered, and must merely vote.

The complex problem of interpreting reactions to politics is well suggested by a letter to a newspaper by an obviously well-informed and sophisticated man, vitally concerned and informed about political issues: ". . . it is better to ignore the news, else the daily anxieties which never get relieved by rational conduct, will drive us further toward insanity. . . . What better way to maintain some degree of rationality in this age than to ignore the current events described in our newspapers and other communication media?"[4] Clearly this man's approach to politics is a conscious withdrawal, alienation based on feelings of futility. It must be a matter of concern as to what extent this feeling is based on reality, and therefore cannot be exorcised by appeals to political responsibility. And yet this response is far different from that of a person who has *never* become "engaged" in the political sphere of life.

The sociologists David Riesman and Nathan Glazer suggest, referring to the extent of the "flight from politics," that its extent may be underestimated if "we look only to such indices as voting and opinion-holding on political questions, as measured by polls, as clues to political interest and participation today. For the indices reflect political action that may, in a greater measure than before, be apolitical."[5] It is possible, therefore, that the overt measures of political interest that we are dealing with here, voting and, to some extent, interest and participation, are inaccurate and miss altogether the possibility that politics now increasingly reflects, at least in the middle class, only group-conformity. Some might criticize this approach focused on voting behavior as missing some of the real historical shifts in the meaning of politics to different groups. This may be a serious criticism, but, as we shall see, differences in the voting turnout of different groups still seem to give meaningful clues to the character of politics

---

[4] San Francisco *Chronicle*, April 23, 1959.
[5] David Riesman and Nathan Glazer, "Criteria for Political Apathy," in Alvin W. Gouldner, ed., *Studies in Leadership* (New York: Harper & Bros., 1950), p. 519.

in modern society, without implying any over-all evaluation of the inner meaning of the voting act.[6]

Patterns of voting participation are strikingly the same in various countries: Germany, Sweden, America, Norway, Finland, and many others for which we have data. Men vote more than women; the better educated, more than the less educated; urban residents, more than rural; those between 35 and 55, more than younger or older voters; married persons, more than unmarried; higher-status persons, more than lower; members of organizations, more than nonmembers.[7] These differences are, however, narrowing in many countries,

[6] Riesman and Glazer are really concerned with the subjective meaning of politics, and its role in the organization of an individual's psyche, while the problem of concern in this chapter is not really apathy as a personal matter, but voting in relation to the fundamental kinds of group differences which affect it. It is of course true that if the act of voting loses all meaning, this poses serious implications for democracy, but that problem, of an almost philosophical character as it is handled by Riesman, is both beyond my scope, and is, in any case, a questionable inference about modern society.

[7] The best single compendium and study of political participation is Herbert Tingsten, *Political Behavior: Studies in Election Statistics* (London: P. S. King & Son, 1937). A summary of generalizations on voting turnout reported in fourteen different studies will be found in Bernard Berelson, Paul F. Lazarsfeld, and William McPhee, *Voting* (Chicago: University of Chicago Press, 1954), pp. 336–37. Robert E. Lane's *Political Life* (Glencoe: The Free Press, 1959) provides a useful summary of the literature relating voting and political participation to various social factors and conditions. See esp. pp. 45–62. Other important materials may be found in Paul F. Lazarsfeld, Bernard Berelson, and Hazel Gaudet, *The People's Choice* (New York: Duell, Sloan & Pearce, 1944), pp. 40–51; Angus Campbell and R. L. Kahn, *The People Elect a President* (Ann Arbor: Survey Research Center, 1952), p. 29; Angus Campbell, Gerald Gurin, and Warren E. Miller, *The Voter Decides* (Evanston: Row, Peterson & Co., 1954), pp. 70–73; for Finnish data see Erik Allardt and Kettil Bruun, "Characteristics of the Finnish Non-Voter," *Transactions of the Westermarck Society*, 3 (1956), pp. 55–76. See also Julian L. Woodward and Elmo Roper, "Political Activity of American Citizens," *American Political Science Review*, 44 (1950), pp. 874–77; Charles E. Merriam and Harold F. Gosnell, *Non-Voting: Causes and Methods of Control* (Chicago: University of Chicago Press, 1924), and Inge B. Powell, "The Non-Voter: Some Questions and

like Sweden, for example, especially in regard to age and sex differences.[8]

As an example of the character of these differences we may look at contemporary Germany where both regular sample surveys and a very large sample of the entire voting population taken in 1953 by the German Bureau of Statistics report consistent differences. Male voting in Germany increased with education and with income. Among farm owners and the self-employed 90 per cent voted in the previous election. The lower-paid among manual workers voted at a 78 per cent rate. Within each occupational category, the better-paid voted more. Also, when the workers were considered by level of skill, fewer of the unskilled than the skilled and semiskilled voted. These differences are significant in view of the unusual size of the samples.[9] They will be discussed later, in terms of the main social factors which seem to explain them best, but it may be noted here that many of the explanations for lower voting among the lower-status groups coincide with the various experiences associated with low-status occupations, that have been cited to account for authoritarian values.[10]

Hypotheses," *Berkeley Publications in Society and Institutions,* 1 (1955), pp. 25–36. For data on female participation, which also includes much material on males as well, see Maurice Duverger, *La participation des femmes à la vie politique* (Paris: UNESCO, 1955), esp. pp. 13–74; and Gabriele Bremme, *Die Politische Rolle der Frau in Deutschland* (Göttingen: Vandenhoeck und Ruprecht, 1956), esp. pp. 28–67.

[8] See Dankwart A. Rustow, *The Politics of Compromise* (Princeton: Princeton University Press, 1955), pp. 137–39. Since voting participation has steadily increased in Sweden from 1924 onward (from a low in that year of 53 per cent to a high in 1948 of almost 83 per cent), part of the decline of differences between groups is undoubtedly due to the increases in all groups rather than direct social influences on particularly low-voting groups.

[9] See Erich Reigrotzki, *Soziale Verflechtungen in der Bundesrepublik* (Tübingen: J. C. B. Mohr, 1956), pp. 63–68 for these figures. See also Juan Linz, *The Social Bases of German Politics* (Ph.D. dissertation, Department of Sociology, Columbia University, 1958).

[10] The effects of low status in creating authoritarian predispositions, as well as withdrawal and apathy, have been analyzed in Chap. 4, "Working-class Authoritarianism."

In addition, many distinct factors rarely occur on the group level except in combination with others operating in the same direction. This makes the task of isolating causal variables difficult.

TABLE I

SOCIAL CHARACTERISTICS CORRELATED WITH VOTING TURNOUT

Higher Turnout	Lower Turnout
High income	Low income
High education	Low education
Occupational groups:	Occupational groups:
Businessmen	Unskilled workers
White-collar employees	Servants
Government employees	Service workers
Commercial-crop farmers	Peasants, subsistence farmers
Miners	
Whites	Negroes
Men	Women
Middle-aged people (35–55)	Young people (under 35)
Older people (over 55)	
Old residents in community	Newcomers in community
Workers in western Europe	Workers in United States
Crisis situations	Normal situations
Married people	Single
Members of organizations	Isolated individuals

The small group of farm laborers in the national German sample was the most apathetic segment of the population. Many of the factors which will be singled out for analysis as separately tending to reduce the voting rate of a social group combine in the case of the farm laborers. They are generally less educated, underprivileged economically, socially isolated, and in close personal contact (especially in Germany, where the farmers are largely peasants, not large absentee land-owners) with their employer. They are little exposed to the mass media, and few are members of unions or other voluntary organizations. In 1953, 48 per cent of the farm laborers

Table II

Social Factors Affecting Rates of Voting Turnout

1. The relevance of government policies to the individual:
   a. Dependence on government as one's employer
   b. Exposure to economic pressures requiring government action
   c. Exposure to government economic restrictions
   d. Possession of moral or religious values affected by government policies
   e. Availability of relevant policy alternatives
   f. General crisis situations

2. Access to information:
   a. Direct visibility of effects of government policies
   b. Occupational training and experience making for general insight
   c. Contact and communication
   d. Amount of leisure

3. Group pressure to vote:
   a. Underprivilege and alienation
   b. Strength of class political organization
   c. Extent of social contacts
   d. Group norms opposing voting

4. Cross-pressures:
   a. Conflicting interests
   b. Conflicting information
   c. Conflicting group pressures

interviewed were "indifferent" about the outcome of the election, as compared to 28 per cent of the urban manual workers and 16 per cent of the farm owners.[11] Thus, farm labor-

[11] See Juan Linz, *op. cit.*, pp. 747 ff. The actual differences in voting in 1949 were much less since 75 per cent of the farm laborers voted as compared to 87 per cent of the farmers and 83 per cent of the nonfarm workers, but it is quite likely that in Germany there is a widespread feeling of moral obligation to vote, but not such a strong norm regarding interest in, or knowledge of, the candidates and the issues. On other measures of interest, the farm laborers were consistently lower than other occupational groups. A sample of 12,000 cases from five American national surveys found that service workers, subject to essentially the same conditions as the farm laborers, had the lowest voting rate (56 per cent). See G. M. Connelly and H. H. Field, "The Non-Voter, Who He Is, and What He Thinks," *Public Opinion Quarterly*, 8 (1944), pp. 175–87.

ers and domestic workers are the social groups most likely to have an extremely low voting rate, and this is borne out by available data from many countries.

Some descriptive differences in voting turnout which have been located in a multitude of studies are listed in Table I. The specific explanations for these differences may be summarized under four very general explanatory propositions. A group will have a higher rate of voting if (1) its interests are strongly affected by government policies; (2) it has access to information about the relevance of political decisions to its interests; (3) it is exposed to social pressures demanding voting; (4) it is not pressed to vote for different political parties. A further classification of these factors found in concrete social groups is presented in Table II.[12]

The Relevance of Government Policies

Although it may be argued that everyone is affected by government policies, some groups are more affected than others, and these groups might be expected to show a higher turnout at the polls than the public at large. The purest case of involvement in government policies is naturally that of government employees whose whole economic position and working life is affected. Data from national and local elections in both the United States and many European countries show that government employees have the highest turnout of any occupational group.[13]

[12] Most official statistics and opinion surveys do not, however, give direct information about these categories. Their classifications are set up for immediate practical purposes: age, sex, income, occupation, religion, region, etc., and the analyst must draw upon his additional knowledge of the social groups which these categories imply in order to "interpret" them in these other terms.

[13] H. Tingsten, op. cit., pp. 120–81, passim. G. Dupeux documents this point for a French departmental capital in "Le Probleme des abstentions dans le département du Loir-et-Cher au début de la troisième république," Revue française de science politique, 2 (1952), pp. 71–95. See also D. Anderson, P. E. Davidson, Ballots and the Democratic Class Struggle (Stanford: Stanford University Press, 1943); Roscoe C. Martin, "The Municipal Electorate: A Case Study," Southwestern Social Science Quarterly, 14 (1933), pp. 213–

Groups subjected to economic pressures with which individuals cannot cope, such as inflation, depression, monopolistic exploitation, or structural change in the economy, might also be expected to turn to government action as a solution and to show a high voting average. This has certainly been the case with farmers who produce for national and world markets, like the wheat farmers.[14] Long subject to periodic collapses in the price of their product and to the monopolistic power of banks, railroads, processors, and dealers, these farmers in almost every advanced country have developed a high degree of political "countervailing power." Thanks to a high rate of organizational activity and a high turnout at the polls they now enjoy government price supports, crop insurance, regulation of railroads, banking, etc., which in effect guarantee a large part of their incomes. Miners, particularly vulnerable both to periodic crises and to structural changes in the economy, also have a high turnout compared to other workers.[15]

On the other hand, there are many cases where drastic economic need is accompanied by low political participation. For instance, Marie Lazarsfeld-Jahoda and Hans Zeisel, studying Austrian urban unemployed during the depression, reported that "subscriptions to a very low-priced workers' political publication dropped by about 60 per cent; whereas subscriptions to another publication which had the same political direction . . . [but was] . . . more concerned with entertainment than with politics . . . declined only by about 27 per cent, in spite of its higher price."[16] The American

14. A 1957 Norwegian survey found that of all male occupational groups, the salaried public employees had the highest rate of voting and participation in political activity. Unpublished survey conducted by the Institute of Social Research, Oslo, kindly made available by Dr. Stein Rokkan.

[14] See S. M. Lipset, *Agrarian Socialism* (Berkeley: University of California Press, 1950).

[15] For Britain, among many others, see D. E. Butler, *The British General Election of 1951* (London: Macmillan, 1951), p. 266.

[16] Marie Lazarsfeld-Jahoda and Hans Zeisel, *Die Arbeitslosen von Marienthal* (Leipzig: Hirzel, 1932), pp. 35–37.

sociologist E. Wight Bakke has reported comparable findings in studies of unemployment in England and America.[17] Need alone does not appear to be sufficient, and some of the sources of low turnout among the unemployed will be discussed later in this chapter.

In most countries businessmen are drastically affected by government economic policies. In the nineteenth century there were old government restraints to be cleared away and government benefits to be sought. In the twentieth, government has again become the source of severe restrictions on business, to the point that taxes and regulations are among the most important economic factors with which the businessman must reckon. The voting record of businessmen in almost every country undoubtedly reflects these facts.[18]

But economic interests are not the only interests that motivate voting. The high voting rate of Jews in recent years has been explained as a reaction to Nazism and political anti-Semitism.[19] The antireligious threat implied by Communism is said to be effective in bringing out Catholic voters. Catholic voting may also be increased whenever issues like the legalization of birth control or government aid to religious schools, which bear specifically on Catholic values, are raised in elections.

Morality issues like prohibition and gambling appear to bring out a higher women's vote, both in the United States and in Europe.[20] The prominence of the "corruption and

[17] E. Wight Bakke, Citizens Without Work (New Haven: Yale University Press, 1940), p. 46.

[18] H. Tingsten, op. cit., Chap. III; L. Harris, Is There a Republican Majority? (New York: Harper & Bros., 1954), pp. 16–17; A. Campbell and R. L. Kahn, op. cit., p. 109. The latter study found that 75 per cent of the executives and 74 per cent of the professionals voted, as compared with 47 per cent among workers in 1948 and 1952.

[19] H. Tingsten, op. cit., p. 215; S. J. Korchin, Psychological Variables in the Behavior of Voters (unpublished Ph.D. thesis, Department of Social Relations, Harvard University, 1946), Chap. IV.

[20] H. Tingsten, op. cit., pp. 12, 72. In the Norwegian advisory referendums on prohibition (1919 and 1926) the difference in electoral participation between the sexes was most marked in the dis-

Communism" issue in the 1952 American elections may account for the unprecedented number of female voters—estimated at 55 per cent, compared with the previous high in 1940 of 49 per cent.[21]

Proposals for new programs of government action also seem to increase voting among the group affected. Precise statistical data are hard to come by, but it would be interesting to find out whether the introduction of old-age pension proposals increased the turnout of old people at the polls or whether veteran-benefit proposals bring out more veterans. The New Deal's federal work-relief program during the 1930s was paralleled by a sizable increase in voting by low-income people who presumably had their first real and visible stake in national politics.

In Europe new parties and programs representing the workers' interests developed together with the increase in working-class voting in the late nineteenth and early twentieth centuries. The lower turnout of American workers, especially between 1920 and 1932, has been attributed to the lack of overt class issues dividing the parties in this period. Even after the New Deal revived such issues, over half of the voters were reported as saying that "there are no differences" between the two parties, or were unable to state what the differences are.[22] Although American workers are overwhelmingly Democratic, the party's low emphasis on ideology and

---

tricts where the anti-prohibitionists were in a majority and considerably smaller where the prohibitionists had a clear majority, as Tingsten's data show (p. 16); for detailed summary of evidence on moralistic concerns of American women, see Robert E. Lane, *op. cit.*, pp. 212–14.

In Italy, where Catholic organizations have been stating that nonvoters "betray the Church," and that abstention means "to vote indirectly for the Communists and the atheists," women, who tend to be very religious, do not have a higher non-voting rate than men. See Mattei Dogan, "Le Comportement politique des Italiens," *Revue française de science politique*, 9 (1959), pp. 383–84.

[21] L. Harris, *op. cit.*, Chap. VI.

[22] H. Cantril and J. Harding, "The 1942 Election: A Case Study in Political Psychology," *Public Opinion Quarterly*, 7 (1943), pp. 222–41.

class organization does not encourage political interest among the workers as do those European "workers" parties which have been to some degree parties of integration.[23]

When a nation faces a crisis—major changes in its social, economic, or political system or in its international position—the electorate as a whole takes a greater interest in politics. André Siegfried[24] has documented the effect of "crisis elections" on turnout during the period 1876–1906 in France. During these elections when the issue of republican or monarchical government was crucial, turnout was high; from 1881–98 this issue was more or less in abeyance and turnout fell. The crisis over the position of the Catholic Church brought a new high from 1902–6. American studies suggest that the economic crisis situations of 1896 and 1936 and the international crises of 1916, 1940, and 1952 similarly provoked unusually high turnouts.[25] In Germany and Austria, the normally high turnout reached its greatest heights in 1932–33, in the last elections before the destruction of the democratic system itself.[26]

An interesting relationship between political crisis and political interest was suggested by the French sociologist Maurice Halbwachs. Starting with the observation that during wartime suicide rates decline greatly, Halbwachs argued that people feel more integrated in social groups during crises and therefore political crises in France should also reduce suicide rates. He studied changes in these rates for a hundred-year period from 1827 and 1927, and found that suicide rates did indeed decline during such major political controversies as the 1830 and 1848 revolutions, the 1851 *coup d'état*, of

[23] See Chap. III, pp. 74–76, for a discussion of "parties of integration."

[24] A. Siegfried, *Tableau politique de la France de l'ouest sous la troisième république* (Paris: Librairie Armand Colin, 1913), pp. 499–506; *Géographie électorale de l'Ardeche sous le troisième république* (Paris: Librairie Armand Colin, 1949), pp. 101–3.

[25] Harold F. Gosnell, *Why Europe Votes* (Chicago: University of Chicago Press, 1930), pp. 196–97; V. O. Key, Jr., *op. cit.*, pp. 624–26; L. Harris, *op. cit.*, p. 177.

[26] H. Tingsten, *op. cit.*, pp. 225–26. See Chap. 5, pp. 148–52.

Napoleon III, the Boulanger crisis of 1889–90, and throughout the intense battles of the Dreyfus affair from 1899 to 1905.[27] Halbwachs then suggested that the effect of political crises on suicide rates should vary with the extent to which different districts (*départements*) of France were involved in politics. As anticipated, during political crises suicide rates dropped most in Paris, somewhat less in other major urban centers, and very little in the more isolated provincial areas. It would be interesting to see whether other peoples with a less revolutionary tradition than the French also react to political controversies with such intensity that their group cohesion is affected. I suspect that Halbwachs' findings merely demonstrate again the bitterness of the political divisions of Frenchmen discussed briefly in Chapter 3. But regardless of what the findings tell us about France, they clearly indicate that crises increase interest and involvement in politics.

Access to Information

While great social problems can lead to high participation in elections, they by no means always do. Often those subject to the most severe economic distress—poor workers, the unemployed, peasants—have the lowest rate of voting. Although this may result from the distressed group's inability to find an available party to represent its interests, there are many examples where voting would greatly further the interests of a group, and still the turnout of that group is low.

Difficulties of social perception and communication provide a partial explanation for such cases. Two groups may have an equal stake in government policies, but one group may have easier access to information about this stake than the other. The impact of government policies on government employees, for example, is not only objectively great, but

[27] The most complete report of this aspect of Halbwachs' research is contained in a book by Robert E. L. Faris, who was a student of his at the University of Chicago, *Social Disorganization* (New York: Ronald Press, 1948), pp. 213–17. Halbwachs' own report appears in his *Les Causes de suicide* (Paris: F. Alcan, 1930).

transparently obvious, as are agricultural policies benefiting the farmers and controls and taxes levied upon businessmen. On the other hand, the impact of a whole collection of government policies (tariffs, controls, antitrust policies, taxation, subsidies, etc.) on a worker or white-collar employee may be very large, but it is hidden and indirect. Some policies require expert professional training to trace their effects, and this often enters into the lawmaker's choice of policies. A sales tax, for example, collected at the point of sale is a constant reminder, but one collected at the manufacturer's level is invisible to the consumer. (This principle is well known to Soviet tax-policy makers.) The low turnout of workers and other low-income people may also reflect the relative indirectness and invisibility of crucial economic relationships.[28]

Where economic relationships are not easily visible to those affected, general insight and sophistication become important. Insight into complex social problems can result from education and no doubt contributes to the higher voting among the more educated groups.[29] But it seems to depend even more on the social experiences flowing from one's work.

[28] Forty-five per cent of the lowest income and occupational group did not vote in the United States in 1952, according to a national sample. See Morris Janowitz and Dwaine Marvick, *Competitive Pressure and Democratic Consent*, Michigan Governmental Studies, No. 32 (Ann Arbor, University of Michigan Press, 1956), p. 26. A British study of the 1950 election found that 66 per cent of the lower-class persons in their sample were "uninterested" in politics, as compared with 29 per cent of the middle and upper-class persons. See M. Benney, A. P. Gray, and R. H. Pear, *How People Vote* (London: Routledge and Kegan Paul, 1956), p. 127.

[29] Paul F. Lazarsfeld, B. Berelson, and Hazel Gaudet, *op. cit.*, p. 47. G. M. Connelly and H. H. Field found when they controlled income and education that, while both factors contributed independently to voting, income contributed much more. See Connelly and Field, *op. cit.*, pp. 179–80. Similarly, S. J. Korchin in his study, already cited, of the 1944 U.S. presidential election found that education had almost no independent effect when socioeconomic status was held constant. For 1948 see A. Campbell and R. Kahn, *op. cit.*, p. 109. Another aspect of this lack of sophistication, fundamentally related to education—its authoritarian consequences—is dealt with in Chap. 4. The 1957 data from Norway indicate the same pattern (survey already cited).

The upper occupational groups not only have more education, their job activities continue their intellectual development, at least along certain practical lines. Most executives
and business owners and many branches of the professions
deal daily with complex legal, economic, and technical problems which develop their understanding of the workings of
complex social and political mechanisms. Routine clerical
and manual jobs, on the other hand, allow little opportunity
for acquiring such insight. The housewife is at a great disadvantage in this respect, a fact that may help to account for
the lower voting rate of women in general.

The relationship of occupational activities to political skills
has long been evident in the backgrounds of the organizers
and leaders of political movements. Many workers' and farmers' political movements have drawn their leaders from the
professions—law, journalism, teaching, the ministry—which
necessarily involve public speaking, writing, and organizing.[30]
Leaders who come from the working class generally do so by
way of trade-union office—the one position directly available
to a worker in which he can learn political skills. It has been
pointed out that the British trade-unions and Chartist movements recruited an important part of their early leadership
from workers who had first learned "political skills" as lay
ministers and Sunday School teachers in the nonconformist
churches.[31] Printers—the first literate group of manual work-

[30] See Robert Michels, *Political Parties* (Glencoe: The Free Press,
1949), pp. 238–39, on the role of the bourgeois intellectuals in a
new labor movement. See also Willy Kremer, *Der Soziale Aufbau
der Parteien des Deutschen Reichstages von 1871–1928* (Ph.D. thesis,
University of Köln, 1934). In 1945, 48.5 per cent of the Labor
M.P.'s in Britain and 61 per cent of the Conservatives were in the
liberal professions, managers, or officers. See Jacques Cadert, "Régime
electoral et régime parlementaire en Grand Bretagne," *Cahiers de la
fondation nationale des sciences politiques*, No. 5 (Paris: Librairie
Armand Colin, 1948), p. 84. For the role of the intellectuals in the
Balkan peasant parties see David Mitrany, *Marx and the Peasant*
(Chapel Hill: University of North Carolina Press, 1951), pp. 131–33.

[31] See Sidney Webb, *The Story of the Durham Miners 1662–1924*
(London: Labour Publishing Co., 1929), p. 21; and A. D. Belden,
George Whitefield, the Awakener (London: S. Marston and Co.,
1930), pp. 247 ff.

ers—were pioneer organizers of trade-unions and labor parties in many countries, another reflection of the impact of occupational activities on intellectual and organizational skills.[32]

It was such considerations as these that led Marx and Engels to urge that a greater diversification of the individual's activities—in fact, the complete "abolition" of the division of labor—was a necessary condition for a completely equalitarian and anarchist society. A somewhat similar suggestion has been made in less utopian form by an admirer of the American corporation, the sociologist Peter Drucker, who would expand the scope of the worker's role in industry to include management of all the welfare activities of the "plant community," so that he can acquire "political" skills in the course of his work.[33]

Another way in which social position can contribute to political awareness is by facilitating contacts with others who have more or less identical problems. This was the assumption underlying Marx's thesis that farmers—isolated in small plots or small villages scattered over the country by the nature of their work—could not develop political class consciousness, while workers—concentrated in large plants and in the working-class districts of great cities—could become conscious of their common interests and then politically active.[34] However Marx's statement concerned an illiterate peasantry before railroads, electrical communications, the mass media, and automobiles penetrated the rural scene. With the development of modern communications, many farmers have

[32] For a further discussion and detailed reference to different countries see S. M. Lipset, M. Trow, and J. S. Coleman, *Union Democracy* (Glencoe: The Free Press, 1956), esp. pp. 25–30.

[33] Peter Drucker, *The New Society* (New York: Harper & Bros., 1949).

[34] See Karl Marx, "The Eighteenth Brumaire of Louis Bonaparte," in his *Selected Works*, Vol. I (New York: International Publishers, 1933), p. 109; see also R. Bendix and S. M. Lipset, "Karl Marx's Theory of Social Class," in R. Bendix and S. M. Lipset, eds., *Class, Status and Power* (Glencoe: The Free Press, 1953), pp. 26–35; Karl Marx and F. Engels, "Manifesto of the Communist Party," in Karl Marx, *op. cit.*, pp. 21–61.

become more integrated in a class network, and are more like workers living in a working-class community. Farmers have in fact been quite successful in building politically potent organizations.

In general, members of occupations which guarantee a great deal of in-group interaction in many activities and roles, and which involve leadership skills and knowledge about large problems, are more politically aware, vote more, and have a greater commitment to such occupationally linked organizations as trade-unions. Thus the sociologist Robert K. Merton analyzed a New Jersey shipyard workers' housing project which was forced to incorporate as a town solely inhabited by workers. Manual workers had to take positions as town executives, school board members, library officials, political party committeemen, and so forth.[35] One effect of forcing workers into these activities was to increase the level of participation in elections and other community activities far above the "normal" level for manual workers in a heterogeneous environment in which people of middle-class background would normally hold such positions.

Similarly, in the province of Saskatchewan, Canada, a combination of geographical circumstances and constitutional provisions made it incumbent on the wheat farmers, who comprised almost all the farmers in the area, to set up and run a large number of governmental and voluntary services. The resultant network of farmer participation in community leadership roles and organizations led to a heightened level of vocational political activity, much higher than is reported in circumstances where urban middle-class people can fulfill the same leadership roles, e.g., county and school board officers, which occur in most other areas.[36] Again, where circumstances create an occupational community, workers must provide a variety of organized services for themselves which

[35] Robert K. Merton, Patricia S. West, and Marie Jahoda, *Patterns of Social Life: Explorations in the Sociology and Social Psychology of Housing* (New York: Bureau of Applied Social Research, mimeographed).

[36] S. M. Lipset, *Agrarian Socialism, op. cit.*, esp. pp. 199–219.

are normally provided by other strata and agencies, and, even more important, they develop their own leaders. This situation makes for high levels of general participation. For example, miners (as we have already noted) must live in communities apart from the rest of society, and their social contacts, whether in church, lodge, school, or town council, are with fellow miners. English mining districts have higher voting rates than any other constituencies in the country, even though these districts often vote Labor by ratios of from three to one to twenty to one.[37]

Related to this factor of high interaction with those with the same background and needs is the development of interest-group organizations devoted specifically to arousing awareness of common problems and organizing participation in politics. In every country businessmen have well-developed organizations, and a large part of the press represents their viewpoint. Workers are by no means always so well organized. The American worker, for instance, even when he is a union member, is seldom exposed to as much propaganda and persuasion to take an interest in politics as is the businessman, and he votes much less.

Moreover, the normal operation of the social structure intensifies the intra-class communications network of the higher strata and weakens in-group communications further down the class ladder. In every country for which we have data, half or more of the adult population does not belong to any formal organization other than trade-unions. But within each country, those higher up in the social structure are much more likely to belong to organizations than those below them. Among Americans interviewed in 1955, in the lowest of five socioeconomic classes only 8 per cent belonged to any organization, as contrasted with 82 per cent in the highest class. That the more privileged are more involved in organizational activities has been found in every comparison between higher and lower status, whether the difference is between occupational strata, different educational levels, income, owners and

[37] H. G. Nicholas, *The British General Election of 1950* (London: Macmillan, 1951), pp. 42, 61, 318.

renters, or those employing servants as compared with those who do not.[38]

The fact that membership in nonpolitical voluntary associations is class-linked has important political consequences. W. Lloyd Warner has documented the crucial role of these associations in linking the citizen to other community institutions.[39] A recent Finnish study has shown the cumulative effect of involvement in any kind of activity. Those participating in one specific type of organization were more likely to be active in others, to attend political meetings, to read more, to have more friends and so on.[40] In Germany, according to a 1953 survey, those who belonged to various associations, such as sports clubs, social clubs, and so forth, were more interested in politics, listened to political radio programs more, read more newspapers, and intended to vote in greater numbers within every stratum.[41] Among the German male workers, for example, 83 per cent of those who belonged to associations other than trade-unions were voters as contrasted with 72 per cent among those who did not belong to an association.

The mechanisms through which participation in nonpo-

[38] See Herbert H. Hyman and Charles Wright, "Voluntary Association Membership of American Adults: Evidence from National Sample Surveys," *American Sociological Review*, 23 (1958), pp. 288–89. Numerous national and local studies, some of which are cited in the Hyman and Wright article, and others mentioned on p. 53 of this book show the same pattern. For example, a Columbia sociologist, Mirra Komarovsky, has collected data in New York City which indicate that well over 80 per cent of both men and women whose occupational status is professional belong to voluntary associations, as contrasted with 32 per cent among men and 9 per cent among women at the unskilled labor level. See Mirra Komarovsky, "The Voluntary Associations of Urban Dwellers," *American Sociological Review*, 9 (1946), p. 688.

[39] W. L. Warner and Paul S. Lunt, *The Social Life of a Modern Community* (New Haven: Yale University Press, 1941), p. 301.

[40] See Erik Allardt, P. Jartti, F. Jyrkila, and Y. Littunen, "On the Cumulative Nature of Leisure Activities," *Acta Sociologica*, 3, No. 4 (1958), pp. 165–72. Unfortunately, the authors did not include any information on the class backgrounds of the members of their sample.

[41] Juan Linz, *op. cit.*, pp. 804–5.

litical groups activates political involvement are many, but one suggested by the authors of the first major survey-type election study, *The People's Choice*, warrants elaboration. They point out that a certain minority of the population are "opinion leaders"—individuals whose greater knowledge, interest, and personality make them influential among their friends and acquaintances. Contact with an opinion leader is more important than exposure to formal propaganda in its effect on political behavior. Opinion leaders are to be found disproportionately among the better educated and more well to do, and also tend to be more active in associations of all kinds. Hence one would expect that members of organizations would be likely to be exposed to a political opinion leader, someone who is knowledgeable and opinionated, and has the same social background as their own. And since a larger proportion of middle-class persons than workers take an active interest in politics, nonpolitical middle-class clubs should contain more politically interested individuals than most workers' organizations. There is in fact much evidence that involvement in organizations has more positive effect on political activity among the middle class than among the workers.[42] Among manual workers, only trade-unions (which have a professional cadre of politically interested leaders) have a strong effect on participation.[43]

In many European countries class-conscious political movements like Communism and socialism have created an organized subculture which cuts workers off from the rest of the

[42] Paul F. Lazarsfeld, Bernard Berelson, and Hazel Gaudet, *op. cit.*, p. 146; A. Campbell and R. L. Kahn, *op. cit.*, pp. 24–28. See also S. M. Lipset, M. Trow, and J. S. Coleman, *op. cit.*, pp. 97–105 for elaboration of this thesis.

[43] In Germany, where the Christian Democratic party attempts to be the spokesman of both Catholicism and Protestantism, whether Catholics or Protestants attend church affects their political participation considerably. The Protestant men in a 1953 survey who attended church regularly voted at the rate of 92 per cent; those who attended irregularly, 90 per cent; seldom, 81 per cent; and never, 80 per cent. Similar differences were found between active and inactive Catholic men, and both Protestant and Catholic women. See E. Reigrotzki, *op. cit.*, pp. 69–70.

society. Parties of integration have attempted to organize
completely the lives of workers by having them belong to
party-controlled unions, live in workers' co-operative housing,
belong to party-aligned sports and social clubs, attend cultural
and musical activities sponsored by the party or the unions,
and read party newspapers and magazines. Children are supposed to grow up belonging to party youth groups. Where
such conditions have had some success, the usual class differential in voting turnout has been entirely eliminated or
even reversed. In Vienna before 1934, for instance, no less
than 94 per cent of the workers turned out to vote in crucial
elections, and in the working-class districts of Berlin the turnout has exceeded 90 per cent, surpassing the voting record
of the businessmen, professionals, and white-collar workers.
Similar results have been reported for France where the
Communist party has organized the lives of many workers.[44]

Occupationally determined activities affect not only the
individual's participation in the organized communications
network of society, and hence his consciousness of political
issues, but also his ability to engage in political activity. Max
Weber pointed out that the lawyer's work, for instance, gives
him not only the skills which we have already discussed but
also the time necessary to be politically active, while the physician's is so demanding of time that it is difficult for him to
participate.[45] Weber's thesis refers to the more active levels

[44] For Vienna see H. Tingsten, *op. cit.*, p. 154; for Berlin see
Stephanie Munke and A. R. L. Gurland, *Wahlkampf und Machtverschiebung: Geschichte und Analyse der Berliner Wahlen von 3 Dezember, 1950* (Berlin: Institut für Politische Wissenschaft, Duncker
und Humbolt, 1952), pp. 175–76. For comparable French findings
see Jean Stoetzel, "Voting Behavior in France," *British Journal of
Sociology*, 6 (1955), p. 115. See also Maximilian Meyer, "Der
Nichtwähler," *Allgemeines Statistisches Archiv*, 21 (1931), pp.
520–21.

[45] Max Weber, "Politics as a Vocation," in his *Essays in Sociology*,
edited by H. H. Gerth and C. W. Mills (New York: Oxford University Press, 1946), pp. 83 ff. In discussing politics as a vocation
Weber suggests that the professional politician must also be economically "dispensable," that is, his income must not depend primarily on his ability to hold public office.

of participation, but it must be remembered that even the limited act of voting is not just a matter of spending an hour going to the polls, but is—for the interested voters at least—an outgrowth of spending much more time in reading, listening, and thinking about politics. Leisure-time activities (as we have seen) are important in developing political awareness. But certain occupations provide very little either actual leisure time or, even more important, *psychic* leisure time free of anxieties that can be devoted to nonpersonal problems. These are occupations which on the whole also provide the least mental stimulation during working hours. The manual or clerical worker or the poor peasant who must work long regular hours to earn his living cannot be as politically active as those with more security and flexible working hours —the trade-union officer, the journalist, or (the extreme case of the man who has practically nothing to do) the *rentier*, who has played such an important role in the politics of England. The low participation of the very poor—impoverished peasants or unemployed workers—is partly attributable to the struggle for existence which leaves no energy for "investment" in political activity, the results of which are in any case dubious.[46] Genevieve Knupfer points out in her summary of the major findings on the social situation of the lower strata that their lower availability for politics reflects a deeper isolation from extra-familial concerns and activities. Lower-class individuals have fewer friends and a narrower geographic range of social contacts than those in higher strata; they read few books and magazines, and consume less of the "serious"

[46] For an excellent description of the way in which extreme poverty reduces the motivation to participate in any kind of community or political activity see Edward Banfield, *The Moral Basis of a Backward Society* (Glencoe: The Free Press, 1958). The various studies of unemployment also illustrate how economic insecurity sharply reduces the energies which people have to give to politics. See the earlier discussion on p. 192 in this chapter. W. Mattes, *Die Bayerischen Bauernräte: Eine Soziologische und Historische Untersuchung uber bauerliche Politik* (Munchener Volkswirtschaftliche Studien, No. 144) (Stuttgart: J. G. Cotta'sche Buchhandlung Nachfolger, 1921) discusses the limits on peasant participation in politics.

materials which would contribute to a deeper involvement in the polity. I have already pointed out in discussing working-class authoritarianism that low status appears to isolate people from involvement in the larger culture, and restricts their attention to the more trivial aspects of life.[47]

In addition to the situation of low-status occupational groups, the position of the married woman illustrates the problem of available time or dispensability as a determinant of political activity. The sheer demands on a housewife and mother mean that she has little opportunity or need to gain politically relevant experiences. Women might thus be expected to have less concern with politics, and in almost every country they do vote less than men.[48] However, those women who are freed from some of the burdens of the housewife should come closer to approximating the political role of men. Middle- and upper-class American wives have fewer children and more servants and labor-saving devices, and thus have the time to participate in formal and informal activities with women in their own stratum. The tens of thousands of women's clubs are for the most part composed of middle- and upper-class women. The sociologists W. Lloyd Warner and Paul S. Lunt in their study of "Yankee City" found that in the three highest social classes more women than men were active in associations, a pattern which was reversed among the lower strata. The Swedish political scientist Herbert Tingsten has reported that in different European countries middle-class women participated politically to much the same extent as did the men in their stratum and that,

[47] Genevieve Knupfer, "Portrait of the Underdog," *Public Opinion Quarterly*, 11 (1947), pp. 103–14. See also Roger Girod, "Facteurs de l'abstentionnisme en Suisse," *Revue française de science politique*, 3 (1953), pp. 349–76.

[48] See H. Tingsten, *op. cit.*, p. 229; the previously cited 1957 Norwegian election survey; R. S. Milne and H. C. Mackenzie, *Marginal Seat: 1955* (London: The Hansard Society for Parliamentary Government, 1958), p. 69; Gabriele Bremme, *op. cit.*, pp. 231–39; Mattei Dogan and Jacques Narbonne, "L'abstentionnisme electoral en France," *Revue française de science politique*, 4 (1954), pp. 6–11; and Maurice Duverger, *op. cit.*, pp. 15–20 and 26–46.

as in America, working-class women showed the lowest voting rates.[49] In Finland, where the Swedish-speaking population as a group is disproportionately well to do as compared to the Finnish majority, Swedish women have a higher rate of turnout than do the Finnish men.[50]

If increased leisure or flexible working hours facilitate political participation, a constant decrease in the length of the work week should result in higher levels of participation. Many nineteenth-century reformers had great hopes for the increased interest and sophistication of the masses in political matters. The sociologists Robert and Helen Lynd, writing in 1929, pointed out, however, that electoral participation was actually decreasing, and suggested that politics could no longer adequately compete as an entertainment form with new commercial ventures—movies, radio, commercial sports—and that politics has lost one of its major functions.[51] The political scientist Robert E. Lane, writing thirty years later, suggests that this trend has not continued, that the "proportion of the eligible voters making use of their franchise declined from the post-Civil War election of 1876 to 1928 when the trend (interrupted by the war) was reversed, and this proportion shows a tendency to increase."[52] However, the evidence of long-term trends in voting or other levels of participation is not very satisfactory because of deficiencies in the data.

Group Pressure to Vote

Even if people are not aware of a personal stake in the electoral decision, they may still be induced to vote by so-

[49] W. L. Warner and P. S. Lunt, *op. cit.*, pp. 337–38; H. Tingsten, *op. cit.*, pp. 146–47. See also Gabriele Bremme, *op. cit.*, p. 53; and Maurice Duverger, *op. cit.*, p. 40.

[50] Erik Allardt, *Social Struktur och Politisk Aktivitet* (Helsingfors: Söderstrom and Co., 1955), p. 38. These data are also presented in less detail in E. Allardt and K. Bruun, *op. cit.*, pp. 55–76.

[51] R. S. Lynd and H. M. Lynd, *Middletown* (New York: Harcourt, Brace & Co., 1929), pp. 416–20.

[52] Robert E. Lane, *op. cit.*, p. 26.

cial pressures and inner feelings of social obligation. The variations in voting behavior which correlate with socioeconomic class may also be related to different degrees of conformity to the dominant norms in various societies. Almost every study of social behavior indicates that conformity to these norms is related to social status. Kinsey has shown the wide variations between middle-class and working-class sexual behavior, with the middle class being much more conventional in its behavior.[53] Attitudes toward corruption and crime also vary with class position. Lower-class persons, for example, tend to be much more tolerant of corruption than do middle-class persons.[54] Attitudes toward the intrinsic worth of hard work and study also vary with class position. In general, middle-class people tend to conform more to the dominant values of the society, and to accept the notion that this conformity will be rewarded by attaining one's personal goals.[55]

Attitudes to politics should not differ much from these general patterns. We should expect being "a good citizen" and "exercising one's duty to vote" to be associated with a middle-class outlook; cynicism or apathy about politics to be related to nonconformity in other areas. The worker who does not anticipate being rewarded for good work is also not likely to anticipate reward for being a good citizen. The force of middle-class norms of behavior is notoriously less in groups that are deprived of middle-class living standards and social acceptance. The low voting rate of very low income groups that occurs in the United States may be part of this general pattern. The extremely low turnout of Negroes, even in the North, may partly reflect the weakness of social conformity

[53] A. C. Kinsey, W. B. Pomeroy, and C. E. Martin, *Sexual Behavior in the Human Male* (Philadelphia: Saunders, 1948).

[54] See Jerome S. Bruner and S. J. Korchin, "The Boss and the Vote: Case Study in City Politics," *Public Opinion Quarterly*, 10 (1946), pp. 8–9, 22. Mayor Curley of Boston, a convicted criminal, received heavy lower-class support, as this study showed.

[55] See Robert K. Merton, "Social Structure and Anomie," in his *Social Theory and Social Structure* (Glencoe: The Free Press, 2d ed., 1956), pp. 131–61.

norms among a group which is denied the normal rewards of conformity.[56]

Besides the general social norm of voting as "good citizenship," there are many interest groups which demand that their members turn out to vote for the good of the group. Thus the high turnout of European working-class districts probably depends a good deal on the existence of such groups, while the low turnout generally found among American workers may reflect the fact that they have not developed integrated class institutions and intense political norms of their own. It has already been noted that workers who belong to unions have a much higher turnout than workers who are nonmembers,[57] and political machines in poor urban districts in America have traditionally appealed to ethnic- and religious-group solidarity as a way of exerting pressure to vote.[58]

Such conformity-pressures obviously depend on the amount of contact an individual has with the dominant social groups. Comparative newcomers in a community, for example, tend to vote less than long-time residents—a fact which has been reported for many communities in the United States, Switzerland, Finland, and England.[59] The same factor may

[56] E. H. Litchfield, "A Case Study of Negro Political Behavior in Detroit," *Public Opinion Quarterly*, 5 (1941), pp. 267–74; Gunnar Myrdal, *An American Dilemma* (New York: Harper & Bros., 1944), pp. 493–94. See also Bureau of Applied Social Research, *Voting Behavior of American Ethnic Groups* (New York: mimeographed, 1946).

[57] For data on the 1954 election in the United States see A. Campbell and H. C. Cooper, *Group Differences in Attitudes and Votes* (Ann Arbor: Survey Research Center, 1956), pp. 31–32. They found that union laborers voted much more than nonunion persons in the same occupations. This was true for 1948, 1952, and 1954. In England, the study of Greenwich found that trade-union members were much more likely to vote than nonunion workers. See M. Benney, A. P. Gray, and R. H. Pear, *op. cit.*, pp. 181–88.

[58] V. O. Key, Jr., *op. cit.*, Chap. 10; F. J. Brown and J. S. Roucek, eds., *One America* (New York: Prentice-Hall, 1945), Chaps. 15–16.

[59] H. Tingsten, *op. cit.*, p. 215; C. E. Merriam and H. F. Gosnell, *op. cit.*, pp. 31 ff.; B. C. Arneson, "Non-Voting in a Typical Ohio

contribute to the lower voting of young people (discussed later), who have not yet taken a place in the organized social life of the adult community, and of the very old, who are losing their social contacts through retirement, infirmity, and death within their age group.

The highest pressure to vote as a symbol of conformity is found where the objective significance of the vote is least: in totalitarian "show" elections. In Nazi Germany and the Soviet Union enormous efforts have been devoted to contacting the entire electorate and requiring it to vote. In the 1946 elections to the Supreme Soviet, we are told that 99.7 per cent of the electorate of over 100 million people turned out to vote—99.2 per cent of them for the single official list.[60] If the sense of external threat to American society increases, we may expect an increasing emphasis to be laid on voting as a symbol of loyalty and satisfaction with the existing political system. But unless the increase is accompanied by a corresponding increase in concern with the issues, it will hardly be related to the ideal of rational participation in self-government.

In some cases group pressures are directed against voting. The universally lower vote of women may be due in part to the traditional idea of "women's place." In the United States this does not seem to prevent women who are interested from voting; however, women with little interest feel free not to vote, while similarly disinterested men feel more called upon to go to the polls.[61] In parts of the American South today

Community," *American Political Science Review*, 19 (1925), pp. 816–25; A. H. Birch, "The Habit of Voting," *The Manchester School of Economic and Social Studies*, 18 (1950), pp. 75–82; R. Girod, *op. cit.*, p. 368; E. Allardt and K. Bruun, *op. cit.*, p. 75; Charles H. Titus, *Voting Behavior in the United States* (Berkeley: University of California Press, 1935), p. 68. See also Robert E. Lane, *op. cit.*, pp. 267–69.

[60] J. Towster, *Political Power in the U.S.S.R.—1917–1947* (New York: Oxford University Press, 1948), p. 197.

[61] P. F. Lazarsfeld, B. Berelson, and Hazel Gaudet, *op. cit.*, pp. 48–49; Alice Kitt and D. B. Gleicher, "Determinants of Voting Behavior," *Public Opinion Quarterly*, 14 (1950), pp. 393–412.

the norms laid down by the dominant white group for the behavior of Negroes include a prohibition on voting.[62]

Another type of norm opposing voting occurs in some extreme, radical groups which urge abstention as a protest against "bourgeois democracy." "Voting means accepting slavery" was the theme of an intensive campaign of the Spanish Anarcho-syndicalist National Confederation of Workers, which comprised more than half of the organized workers, in the Spanish elections of 1933. Nonvoting as a means of protest has often been used in "semi-free" elections by the opposition. Similarly in plebiscites in which none of the alternatives was considered acceptable, massive nonvoting has sometimes appeared as a way of expressing political opinions.

Within groups where the norms oppose voting, the usual situation is reversed: the conformists become the nonvoters, and the nonconformists—the "nonclass-conscious worker," the "Negro who doesn't know his place,"—the voters.

Cross-pressures

In general, the more pressures brought to bear on individuals or groups which operate in opposing directions, the more likely are prospective voters to withdraw from the situation by "losing interest" and not making a choice. The first intensive American study of how the voter makes up his mind (employing the "panel" method of repeated interviews over time with the same sample) reported that "many voters subject to cross-pressures tended to belittle the whole affair. They escaped from any real conflict by losing interest in the election. . . . Those with no cross-pressures showed most interest in the election; even one cross-pressure meant a substantial increase in the proportion of voters who felt less interested in the election. And as the number of cross-pressures in-

[62] J. Dollard, *Caste and Class in a Southern Town* (New York: Harper & Bros., 1937); G. Myrdal, *op. cit.,* Chap. 22. The report, released in September, 1959, of President Eisenhower's Civil Rights Commission, further documents this continuing prohibition.

creases the degree of interest shows a steady decline."[63]
Studies of elections in America and Great Britain have shown
comparable findings.[64] An interview study of the members
of a trade-union in which Communist and Catholic factions
were contesting for power reported the same results. Those
union members who were actually reached by propaganda
from both sides reacted by refusing to make a choice between
them.[65]

Perhaps the most striking evidence that political cross-
pressures pulling individuals toward different parties make
some people politically impotent comes from a German study
of void ballots. Ballots are voided when a voter marks his
ballot for two parties rather than one. If such "errors" were
a result of accident or ignorance of how to vote, then the
two parties which were marked on the same ballots should
have been more or less randomly distributed. An examination of such ballots in Bavaria found, however, that when
people voted for two parties, they almost invariably voted
for two which were ideologically relatively close to each other.
Thus a void ballot marked for the Social Democrats would
usually also be marked either by a vote for a small left-wing
party, immediately to the left of the socialists, or for the
Christian Democrats, immediately to the right of them. Similarly, most of the void ballots marked for the Christian Democrats were also marked for the Social Democrats just to the
left (43 per cent) or for the Bavarian Farmers' party (31 per

[63] P. F. Lazarsfeld, B. Berelson, and Hazel Gaudet, *op. cit.*, p. 62.
As was already noted in Chap. 3, p. 77 the cross-pressure theory
was first advanced over fifty years ago by the German sociologist,
Georg Simmel. Its first detailed application to voting research may
be found in the work of Herbert Tingsten, in his "law of the social
center of gravity," in which he shows that the participation of a
group rises with the strength of the group in a given district. See
H. Tingsten, *op. cit.*, pp. 230–31. For a summary of recent American
work using this thesis, see Robert E. Lane, *op. cit.*, pp. 197–203.

[64] B. Berelson, P. F. Lazarsfeld, and W. McPhee, *op. cit.*, pp.
27, 130–31; M. Benney, A. P. Gray, and R. H. Pear, *op. cit.*, pp.
178–82; S. J. Korchin, *op. cit.*, Chap. V.

[65] Martin Kriesberg, "Cross-Pressures and Attitudes," *Public Opinion Quarterly*, 13 (1949), pp. 5–16.

cent) just to the right. The more conservative Farmers' party void votes also contained votes for the Christian Democrats on their left (47 per cent) or the German party on their right (13 per cent). Most of these void ballots thus contained a second vote which was for the closest party to the right or the left, indicating that these were not the result of errors, but reflected the inability of some voters to decide between two parties that strongly appealed to them.[66]

The cross-pressures hypothesis may help to account for some of the differences in the behavior of various groups cited earlier. For example, we know that workers tend to vote less than middle- and upper-class people, and that even in countries like Great Britain, where the differences between the classes in voting rates is not so great as in America, there is still a considerable variation in the degree of interest and involvement in politics. Thus a British panel study found a spread of from 34 per cent of the lowest classes to 71 per cent of the upper classes in the proportion interested in the elections.[67] These differences may be due in part to the fact that the lower strata in every society are influenced by their life experiences and their class organizations to favor those parties which advocate social and economic reforms, but at the same time they are exposed to strong upper-class and conservative influences through the press, radio, schools, churches, and so forth. Though their social and economic inferiority predisposes them against the *status quo*, the existing system has many traditional claims to legitimacy which influence them. The lower strata are, therefore, placed in a situation of not only less but also conflicting information, and of opposing group pressures.

Members of the more well-to-do classes, on the other hand, are seldom exposed to equivalent sets of cross-pressures. They live in a relatively "homogeneous political environment,"

[66] R. Schachtner, "Wahlbereditigte, Wahlbetelligung, Nichtwahler und Falschwahler," *Bayern in Zahlen: Monatshefte des Bayerischen Statistischen Amtes*, January 1952, pp. 18–21.

[67] M. Benney, A. P. Gray and R. H. Pear, *op. cit.*, p. 127.

where all influences point in one political direction. While
in most countries the majority of the workers read newspapers opposed to trade-unions and workers' parties, the businessmen of every country read newspapers which reiterate
their basic political opinions.[68]

The sheer operation of the values of a stratified and yet
open society may reduce the political effectiveness of the
lower classes by increasing the objective cross-pressures upon
them. Although lower-class individuals see political issues as
members of an underprivileged group, they are also exposed
to the dominant values of the society through mass communications and are able (at least in certain open societies)
to aspire to higher positions within the social structure. They
are faced with the need of reconciling lower-class norms with
the conflicting sets of values that correspond to the political
and social position of the dominant class. Unless the social
structure isolates them from these cross-class values, they
should be more politically apathetic than upper-class groups
who do not face such a conflict. The latter remain self-con-
fident in their conformity in a conflict-free political environment. As Gunnar Myrdal describes the upper-class situation: "There are closer ties and a more easy understanding between upper class persons. . . . They travel more . . .

[68] See R. S. Milne and H. C. Mackenzie, *Straight Fight* (London:
The Hansard Society, 1956). The authors report that among British
voters, "the number of left-wing papers read by Conservatives was
much smaller than the number of right-wing papers read by Labour
voters" (p. 96).
    In Norway, 69 per cent of all socialist voters regularly read non-
socialist newspapers, 28 per cent do not read any socialist paper.
Among the supporters of the non-socialist parties only 17 per cent
read socialist journals, while over 80 per cent of them read non-
socialist papers. See Stein Rokkan and Per Torsvik, "The Voter, the
Reader, and the Party Press," paper given at Fourth World Congress
of Sociology, Stresa, September 1959. Comparable Swedish findings
are reported by Jörgen Westerståhl and Carl-Gunnar Janson, *Politisk
Press* (Gothenburg: Political Science Institute, 1958), pp. 65, 89,
98. For a general discussion of the problem and statistics see Herbert
Tingsten, "The Press," in J. A. Lauwerys, ed., *Scandinavian Democracy* (Copenhagen: The Danish Institute, 1958), pp. 316–28.

being together on a Pullman train brings people together intimately. They meet constantly for conferences."[69] These differences are another reason for the class differentials in voting turnout. And on a comparative basis we should expect that the more open the class structure of any society, the more politically apathetic its working class should be; and, conversely, the more rigidly stratified a society, the more likely that its lower classes will develop their own strong form of political activity. Those members of the lower strata who are most isolated from contact with middle-class culture or individuals are most likely to be active in the dominant politics of their stratum, while those who are most exposed to cross-class contacts will be least active, interested, and committed. Much of the evidence (some of which has already been presented in other contexts) fits these expectations, such as that dealing with workers in "isolated" industries, in large factories, or in the proletarian districts of large cities, members of "parties of integration" like the pre-1934 Austrian Social Democrats or the Communists, and members of trade-unions.[70]

Districts within cities which are homogeneous, either

[69] G. Myrdal, *op. cit.*, p. 715. In view of the present-day decline in train travel, the contemporary equivalent of the Pullman coach might be the first-class transcontinental airliner, the first-class hotels, and the expensive restaurants which are paid for by expense accounts.

[70] David Truman found in an analysis of survey data in the 1948 U.S. presidential elections that members of the highest socioeconomic classes were most likely to have a homogeneous environment. Among workers, trade-union members had more homogeneous environments than nonunionists, and CIO members were in a more integrated environment than members of the AFL. Since union members on the average work in larger plants and live in larger cities than nonunionists, and CIO members had these characteristics even more than members of the AFL, the sources of their greater homogeneity cannot be credited solely or even primarily to the union's structuring of the environment. Nevertheless, all of these differentials are congruent with our theoretical anticipation. See David Truman, "Political Behavior and Voting," in F. Mosteller, H. Hyman, P. McCarthy, E. Marks, and D. Truman, *The Pre-Election Polls of 1948* (New York: Social Science Research Council, Bulletin No. 60, 1949), pp. 229–30.

largely working class or middle class in Vienna, Amsterdam, Basel, Berlin, Helsinki, parts of Britain, and Norway have a much higher vote than those with a "mixed" population, as various studies made from 1920–57 have reported.[71] The frequently reported low voting record of individuals employed in personal and domestic service, and of farm workers on family farms is perhaps an illustration of the extreme case fitting the pattern. Such workers, though low in status and pay, are also among the least integrated within their class, and most in direct contact with high status individuals.[72]

Several examples from studies of voting in Finland reinforce the cross-pressure hypothesis. Finland is a country with an upper-class Swedish minority, and the sociologist Erik Allardt found that voting districts in which the Swedish-speaking proportion of the population was over 75 per cent had a consistently higher rate of turnout than ethnically mixed or predominantly Finnish districts.[73] Districts with strong political traditions, i.e., districts where the majority was either conservative or leftist both in 1917 and after 1945, had a consistently higher rate of turnout than districts in which conservative and leftist parties had intermittent majorities.[74] Also, districts with one strongly dominating political party had higher rates of voting than districts where several equally strong parties were competing.

The cross-pressure hypothesis also helps account for the differences between the voting of men and women. There is evidence that women in most societies are more conservative and more religious than men, with these differences most accentuated on the working-class level. Such variations in the

---

[71] For Vienna, Amsterdam, and Basel see H. Tingsten, *op. cit.*, pp. 126–27, 155–57; for Berlin see Stephanie Munke and A. R. L. Gurland, *op. cit.*, pp. 175–76; for Britain see D. E. Butler, *op. cit.*, p. 208; for Helsinki see Erik Allardt, *op. cit.*, p. 136. Data from the unpublished 1957 survey in Norway, already cited, also bear out this point.

[72] See M. Meyer, *op. cit.*, pp. 520–21; H. Tingsten, *op. cit.*, pp. 62, 120–81, *passim*; R. Girod, *op. cit.*, esp. Table V.

[73] Erik Allardt, *op. cit.*, p. 34; E. Allardt and K. Bruun, *op. cit.*

[74] Erik Allardt, *op. cit.*, p. 52.

values of the sexes may flow from varying life experiences. Husbands are more exposed, in both their work and their leisure activities, to the modal or predominant opinion of their class. Women, particularly housewives, are less involved in the intra-class communications structure, see fewer politically knowledgeable people with backgrounds and interests similar to their own, and are therefore more likely to retain the dominant conservative values of the larger culture. A second factor which may operate to make working-class women more conservative than their men is the fact that their strong family concerns make them the more status-conscious sex. As Robert and Helen Lynd have pointed out in their *Middletown* books, women are the carriers of the dominant cultural and status values. Concern with status means largely concern with the values and practices of the social class or group immediately above one's own, a class which is likely to have more conservative values than one's own. Thus working-class women are pushed to the left by their class position and the values their husbands bring home from the factory, but are pushed to the right by these other elements in their experience, and hence will be more under cross-pressures than their husbands, and more likely to withdraw completely from political decision.

In European countries like France and Austria, where most working-class men back anticlerical leftist parties, their often religious wives are faced with a conflict between voting with their church or with their class and their husbands. This vivid and not uncommon conflict situation undoubtedly contributes greatly to the low voting rates of working-class women.[75]

Mobility, whether residential, social, or job, should also decrease involvement in politics, since the various types of mobility both reduce the extent to which individuals are engaged in different forms of activity, and increase the pos-

[75] In France, however, those working-class women who do vote are more likely to vote like their husbands than are middle-class women. See Maurice Duverger, *La participation des femmes à la vie politique, op. cit.*, pp. 47–48.

sibility that they will be exposed to politically relevant cross-pressures. Evidence showing that newcomers to an area are much less likely to vote than old residents has already been cited.[76] Research studies of activity in American trade-unions provide data that workers who have changed their residence or job recently are also less likely to be active in their unions than are workers who have remained in one community and on one job for a length of time.[77]

But while the negative effect of job and residential mobility on voting may reflect only in part heightened cross-pressures on those involved, social mobility both upward and downward, together with the hopes which many individuals have of improving their position in the future, should increase political cross-pressures and reduce interest in politics. Persons moving up or down the occupational ladder are likely to enter social groups with a different political orientation from the one which they left. And data from a number of election surveys in the United States, Germany, Sweden, Finland, and Norway indicate that "children in the same [social class] group as their fathers cast a higher vote than children in a different group than their fathers."[78]

Belief in the possibility of future upward mobility may

[76] See footnote 59, p. 209, for references.

[77] See S. M. Lipset and Joan Gordon, "Mobility and Trade Union Membership," in R. Bendix and S. M. Lipset, eds., *Class, Status, and Power* (Glencoe: The Free Press, 1953), pp. 491–500.

[78] The quote is from Erik Allardt and K. Bruun, *op. cit.*, p. 76. Data on the mobility of Finnish voters indicate that mobile persons vote less, consistent with the cross-pressure hypothesis. Eighty per cent of the respondents in the same occupational group as their fathers voted, but only 65 per cent of those in a different stratum. Both downward and upward mobility had this effect, but the persons in a lower occupational group than their father's voted far less. Fifty-three per cent of the workers with white-collar fathers voted (as compared with 78 per cent of the workers with worker-fathers), and 72 per cent of the white-collar persons with worker-fathers voted (as compared with 84 per cent of the white-collar people with white-collar fathers). For further references and data bearing on studies in other countries, see S. M. Lipset and R. Bendix, *Social Mobility in Industrial Society* (Berkeley: University of California Press, 1959), pp. 66–70.

also serve to reduce political activity since those oriented upward may be more influenced by the values and patterns of behavior in the class into which they hope to move, than those who accept their current status as relatively permanent. The hope of changing one's class is strongest among young people, and everywhere they have the lowest electoral turnout. But there are other sources of cross-pressures in the situation of young, particularly first voters, and a discussion of these will further illustrate both the usefulness of the cross-pressure hypothesis and also the problem of attempting to relate behavior determined by a multitude of interacting and conflicting factors to those particular variables which interest the social analyst at the moment.

The youth entering the voting age faces a different situation than the rest of the electorate does since he must make his decision for the first time; he cannot vote as he did in the previous election as do the majority of voters in every country. If we may assume, therefore, that first-voters are in a conflict situation, this may account for the relatively low-voting record of this group everywhere. It also follows that those first-voters with no major source of cross-pressures will be most likely to vote. If the decision is already made, in a sense, for the first-voter by his environment, he will vote; if he is faced with conflict, he is likely to delay reaching a decision. Two studies made in very different environments bear this out. One is the study of the 1948 U.S. presidential election conducted in the strongly Republican upstate New York city of Elmira; the other is a study of the 1950 election in West Berlin, a city which has been dominated by the Socialists ever since 1912, with the exception of the Nazi period.

In Elmira, a middle-class youth grows up in an environment in which everything operates to make him a Republican, while a working-class youth receives Democratic stimuli from his class background and Republican pressure from his exposure to the predominant sentiments and institutions of the community. In Berlin, a working-class young voter is exposed to a strongly organized and socially legitimate socialist environment, while a middle-class youth grows up in an environment in which the middle classes and their parties have remained relatively weak. Table III presents the relations between age, class, and nonvoting in the two cities. From it we see, first of all, that young people are less likely to vote than older ones. Second, when class position is considered, the size of the difference between younger and older voters varies with their class. The nature of this variation differs sharply in the two cities, however. In one context, socialist Berlin, the gap between age groups is wide in the middle class and narrow in the working class; in Republican Elmira, the relationship is just the opposite. In Elmira, the middle-class youth has his mind made up for him; in Berlin it is the working-class first-voter who is in that situation.

Although the data in Table III tend to validate the hypothesis that youth will vote when the decision is made for it by a homogeneous environment and will postpone voting when exposed to conflicting stimuli, even among working-class Berliners and middle-class Elmirans young people vote less than those who are thirty or over. One further explanation for this is that young people just coming to voting age are also establishing new families, finding their way into new jobs, new neighborhoods, and new associations, all of which produce political inconsistencies and conflicts. More of a young person's close associates tend to have conflicting opinions than an older person's, since older people have had a chance to establish a homogeneous environment, either by selecting similar friends and associates or by adjusting to the predominant viewpoint around them. The Elmira study reports that only half of the first-voters agree with the politics of their three best friends, and as many as 30 per cent disagree with two or all three of them. In the group aged thirty-five to forty-four, 75 per cent agree with their three best friends and only 10 per cent disagree with two or more friends.[79] A French study reports that among those over fifty years of age husbands and wives voted alike in 97 per

[79] B. Berelson, P. F. Lazarsfeld, and W. McPhee, *op. cit.*, pp. 96–97.

cent of the cases, as compared with 80 per cent among those under fifty.[80]

The almost universal difference between single and mar-

TABLE III

PERCENTAGES VOTING IN ELMIRA AND IN BERLIN*

Elmira—1948

Birth Year	Age	Business and White-collar	Wage Workers
1927–1924	21–24	74	35
1923–1914	25–34	75	65
1913–1894	35–54	85	79
1893 or earlier	55 +	80	82

Berlin—1950†

		Working-class district Tiergarten	Middle and upper-class district Zehlendorf
1930	20	88.9	67.0
1929	21	92.3	71.8
1928	22	90.9	74.3
1927	23	90.9	72.7
1926	24	92.9	76.7
1925–1921	25–29	92.7	77.5
1920–1916	30–34	94.3	81.7
1915–1911	35–39	94.7	84.9
1910–1906	40–44	95.1	88.4
1905–1901	45–49	94.9	89.0
	All Ages	94.1	85.3

* S. Munke and A. R. L. Gurland, *Wahlkampf und Machtverschiebung: Geschichte und Analyse der Berliner Wahlen von 3 Dezember, 1950* (Berlin: Institut für Politische Wissenschaft, Duncker und Humbolt, 1952), pp. 254–55; unpublished data from study reported in B. Berelson *et al.*, *Voting* (Chicago: University of Chicago Press, 1954).

† Other working-class districts are similar to Tiergarten, and other middle-class districts are similar to Zehlendorf.

[80] Maurice Duverger, *op. cit.*, p. 48.

ried people—the former vote less than the latter—may, like
the age differences to which it is linked, reflect lesser cross-
pressures among the married, who have a more stable existence, more homogeneous ties in the community, and,
especially among the workers, less geographic and social mobility.[81]

From the above propositions and empirical findings, it is
possible to deduce another fact about first-voters—that they
will be more likely to exhibit "hereditary" voting patterns,
that is, to vote as their fathers do, than older groups of voters,
and if they are pressed to disagree, they will not vote. This
hypothesis is borne out by the data which report a higher
congruence between father's vote and the vote of first-voters
than for any other age group.[82]

This discussion of cross-pressures has attempted to illustrate the utility of the concept to account for a wide variety
of different empirical observations. As I have indicated, it is
often possible to account for any specific difference by an
alternative explanation. "Cross-pressures" is an appealing explanation since it is a relatively simple concept and requires
few assumptions. A more direct test of its usefulness has been
made, however, by estimating the extent to which different
individuals are exposed to objective and subjective cross-pressures. Two American scholars, Morris Janowitz and Dwaine
Marvick, reanalyzed a survey study of the 1952 presidential
elections and devised a measure of cross-pressures from residence, socioeconomic status, and religion (all objective meas-

[81] This is not a "fictitious" finding. It holds regardless of other
factors. In Stavanger, a city in Norway, in 1957, even within a low-
voting working-class ward, married men and women voted more
than the average—80 per cent against 76 per cent. The lowest percentage of voters occurred among the separated and divorced (53
per cent of the men, 63 per cent of the women), less than among
single people. (See the already cited unpublished Norwegian survey.)
Tingsten sums up his comprehensive survey of election statistics
bearing on this point with the observation that "the married show
more active political interest than the unmarried." *Op. cit.*, p. 229.
See also G. Bremme, *op. cit.*, pp. 56–58.

[82] B. Berelson, P. F. Lazarsfeld, and W. McPhee, *op. cit.*, pp.
88–93.

ures of a Democratic or Republican predisposition) and also from party identification, attitudes on campaign issues, and attitudes toward the candidates (subjective measures). Respondents were then ranked from an extremely high Republican predisposition through varying degrees of cross-pressure to a high Democratic predisposition. These measures predicted the behavior of those on the two extremes with a high degree of accuracy. Thus 95 per cent of those under consistent Eisenhower pressure actually voted for him on Election Day, while 80 per cent of those under similar Stevenson pressure cast their ballots for him. Between these extremes, increasing cross-pressures regularly decreased the relevant party vote. Nonvoting also increased regularly with increasing cross-pressures, rising to a high of 37 per cent among those under the most conflicting pressures.[83]

The convergence of all the various causal factors which have been discussed in this chapter is strikingly shown by data on nonvoting in the city of Stavanger, Norway, in a 1957 election. Information on the entire electorate was available for sex, age, marital status, and occupation, all variables which have been shown to affect rates of voting independently. As the analysis here presented calls for, extremely high rates of nonvoting (54 per cent) occurred among the unmarried service workers under thirty years of age. These are precisely the persons least exposed to social pressures to vote, most exposed to interpersonal cross-pressures and contacts with those holding higher-class political values, least exposed to information about the relevance of government policies to their position, and least trained (by experience) in political knowledge and skills. Conversely, only 2.5 per cent of the married male professionals and business managers over sixty-five, the group with the most awareness, knowledge, experience, and social pressure on it, failed to vote.[84]

These data by themselves do not demonstrate the validity of the generalized explanations suggested in this chapter. Nevertheless, the way in which some order (explanation)

[83] Morris Janowitz and Dwaine Marvick, *op. cit.*, p. 94.
[84] From the unpublished Norwegian study cited earlier.

Table IV

Social Factors Related to Rates of Voting Turnout

Awareness of relevance due to:

	Relevance of government policies	Direct visibility	Training, job experience	Contact, communication	Amount of leisure	Social pressure to vote	Absence of cross-pressure	Voting rate
High income	+	+	+	+	+	+	+	Higher
Low income	+	−	−	−	−	−	−	Lower
Miners	+	−	−	+	−	+	+	Higher
Servants	−	−	−	−	−	−	−	Lower
Workers in Europe	+	−	−	+		+	+	Higher
Workers in America	+	−	−	+		−	−	Lower
Government employees	+	+	+			+	+	Higher
Private employees	+	+				−	−	Lower
Wheat farmers	−	+						Higher
Nonmarket farmers	−							Lower

TABLE IV—continued

Awareness of relevance due to:

	Relevance of government policies	Direct visibility	Training, job experience	Contact, communication	Amount of leisure	Social pressure to vote	Absence of cross-pressure	Voting rate
Jews	+							Higher
Non-Jews	−							Lower
Crisis periods	+							Higher
Normal periods	−							Lower
Whites						+	+	Higher
Negroes						−	−	Lower
Old residents						+	+	Higher
Newcomers						−	−	Lower
Age 35–55			+	+	+	+	+	High
Over 55			−	−	−	−	+	Medium
Under 35						−	−	Low
Men						+	+	Higher
Women						−	−	Lower
Totalitarian "elections"						+		High

NOTE: Plus sign indicates condition relatively more favorable to voting; minus sign, one relatively less favorable, with respect to the groups compared.

can be made of the myriad of voting statistics bears elo-
quent testimony, in my judgment, to the power of sociological analysis, and indicates the need for—and the value of—
far more elaborate and systematic comparative analysis of
political behavior than has been possible here. Table IV presents an attempt at systematization of the factors which have
been discussed in this chapter as they affect different social
groups.

Conclusions

A concern with the social roots of political participation
should not lead us to ignore the consequences of different
levels of participation for the stability of the democratic system. At the beginning of this chapter I pointed out that both
totalitarian states and Communist trade-union leaders within
democratic society are concerned with securing a high rate of
participation among their citizens or members, because this
means that the participants are reachable. One of the most
important differences between a traditional conservative oligarchy or dictatorship and a totalitarian regime is that the
former is relatively unconcerned about participation, while
the latter demands it. David Riesman has perceptively noted
that within a totalitarian society, political apathy may be a
major barrier against the complete triumph of the system.[85]

Democratic societies can exist with different levels of participation, although it is clear that varying consequences flow
from them. Those who believe that democracy is best served
by a high level of participation point to the fact that a democratic state, unlike a traditionalist oligarchy, must depend on
the consent of its citizenry. And a state in which a large part
of the population is apathetic, uninterested, and unaware is
one in which consent cannot be taken for granted and in
which consensus may actually be weak. Secondly, as the political scientist V. O. Key, Jr., has pointed out, when the vote

[85] David Riesman, "Some Observations on the Limits of Totalitarian Power," in his *Individualism Reconsidered* (Glencoe: The
Free Press, 1954), pp. 414–25.

is low, this almost always means that the socially and economically disadvantaged groups are underrepresented in government. The combination of a low vote and a relative lack of organization among the lower-status groups means that they will suffer from neglect by the politicians who will be receptive to the wishes of the more privileged, participating, and organized strata.[86] Lack of participation and representation also reflects lack of effective citizenship and consequent lack of loyalty to the system as a whole.

But while the case for higher levels of participation may seem almost self-evident to believers in democracy, as we have come to know more about the characteristics of nonvoters and the conditions under which nations secure high turnouts, some people have questioned whether high participation actually is a good thing. One school of thought welcomes a low voting rate as evidence of the electorate's basic satisfaction with the way things are going. In 1936, the political scientist Francis Wilson put it this way: "In a society in which only fifty per cent of the electorate participates it is clear that politics does satisfy in a way the desire of the mass of the individuals in the state. As the percentage of participation rises above, let us say, ninety per cent, it is apparent that the tensions of political struggle are stretching to the breaking point the will toward the constitutional."[87] The same point was made a short time later by the foremost analyst of the determinants of political participation, the Swede Herbert Tingsten, in concluding his brilliant survey of voting statistics around the world. He pointed to the extremely high vote in various nations like Germany and Austria at the point when their democracies began to break down, and he suggested that a high turnout was a symptom of the decline of consensus.[88]

[86] V. O. Key, Jr., *Southern Politics, op. cit.*, pp. 526–28; and *Politics, Parties, and Pressure Groups, op. cit.*, pp. 642–43.

[87] Francis G. Wilson, "The Inactive Electorate and Social Revolution," *Southwestern Social Science Quarterly*, 16 (1936), p. 76.

[88] See Herbert Tingsten, *op. cit.*, pp. 225–26; for more recent statements of comparable points of view see W. H. Morris Jones, "In Defense of Apathy," *Political Studies*, 2 (1954), p. 25; D. N. Hogan, *Election and Representation* (Cork: Cork University Press,

David Riesman has argued also that apathy may reflect the fact that people have more interesting things to do with their time than indulge in politics, and suggests that governmental bodies and large-scale organizations function well in spite of great apathy.[89]

Pessimistic conclusions about the effects of an increase in participation may also be reached from the research on the characteristics of nonvoters. As early as 1928, the American political scientist W. B. Munro argued that increased participation might threaten the workings of democracy since nonvoting was largely located among the most ignorant part of the electorate.[90] And subsequent studies based on survey and questionnaire data, some of which are reported or cited in Chapter 4, indicate that nonvoters differ from voters in having authoritarian attitudes, cynical ideas about democracy and political parties, intolerant sentiments on deviant opinions and ethnic minorities, and in preferring strong leaders in government.[91]

Many of the differences between voters and nonvoters are, of course, a by-product of the fact that nonvoting is concentrated among the least educated and poorest social groups. However, these variations in attitudes hold up even when the major social variables which have been found to affect voting turnout—sex, age, religion, education, and income—are controlled. Thus in a study which controlled all of these factors, the psychologist Philip Hastings reported that, compared to the regular voter, the habitual nonvoter withdraws from social activity, is more concerned with "immediate" issues than long-

1945), pp. 275 ff.; Harold F. Gosnell, *Why Europe Votes, op. cit.*, pp. 208 ff.

[89] See Riesman's remarks, in Herman Finer, Granville Hicks, and David Riesman, "Political Apathy in America," *The University of Chicago Round Table*, No. 657 (Oct. 29, 1950), p. 11.

[90] W. B. Munro, "Is the Slacker Vote a Menace?", *National Municipal Review*, 17 (1928), pp. 80–86. And David Riesman has commented that "Bringing sleepwalkers to the polls simply to increase turnout is no service to democracy." David Riesman, "Private People and Public Policy," *Bulletin of the Atomic Scientists*, 15 (1959), p. 205.

[91] See pp. 102–3.

range ones, is "not even willing to think for himself as far as political matters are concerned" (manifested by his willingness to agree with his "superiors" on political matters), and in general exhibits "a personal sense of inadequacy and insecurity."[92]

The evidence confirms Tingsten's thesis that a sudden increase in the size of the voting electorate probably reflects tension and serious governmental malfunctioning and also introduces as voters individuals whose social attitudes are unhealthy from the point of view of the requirements of the democratic system. On the other hand, a high vote is not necessarily bad. Many stable democratic nations—Australia, New Zealand, Great Britain, and the Scandinavian countries —have much higher rates of participation than does the United States. To the extent that the lower strata have been brought into electoral process *gradually* (through increased organization, an upgrading of the educational system, and a growth in their understanding of the relevance of government action to their interests), increased participation is undoubtedly a good thing for democracy. It is only when a major crisis or an effective authoritarian movement suddenly pulls the normally disaffected habitual nonvoters into the political area that the system is threatened. Thus neither high nor low rates of participation and voting are in themselves good or bad for democracy; the extent and nature of that participation reflect other factors which determine far more decisively the system's chances to develop or survive. But the extent of apathy and the varying levels of participation of different segments of the population do clarify the underlying consensus and conflict within the political process. In the next chapter, we turn to a more direct examination of the sources of diversity which underlie continuous electoral conflict— the lifeblood of the entire democratic system.

[92] See Philip K. Hastings, "The Voter and the Non-Voter," *American Journal of Sociology*, 62 (1956), p. 307; for somewhat similar findings in a study based on 70 depth interviews with middle-class persons, see Morris Rosenberg, "Some Determinants of Political Apathy," *Public Opinion Quarterly*, 18 (1954–55), pp. 349–66.

CHAPTER 7

Elections: The Expression of the Democratic Class Struggle[1]

IN EVERY modern democracy conflict among different groups is expressed through political parties which basically represent a "democratic translation of the class struggle." Even though many parties renounce the principle of class conflict or loyalty, an analysis of their appeals and their support suggests that they do represent the interests of different classes. On a world scale, the principal generalization which can be made is that parties are primarily based on either the lower classes or the middle and upper classes. This generalization even holds true for the American parties, which have traditionally been considered an exception to the class-cleavage pattern of Europe. The Democrats from the beginning of their history have drawn more support from the lower strata of the society, while the Federalist, Whig, and Republican parties have held the loyalties of the more privileged groups.[2]

There have been important exceptions to these generalizations, of course, and class is only one of the structural divisions in society which is related to party support. In every

[1] This apt phrase was taken from the title of the book by Dewey Anderson and Percy Davidson, *Ballots and the Democratic Class Struggle* (Stanford: Stanford University Press, 1943). This book and the earlier one by the sociologist Stuart A. Rice, *Quantitative Methods in Politics* (New York: Alfred A. Knopf, 1928) deserve to stand as the first American classics of the political-behavior field. Rice did the first panel (repeat interview) study in 1924, made the first statistical studies of the sources of voting behavior by legislators, and correlated changes in party support over periods of time with changes in the business cycle. Anderson and Davidson also analyzed who among voters changed their party in the early 1930s.

[2] See Chap. 9 for a more detailed analysis of American politics.

country which has more than one important religion, or where there is a distinct difference between religious adherents and secularists, religious differences have contributed to the support of one party or another. In some countries religious belief has formed the basis for the formation of religious political parties, dedicated to meeting the needs of specific churches. Similarly, ethnic or nationality divisions within countries have been reflected in group identification with specific parties, or by the formation of ethnic or nationality parties. Religious and ethnic differences, however, have correlated with socioeconomic divisions, so that there has been an admixture of class and ethnic support. In the United States, Canada, Great Britain, and Australia, the conservative parties have been supported by the more well to do, by the members of the historic privileged religions like the Anglican-Episcopal church and the Congregationalists, and by the ethnic group which has highest status (also disproportionately composed of wealthier individuals).

Regional loyalties are another major factor which has affected party support. In many countries certain regions have developed historic loyalties to one or another political party, which have been maintained long after the specific event which gave rise to the allegiance has lost its relevance.

In practically every country for which we have data (except perhaps the United States), women tend to support the conservative parties more than men do. But this relationship is somewhat different from the preceding four, since the parties which are backed by women cannot be considered as representing women's interests against those of men. The differences are probably due to the different social role of women, and the way in which this leads them to accept values identified with conservative parties.

A sixth distinct factor affecting political opinions and loyalties is age, considered in more detail in Chapter 8. Unlike the others, however, there is no regular and distinct correlation between age and party support. In some countries and historical periods, the young voters (or the aged) are likely to be found on the left, in others they are more conservative. Different age groups react to their political environment according to the significant experiences of their generation. Any analysis of party support must take age into account as a relevant source of political differentiation, but party conflict cannot be interpreted as an age conflict.

The differences between rural and urban populations have constituted an additional basis of cleavage in many countries. In some the rural population has formed the backbone of an independent agrarian party, while in others farmers have identified with other major parties. The concept of a rural group and its needs opposing the rest of the country often conceals the fact that most rural societies are as internally differentiated as urban areas between rich and poor, and into ethnic, religious, and regional groups. Differences between crop areas have also constituted an important source of cleavage. For example, in many countries wheat farmers have often been much more radical than farmers raising mixed crops.

The fact that many interests and groups which are not social classes take part in the party struggle does not vitiate the thesis that "the rationale of the party-system depends on the alignment of opinion from right to left," as the sociologist and political philosopher Robert MacIver has pointed out. "The right is always the party sector associated with the interests of the upper or dominant classes, the left the sector expressive of the lower economic or social classes, and the center that of the middle classes. Historically this criterion seems acceptable. The conservative right has defended entrenched prerogatives, privileges and powers; the left has attacked them. The right has been more favorable to the aristocratic position, to the hierarchy of birth or of wealth; the left has fought for the equalization of advantage or of opportunity, for the claims of the less advantaged. Defense and attack have met, under democratic conditions, not in the name of class but in the name of principle; but the opposing principles have broadly corresponded to the interests of the different classes."[3]

[3] Robert M. MacIver, *The Web of Government* (New York: Macmillan, 1947), pp. 216, 315. It is interesting to note that Talcott

Such terms as "left," "liberal," and "progressive," and their opposites, "right," "conservative," and "reactionary," have been defined on the basis of many different issues—political democracy versus monarchy, the free market system versus traditional economic restrictions, secularism versus clericalism, agrarian reform versus landlordism and urban exploitation of the countryside, social reform versus *laissez-faire*, socialism versus capitalism. The parties and social groups which have been "left" on one of these issues have by no means always been "left" on another, and the "center" has emerged to oppose both left and right parties. Nevertheless, at any given period and place it is usually possible to locate parties on a left to right continuum.[4]

The issue of equality and social change has been a dominant one in most countries over the last two or three generations, and overlaps the older left-right issues like democracy versus monarchy and clericalism versus secularism. The most significant issue cutting across the left-right dimension today is political democracy versus totalitarianism, which was discussed earlier.[5] In some countries, as I have already docu-

Parsons, whose sociology has often been criticized for deprecating problems of conflict and overemphasizing the degree of cohesion in society, has stressed the need to analyze American political history and voting contests in terms of an enduring conflict between the left and the right: those oriented to the lower strata and change, and those more concerned with stability and the needs of the more well to do. See his "Voting and the Equilibrium of the American Political System," in E. Burdick and A. Brodbeck, eds., *American Voting Behavior* (Glencoe: The Free Press, 1959), p. 88.

[4] M. Duverger, *Political Parties* (London: Methuen and Co., 1954), pp. 215–16, 228–39; M. Duverger, "Public Opinion and Political Parties in France," *American Political Science Review*, 46 (1952), pp. 1069–78. Of course, this groups together parties which have quite different approaches to social change and which may in practice be bitterly hostile toward one another. It ignores the question of the finer degrees of "left" and "right" and neglects other issues which at times cut completely across the left-right dimension as defined here, such as regional autonomy vs. centralism, national self-determination vs. imperialism, and, most recently, political democracy vs. totalitarianism.

[5] See also Edward Shils, "Authoritarianism: 'Right' and 'Left,'" in R. Christie and M. Jahoda, eds., *Studies in the Scope and Method*

mented, the great majority of the traditional leftist vote goes
to totalitarian Communist parties, while in others the traditional centrist and rightist vote has gone to various forms
of "fascism." But even in such cases the economic and stratification left-right issues are probably much in the minds of
the rank-and-file voters. More than anything else the party
struggle is a conflict among classes, and the most impressive
single fact about political party support is that in virtually
every economically developed country the lower-income
groups vote mainly for parties of the left, while the higher-
income groups vote mainly for parties of the right.

The differences in political preference between lower- and
upper-income groups which are typical of many countries are
illustrated in Tables I and II which report on the support
of French and Italian parties. In both countries the industrial
and agricultural workers give strong support to the Communists, and in Italy to the left (Nenni) Socialists as well, and
the middle and upper classes back the parties of the center
and the right.

Though this broad pattern holds, there is a great amount
of variation within income groups. In the middle-income
groups white-collar workers and teachers give strong support
to the moderate socialists in France and the Saragat (right-
wing) socialists in Italy. The considerable variation within
lower-income groups in the two countries is also shown in
these tables. The lower the economic level of the worker,
the more likely he is to vote Communist. The higher-income
workers prefer the moderate socialist parties or the center
parties.

The same pattern holds in countries with stable two-party
systems. As Table III shows, in Great Britain the higher one
goes in the social structure, the smaller the support for the
Labor party, until among top businessmen and higher-level
professionals the party is supported by less than 10 per cent
of the class. Almost identical patterns differentiate the back-

of 'The Authoritarian Personality' (Glencoe: The Free Press, 1954),
pp. 24–49.

Table I
Support of Political Parties in France among Different Occupational Groups
1956*

	Industrial Workers	Agric. Workers	White Collar	Civil Servants and Teachers	Merchant	Farm Owner	Professional
Communist	39%	37%	16%	14%	7%	5%	11%
Socialist	31	19	33	48	21	17	23
Radical	11	13	7	21	12	13	20
M.R.P. (Catholic)	8	9	21	9	17	14	13
Independent	3	17	11	3	21	45	20
U.R.A.S. (De Gaulle)	4	–	10	5	3	4	8
Poujade	4	4	2	–	19	2	5
Total	100%	99%	100%	100%	100%	100%	100%
(N)	(169)	(67)	(61)	(58)	(81)	(180)	(64)

* Computed by author from cards of a national opinion survey conducted in May 1956 by the Institut national d'études demographiques. I am indebted to Alain Girard for use of the data.

TABLE I—continued

1954†

| Occupation | Industrial Workers | | | Farmers | | | |
Economic Level	B Above Average	C Average	D Poor	A Wealthy	B Above Average	C Average	D Poor
Party Choice							
Communist	18%	40%	45%	4%	9%	27%	43%
Socialist	41	27	22	12	28	14	10
Radical	4	7	5	9	12	24	10
M.R.P.	17	7	10	12	12	10	10
Independent	18	15	18	60	30	23	26
R.P.F. (De Gaulle)	2	5	–	3	8	1	–
Total	100%	101%	100%	100%	99%	99%	99%

† Recomputed from J. Stoetzel "Voting Behavior in France," *British Journal of Sociology*, 4 (1955), pp. 118–19.

TABLE II

OCCUPATION AND PARTY CHOICE IN ITALY*

(1953—males only)

	Employers Professionals	Farm				Artisan	White Collar	Workers (Socioeconomic Levels)		
		Large Owner	Small Owner	Share Tenant	Farm Labor			Middle	Upper Lower	Lower
Communist	–%	5%	4%	33%	58%	7%	5%	24%	31%	53%
Nenni Left Socialist	6	5	4	10	11	17	3	16	32	25
Saragat Right Socialist	11	11	15	3	2	15	26	12	13	3
Republican	2	5	–	–	–	4	–	4	1	–
Christian Democrat	41	29	41	33	17	23	42	36	10	9
Liberal	22	29	10	2	–	4	–	4	–	3
Monarchist	6	14	10	8	–	15	13	–	5	3
Neo-Fascist (M.S.I.)	11	9	15	11	12	15	11	4	8	3
Total per cent	99%	101%	99%	100%	100%	100%	100%	100%	100%	100%
(N)	(46)	(21)	(71)	(61)	(64)	(53)	(38)	(25)	(78)	(32)

* Computed by author from cards of a national opinion survey conducted by International Public Opinion Research for the M.I.T. Center for International Studies.

TABLE III

ESTIMATED PERCENTAGES OF PERSONS IN DIFFERENT OCCU-
PATIONS VOTING LABOR OR CONSERVATIVE, GREAT BRITAIN,
1951*

Business Group	Conservative (%)	Labor (%)
Top Business	80	8
Middle Business	73	10
Small Business	64	15
Managerial	65	19
Professional Group		
Higher Professional	78	6
Lower Professional	52	24
White Collar Group		
Higher Office	63	13
Lower Office	48	29
Intermediate Group	41	39
Manual Workers	28	51
Whole Adult Population	40	41

* John Bonham, *The Middle Class Vote* (London: Faber & Faber,
1954), pp. 129 and 173. The figures for the manual workers were
compiled from a graph on p. 173. All figures were estimated from
survey data from the British Institute of Public Opinion. The difference between the per cent secured by the two main parties and
100 per cent is accounted for by nonvoters and third-party voters.

ing of the Democrats and Republicans in the United States,
a point which will be documented in detail in Chapter 9.

Further striking evidence of the pervasiveness of the effect
of class position on political attitudes comes from a country
in which real party competition does not exist: Communist
Poland. In 1957 the young Polish sociologist Andrzej Malewski conducted a public opinion survey on attitudes concerning
the proper level of differences in income for different occupations—an issue which in capitalist countries is strongly linked
to leftist or conservative views. As in the capitalist countries
he found "that there is a strong correlation between the incomes of people and their views concerning a maximum scale
of income differences. . . . The poll shows that factory work-

ers, technicians, and certain groups of the intelligentsia with low salaries (teachers, post office workers, social service officials, etc.) are in favour of egalitarianism. On the other hand, an unfavourable attitude prevails among people of whom many have possibilities of high incomes." At the extremes, 54 per cent of the Polish workers interviewed favored "relatively equal incomes" as contrasted with 20 per cent of the executives. Fifty-five per cent of the latter were strongly against sharply narrowing the income gap, as compared with only 8 per cent of the manual workers. So in a Communist country, too, the struggle between the more and the less privileged is reflected in attitudes comparable to those voiced by similarly placed strata in the West. The one major difference is that in a Communist country "both those in favor of the limitation of income scale span and those opposing it often use the traditional slogans of the left."[6]

The simplest explanation for this widespread pattern is simple economic self-interest. The leftist parties represent themselves as instruments of social change in the direction of equality; the lower-income groups support them in order to become economically better off, while the higher-income groups oppose them in order to maintain their economic advantages. The statistical facts can then be taken as evidence of the importance of class factors in political behavior.

This relationship between class position (as measured by education, income, status, power, occupation, or property status) and political opinions or party choice is far from consistent, however. Many poor people vote conservative and

[6] The quotations and the statistics are from an apparently as yet unpublished report by Andrzej Malewski which is translated in part in Leopold Lebedz, *Sociology and Communism 1957–1958* (London: Soviet Survey, 1959), p. 10. A more extensive report of this study may be found in Zeigniew Socha, "Postawy wobee egalitaryzmu," (Attitudes toward egalitarianism), *Przeglad Kulturalny*, No. 3 (333), Warsaw, January 15, 1959. In Denmark, "the Social Democratic Party increases monotonically in relative popularity with decreasing social status, while exactly the opposite regularity applies to the Conservatives," K. Svalastoga, *Prestige, Class and Mobility* (Copenhagen: Scandinavian Universities Press, 1959), pp. 264–65.

some wealthy ones are socialists or Communists. Part of the explanation of these deviations has already been pointed out: other characteristics and group affiliations such as religious belief are more salient in particular situations than high or low social and economic position. But the deviations are also a consequence of the complexity of the stratification system itself. In modern society, men are subjected to a variety of experiences and pressures which have conflicting political consequences because men have disparate positions in the class structure. Men may hold power, like some civil servants, but have a low income or status; they may enjoy high occupational prestige, like many intellectuals, but receive low income; they may enjoy a relatively high income, but have low social status like members of some ethnic minorities or *nouveaux riches* businessmen, and so forth. Some of their social positions may predispose them to be conservative, while others favor a more leftist political outlook. When faced with such conflicting social pressures, some men will respond more to one than to another, and therefore appear to deviate from the pattern of class voting.

These conflicting and overlapping social positions probably injure the leftist lower-class-based parties more than they do the conservative right. Men are constantly struggling to see themselves favorably, and some of their status-attributes will produce a favorable self-evaluation, others a negative one. It seems logical to assume that men will arrange their impressions of their environment and themselves so as to maximize their sense of being superior to others. Thus the white-collar worker will stress the identification of white-collar work with middle-class status (a point to be discussed further later); the low-income white worker will regard himself as superior to the Negro, and so forth. A variety of evidence gathered in the course of research on social mobility indicates that those who are occupationally upwardly mobile seek to get rid of the characteristics which still link them to their past status. The man who succeeds will in fact often change his neighborhood, seek to find new, higher-status friends, perhaps leave his church for one whose members are higher in status, and also vote more conservatively. The more conservative parties have the advantage of being identified with the more prestigeful classes in the population, an asset which helps to overcome the left's appeal to the economic interests of the lower strata.

Although it is not always possible to predict whether a right or a left political direction will result from specific status-discrepancies, the concept itself points up sources of change in political values flowing from the tensions of contradictory social positions. A discrepancy in status may even lead an old but declining upper class to be more liberal in its political orientation. For example, most observers of British politics have suggested that the emergence of Tory socialism, the willingness of British nineteenth-century conservatism to enact reforms which benefited the working class, was a consequence of the felt hostility of the old English landed aristocracy to the rising business class, which was threatening its status and power. Some of the sources of comparable American upper-class liberalism will be discussed in more detail in Chapter 9.

But although variations in the political behavior of the more privileged strata constitute one of the more fascinating problems of political analysis, the available reliable evidence which permits us to specify why people differ in their political allegiances is largely limited to the largest segments of the population, particularly workers and farmers. Public opinion surveys and studies of the voting patterns of different rural districts can deal statistically with different types of workers and farmers in ways that cannot as yet be done on a comparative international level for most sections of the urban middle and upper classes. Discussion, therefore, of variations in the political affiliations of the latter groups has been limited to American materials and is presented in the next section of this book (see Chapters 9 and 10). This chapter focuses primarily on the politics of the lower and more numerous strata.

TABLE IV

SOCIAL CHARACTERISTICS CORRELATED WITH VARIATIONS IN LEFTIST
VOTING IN THE LOWER-INCOME GROUPS WITHIN DIFFERENT
COUNTRIES*

Higher Leftist Vote	*Lower Leftist* Vote
Larger cities	Smaller towns, country
Larger plants	Smaller plants
Groups with high unemployment rates	Groups with low unemployment rates
Minority ethnic or religious groups	Majority ethnic or religious groups
Men	Women
Economically advanced regions	Economically backward regions
Manual workers	White-collar workers
Specific occupations:	Specific occupations:
Miners	Servants, service workers
Fishermen	Peasant, subsistence farmers
Commercial farmers	
Sailors, longshoremen	
Forestry workers	
Less skilled workers	More skilled workers

* The major exceptions to some of these patterns are discussed
below.

Table IV presents a summary of the social characteristics
that are related to these variations within the lower-income
group, i.e., those whose standard of living ranges from poor
to just adequate by local middle-class standards—most workers, working farmers, lower white-collar workers, etc. In comparing international political behavior, it is difficult to make
a more precise classification.

These generalizations are made on the basis of having
examined public opinion or survey data from a large number
of countries including the United States, Argentina, Chile,
Brazil, Canada, Australia, Japan, India, Finland, Norway,

Sweden, Denmark, Germany, the Netherlands, Belgium, France, Austria, Italy, Great Britain, and Hungary.[7]

Left Voting: A Response to Group Needs

Leftist voting is generally interpreted as an expression of discontent, an indication that needs are not being met. Students of voting behavior have suggested the following needs as central:

1. The need for security of income. This is quite closely related to the desire for higher income as such; however, the effect of periodic unemployment or a collapse of produce prices, for example, seems to be important in itself.

2. The need for satisfying work—work which provides the opportunity for self-control and self-expression and which is free from arbitrary authority.

3. The need for status, for social recognition of one's value and freedom from degrading discrimination in social relations.

In terms of this list, let us see how various groups vote.

INSECURITY OF INCOME

Certain occupational groups in the lower-income category suffer from extreme insecurity of income—one-crop farmers,

[7] Most of the published sources are referred to in various parts of this book, and I will not reiterate them here. Many of the statements made in this chapter are based on as yet unpublished results of analyses of studies made by academic or commercial survey research organizations who have either turned over duplicate copies of their IBM cards to me, or have made new computations at my request. I hope to publish a more detailed report on such comparative research in the future. There are a number of good compendia of such data from various countries. These include J. J. de Jong, *Overheid en Onderdaan* (Wageningen: N. V. Gebr. Zomer and Keunings Uitgeversmij, 1956), esp. pp. 75–121, *passim*; Michael P. Fogarty, *Christian Democracy in Western Europe* (London: Routledge and Kegan Paul, 1957), esp. pp. 352–76; Hadley Cantril, ed., *Public Opinion, 1935–1946* (Princeton: Princeton University Press, 1951), esp. pp. 602, 623, 627, and 630 for the United States; p. 197 for Great Britain.

fishermen, miners, and lumbermen—and these groups have histories of high rates of leftist voting.

The prototype of a "boom-and-bust" agricultural economy is the North American wheat area. Depression or drought, or both, have hit the wheat belt in every generation since it was settled. Many studies of the political behavior of this region have been made, and all agree that the wheat farmers are the most leftist of all farmers in times of economic crisis. They have formed the core of the great agrarian radical movements—the Greenbackers, Populists, and Non-Partisan League in the United States, and in Canada the Progressives, Social Credit, and the Cooperative Commonwealth Federation.[8] The only socialist government in North America above the local level is the Cooperative Commonwealth Federation provincial government of Saskatchewan, a one-crop wheat area.

Studies of one-crop commercial farmers in other parts of the world show that they too tend to support periodic protest movements which are often (as we have seen earlier) authoritarian in character.[9] In contrast, farmers whose crops are diversified, who depend on local rather than world markets, and even very poor subsistence farmers whose level of income is steady and reliable tend to support conservative parties.

Fishermen selling to national or international markets are

[8] S. M. Lipset, *Agrarian Socialism* (Berkeley: University of California Press, 1950); J. D. Hicks, *The Populist Revolt* (Minneapolis: University of Minnesota Press, 1931); S. A. Rice, *Farmers and Workers in American Politics* (New York: Columbia University Press, 1924), Chap. II; V. O. Key, Jr., *Politics, Parties, and Pressure Groups* (New York: Crowell, 4th ed., 1952), Chap. II; C. B. MacPherson, *Democracy in Alberta* (Toronto: University of Toronto Press, 1953).

[9] A. Siegfried, *Tableau politique de la France de l'ouest sous la troisième république* (Paris: Librairie Armand Colin, 1913), Chap. 44; R. Heberle, *From Democracy to Nazism* (Baton Rouge: Louisiana State University Press, 1943), Chap. III; Charles P. Loomis and J. Allen Beegle, "The Spread of German Nazism in Rural Areas," *American Sociological Review*, 2 (1946), pp. 724–34; S. S. Nilson, *Histoire et sciences politiques* (Bergen: Chr. Michelsens Institut, 1950); S. S. Nilson, "Aspects de la vie politique en Norvege," *Revue française de science politique*, 3 (1953), pp. 556–79.

in much the same position as the wheat farmers, and commercial fishermen vote left around the world. In Norway, the first labor representatives in the Storting were elected from a fishing district.[10] In Iceland, the fishermen support the second strongest Communist party in Scandinavia.[11] André Siegfried in his pioneer study of voting statistics in western France in 1913 found the fishermen to be a strong leftist group.[12] The fishermen of British Columbia are a strong source of support for the leftist unions.[13] In the United States the West Coast fishermen are traditionally militant and have been organized in a Communist-dominated union, even though they are mostly owners or part owners of their own boats. Great Lakes fishermen have been disproportionately Democratic. And in Great Britain fishing districts are Labor party strongholds.[14]

Miners are among the working-class groups most exposed to unemployment, and the fact that they are one of the strongest leftist groups throughout the world has already been noted. In the British elections of 1950, the thirty-seven Labor party candidates sponsored by the National Union of Mineworkers were elected with a median vote of 73 per cent.[15]

---

[10] E. Bull, *Arbeiderklassen i Norsk Historie* (Oslo: Tilden Norsk Forlag, 1948).

[11] S. S. Nilson, "Le Communisme dans les pays du nord—les élections depuis 1945," *Revue française de science politique*, 1 (1951), pp. 167–80. Rudolf Heberle reports on the success of the leftist parties among the fishermen in Schleswig-Holstein in *From Democracy to Nazism, op. cit.*, p. 104.

[12] See also B. Leger, *Les opinions politiques des provinces françaises*, 2d ed. (Paris: Recuiel Sirey, 1936), pp. 49–50.

[13] S. Jamieson and P. Gladstone, "Unionism in the Fishing Industry in British Columbia," *Canadian Journal of Economics and Political Science*, 16 (1950), pp. 1–11 and 146–71.

[14] J. K. Pollock and S. J. Eldersveld, *Michigan Politics in Transition* (Ann Arbor: University of Michigan Press, Michigan Governmental Studies, No. 10, 1942), p. 54. For the behavior of British fishermen see *The Economist* (Aug. 15, 1959), p. 435.

[15] H. G. Nicholas, *The British General Election of 1950* (London: Macmillan, 1951), pp. 42, 61. See also J. F. S. Ross, *Parliamentary Representation* (New Haven: Yale University Press, 1944), pp. 58–77.

In Canada, the only eastern district which has elected a socialist on different occasions is a coal-mining area in Nova Scotia; the only Quebec constituency ever to elect a socialist to the provincial legislature was a metal-mining area. Studies in the United States show that coal miners are among the most consistent supporters of the Democratic party.[16]

In France, where workers in nationalized industries elect representatives to Works Councils, the underground workers in coal mines gave the Communist-controlled C.G.T. 80 per cent of their votes—a higher figure than that for any other group, including railroad, rapid transit, public utility, shipyard, aircraft, and automobile workers. Data from Germany indicate that in pre-1933 elections as well as in elections to Works Councils in the 1950s, mining areas gave heavy support to the Communists.[17] An ecological analysis of voting in Chile in 1947 showed that the small Communist party had its greatest strength in mining areas. In the coal, copper, and other mineral mining areas the Communists received from 50 to 80 per cent of the votes as compared to only 10 per cent in the country as a whole.[18]

Lumber workers are also subject to severe cyclical fluctuations. In Sweden lumbering areas give the Communists a higher vote than do the large industrial centers.[19] Analysis of the results of an Austrian provincial election in 1952 showed that 85 per cent of the forestry workers voted for the Socialist party.[20] California and Michigan data indicate

[16] H. F. Gosnell, *Grass Roots Politics: National Voting Behavior of Typical States* (Washington: America Council on Public Affairs, 1942), pp. 31–32; see also Malcolm Moos, *Politics, Presidents, and Coattails* (Baltimore: The Johns Hopkins Press, 1952), pp. 47–48.

[17] O. K. Flechtheim, *Die Kommunistische Partei Deutschlands in der Weimarer Republik* (Offenbach am Main: Bollwerk-Verlag Karl Drott, 1948), p. 211, for pre-1933 data; for statistics on Works Councils elections in the 1950s see Michael Fogarty, *op. cit.*, p. 213.

[18] Ricardo Cruz Coke, *Geografía electoral de Chile* (Santiago de Chile: Editorial del Pacífico, S.A., 1952), pp. 53, 81–82.

[19] S. S. Nilson, "Le Communisme dans les pays du nord—les élections depuis 1945," *op. cit.*, pp. 167–80.

[20] Walter B. Simon, *The Political Parties of Austria* (Ph.D. thesis, Department of Sociology, Columbia University, 1957, Microfilm 57–2894 University Microfilms, Ann Arbor, Michigan), p. 263.

that lumber areas give more support to leftist candidates than do other areas,[21] and lumber workers were prominent in the old Industrial Workers of the World (I.W.W.).

An occupation which in many respects resembles lumbering both in economic insecurity and social isolation is sheep-shearing, especially in Australia. Australia has tremendous sheep stations which are usually located far from population centers. The sheepshearers live in camps somewhat like lumber camps, and stay at a station for some time cutting the wool from the sheep. The workers are migratory, moving from one sheep station to another. They are reported to have strong group-consciousness and solidarity. Though there are no voting data reported which have separated out the votes of the sheep station workers, reports on their union behavior suggest that they are militant and radical.[22]

A general depression makes economic insecurity widespread, and in the elections of 1932 and 1936 the counties in the U.S. which were hardest hit by the Depression were the most strongly pro-Roosevelt. Survey data pinpoint the fact that in 1936 and 1940, of all low-income people, those on relief were the most strongly Democratic—over 80 per cent.[23] A study of political attitudes in 1944 found that among American manual workers who had never been unemployed, 43 per cent were "conservative" as compared with only 14 per cent conservative among those who had experienced more than a year of unemployment.[24]

Comparable findings are reported from Great Britain—the higher the unemployment in an area, the stronger the Labor vote. Moreover, the extent of unemployment in the 1930s was still affecting voting during the full-employment year of 1950—the districts that showed the least decline in Labor vote between 1945 and 1950 were those with the most de-

[21] H. F. Gosnell, *op. cit.*, p. 77, and J. K. Pollock and S. J. Eldersveld, *op. cit.*, p. 54.

[22] See T. C. Truman, *The Pressure Groups, Parties and Politics of the Australian Labor Movement* (unpublished M.A. thesis, University of Queensland, 1953), Chap. IV, pp. 70–72.

[23] H. F. Gosnell, *op. cit.*, pp. 3, 32, 37, 90.

[24] R. Centers, *The Psychology of Social Classes* (Princeton: Princeton University Press, 1949), pp. 177–79.

pression-time unemployment.[25] Similarly in Finland, areas with the most depression-time unemployment gave highest support to the Communist party in 1951–54.[26] In Germany, the extent of unemployment was directly related to the size of the Communist vote in the 1932 elections. A French public opinion poll of 1956 states that 62 per cent of the members of the Communist trade-union movement, the C.G.T., report having been unemployed at some time in the past, as compared to 43 per cent of the members of the socialist *Force Ouvrier*, and 33 per cent of the members of the Catholic C.F.T.C.[27]

The relative conservatism of white-collar workers in the United States may be due to their greater job security during the Depression. Only about 4 per cent of the white-collar workers were unemployed in 1930, as compared to 13 per cent of urban unskilled workers. In 1937, 11 per cent of the former and a quarter of the latter were out of work.[28] In Germany this middle-class group was much more affected by the postwar economic crisis than in the United States. The German white-collar workers tended to turn to the fascist movement rather than to the leftist parties with their doctrinaire emphasis on the proletariat.[29]

UNSATISFYING WORK

Students of working-class movements have often suggested that the nature of the work situation itself, aside from wages and security, is an important factor in creating satisfaction

[25] H. G. Nicholas, *op. cit.*, pp. 297–98; Wilma George, "Social Conditions and the Labor Vote in the County Boroughs of England and Wales," *British Journal of Sociology*, 2 (1951), pp. 255–59.

[26] Erik Allardt, *Social Struktur och Politisk Aktivitet* (Helsingfors: Söderstrom and Co., 1956), p. 84.

[27] *Réalités*, No. 65, April 1956.

[28] C. W. Mills, *White Collar* (New York: Oxford University Press, 1951), p. 281.

[29] T. Geiger, *Die Soziale Schichtung des Deutschen Volkes* (Stuttgart: Ferdinand Enke, 1932), pp. 109–22; Samuel Pratt, *The Social Basis of Nazism and Communism in Urban Germany* (unpublished M.A. thesis, Department of Sociology, Michigan State University, 1948), Chap. 8.

or dissatisfaction. The factory worker spends his days under the control of others, often subject to arbitrary discipline. And workers in mass-production industries with minutely segmented, routine tasks have little opportunity to interest themselves in their work and to exercise creative abilities.[30]

From this it should follow that the more arbitrary the managerial authority and the more monotonous the work, the more discontented the workers would be and the more likely to support political movements aiming at social change. And there is evidence that the larger the industrial plant (and therefore, usually, the more segmented the work) the more leftist the workers. A study of voting in large German cities before 1933 found that the higher the proportion of workers in large plants the higher the Communist vote.[31] A study of the American printing industry has likewise found a relation between political leftism and size of shop.[32]

In general, the more skilled are almost everywhere the more conservative among manual workers. Whether job satisfaction and creativity contribute independently to political behavior over and beyond differences in status and economic conditions is still, however, not proved.

STATUS

Feelings of deprivation and consequent political radicalism on the part of those in lowly occupations are not solely due to the objective economic situation. All societies are stratified by status (prestige) as well as by economic rewards, and while status and income tend to be related, they are far

[30] The difference in job satisfaction between such jobs and those allowing more creativity are documented, with a review of the literature, in R. Blauner, "Attitudes Toward Work," in W. Galenson and S. M. Lipset, eds., *Readings in the Economics and Sociology of Trade Unions* (New York: John Wiley & Sons, 1960).

[31] S. Pratt, *loc. cit.*

[32] Unpublished data from a study of the International Typographical Union. For other details of this study see S. M. Lipset, M. Trow, and J. Coleman, *Union Democracy* (Glencoe: The Free Press, 1956), esp. pp. 150–97, which discuss the differences in environments in small and large shops.

from identical. Status involves invidious distinctions—men and groups defined as superior or inferior to others—and it does not follow from what we know about human behavior that men will accept a low social evaluation with equanimity. Wherever the possibility exists, therefore, people will try either to improve their prestige position through individual efforts (social mobility) or to improve the position of their group through collective action of some sort. And if self-interest describes the motivation flowing from the desire to improve the material conditions of existence, then *resentment* describes the feelings of lowly placed persons toward the social system and those who are high in prestige.[33]

The lack of respect with which workers are treated by office personnel, salespeople, clerks, minor officials, etc., and the general failure of middle-class society to recognize the workers' economic contributions and personal abilities undoubtedly contribute to dissatisfaction with the *status quo* and to political leftism.

While low prestige plus low income and high prestige plus high income join together to reinforce leftist or conservative political motivation, situations in which one factor places the individual much higher or lower on relative ranking scales help, as has been already noted, to account for seemingly deviant patterns of behavior. In all societies for which we have data, white-collar workers receive more prestige than manual workers, and identify in many ways (dress, speech, family patterns) with those higher in the system, even when their income is not higher than that of skilled manual workers.[34] And many studies show that the white-collar workers in different countries are much more likely to vote for the more conservative parties than are manual workers—in general, taking a position midway between that of the higher

[33] For a more detailed discussion of the reactions to position in the status structure see S. M. Lipset and Hans Zetterberg, "Social Mobility in Industrial Societies," in S. M. Lipset and R. Bendix, *Social Mobility in Industrial Society* (Berkeley: University of California Press, 1959), pp. 60–64.

[34] For a detailed summary of evidence bearing on this point from many countries, see *ibid.*, pp. 14–17.

business strata and the manual workers on the left-right continuum.[35] This greater conservatism is not due solely to higher income. A study of voting in the 1949 Norwegian election showed that the vote for leftist parties (Communist and socialist) was almost twice as high among manual workers as it was for white-collar workers on each income level (see Table V). A survey study of political affiliation in Germany gave similar results.[36]

TABLE V

PERCENTAGE VOTING FOR LABOR AND COMMUNIST PARTIES BY OCCUPATIONAL GROUP AND INCOME IN NORWAY—1949*

Yearly income in Kroner	Industrial workers	White-collar workers
Under 4,000	56	35
4,000–7,000	70	28
7,000–12,000	69	24
Over 12,000	–†	13

* A. H. Barton, *Sociological and Psychological Implications of Economic Planning in Norway* (unpublished Ph.D. thesis, Department of Sociology, Columbia University, 1954), p. 327.

† Too few cases.

Direct evidence of the importance of the status motive in white-collar political behavior is provided by a study of "class identification" in the United States where 61 per cent of white-collar workers called themselves "middle-class," as against only 19 per cent of manual workers. Among the white-

[35] G. Gallup, *The Gallup Political Almanac for 1948* (Princeton: American Institute of Public Opinion, 1948), p. 9; R. Centers, *op. cit.*, p. 38; E. G. Benson and Evelyn Wicoff, "Voters Pick Their Party," *Public Opinion Quarterly*, 8 (1944), pp. 165–74; L. Harris, *Is There a Republican Majority?* (New York: Harper & Bros., 1954); H. Cantril, *op. cit.*

[36] Institut für Marktforschung und Meinungsforschung, E.M.N. I.D., *Zur Resonanz der Parteien bei Männer und Frauen in den Soziologischen Gruppen* (Bielefeld: mimeographed, no date), pp. 5, 7, 9.

collar workers this self-labeling made a great difference in
political attitudes—65 per cent of those who considered themselves "middle-class" had conservative attitudes, compared
with 38 per cent of the "working-class" white-collar workers.
Among manual workers, subjective class identification made
much less difference in attitudes—37 per cent of "middle-
class" manual workers had conservative attitudes, compared
with 25 per cent of the "working-class" workers.[37]

The political role of the white-collar workers was studied
intensively in Germany, but unfortunately before the days
of sampling surveys.[38] Studies using available area voting
statistics suggest that the white-collar vote swung from the
centrist parties to the Nazis under the impact of the Depression of 1929.[39] A strong correlation existed between the
proportion of the unemployed among the white-collar workers
in German cities and the Nazi vote.[40] The usual explanation
offered by Germans for this is that the Nazis represented a
hope for solving the economic crisis and at the same time
for maintaining the status position of the white-collar workers, while the Marxist parties offered them economic gains
only at the cost of "proletarianization."[41]

Some of the variations in the way workers vote in different
countries may possibly be explained by differences in the
rigidity of the status-hierarchy. The data on political party
choices of Australian, British, American, French, and Italian
workers all suggest that the lower the socioeconomic position
of a worker, the more likely he is to vote for a party of the
left. On the other hand, in Germany and Sweden the lowest

[37] R. Centers, op. cit., pp. 130–32.

[38] T. Geiger, op. cit., pp. 109–22.

[39] W. Dittmann, Das Politische Deutschland vor Hitler (Zurich:
Europa Verlag, 1945); A. Dix, Die Deutschen Reichstagswahlen,
1871–1930, und die Wandlungen der Volksgliederung (Tübingen:
J. B. C. Mohr, Paul Siebeck, 1930); W. Stephan, "Zur Soziologie
der Nationalsozialistischen Deutschen Arbeiterpartei," Zeitschrift für
Politik, 20 (1931), pp. 293–300. See also Chap. 5.

[40] S. Pratt, op. cit., Chap. 8.

[41] T. Geiger, op. cit., p. 114.

stratum of workers is most likely to back the nonlabor oriented parties. In these countries the higher strata within the working class are more prone to support left parties.[42] For each level of skill in a sample of workers in Germany, the workers earning over 250 marks per month were more likely to support left (Socialist and Communist) parties than workers earning less than that amount. Nearly half of the workers in every group supported these parties, but the lowest support was found in the unskilled, low-income group (45 per cent going to those parties) and the highest (65 per cent) in the skilled, better-paid group (see Table VI).

TABLE VI

PROPORTION OF MALE WORKERS SUPPORTING THE SOCIAL DEMOCRATIC AND COMMUNIST PARTIES IN GERMANY—1953*

Skill Level and Income

All Skilled Workers		61%	(230)
Over 250 Marks per Month	65		(140)
Under 250 Marks per Month	55		(94)
All Semiskilled		58	(209)
Over 250 Marks per Month	65		(113)
Under 250 Marks per Month	50		(96)
All Unskilled		51	(97)
Over 250 Marks per Month	59		(42)
Under 250 Marks per Month	45		(55)

* Computations made for the purposes of this study from IBM cards kindly supplied by the UNESCO Institute, Cologne, Germany, from their survey of the 1953 German population.

[42] Similar German findings are also reported in Institut für Marktforschung und Meinungsforschung, E.M.N.I.D., *op. cit.*, and in Divo Institut, *Umfragen 1957* (Frankfurt: Europaiische Verlaganstalt, 1958), p. 53. Thus three different research institutes report that the more skilled in Germany are more radical than the less skilled. The Divo Institut found these results in both its surveys of the 1953 and 1957 elections. In the latter year 62 per cent of the skilled workers who voted were for the Social Democrats as contrasted with 43 per cent among the semiskilled and unskilled, p. 5. For Sweden see Elis Hastad, *et al.*, eds., *"Gallup" och den Svenska Valjarkaren* (Uppsala: Hugo Gebers Forlag, 1950), pp. 157–70.

In absence of more detailed investigations of the varying situation of workers in these two countries as compared with others, it would be foolhardy to attempt to explain these striking differences. The one hypothesis which some people more familiar with life in different parts of Europe than I am have suggested is that there is more frustration among the upper levels of the working class in Germany and perhaps Sweden precisely because these nations remain among the most status-differentiated countries in the Western world. The nobility retained power and influence in these countries until well into the twentieth century, and interpersonal relations still reflect a considerable explicit emphasis on status. Superiority and inferiority in status position are expressed in many formal and informal ways. Conversely, Australia, Britain, America, and France are nations in which these status differences have declined in importance, given the decline or absence of aristocracy. And an emphasis on status differentiation should affect the more skilled and better-paid workers more than their less privileged class brethren. While the more skilled are better off than other workers, their very economic success makes more obvious to them their rejection by the middle classes. They are in a sense like successful Negroes or Jews in societies which discriminate socially against members of these groups. The more successful among them are more likely to be aware of, and consequently resentful of, their status inferiority. The lower group of workers, Negroes, or Jews, will be less likely to feel deprived of status.

Thus the tentative hypothesis may be offered that the more open the status-linked social relations of a given society, the more likely well-paid workers are to become conservatives politically. In an "open" society, relative economic deprivation will differentiate among the workers as it has traditionally done in the United States and Australia. In a more "closed" society, the upper level of the workers will feel deprived and hence support left-wing parties. Whether these hypotheses correspond to the actual facts is a moot question. It is a fact, however, that these differences in political behavior exist. We need more research to account for their sources.

A second prestige hierarchy is based on religious or ethnic differences. Minority religions, nationalities, and races are usually subjected to various forms of social discrimination, and the low-income member of a minority group consequently faces additional obstacles to economic and social achievement. The poor majority group member, on the other hand, may find substitute gratifications in his ethnic or religious "superiority." High-income members of a low-status ethnic or religious group are therefore, as we have noted, in a situation comparable to the upper level of the working class in those countries with "closed" status systems.

In the English-speaking countries, studies show that among the various Christian denominations, the more well to do the *average* socioeconomic status of the church members, the more likely the lower-status members are to vote for the more conservative party. In Britain, Australia, Canada, and the United States, workers belonging to the more well-to-do churches like the Anglican (Episcopal in the U.S.) are more likely to back the more conservative party than workers belonging to poorer churches.

Similarly, middle-class voters who belong to a relatively less well-to-do church like the Catholic or the Baptist are more prone to be Laborites or Democrats than their class peers in other denominations. One British study reports that among industrial workers voting in the 1951 elections, the percentage backing the Labor party was 73 among Catholics, 64 among Nonconformists, and 43 among Anglicans. "The proportion of Anglicans who voted Conservative is almost exactly twice as great as the proportion of non-Anglicans who did so; and three-fifths of all the industrial workers who voted Conservative were Anglicans."[43]

[43] A. H. Birch, *Small-Town Politics* (London: Oxford University Press, 1959), p. 112; for national data on British voting see H. J. Eysenck, *The Psychology of Politics* (London: Routledge and Kegan Paul, 1954), p. 21, and M. Benney, A. P. Gray, and R. H. Pear, *How People Vote: A Study of Electoral Behavior in Greenwich* (London: Routledge and Kegan Paul, 1956), p. 111; for data dealing with Britain and the United States see Michael Argyle, *Religious Behavior* (Glencoe: The Free Press, 1959), pp. 81–83; for a more detailed

In Australia in 1951 and 1955, Gallup Poll data indicate that approximately 50 per cent of the Catholics in urban nonmanual jobs backed the Labor party, as contrasted with less than 30 per cent of the Anglicans in comparable positions. Similarly, among manual workers, Australian Catholics have been more heavily Laborite than any other denomination.[44]

In all of the above countries, Jews, although relatively well to do, are politically the least conservative denomination, a pattern which holds as well in many non-English-speaking Western nations. Electoral data in Austria show that the Jewish districts of Vienna, although middle class, were disproportionately Socialist in many elections before 1933.[45] A study of voting in Amsterdam, the Netherlands, also indicated that the predominantly Jewish district of that city was a strong Social Democratic center.[46] The leftist voting patterns of the Jews have been explained as flowing from their inferior status position (social discrimination) rather than from elements inherent in their religious creed.[47]

The differential impact of religious affiliation on political allegiances does not flow solely from the current status position of the different denominations. In a number of coun-

---

discussion of religion and politics in the United States together with further bibliographic references see Chap. 9, pp. 307–8; for published Australian data see Louise Overacker, *The Australian Party System* (New Haven: Yale University Press, 1952), pp. 166–70, 298, 305–6, and Leicester Webb, *Communism and Democracy in Australia* (Melbourne: F. W. Cheshire, 1954), pp. 91–100. The Australian Gallup Poll has made available considerable data which show the relationship between political affiliation and religion. The references to Canada are based on an inspection of unpublished data collected by the Canadian Gallup Poll.

[44] All the Australian Labor parties are considered as Labor for the purposes of this analysis, although the dissident right-wing Labor parties are largely based on the Catholics.

[45] Walter B. Simon, *op. cit.*, pp. 335, 338–41.

[46] J. P. Kruijt, *De Onkerkelikheid in Nederland* (Groningen: P. Noordhoff, N. V., 1933), pp. 265, 267.

[47] See Robert Michels, *Political Parties* (Glencoe: The Free Press, 1949), pp. 261–62, for an analysis of the sources of Jewish radicalism in Wilhelmine Germany that still seems applicable to other countries.

tries churches which have been established, protected by the state, and linked to the landed aristocracy often provide the base for a religious political party which seeks to defend or restore religious rights and influence against the attacks of more left-wing and anticlerical political movements. Thus in Catholic Europe working-class Catholics have disproportionately voted for the more conservative and Catholic parties, while middle-class Protestants, Jews, and free-thinkers have been more leftist, even to the point of backing Marxist parties.[48]

The close link between political behavior patterns and religious practice in two European countries, France and the Netherlands, may be seen in Table VII. The sharp differences in party choice between those who attend church and those who do not are apparent from the tables. In France, for example, 68 per cent of the practicing Catholics supported either the M.R.P. or the Independent party, both conservative, but 56 per cent of the nonpracticing and 63 per cent of the "indifferent" Catholics supported either the Communists or the Socialists. There were not enough Protestants in the sample to differentiate between degrees of religious practice, but among these members of a formerly persecuted minority, 39 per cent supported the leftist parties, and another 34 per cent backed the Radical party, the liberal anticlerical party. Among those with no religion 79 per cent supported the Marxist parties.

In the Netherlands information was available on church attendance for the three major religious groups, and here again, striking differences are evident in the voting choices

[48] See Stuart R. Schram, *Protestantism and Politics in France* (Alençon, France: Corbiere and Jugain, 1954), pp. 183–86. For example, 55.5 per cent of the registered voters in the Protestant communes (in the *Gard*) voted Communist or Socialist in 1951, as against only 35.1 per cent in the Catholic communes. On the whole, the Protestant communes are more well to do than the Catholic ones. For the best discussion of the characteristics of Catholic and other religious political parties in Europe, see Michael Fogarty, *op. cit.*, Chap. 22.

TABLE VII

RELIGION AND PARTY CHOICE BY CHURCH ATTENDANCE

France—1956*

	Catholics			Protestants	No Religion
	Practicing	Non-practicing	Indifferent		
Communist	2%	17%	18%	5%	49%
Socialist	9	39	45	34	30
Radical	10	17	17	34	8
M.R.P.	34	4	2	7	1
Independent	34	14	12	10	4
R.P.F.	6	3	2	2	1
Poujade	5	6	4	7	6
Total	100%	100%	100%	99%	99%
(N)	(609)	(507)	(168)	(41)	(144)

The Netherlands—1956†

Party Choice	Catholic		Moderate Protestant		Calvinist		No Religion
	Church Attendance						
	Yes	No	Yes	No	Yes	No	No
Catholic	94%	52%	—%	—%	—%	—%	1%
Socialist	3	30	22	51	2	27	75
Antirevolutionary (Calvinist)	—	6	17	6	90	63	—
Christian Historical (Moderate Protestant)	—	—	45	19	3	—	—
Liberal	—	9	7	18	—	—	11
Communist	—	—	—	—	—	—	7
Calvinist Splinter	—	—	5	3	1	5	—
Other	2	3	4	3	4	5	6
Total	99%	100%	100%	100%	100%	100%	100%
(N)	(329)	(33)	(134)	(236)	(101)	(22)	(218)

* Computed by author from the IBM cards of a national opinion survey conducted in May 1956 by the Institut national d'études demographiques.

† Computed by author from the IBM cards of a Netherlands Institute of Public Opinion survey conducted in May 1956.

of the different denominations.[49] Fully 94 per cent of the practicing Catholics supported the Catholic party, but only 52 per cent of those nonpracticing did, with 30 per cent of their choices going to the Socialists. Ninety per cent of the practicing Calvinists supported the Calvinist Antirevolutionary party, as compared with 63 per cent of the nonchurchgoing. The difference is far less significant among the moderate Protestant practicing members, whose religious patterns are more nearly like those of American Protestants and who are therefore under less social pressure to vote for their party. The Christian Historical party commanded 45 per cent of the practicing church members' allegiances, and 19 per cent among those nonpracticing.

In West Germany Catholics and Protestants are linked to direct political action through one religious party, the Christian Democrats. And there also, the more involved a man is in church activity, the more likely he is to back a religious party.[50]

Although we have ignored other factors in reporting the impact of religion in these countries, it is important to note that class factors continued to operate within each denomi-

[49] The full extent of the unity of the religious and political cleavage in the Netherlands is clear from the numbers of persons who do not practice their religion. Whereas in France the number of nonpracticing Catholics was almost as great as those practicing, in the Netherlands they formed only one tenth of the total of Catholics, and the nonpracticing Calvinists were only one sixth of the total of Calvinists. The number of nonpracticing moderate Protestants was almost twice as many as those practicing, but the differences in voting behavior were equally plain. These polls were taken on the basis of random samples of the entire population, so that it is legitimate to infer that the proportion of those practicing their religion is representative.

[50] In Germany, 60 per cent of the male Catholic churchgoers support either the C.D.U. or the *Zentrum*, while only 33 per cent of the nonchurchgoing Catholics support these parties. See Juan Linz, *The Social Bases of German Politics* (unpublished Ph.D. thesis, Department of Sociology, Columbia University, 1958), p. 700. See J. J. de Jong, *op. cit.*, pp. 179–87, for further data on Holland. This book also presents a survey of voting patterns in different European countries for different occupations, age groups, and other aspects of social structure.

nation. Among French Catholics, as among Dutch and German Protestants and Catholics, those who voted for the leftist parties were predominantly manual workers. The available evidence suggests that workers in these countries are much more subject to tensions flowing from the conflict between their religious and class positions than members of the middle strata. While most religious workers resolve this tension, at least as far as voting is concerned, by backing the religious party, a significant minority, particularly among the less faithful church attenders, backs the Socialists. It may be that this tension leads some workers into the ranks of the free-thinkers.

Where the conflict between religious groups and anticlerical parties is a major element in political life, as it is in various European states, there are also important differences in the sex composition of the supporters of the different parties, since everywhere in the Western world women are more faithful religious adherents than men.[51] In France, Germany, the Netherlands, Belgium, Austria, and other countries the anticlerical parties, Marxist and liberal alike, get a much larger segment of the male electorate than of the female voters. In Germany, according to a 1953 survey, 60 per cent of all Socialist voters were men, while 58 per cent of the Christian Democrats were women.[52] In the United States, on the other hand, where there is no conflict between religion and irreligion as such, there is also no difference in the support given to the two parties by men and women.[53]

[51] For instance, studies in France in 1952 and in the diocese of Mantua, Italy, in 1948 show that almost twice as many Catholic women as Catholic men were regular attenders at Sunday Mass. See M. Fogarty, op. cit., pp. 352–53.

[52] Juan Linz, op. cit., p. 234.

[53] A. Campbell, G. Gurin, and W. E. Miller, The Voter Decides (Evanston, Ill.: Row, Peterson and Co., 1954), p. 70; B. Berelson, P. F. Lazarsfeld, and W. M. McPhee, Voting (Chicago: University of Chicago Press, 1954), pp. 73, 75. It should be noted, however, that when morality issues such as corruption or prohibition have been salient in American elections, women have voted disproportionately for the more "moral" candidate. See Stuart A. Rice, Quantitative Methods in Politics, op. cit., pp. 177–79, for discussion of women's voting, circa 1917–20, when sex differences held up.

Many ethnic and religious minorities suffering social or economic discrimination support the more left parties in different countries, although this pattern is most commonly found in the Jews. In the United States, the Negro minority tends to be more Democratic than whites on a given income level; indeed, within the Negro group economic status makes little difference in voting.[54] Other examples can be found in Asia. In India the Andhras, a large linguistic minority, have been among the strongest supporters of the Communist party,[55] while in Ceylon the Communists are disproportionally strong among the Indian minority. In Japan the Korean minority gives considerable support to the Communists.[56] In Israel the Arab minority and in Syria the Christian minority have been relatively pro-Communist.[57]

Social Conditions Affecting Left Voting

Granted that a group of people is suffering from some deprivation under the existing socioeconomic system, it does not automatically follow that they will support political parties aiming at social change. Three conditions facilitate such a response: effective channels of communication, low belief in the possibility of individual social mobility, and the absence of traditionalist ties to a conservative party.

The best discussion and most comparative data on women's voting are in Mattei Dogan, "*Il voto delle donne in Italia e in altre democrazie,*" *Tempi Moderni,* n. 11–12 (Jan.-Feb. 1959), pp. 621–44.

[54] J. A. Morsell, *The Political Behavior of Negroes in New York City* (Ph.D. thesis, Department of Sociology, Columbia University, 1951).

[55] S. S. Harrison, "Caste and the Andhra Communists," *American Political Science Review,* 50 (1956), pp. 378–404.

[56] R. Swearingen and P. Langer, *Red Flag in Japan: International Communism in Action, 1919–1951* (Cambridge: Harvard University Press, 1952), pp. 181–84.

[57] Bureau of Applied Social Research, *Syrian Attitudes Toward America and Russia* (New York: Columbia University, 1952), mimeographed.

CHANNELS OF COMMUNICATION

Perhaps the most important condition is the presence of good communications among people who have a common problem. Close personal contacts between such people further awareness of a community of interests and of the possibilities of collective action, including political action, to solve the common problems. When informal contacts are supplemented by formal organization in trade-unions, farm groups, or class political movements, with all their machinery of organizers, speakers, newspapers, and so forth, political awareness will be intensified still more.

For example, Paul Lazarsfeld has shown that membership in social or other organizations reinforces the tendency to vote Republican among upper- and middle-class people. Similarly, among the lower socioeconomic groups "only 31 per cent of those who were union members, but 53 per cent of those who were not union members voted Republican."[58] The greater political interest and more leftist vote of trade-union members has been documented by studies in a number of countries.[59]

[58] P. F. Lazarsfeld, B. Berelson, and H. Gaudet, *The People's Choice* (New York: Duell, Sloan & Pearce, 1944), pp. 146–47.

[59] Other studies in the United States are A. Campbell, G. Gurin, and W. E. Miller, *op. cit.*, p. 73. B. Berelson, P. F. Lazarsfeld, and W. N. McPhee show that the more involved in union activities the members are the more likely they are to vote Democratic, *op. cit.*, pp. 49–52. This study also shows the reinforcing effect of organization membership upon Republican votes among the middle and upper classes. Ruth Kornhauser has demonstrated that the relationship between Democratic vote and union membership holds in all sizes of community, though more strongly in the larger cities. "Some Determinants of Union Membership," (mimeographed, Institute of Industrial Relations, Berkeley, 1959).

In Britain, 66 per cent of trade-union members in Droylsden, England, in 1951 voted Labor as against 53 per cent of other employees, P. Campbell, D. Donnison, and A. Potter, "Voting Behavior in Droylsden in October 1951," *Journal of the Manchester School of Economics and Social Studies*, 20 (1952), p. 63. R. S. Milne and H. C. Mackenzie found an even stronger relationship between union membership and Labor vote, *Straight Fight; A Study of Voting in the Constituency of Bristol North-East at the General*

We have already discussed several occupational groups which suffer from severe insecurity of income and which vote strongly leftist in different countries—one-crop farmers, fishermen, miners, sheepshearers, and lumbermen. In each of these groups there was not only a strong reason for social discontent but also, as has been pointed out in detail earlier, a social structure favorable to intragroup communications and unfavorable to cross-class communications, an "occupational community."

In contrast to such groups the service industries generally are composed of small units scattered among the well-to-do populations they serve, and their workers tend to be not only less politically active but also more conservative. The white-collar workers' well-known lack of organization and class consciousness may also be partly due to the small units in which they work and to their scattering among higher-level managerial personnel.[60]

Two general social factors that correlate with leftist voting are size of industrial plants and size of city. We have already noted that there was a correlation between size of plant and leftist vote in German elections before 1933, a finding which was reiterated in a 1953 German survey (see Table VIII). Among workers the combined Socialist and Communist vote increased with size of the plants. Twenty-eight per cent of the workers in plants with under ten workers voted left; as contrasted with 57 per cent of those in establishments of over a thousand. Similarly, the vote for the Christian Democrats and the conservative parties was smaller

Election of 1951 (London: The Hansard Society, 1954), pp. 62–64; see also M. Benney, A. P. Gray, and R. H. Pear, *op. cit.*, p. 112. Data supplied by the Canadian Institute of Public Opinion Research indicate that union members give greater support to the C.C.F. (socialists) and the Communists than do nonunionized workers. In Germany union members are twice as likely to support the Socialist party as those workers who do not belong to any voluntary associations, Juan Linz, *op. cit.*, pp. 215, 828–30.

[60] C. Dreyfuss, "Prestige Grading: A Mechanism of Control," in R. K. Merton, *et al.*, eds., *Reader in Bureaucracy* (Glencoe: The Free Press, 1952), pp. 258–64.

for each larger category of plant size. Interestingly enough, the percentage of workers preferring no party also decreased with increasing plant size, indicating both social pressure to vote left, and simply pressure to vote. The earlier study also found a relation between over-all city size and leftist vote.[61]

A later German study (1955) showed that among men the leftist vote increased with size of city in every occupational group except that of people with independent means. But the increase was greatest among manual workers (see Table VIII).[62] Similar results are indicated by an analysis of the election returns for Works Councils in Italy in 1954 and 1955. The larger the city and the larger the factory, the more votes received by the Communist-controlled C.G.I.L. (General Confederation of Italian Labor) in elections to Works Councils. The Communist union federation secured 60 per cent of the vote in cities with less than 40,000 population and 75 per cent in cities with over a million people. The same pattern held up when comparing union strength by size of factory for the entire country, and even within most specific industries. For example, in the textile industry, the Communist-controlled union secured 29 per cent of the vote in plants employing 50–100 people (the smallest size reported for this industry) and 79 per cent in plants employing over 2,000.[63]

[61] S. Pratt, op. cit., Chap. 3.
[62] See also Juan Linz, op. cit., pp. 347 ff. Both men and women and male workers at each skill level were more leftist in larger cities.
[63] For detailed statistical breakdowns of specific cities and plants see L'Avanzata della C.I.S.L. nolle commissioni interne (Rome: Confederazione Italiana Sindacati Lavoratori, 1955), pp. 46–95. This report was prepared by an anti-Communist labor federation. The categories in which data are given for size of factories for each industry vary from industry to industry so that it was impossible to add the data to get an over-all statistic. However, the differences are consistent, and the report in any case does not give all the returns for the entire country. A number of British factory studies by the Acton Society Trust have reported a "clear relationship . . . between size and sick-leave; between size and the number of accidents . . ." and various other indices of worker morale. See Acton Society Trust, Size and Morale (London: 1953); The Worker's Point of

TABLE VIII

PERCENTAGE OF MALE WORKERS VOTING FOR DIFFERENT PARTIES,
BY SIZE OF CITY AND SIZE OF PLANT

(Germany—1955)*

Size of City	Percentage of Socialist and Communist Votes	(N)
Less than 2,000	43%	(453)
2,000–10,000	46	(587)
10,000–100,000	51	(526)
More than 100,000	54	(862)

(Germany—1953)†

Party Choice	Size of Plant				
	Under 10 workers	10–49 workers	50–299 workers	300–999 workers	Over 1,000 workers
Socialist and Communist‡	28%	40%	45%	45%	57%
Christian Democrat	22	20	18	22	15
Bourgeois Parties	21	16	13	7	5
No Party	26	22	23	22	15
Total	97%	98%	99%	96%	92%
(N)	(134)	(116)	(163)	(124)	(130)

* E.M.N.I.D., *Zur Resonanz der Parteien bei Männer und Frauen in den Soziologischen Gruppen* (Bielefeld: mimeographed, no date), p. 4.

† Computed by author from cards supplied by the UNESCO Institute at Cologne, Germany.

‡ Less than 2 per cent Communist.

The same relationship between size of community and party choice is to be found in France, Australia, and the United States.[64] The Australian Gallup Poll isolates the re-

View (London: 1953); and *Size and Morale, II* (London: 1957). Somewhat comparable American findings are reported in Sherrill Cleland, *The Influence of Plant Size on Industrial Relations* (Princeton: Princeton University Press, 1955).

[64] R. Centers, *op. cit.*, pp. 58, 185–90; P. Ennis, "Contextual Factors in Voting Decisions," in W. N. McPhee, ed., *Progress*

sponses of those living in mining communities from those living in other smaller communities and finds, as should be anticipated, that the "isolated" miners are less likely to back middle-class-based parties than are manual workers in large cities (see Table IX). These Australian data further show that, although the skilled workers were less likely to vote

TABLE IX

SIZE OF COMMUNITY AND WORKERS' PARTY PREFERENCE IN AUSTRALIA—1955*

Party Choice	Community Size					
	Large Cities		Small Cities		Mining Communities†	
	Skilled workers	Semi- and unskilled workers	Skilled workers	Semi- and unskilled workers	Skilled workers	Semi- and unskilled workers
Liberal	35%	19%	44%	29%	15%	17%
Labor	64	81	56	71	77	83
Total	99%	100%	100%	100%	92%‡	100%
(N)	(333)	(241)	(96)	(107)	(13)	(6)

* Computed from IBM cards of a 1955 election survey conducted by the Australian Gallup Poll and kindly supplied to the author for further analysis.

† The number of cases is, of course, too small to justify any inferences from one sample, but previous surveys show comparable results. For example, a survey of the 1951 electorate indicates that 12 out of 13 manual workers living in mining towns were Labor voters.

‡ One respondent preferred one of the minor parties.

Report of the 1950 Congressional Voting Study (New York: Bureau of Applied Social Reseach, Columbia University, 1952), mimeographed. Leon Epstein demonstrates that in Wisconsin gubernatorial elections, the Democratic vote increased consistently with size of city, "Size of Place and the Division of the Two-Party Vote in Wisconsin," *Western Political Quarterly*, 9 (1956), p. 141. N. A. Masters and D. S. Wright show that though workers are distinctly less inclined to vote Democratic in small cities than in large ones, people in the managerial group tend to vote Republican in the same degree regardless of the size of the city they live in. "Trends and Variations in the Two-Party Vote: The Case of Michigan," *American Political Science Review*, 52 (1958), p. 1088.

Labor than the semi- and unskilled workers, both groups voted Labor more heavily in the large cities than in the small ones.

In all these cases the communications factor may be involved. A large plant makes for a higher degree of intraclass communication and less personal contact with people on higher economic levels. In large cities social interaction is also more likely to be within economic classes. In certain cases the working-class districts of large cities have been so thoroughly organized by working-class political movements that the workers live in a virtual world of their own, and it is in these centers that the workers are the most solidly behind leftist candidates, and, as we have already seen, vote most heavily.

BELIEF IN OPPORTUNITIES FOR INDIVIDUAL MOBILITY

Instead of taking political action, some discontented individuals attempt to better their lot within the existing economic system by working their way up the ladder of success. If such a possibility seems to exist, there will be a corresponding reduction in collective efforts at social change, such as the support of unions and leftist parties.

This has long been the major explanation offered for the fact that American workers tend to vote for mildly reformist parties, while European workers normally vote socialist or Communist. Supposedly living in an open-class society, with a developing economy which continually creates new jobs above the manual-labor level, the American worker is presumably more likely to believe in individual opportunity. His European counterpart, accepting the image of a closed-class society which does not even pretend to offer the worker a chance to rise, is impelled to act collectively for social change. While these stereotypes of the relative degree of social mobility in Europe and America do not correspond to reality, their acceptance may well affect voting.[65]

[65] A recent survey of the literature and research relating to mobility in many different countries found that the total vertical mobility (movement from lower- or working-class occupations to nonmanual

Unfortunately, it is not easy to give precise statistical validation for this explanation, since there are so many other ways in which European and American society differ. In America the working class as a whole has risen, through a large long-term increase in real wages, to a position which in other countries would be termed "middle class." There is a good deal of evidence that American workers believe in individual opportunity; various surveys show about half the workers saying that they have "a good chance for personal advancement in the years ahead."[66] A study in Chicago in 1937 during the Great Depression found that no less than 85 to 90 per cent of every economic group believed that their *children* had a good chance to be better off economically.[67] The most recent data indicate that *actual* social mobility in Europe is as high as it is in the United States but the *belief* in mobility differs. A relatively high rate of actual social mobility appears to be characteristic of all industrial societies.

Two factors are involved in the differential *belief* in mobility: the differences between the United States and Western Europe in total national income and its distribution and, second, the different value systems of the American and European upper classes. As I have put it elsewhere: "Income, in every class, is so much greater in America, and the gap between the living styles of the different social classes so much narrower, that in effect the egalitarian society envis-

---

or higher-prestige occupations) in the United States was not substantially different (30 per cent of the population) than in most other relatively developed countries. Other rates were Germany, 31 per cent; Sweden, 29 per cent; Japan, 27 per cent; France, 27 per cent; Denmark, 31 per cent; Great Britain, 29 per cent. Slightly lower was Switzerland, 23 per cent, and the lowest country in Western Europe was Italy at 16 per cent. These studies are fully reported in S. M. Lipset and R. Bendix, *op. cit.*, Chap. II.

[66] E. Roper, "Fortune Survey: A Self-Portrait of the American People," *Fortune*, 35 (1947), pp. 5–16.

[67] A. W. Kornhauser, "Analysis of Class Structure of Contemporary American Society," in G. W. Hartmann and T. M. Newcomb, eds., *Industrial Conflict* (New York: The Cordon Co., 1939), pp. 199–264.

aged by the proponents of high social mobility is much more closely approximated here than in Europe. While Europeans rise in the occupational scale as often as we [Americans] do, the marked contrast between the ways of life of the different classes continues to exist. Thus, in the United States workers and middle-class people have cars, while in Europe only the middle class can own an automobile."[68]

But divergent value systems also play a role here, since the American and European upper classes differ sharply in their conceptions of egalitarianism. The rags-to-riches myth is proudly propagated by the successful American businessman. Actual differences in rank and authority are justified as rewards for demonstrated ability. In Europe aristocratic values and patterns of inherited privilege and position are still upheld by many of the upper class, and therefore the European conservative wishes to minimize the extent of social mobility.

Given the much wider discrepancy in consumption styles between the European and American middle and working class, one would expect the upwardly mobile European of working-class origin to have somewhat greater difficulties in adjusting to his higher status, and to feel more discriminated against than his American counterpart, much like the successfully upwardly mobile Negro or other minority ethnic member in America comparing himself with a native-born Protestant white. The comparative materials bearing on the effect of mobility on party choice are, in fact, consistent with the hypothesis that Europeans remain more dissatisfied or retain more ties with their previous status. Surveys in five European nations—Sweden, Finland, Germany, Norway, and Britain—find that upward-mobile Europeans are more likely to vote for left parties than are their fellow countrymen who were born into the middle class, while in the United States, three different survey studies report that the upward mobile are more conservative (Republican) than those who grew

[68] S. M. Lipset and Natalie Rogoff, "Class and Opportunity in Europe and the United States," *Commentary*, 18 (1954), pp. 562–68.

up in middle-class families.[69] Some indication that the propensity to adjust to the cultural style of the class into which
one moves is associated with political views is suggested by
Swedish data which indicate that men in nonmanual occupations who have risen from the working class will continue
to vote for the left party unless they change their consumption styles (symbolized in Table X by the automobile).
Conversely, among those still in the class in which they grew
up, variations in consumption style seem to have no relationship to voting choice.

The American version of this difference in "consumption
styles" may be the move to the suburb, and several studies
have shown the differences in the political behavior of lower-
status persons who make such a move. A re-analysis of the
1952 survey conducted by the Survey Research Center at
Michigan (and analyzed generally in *The Voter Decides*)
along lines of suburban-urban differences found that there
were indeed shifts in party loyalties which could not be explained simply as the movement of already conservative people to the suburbs. Both hypotheses suggested by the authors
of this study are consistent with the thesis suggested here of
the impact of social mobility upon lower-class people.
Whether self-selection is the crucial factor (implying that the
new suburbanites are upwardly mobile and anxious to become socialized into a higher environment, which means voting Republican) or whether the effects of being exposed to a
more Republican environment—friends and neighbors—accounts for greater conservative voting, the data show that
mobility of this kind produces higher Republican voting on
the part of previously Democratic voters.[70] When occupation was held constant, in both "medium" and "high" status

[69] See S. M. Lipset and Hans Zetterberg, *op. cit.*, pp. 64–72, for
a detailed report on the political consequences of social mobility.
Data which indicate that the relationship between upward mobility
and vote choice in England is like that in other European countries
rather than the United States may be found in R. S. Milne and H.
C. Mackenzie, *op. cit.*, p. 58.

[70] See Fred I. Greenstein and Raymond E. Wolfinger, "The
Suburbs and Shifting Party Loyalties," *Public Opinion Quarterly*,

TABLE X

RELATIONSHIP BETWEEN SOCIAL ORIGIN, CONSUMPTION PATTERNS, AND VOTING BEHAVIOR AMONG MEN IN SWEDEN.*

	Manual from manual homes		Nonmanual from manual homes		Nonmanual from nonmanual homes	
	Without Car	With Car	Without Car	With Car	Without Car	With Car
Non-Socialist	15%	14%	38%	74%	79%	83%
Socialist	85	86	63	26	21	17
(N)	(221)	(72)	(78)	(55)	(170)	(145)

* H. L. Zetterberg, "Overages Erlander," *Vecko-Journalen*, 48 (1957), pp. 18, 36. Reproduced in S. M. Lipset and Reinhard Bendix, *Social Mobility in Industrial Society*, p. 68.

occupations there was considerably more Republican voting in the suburbs.[71]

While most discussions of the impact of mobility on the political and social systems emphasize the supposed consequences of different rates of upward mobility, considerable evidence indicates that there is a substantial degree of downward movement from one generation to another in every

22 (1958), pp. 473–83. Another study which dealt with one city rather than the whole country found little political change in the suburb of Kalamazoo, Michigan, and its authors concluded that the effect of the suburb has been overestimated. Yet, as their data show, the suburb from which they drew their interpretation was far from typical of the tract-type, relatively low-priced suburb which attracts the low-income buyer with aspirations to better himself and his family's future. Most of the homes were high priced for the area, 83 per cent of the respondents voted for Eisenhower in 1956, and 85 per cent were Protestants. It is not surprising that in an area like this, in which almost everyone was already a Republican, the effects of mobility upon political choice were not to be seen. For a report of this study see Jerome G. Manis and Leo C. Stine, "Suburban Residence and Political Behavior," *Public Opinion Quarterly*, 22 (1958), pp. 483–90.

71 Samuel Lubell, *The Revolt of the Moderates* (New York: Harper & Bros., 1956) and William H. Whyte, *The Organization Man* (New York: Simon and Schuster, 1956) discuss the political impact of suburbia. Lubell also sees a rising Republican trend in the cities, as part of general social trends not confined to the suburbs.

modern industrial society—a father's high position is no guarantee of a similar position for his children. And the most recent American data do in fact indicate that about one third of the sons of professionals, semi-professionals, proprietors, managers, and officials—the most privileged occupations—are in manual employment.[72] Similarly, there is extensive movement from rural to urban areas in most societies, much of which helps to fill the ranks of the manual workers.

These rather extensive movements into the industrial proletariat are one of the major sources of conservative politics within that class. In every country for which data are available—Germany, Finland, Britain, Sweden, Norway, and the United States—workers of middle-class parentage are much more likely to vote for the conservative parties than are workers whose fathers are of the same class. Those of rural background are also relatively more conservative. The difference is even more accentuated when variations in background over three generations are compared. In Germany a 1953 survey found that 75 per cent of the workers whose grandparents were workers voted for the Socialists or the Communists, but only 24 per cent of the workers with a middle-class father did.[73] In Finland, a similar study in 1948 showed that 82 per cent of the workers whose father and paternal grandfathers were workers voted for left parties as compared with 67 per cent of those with a rural background, and 42 per cent of those of middle-class parents.

Given the fact of extensive social mobility in all industrial societies, perhaps the most important effect of mobility on politics which should be noted is that the bulk of the socially mobile, whether their direction be upward or downward, vote for the more conservative parties. In Germany, where over three quarters of the manual workers of middle-class parentage voted for the nonsocialist parties in 1953, almost 70 per cent of those in nonmanual positions of working-class family background also opted for the "middle-class"

---

[72] S. M. Lipset and R. Bendix, *op. cit.*, pp. 87–91.
[73] Data computed from materials supplied by the UNESCO Institute in Cologne, Germany.

parties. Similarly in Finland, two thirds of the workers of middle-class origin remained loyal to nonleftist parties, while less than a quarter of those who had risen into middle-class occupations from working-class family background voted for the Socialists or Communists.[74] These findings illustrate the pervasive influence of contact with superior status on attitudes and behavior. Those subject to a cross-pressure between the political values congruent with a higher and a lower status as a result of having been in both positions are much more likely to resolve the conflict in favor of the former.

TRADITIONALISM

One of the most striking cases of deviation from leftist voting within the lower-income group is presented by some relatively poor and economically less-developed regions that regularly vote for conservative candidates. Such areas are found in the southern states of the United States, in southern Italy,[75] in Quebec in Canada, in the Scottish Highlands in Great Britain, and in the west of Norway. The political pattern of such regions has been summed up in the statement, "Every country has a South." All these areas have a special regional flavor in their politics which separates them from the main lines of political division within the country and sometimes produces regional or separatist parties.[76]

One obvious explanation, which was discussed above, is that poverty can be so extreme that it prevents effective organization and destroys all hope of being better off. Extreme

[74] Data supplied by Dr. Erik Allardt of the University of Helsinki, and based on two surveys conducted by the Finnish Gallup Poll. Both German and Finnish studies are reported in more detail in Lipset and Bendix, *op. cit.*, pp. 69–71.

[75] G. Schepis, "Sociologia elettorales della Sicilia," *Revista italiana di economia demografia a statistica*, 4 (1950), No. 3–4, pp. 491–98.

[76] R. V. Burks, "Catholic Parties in Latin Europe," *Journal of Modern History*, 24 (1952), pp. 269–86. Even in Sweden where regional parties are unknown, regional differences have persisted for many decades with "parties of the left . . . stronger in the North and parties of the right stronger in the South," Dankwart A. Rustow, *The Politics of Compromise* (Princeton: Princeton University Press, 1955), pp. 136–37.

ignorance and illiteracy make communication and understanding of any political program difficult. People completely occupied by the day-to-day task of keeping alive have no surplus of time and energy to invest in long-run ventures for betterment through political action.[77] They may also be too powerless to stand up to the economic pressure or violence used against them by local privileged classes. Thus the tenant farmer and the farm laborer in America have never been able to build effective economic and political organizations, even when they have had sympathetic help from government agencies like the Farm Security Administration under the New Deal.

The most powerful deterrent to leftist political action by the impoverished workers and peasants of backward areas, however, is the extent to which their minds are dominated by "traditionalistic" values—resignation to a traditional standard of living and loyalty to the "powers that be." In these areas the social structure remains in some part the way it was before the age of capitalism and the free-market economy. The positions of rich and poor are defined as the natural order of things and are supported by personal, family, and local loyalties rather than viewed as a product of impersonal economic and social forces, subject to change through political action. At the same time the poor peasant or worker performs a role which has an obvious meaning and value, and he derives gratification from stable personal relationships and ceremonial activities embracing the whole community. Religious belief tends to be strong and to support the *status quo*.[78]

In contrast, the position of a commercial farmer or urban worker in a rationalized market economy offers no such stable structure of relationship. The personal relationships and local institutions that rewarded loyalty and punished deviation from traditional beliefs have been swept away, and aspira-

[77] For a discussion of southern Italy see Edward Banfield, *The Moral Basis of a Backward Society* (Glencoe: The Free Press, 1958).

[78] A. Siegfried, *Tableau politique de la France de l'ouest sous la troisième république, op. cit.*

tions for economic betterment are encouraged. The railroad corporation or the grain elevator operation are protected by none of the ancient legitimacy which hallows the power of a great landowning family. The commercial farmer is free to respond to frustration with militant support of parties favoring social change.

Backward, agrarian areas sometimes burst into flames of revolt, however, and once shaken loose from the acceptance of traditional values, they may swing to the most radical extremes. Even in the American South, the 1890s saw an explosive growth of radical Populism, mobilizing some of the poorest farmers in the country, both white and Negro. This electoral uprising met with failure and disappeared, leaving hardly a trace. In the impoverished Italian South, the Communists and the neo-Fascists have been disproportionately strong.[79] The two most drastic political transformations of our time, the Russian and the Chinese Communist revolutions, took place in countries with an almost wholly backward, traditionalistic rural social structure.

Little is actually known about the conditions under which a backward area can be suddenly transformed from one end of the political spectrum to the other. Studies of political attitudes in the Near East suggest that communications from the outside can play an important part by creating discontent and holding out the example of an American or a Russian utopia in which ordinary workers or farmers live well.[80] But the problem of political behavior in backward areas is one of the most important and perplexing in the world today from the viewpoint of advocates of political and social democracy. A large part of the "free world," and particularly of the countries bordering on the Soviet sphere, is made up of just such areas.

Traditionalism may help to account for the greater con-

[79] Department of State, United States Division of Research for Europe, *A Statistical Analysis of the Italian Election Results* (Washington, 1948). See discussion in Chap. 5 of Italy.

[80] Daniel Lerner, *The Passing of Traditional Society* (Glencoe: The Free Press, 1958).

TABLE XI

EXPLANATORY FACTORS RELATED TO ORIGINAL STATISTICAL REGULARITIES IN VOTING WITHIN THE LOWER-INCOME GROUPS

Types of deprivation:

	Insecurity of income	Unsatisfying work	Low prestige status
Workers in:			
Large plants	+	+	+
Small plants	+	−	+
Workers in:			
Large cities			
Small towns			
Workers in:			
Europe			
United States			
Manual workers			+
White-collar			−
Minority group			+
Majority group			−
Commercial farmers, fishermen	+	−	
Local market, subsistence farmers	−	−	
Miners, lumbermen	+	+	+
Servants, service workers			
Economically advanced areas	+		
Backward areas	−		
Men			
Women			

NOTE: Plus signs indicate factors favoring leftist voting in lower classes.

TABLE XI (continued)

Good intra-class communications	Low expectation of mobility	Lack of traditionalism	Left vote
		Facilitating conditions:	
+	+	+	Higher
−	−	−	Lower
+		+	Higher
−		−	Lower
+	+		Higher
−	−		Lower
+			Higher
−			Lower
			Higher
			Lower
	+		Higher
			Lower
+		+	Higher
−			Lower
+		+	Higher
−			Lower
+		+	Higher
−			Lower

servatism of women, particularly in Europe, which was noted earlier. Women are usually more influenced by traditional religious beliefs which uphold the existing social order.[81] Direct evidence of this has been found in opinion surveys in France—47 per cent of the women said they paid "much" or "a little" attention to the position of the church when deciding how to vote, as compared with only 33 per cent of the men.[82] The greater conservatism of workers in small towns may also reflect the remnants of traditionalistic attitudes and relationships.

The effort to account for the variations in the electoral behavior of different groups by pointing up different aspects of the class structure in various societies has involved a discussion of several factors, many of which operate simultaneously. It is obvious that an explanation of the behavior of any one group involves treating a whole pattern, and in discussing each factor separately, it is perhaps difficult to see all the variables at work on any one group, like the miners whose behavior has been cited a number of times to illustrate the operation of different factors. Table XI indicates some of the ways in which different sets of variables combine to form a pattern in the separate groups.

Although it seems evident that most of the structural factors which determine party choice in modern society can be viewed as aspects of the stratification system, there are clearly many other social variables which interact with class and politics. The next chapter continues the discussion of the conditions of the democratic order by analyzing one such major determinant of electoral behavior—variations in the experiences of different generations—and by treating the related issue of historical change in voting patterns.

[81] H. Tingsten, *Political Behavior: Studies in Election Statistics*, Stockholm Economic Studies, No. 7 (London: P. S. King, 1937), pp. 42–45; for a summary of evidence on sex and religiosity, see Michael Argyle, *op. cit.*, pp. 71–79.
[82] French Institute of Public Opinion, "La verité sur la pratiques et les sentiments religeux des Français," *Réalités*, 32 (1952), pp. 36–44. See also "La France est-elle encore Catholique?" *Sondages*, 14 (1952), No. 4.

CHAPTER 8

Elections: The Expression of the Democratic Class Struggle—Continuity and Change

Generations and Political Behavior

ALL SURVEYS of voting choice report major differences in the political allegiances of different age groups within specific strata, educational, religious, or ethnic groups. Different ages imply variations in life experiences and affect left or right political behavior in at least two ways: through generational differences (with the crucial experiences of adolescence sometimes shaping the political outlook of an entire age group) and through differences in the typical patterns of social experience associated with different age groups: adolescence, maturity, and old age. Many such more or less significant variations may be cited. For the middle classes, for example, age is largely correlated with career. That is, the older a person (up to a certain age), the more likely he is to have moved up in socioeconomic position. Age may also reflect other status variations, such as being the primary or the supplementary breadwinner, and may be related to membership in different types of groups, or to a more exposed position in the economic structure.[1]

A number of sociologists in pre-Hitler Germany suggested that the concept of the "generation" had to be added to such

[1] For a general discussion of age differences see Robert E. Lane, *Political Life* (Glencoe: The Free Press, 1959), pp. 216–19; and Herbert H. Hyman, *Political Socialization* (Glencoe: The Free Press, 1959), *passim*. The latter book is the best American discussion of the formation of generations in politics.

structural categories as class or ethnic group to explain political behavior.[2] They argued that just as men's attitudes differ as a consequence of their being in a different position in the stratification hierarchy, so men also differ as a result of belonging to different generations. Karl Mannheim, a leading exponent of this concept, emphasized that common experiences at a given point—largely, in his opinion, late adolescence—create a common frame of reference within which people of the same age group tend to view their subsequent political experiences.

This suggests that the political frame of reference in terms of which one first begins to think seriously about politics may remain in force for the rest of one's life. Thus, Mannheim and others argue, to understand the basic values underlying the approach of the middle-aged groups who dominate the political life of any given society, one must go back and examine the political climate and problems which existed when they were young.

This focus on the specific political environment of late adolescence is actually a sociological counterpart of the psychological concern with the life-cycle. The psychologist Edward Spranger recognized this problem and began his discussion of adolescent politics by pointing out that "the political position of youth changes with specific historical circumstances."[3]

Unfortunately there has been no attempt to study systematically the effect of generation experiences with modern

[2] K. Mannheim, "The Sociological Problem of Generations," in P. Kecskemeti, ed., *Essays on the Sociology of Knowledge* (New York: Oxford University Press, 1952), pp. 276–322; R. Behrendt, "Die öffentliche Meinung und das Generationsproblem," *Kölner Vierteljahrshefte für Soziologie*, 11 (1932), pp. 290–309; Sigmund Neumann, "The Conflict of Generations in Contemporary Europe," *Vital Speeches*, 5 (1939), pp. 623–28; Sigmund Neumann, *Permanent Revolution* (New York: Harper & Bros., 1942); Rudolf Heberle, *Social Movements* (New York: Appleton-Century-Crofts, 1951), Chap. 6.

[3] Edward Spranger, *Psychologie des Jugendalters* (Leipzig: Quelle und Meyer, 1925), p. 212.

survey research techniques. A pre-Hitler student of German society, Arthur Dix, did set up in tabular form the types of data that would be necessary for such research. He broke down the 1930 German electorate into age groupings and presented data for each group on the political climate surrounding the first election in which they participated. From these data, he made assumptions concerning the role these earlier events played in the political events of the 1930s.[4] And the age composition and life experiences of members of the Nazi and Socialist parties reported at that time, tended to confirm some of the hypotheses about the role of different generations in German society.[5]

Some American studies also illustrate the usefulness of the generation concept. In a study of Negro voting in Harlem in 1944, the sociologist John Morsell found that 82 per cent of the Negroes under forty-four years old voted for Roosevelt, as compared with 59 per cent of those over that age. Many of the older Negroes may have been still responding to an image of the Republican party as the party of Lincoln.[6]

Panel studies of the elections of 1940, 1944, and 1948 have shown that younger Catholics were more likely to vote Republican than their elders, while younger Protestants were more prone to be Democratic than older ones.[7] These dif-

---

[4] Arthur Dix, *Die Deutschen Reichstagswahlen, 1871–1930, und die Wandlungen der Volkgliederung* (Tübingen: J. B. C. Mohr, Paul Siebeck, 1930), pp. 34–35.

[5] Hans Gerth, "The Nazi Party: Its Leadership and Composition," *American Journal of Sociology*, 55 (1940), pp. 530–41.

[6] John Morsell, *The Political Behavior of Negroes in New York City* (unpublished Ph.D. thesis, Department of Sociology, Columbia University, 1951).

[7] Paul F. Lazarsfeld, Bernard Berelson, and Hazel Gaudet, *The People's Choice* (New York: Duell, Sloan & Pearce, 1944), p. 24; Bernard Berelson, Paul F. Lazarsfeld, and William McPhee, *Voting* (Chicago: University of Chicago Press, 1954), p. 70; S. J. Korchin, *Psychological Variables in the Behavior of Voters* (unpublished Ph.D. thesis, Department of Social Relations, Harvard University, 1946).

ferences might reflect sheer rebellion against tradition, but
are probably another result of the experiences of different
generations. The older Catholics and Protestants may have
been still reacting to the pre-Depression voting situation
when religion was more important than class in creating a
political predisposition. The younger voters, however, formed
their political beliefs in the thirties and forties, when class
became more important. The apparent contradiction between parents and children, therefore, appears to be a product of middle-class young Catholics becoming Republicans
and young working-class Protestants becoming Democrats.
These shifts indicate that traditional family allegiances are
affected by other statuses and experiences.

Studies of the 1948 and 1952 elections indicate that the
new political generation is more Republican than that which
immediately preceded it. In Elmira, New York, in 1948 only
38 per cent of the wage workers aged twenty-one to twenty-
four voted for Truman, as compared with 54 per cent among
those aged twenty-five to thirty-four;[8] using national survey
data, the pollster Louis Harris reported that 44 per cent of
the twenty-one to twenty-four age group were for Eisenhower
in 1952, as compared with 38 per cent of the twenty-five to
thirty-four group.

These differences may be the result of a situation in which
people who came of age during the Depression or war developed Democratic ties; whereas those who know these events
only as history and whose first vote was cast in a period of
prosperity turned toward the Republican party. If, in fact,
generations tend to vote left or right depending on which
group was in the ascendancy during their coming of age,
then it may be necessary to reconsider the popularly held
idea that conservatism is associated with increasing age. The
empirical evidence for this belief was gathered during periods
of tremendous social instability—the 1930s and 1940s—when
youth turned leftist while their elders tended to retain the

[8] B. Berelson, P. Lazarsfeld, and W. McPhee, op. cit., p. 96; L.
Harris, Is There a Republican Majority? (New York: Harper &
Bros., 1954), p. 218.

more conservative beliefs of their youth. If a society should move from prolonged instability to stability, it may well be that older people would retain the leftist ideas of their youth, and the younger generations would adopt conservative philosophies.

Increasing age is often associated with advancement in income or status. People marry, change their residences, their jobs, and form new associations. It would seem obvious that such changes in social position should be related to opinion formation and political behavior. Unhappily, public opinion surveys rarely collect much information on variations in the past experience of individuals. Studies of labor mobility indicate that many people have an extremely varied work history. Manual workers over thirty-one years old in one such survey spent 20 per cent of their work history in nonmanual positions, while those in nonmanual employment indicated that about 25 per cent of their work history had been spent in manual employment.[9] These studies did not deal with politics, but the American one did consider trade-union membership and activity, which is usually related to politics. It was found that the larger the proportion of his career a presently employed manual worker had spent in that category, the more likely he was to be an active member of his union and, one would guess, a Democrat.

Other changes in political outlook related to increasing age are due to the requirements of family life. There is a tendency for irreligious parents to feel the need to send their children to Sunday school and, in the process, to become themselves reintegrated in the religious, and usually more conservative, community. Among middle-class and well-paid working-class parents, children are one of the prime reasons for the move to the suburbs. The concern for the welfare of children may also have more subtle psychological effects, causing a parent to become aware, often for the first time, of

[9] S. M. Lipset and R. Bendix, *Social Mobility in Industrial Society* (Berkeley: University of California Press, 1959), p. 166. This book also reports on other American studies as well as surveys in a number of European and Asian states.

the positive functions of authority mechanisms in a society.

Children may also serve to restrain any propensity for deviant behavior on the part of their parents. No one is more "conservative" or conformist than a young child. But the way in which the child may force his parents to change has been ignored for the most part by students of the family.

The pattern has been explicitly recognized only in the literature dealing with the relationship between immigrant parents and their American children.[10] Such studies have called attention to the role of children in "Americanizing" their parents (changing their attitudes and values). Northern liberals who move to the South furnish another example of a process which is continually going on. The child whose parents tell him that Negroes are equal is exposed to punishment by the other members of his peer group. If he adapts to the peer group's standards, he is punished at home. Undoubtedly, many parents find it easier to adapt to the community's social or political values than continually to expose their children to punishment. In less obvious ways, similar processes probably occur whenever people with children move from one political environment to another.

Another indication of the way that changing social position, as a correlate of increasing age, can affect attitudes is furnished by the sociologists Mark Benney and Phyllis Geiss, who show that concern with social status grows more marked with age.[11] As people grow older they become more likely to report themselves as middle class rather than working class, and this greater concern with status position may be reflected in political opinions as well.

The great increase in the proportion of elderly people in the population has led experts in various fields to analyze the impact of an aging population on society.[12] The political

[10] O. Handlin, *The Uprooted—The Epic Story of the Great Migrations That Made the American People* (Boston: Little, Brown, 1952); R. E. Park and H. A. Miller, *Old World Traits Transplanted* (New York: Harper & Bros., 1927).

[11] Mark Benney and Phyllis Geiss, "Social Class and Politics in Greenwich," *British Journal of Sociology*, 1 (1950), pp. 310–27.

[12] K. Davis and J. W. Combs, Jr., "The Sociology of an Aging Population," in New York Academy of Medicine, *The Social and*

strength of the aged is already evident from the increasing number of public welfare measures that provide pensions for retired people.

There are at least two parallel processes going on which may affect the political behavior of the aged. On one hand, as we indicated earlier, people are likely to retain the perspectives and loyalties of their youth. Thus, in the present day, an older population will probably slow down political changes. On the other hand, the aged in modern industrial society are largely an underprivileged group; they have no useful role to perform as they had in rural societies, nor are they well supported by, or integrated into, families. As a group, therefore, they are especially dependent on the state. Moreover, because of the rigidity of fixed incomes from pensions or savings, they are more exposed to the effects of inflation than those with greater bargaining power. Depressions are likely to affect the aged disproportionately, since the number of jobs available to them on a part-time or full-time basis is reduced even more than for the population as a whole, and contributions from relatives also tend to decline.

Such conditions may actually result in the radicalization of part of the aged population, although their isolation and relatively poor communication facilities restrict their political effectiveness. As a have-not group dependent on state support, they may find that only the leftist parties advocate extension of welfare state measures. The growth of mass movements of the aged, like the Townsend Plan, is one indication of old people's propensity to fight for redistribution of the income.[13] And pension movements in the United

Biological Challenge of Our Aging Population (New York: Columbia University Press, 1950), pp. 146–70; O. Pollak, "Conservatism in Later Maturity and Old Age," American Sociological Review, 8 (1943), pp. 175–79; L. H. Fisher, "The Politics of Age," in M. Derber, ed., The Aged and Society (Champaign: Industrial Relations Research Association, 1950), pp. 157–67.

[13] H. Cantril, The Psychology of Social Movements (New York: John Wiley & Sons, 1941), p. 192; for a discussion of a powerful old-age movement during postwar prosperity see Frank A. Pinner, Paul Jacobs, and Philip Selznick, Old Age and Political Behavior: A Case Study (Berkeley: University of California Press, 1959).

States have had a tendency to identify or co-operate with radical movements. During the 1930s, for example, the Townsendites worked with some semifascist groups, while the Communists were successful in capturing a number of aged groups on the West coast. In Canada some of the pensioner organizations work with the C.C.F., the socialist party. Samuel Pratt suggests that older persons in small communities in Germany tended to go Nazi.[14] In Holland, public opinion data indicate that the Communists are more successful than the socialists in winning the support of retired workers.[15] In Britain and Denmark, the available data are somewhat contradictory, which suggests that age as such is not a major differentiating element in these countries.[16] On the other hand, contemporary American, German, Swedish, Italian, and French data suggest that the old in these five countries are disproportionately conservative.[17]

The Historical Background of Voting Patterns

Since voting is a recurrent and periodic event in the life of individuals and social groups, we must consider it over longer periods of time, extending our perspective beyond static relationships between social positions, and beyond the immediate events of one election. As Joseph Schumpeter has put it:

[14] Samuel A. Pratt, *The Social Basis of Nazism and Communism in Urban Germany* (unpublished M.A. thesis, Department of Sociology, Michigan State University, 1948).

[15] Wiardi Beckman Institute, *Verkiezingen in Nederland* (Amsterdam: 1951), mimeographed; J. J. de Jong, *Overheid en Onderdaan* (Wageningen: N. V. Gebr. Zomer and Keunings Uitgeversmij, 1956), p. 105.

[16] H. G. Nicholas, *The British General Election of 1950*, p. 303; De Jong, *op. cit.*, pp. 81, 92–93.

[17] L. Harris, *op. cit.*, p. 173; F.I.P.O. (French Institute of Public Opinion), "La verité sur la pratiques et les sentiments religeux des Français," *Réalités*, 82 (1952), pp. 36–44; also "La France est-elle encore Catholique?" *Sondages*, 14 (1952), No. 4; De Jong, *op. cit.*, pp. 98, 109, 114, 119.

No decade in the history of politics, religion, technology, painting, poetry and whatnot ever contains its own explanation. In order to understand the events [of various given periods] . . . you must survey a period of much wider span. Not to do so is the hall-mark of dilettantism.[18]

When we consider that between 1896 and 1932 over 70 per cent of all American counties did not change the majority of their presidential vote from one election to the next, the need to include a historical dimension can be seen. Even in an election like 1932, only 58 per cent changed their party allegiance of four years before. And in the whole period only five counties were on a different side in each election but one.[19] Clearly it is impossible to explain why given areas or groups support specific parties solely by knowing the social correlates associated with different political tendencies, a fact which is pointed up by the two major panel studies of American voting behavior. Both were conducted in individual cities, and both report relatively comparable relationships between the vote and social structure. In each the more well to do were more Republican. The first study, which took place in Sandusky, Ohio, reported on a preponderantly Democratic community, while the second one, in Elmira, New York, reported on an overwhelmingly Republican city.[20] The only way to explain why the cities differed is by their varying histories.

The political scientists V. O. Key, Jr., and Frank Munger have developed this point further in a study of "political swings" in Indiana. Since the social characteristics of voters discussed in most survey-type voting research do not account for a great deal of the variation in political preference, they

[18] Joseph Schumpeter, "The Decade of the Twenties," *American Economic Review Supplement*, 36 (1946), pp. 1–10.
[19] Ralph and Mildred Fletcher, "Consistency in Party Voting, 1896–1932," *Social Forces*, 15 (1936), pp. 281–82.
[20] The Sandusky study is reported in P. F. Lazarsfeld, B. Berelson, and H. Gaudet, *op. cit.*; the Elmira study is in B. Berelson, P. F. Lazarsfeld, and W. McPhee, *op. cit.*

argue that too great an emphasis on the social determinants of the electoral decision may "take the politics out of political behavior." Key and Munger report a high correlation between the votes of counties in Indiana in the years 1868 to 1900 and 1920 to 1948, in spite of major social changes in these periods. They suggest: "The long persistence of county patterns of party affiliation despite changes in interest and the disappearance of the issues that created the pattern, and the existence of contrasting partisan patterns in essentially similar counties point toward a 'political' grouping at least to some extent independent of other social groupings."[21] Thus traditional party identification operates, to some extent, like religion or class, as a determinant of the vote.

Perhaps the major contribution of these authors is their insistence on the necessity of studying the differential relevance of social characteristics at different periods in time. They suggest that social characteristics gain political significance only in the context of an analysis of specific political alternatives. This kind of analysis may help us explain such phenomena as the differential political significance of class and religion for the pre- and post-New Deal generations, with the first gaining at the expense of the second.[22]

Long-term continuities in allegiance to political groups in spite of changes in the issues or in the role of different parties call for a study of the conditions underlying consistency or variation.[23] Over a period of time either the social structure

[21] V. O. Key, Jr., and Frank Munger, "Social Determinism and Electoral Decision: The Case of Indiana," in E. Burdick and A. J. Brodbeck, *American Political Behavior* (Glencoe: The Free Press, 1959), pp. 281–99. Analysis along these lines of the changes in political attitudes between 1952 and 1956, when little change in the social characteristics of the voters took place, but a shift in almost all social groups toward the Republicans, is presented in a re-analysis of data collected by the Survey Research Center in Michigan. See Donald E. Stokes, Angus Campbell, and Warren E. Miller, "Components of Electoral Decision," *American Political Science Review*, 62 (1958), pp. 367–88.

[22] See Chap. 9 for a discussion of this phenomenon.

[23] For discussions of continuities see V. O. Key, Jr., *Southern Politics in State and Nation* (New York: Alfred A. Knopf, 1949);

of an area, the social position of a group, or the role of a
party may remain constant or change. Adherence to a party,
when there is a consistent relationship between the position
of a group and that of a party, does not need explanation.
But when a group continues to support a party after that
party has changed its program or the group has changed its
position in the social structure, the situation requires analysis.

In some situations political allegiances may reinforce the
institutions and sentiments attached to a given social structure which might otherwise lose their meaning and importance. For example, the continued long-term loyalty of a
lower-class ethnic group to the Democratic party may, on
the surface, appear the same as the support given to the
Republican party since the Civil War by the poor hill or
mountain farmers of parts of the South.[24] The first example,
however, represents a case in which a lower-class group continues to support the party of the "underdog." The southern
Republican example, on the other hand, seems to be an out-
dated or "nonlogical" loyalty; the poor mountain farmers
originally supported the direct antecedent of the Republicans, the Whigs, because they were the party advocating
internal improvements, e.g., good roads; then backed the Republicans as the Union party, but continued to support them
long after these issues were dead and economic differences
had reasserted themselves as the main basis of cleavage.[25]
The problems presented by these two types of continuities
are vastly different.

Continuity in allegiance in spite of a change in the social
structure of an area may simply represent a "political lag"
and the failure of the traditional opposition party to realize
that the political potential of the area has changed. In 1948,

R. and M. Fletcher, *op. cit.*, pp. 281–85; and F. Goguel, *Géographie
des élections françaises de 1870 à 1951, Cahiers de la fondation
nationale des sciences politiques*, no. 27 (Paris: Librairie Armand
Colin, 1951).

[24] V. O. Key, Jr., *op. cit.*, pp. 280–85; Alexander Heard, *A Two-
Party South* (Chapel Hill: University of North Carolina Press, 1952),
pp. 40–45.

[25] For a more detailed discussion see Chap. 11, pp. 381–84.

for example, the New Hampshire Democrats complained that no major Democratic campaigner entered the state and little money was given to them for organizational purposes. Yet New Hampshire is now one of the most industrialized states in the Union, and also has a large Catholic population.[26]

Among what may be called the "structural" factors underlying many seemingly "nonlogical" continuities is the fact that the dominant political party in a given area becomes recognized as the only legitimate, socially approved vehicle for political action. In some areas the Republican party or the Democratic party was originally the party of a military enemy and still carries the overtones of being illegitimate or a threat to the community. Catholics in France remember that leftist parties originally were violent opponents of Catholicism and that to support an opposition party meant being identified as an enemy of the community. With the passage of time the original basis for rejecting alternative forms of political action may disappear, but change in political allegiance becomes extremely difficult if the challenge to a party develops only after a group or area has supported it for a number of generations. By then the traditional political allegiance has become so intertwined with other institutions—the church, the family—that to change it often involves change in the other institutional structures as well.

Such an integration of a party with the other segments of the social structure implies that a minority party supporter must accept the role of a social deviant. The political scientist Alexander Heard reports that in small towns and cities in the South many businessmen who openly became Republicans have been socially ostracized and financially ruined. He

[26] For a discussion of why New Hampshire Democrats cannot seem to win elections in spite of a relatively high vote and favorable urban, industrial, and ethnic characteristics, see Duane Lockard, *New England State Politics* (Princeton: Princeton University Press, 1959), pp. 62–65. Lockard attributes this failure mainly to factional warfare between ethnic groups, and the failure of Democratic leaders to organize effectively, because they are more concerned with patronage. Both of these factors may be considered hangovers from a period of minority-party status, part of the political lag of leaders unable to change their view of the party.

also points out that in most Southern counties a person with serious political ambitions can normally hope to achieve them only if he operates within the legitimate one-party political structure.[27] This assures a monopoly of talent for the dominant party.

In such a situation, a self-perpetuating political cycle develops in which the existence of a legitimate political monopoly forces people into operating within that framework to achieve reforms; and since they operate within it, its security is reinforced.

Community definition of a certain avenue of political action as the only legitimate one also limits the frame of reference within which politics may be presented. The elder Senator La Follette pointed this out, when explaining why he did not break with the Republican party, by saying, "People will listen to me because I am a Republican."[28] In North Dakota the socialist founder of the Non-Partisan League, A. C. Townley, made the conscious decision to enter the Republican party because he believed that the farmers of the state would accept politics only under the Republican label.[29] An opposition leadership working within the dominant party

[27] A. Heard, *op. cit.*, pp. 74–75. V. O. Key, Jr., has shown that "the extent to which a party's nominations are contested in the primary by two or more aspirants depends in large measure on the prospects for victory for the nominee in the general election. Uncontested nominations for legislative posts are almost the rule in those districts in which a party's cause seems hopeless, while a large proportion of nominations are contested in relatively sure districts." *American State Politics: An Introduction* (New York: Alfred A. Knopf, 1956), p. 172. W. H. Standing and J. A. Robinson set up detailed criteria for "safe" and "competitive" electoral districts and confirm Key's observations. They found that, on the average, nearly one more contestant (2.31) enters the primary of the dominant party than of the subordinate party (1.39). "Inter-Party Competition and Primary Contesting: The Case of Indiana," *American Political Science Review*, 52 (1958), pp. 1066–77.

[28] E. N. Doan, *The La Follettes and the Wisconsin Idea* (New York: Rinehart, 1947), p. 6.

[29] H. G. Gaston, *The Non-Partisan League* (New York: Henry Holt, 1940); A. A. Bruce, *The Non-Partisan League* (New York: Macmillan, 1921).

may thus help to maintain the legitimacy of a traditional party allegiance by giving it a new content.

Political systems are linked in different societies to ethnic, religious, caste, or regional economic systems. Their perpetuation may seem to be contradictory to one need, such as the economic, but of major relevance to the others. For example, one party may be viewed as the party of the immigrant Catholics, while the other is the party of the Anglo-Saxons. In Massachusetts it has been almost impossible for a person of Irish or Jewish extraction to achieve position in the Republican party. The London *Economist*, discussing contemporary British practices in selecting parliamentary candidates, reports that "The chairman of the Labour party's national executive was excluded from consideration for one seat last year because he was not a Roman Catholic. Despite Disraeli, it is still difficult to get a Tory seat if you are a Jew. . . ."[30] The traditional left-right cleavage in France, as we have seen, is also related to religious affiliation. Secular, anticlerical, or Protestant conservative French businessmen will not vote for a clerical conservative party, and religious radical Catholics will not vote for a radical antireligious party. This seeming irrationality, when politics is viewed along economic-interest or liberal-conservative lines, may actually be an expression of the greater saliency to a group and its members of other values or tensions.[31]

A somewhat similar factor is the conflict between geographical areas or rural and urban divisions. A good deal of internal American state politics involves a cleavage between the big cities and the rest of the state. This kind of interest cleavage restricts the entry of national issues as sources of division.[32]

[30] "How to Get Chosen: An Elementary Guide to Becoming a Member of Parliament," *The Economist*, 191 (May 2, 1959), p. 405.

[31] André Siegfried, *Géographie électorale de l'Ardèche sous le troisième république, Cahiers de la fondation nationale des sciences politiques*, no. 9 (Paris: Librairie Armand Colin, 1949).

[32] Harold F. Gosnell, *Grass Roots Politics: National Voting Behavior of Typical States* (Washington: American Council on Public Affairs, 1942), *passim*.

The primary system in the United States has facilitated the maintenance of continuities, a point elaborated in the next chapter. It permits new strains introduced by changes in social structure to be reflected within the dominant party rather than through support of the opposition party. The commitment to factional politics within a party then helps carry the national ticket. We know little, however, about how individual voters reconcile the strains of voting for a radical faction in the primaries, and then voting for a conservative party in the national elections, as has occurred in North Dakota and other states.

Underlying these "structural" factors are some, more psychological in character, which further help to account for historical continuities in voting patterns. A sharp break with a traditional political allegiance, or continuity, by a group can occur only when some experience is perceived as clearly affecting the group's interests and requiring a new political orientation. The necessary ambiguity of democratic politics, especially in two-party countries, prevents this sharp challenge to an institutionalized voting pattern from occurring often. If we think of different kinds of elections in the United States, those which present a clear-cut, important policy division that is easily understood and has major consequences for a large number of voters, like 1896 and 1936, are the exception rather than the rule. Both parties in a two-party election seek to appeal to almost every group of voters, and most especially to those who have some tradition of loyalty to the party. Given an ambiguous, complex stimulus without clear alternatives, many voters fall back on older loyalties and habits which are usually reinforced by present social relationships.

An additional factor that intensifies the effect of the ambiguity, though in part it may flow from it, is the fact that the overwhelming majority of voters in most stable democracies are relatively indifferent to politics under normal conditions. Most studies have reported that only about 20 to 40 per cent of the electorate say that they get worked up over politics, or that they believe they can influence government,

or that they take an active part in political discussions. The
"indifferent majority" is even more likely to react in terms
of the existent group pattern. When vote changes occur, this
large group will tend to retard the impact, since the political
stimuli which determine the changes affect them least. For
example, those American Catholics who in the 1940s still
voted along the religious cleavage lines of the 1920s rather
than along the class lines of the 1940s were the least involved or interested in politics.[33]

The problem of analyzing change of political allegiance is
similar to that of continuity. Most explanations of group
change state that a party no longer represents the needs of a
specific group and the group therefore changes; or that the
position and needs of a group have changed, and therefore
they change their political allegiance.[34] Given the fact that
there are many situations in which these patterns occur but
change does not take place, it is clear that such analyses
must include the fact that political allegiances not only have
a "life of their own" and may persist long after their rational
basis is gone, but also that a group may be wrested from its
traditional party by political tactics, novel appeals, an attractive candidate, and other methods unrelated to social structure and the correspondence we normally expect between
party program and group support.

Even with this qualification, however, long-term shifts in
the social position of a group can usually be correlated with
changes in their political (left or right) complexion, even if
not immediately or directly. It may be suggested, for example,
that left or reform governments initiate a self-destroying proc-

[33] B. Berelson, P. F. Lazarsfeld, and W. McPhee, *op. cit.*, pp.
69–70.
[34] There is a curious discrepancy between the analysis of electoral
change in groups and individuals. When dealing with groups, political scientists explain the change as a rational reaction to new
situations or factors. On the individual level, sociologists and social
psychologists analyze change in terms of group pressures on the individual or as a response to personal needs, some of which are rational but many of which are latent or unconscious. There is as yet
little theoretical integration of these contrasting modes of analysis.

ess by integrating depressed groups into the national structure. By granting the demands of the have-nots, reform movements may shift some of them into the conservative ranks. I have argued this thesis elsewhere to explain the ebb and flow of agrarian radicalism:

New Zealand farmers supported the guaranteed price policy of the Labor Party in the depths of the depression in 1935, when low prices threatened their security. When the depression ended, however, the rural districts turned against Labor's planning program, which called for maximum prices as well as minimum ones, and increased the incomes of the poorer groups. In the United States, President Roosevelt established the guaranteed parity prices and crop insurance demanded by organized farmers. In so doing, however, he lost the support of the rural areas, including the once-radical wheat belt. In Russia the Bolsheviks lost the support of the peasants after they gave them title to the land.[35]

The fact that Negroes in the United States and the poorer workers in Great Britain have of late proved resistant to conservative trends which have affected most other strata in a period of great prosperity may be an indication of the fact that the improvement in their position has not been enough to change their perception of the situation and they remain dissatisfied, while other segments of the lower strata have benefited sufficiently to begin to break with tradition.[36] Conservatives in office are similarly subject to inherent instability of support because of their resistance to enacting needed changes.

Another source of change lies in the compromising char-

[35] S. M. Lipset, *Agrarian Socialism* (Berkeley: University of California Press, 1950), p. 229.

[36] For Negro patterns see E. Litchfield, *Voting Behavior in a Metropolitan Area*, Michigan Governmental Studies, No. 7 (Ann Arbor: University of Michigan Press, 1941), pp. 58–59; Louis Harris, *op. cit.*, pp. 152–60; for Britain see John Bonham, *The Middle Class Vote* (London: Faber & Faber, 1954), pp. 154–55.

acter of political power in a democracy. This is self-destruc-
tive because politicians in office must necessarily alienate
support in deciding among conflicting interests. Over a period
of time the accumulation of such grievances may show up in
the slow ebb of popular support, even among those groups
who are most consistently benefited.

If most shifts by groups from one party to another occur
as reactions to a rational contradiction, in which the interests
or social position of a group and the program of its traditional
party are at variance, then the more salient and clear-cut the
issue, the more likely it is that a group will react in terms
of its defined interests and change accordingly. Negroes
shifted to the Democrats, for example, after it became clear
that the policies of the New Deal were more beneficial to
them than those of the Republicans. The issue of race relations, to the Negroes, is both salient and less ambiguously
defined than most issues affecting other groups in the society.

A discussion of the changes in the electoral behavior of
British voters in the various by-elections since the 1955 general elections points up many of the themes presented in
these three chapters dealing with participation and electoral
choice. The authoritative British pollster Mark Abrams explains an increase in the proportion of the vote received by
the Labor party and a drop-off from 77 to 64 per cent in
the percentage actually voting by the fact that one key source
of Conservative support has been weakening in its party
allegiance. According to various public opinion surveys, these
are largely older working-class Tories, people who have voted
Conservative all their lives. In their old age they need and
appreciate the benefits of the welfare state, and resent the
fact that Tory fiscal policies have reduced these somewhat.
Faced with a cross-pressure between their traditional party
loyalties and felt political needs, a large segment of the older
Tory working class has retreated into indecision and nonvoting, or has actually shifted over to the Labor party. Conversely, however, Abrams notes the reverse process going on
among skilled manual workers whose income and economic
security has sharply improved since 1940. This group is grad-

ually acquiring middle-class tastes and aspirations, and this shift in values is accompanied by a drift toward the Tories among them.[37] Consequently the Tories, rather than Labor, have been making the more enduring gains.

Conclusions

The emphasis on social class as the main determinant of party choice and party division seems to validate the fears of many nineteenth-century conservatives that the poor would vote for their self-interests if given the franchise. Because of this belief conservatives in almost every Western country fought the creation of a political system in which a government representing the majority of the adult population could enact any legislation it wished.[38]

But while those who predicted that men would vote along class lines in a democratic society have on the whole been proved right, those who challenged the view that universal suffrage would automatically mean the permanent supremacy of the lower-class-based party—an occurrence which would have meant the end of democracy—have also been confirmed in their belief. The latter group, including some major conservative figures, felt that a socially responsible upper class could retain the loyalty of a large enough segment of the lower classes to maintain its leadership role. Disraeli, for

[37] See Mark Abrams, "Press, Polls and Votes in Britain since the 1955 General Elections," *Public Opinion Quarterly*, 21 (1957–58), pp. 543–47.

[38] Many of the restrictions on direct democracy persisted in large parts of the Western world until World War I; some, until after World War II; and some are still maintained today. The House of Lords' veto power on British legislation was not modified until 1911, and it retained considerable delaying power until 1948. Double-votes for property holders and university graduates were abolished by the British only after the Labor victory in 1945. The three-chamber system of elections, in which a government based on a lower-class majority was impossible, lasted until 1918 in Prussia. Direct election of United States Senators was not enacted until 1916. Similar restrictions remain, or were only recently abolished, in Australia, Canada, Belgium, Italy, and other countries.

example, strongly expressed his belief that "the honest, brave, and good-natured people of England" would not abuse manhood suffrage. It should be noted, however, that Disraeli represented the rural upper-class party, whose confidence in its ability to rule was based on the success of paternalism in the rural areas, and believed that similar relationships could be introduced in the nation as a whole.[39]

On the other side of the political spectrum, Karl Marx likewise did not assume that the poor were necessarily an effective left political force. He recognized that sections of the lower classes actually supported the *status quo*. Marx accounted for such support (which he called "false consciousness") by postulating (1) that the lower classes enter the body politic accepting the legitimacy of the existing stratification arrangements, and (2) that the basic institutions of a society—religion, education, the mass media—propagate ideas and values which support the existing order and are necessarily accepted by all social strata to some extent. Marx was much more pessimistic about the possibilities for successful seizure of power by the lower class than were many conservatives who projected their own assumptions about rational self-interest onto the poor.

There are a variety of reasons, some already discussed, why a closer relationship between class and voting does not exist. Perhaps the most important one (not derivable from a study of voters) is the constant adjustments made by the main actors in the democratic game—the parties and their leaders—to the requirement that the system be kept in balance. The parties are concerned with preserving the possibility that the fortunes of the next election will keep them in or return them to office. Consequently, as historical events change the felt needs of the electorate, democratic parties

[39] In 1861, Napoleon III had advised the Prussian government to introduce universal suffrage "by means of which the conservative rural population could outvote the Liberals in the cities." See F. Meinecke, *Weltburgertum und Nationalstaat, Genesis des Deutschen Nationalstaats* (München: G. R. Oldenbourg, 1922, 6th ed.), pp. 517–18, and F. Naumann, *Die Politischen Parteien* (Berlin: Schonberg, Buchverlag der Hilfe, 1910), pp. 16–17.

shift their programs so as to retain or secure votes. The classic model of a conservative statesman who knew how to keep the system in balance under pressure from the left is Benjamin Disraeli. He recognized that a Conservative party would have to find a basis for appealing to the working class and suggested, therefore, the formation of Conservative working-men's associations. These associations, formed by the Tory party throughout England, made a conscious effort to appeal to the working class. Trade-union leaders and other representatives of the workers were invited to join. Disraeli hoped that concessions of various kinds to the workers—adult suffrage and laws designed to improve working and living conditions—would win their loyalty to the Conservatives. He believed that the traditional explicit upper-class position of the Conservatives could not be maintained with adult suffrage and was convinced that, by representing the workers, the Tories could hold their loyalty. The history of British politics would seem to bear Disraeli out in part, since the Tories were able to gain and retain a considerable proportion of the working-class vote. One out of every two Tory voters today is a manual worker.

But the fact remains, that in most stable democracies there is an inherent drive to the left. Over time, the left parties win support for measures which increase the relative power and security of the lower strata. Measures which in the nineteenth century were denounced as rank socialism are today pointed to with pride by conservative orators. The Conservatives in Britain, for example, retain their leadership role by "more effectively administering socialism." Their ability to do this is both their triumph and their tragedy—triumph because they remain at the head of society, tragedy because they must give up much of what they value.

Constant yielding to the program of their opponents is not a palatable solution for any political tendency, however, and conservative parties have enormous resources on their side, which they use effectively to retard left reforms. Just as the left is benefited when class differences are recognized as the principal basis of political division, the right often gains the advantage when nonclass issues—foreign policy, morality, administrative efficiency, the personality of the candidates—are of central concern to voters. To the extent, therefore, that the conservative parties can make elections revolve around noneconomic issues, they can reduce the pressure for reform and increase their chances of electoral victory. Their greater access to the press and other mass media helps them to define the issues of the election, particularly in periods of prosperity when economic needs are not salient.

A democratic party system based on two political parties tied to the more and the less privileged strata in the country has existed longer in the United States than in any other country in the world. A look at the way it has handled the problem of institutionalizing the class struggle sheds further light on the mechanisms required for stable democracy. The next section of this book, then, turns to an examination of many of the topics discussed here, within the framework of American society.

PART III

POLITICAL BEHAVIOR IN AMERICAN SOCIETY

CHAPTER 9

Classes and Parties in American Politics

IT OFTEN comes as a shock, especially to Europeans, to be reminded that the first political parties in history with "labor" or "workingman" in their names developed in America in the 1820s and 1830s. The emphasis on "classlessness" in American political ideology has led many European and American political commentators to conclude that party divisions in America are less related to class cleavages than they are in other Western countries. Polling studies, however, belie this conclusion, showing that in every American election since 1936 (studies of the question were not made before then), the proportion voting Democratic increases sharply as one moves down the occupational or income ladder. In 1948 almost 80 per cent of the workers voted Democratic, a percentage which is higher than has ever been reported for left-wing parties in such countries as Britain, France, Italy, and Germany. Each year the lower-paid and less skilled workers are the most Democratic; even in 1952, two thirds of the unskilled workers were for Stevenson, though the proportion of all manual workers backing the Democrats dropped to 55 per cent in that year—a drop-off which was in large measure a result of Eisenhower's personal "above the parties" appeal rather than a basic swing away from the Democratic party by the lower strata.[1]

[1] See Herbert Hyman and Paul B. Sheatsley, "The Political Appeal of President Eisenhower," *Public Opinion Quarterly*, 17 (1953), pp. 443–60. They demonstrate this on the basis of poll results from 1947–48, which already indicated that Eisenhower could win the presidency under the banner of either party.

TABLE I

Per Cent Republican Voting or Voting Preference Among
Occupational Groups and Trade-union Members*

	1940	1948	1952	1954	1956
Business and Professional	64	77	64	61	68
White-collar Workers	52	48	60	52	63
Manual Workers (skilled and unskilled)	35	22	45	35	50
Farmers	46	32	67	56	54
Trade-union Members	28	13	39	27	43

* The 1940 figures represent pre-election voting preferences, and
are recomputed from Hadley Cantril, *Public Opinion, 1935–1946*
(Princeton: Princeton University Press, 1951), p. 602. Since the
number of cases is not given in the table, estimates from census
data on the relative proportion of persons in a given occupational
category were made to facilitate the combination of several of them.
The 1948 figures represent the actual voting reported by a national
random sample, and are taken from Angus Campbell, Gerald Gurin,
and Warren E. Miller, *The Voter Decides* (Evanston: Row, Peterson and Co., 1954), pp. 72–73. The remaining data may be found
in an American Institute of Public Opinion news release, October
12, 1958, and also represent actual voting results.

In general, the bulk of the workers, even many who voted
for Eisenhower in 1952 and 1956, still regard themselves as
Democrats, and the results of the 1954 and 1958 congressional elections show that there has been no shift of the traditional Democratic voting base to the Republicans. Two
thirds of the workers polled by Gallup in 1958 voted for a
Democrat for Congress.

The same relationship between class, considered now as a
very general differentiating factor, and party support exists
within the middle and upper classes. The Democrats have
been in a minority among the nonmanual strata, and, except
among the intellectual professions (see Chapter 10), the
Democratic proportion of the nonmanually occupied electorate declines inexorably with income and occupational status
to the point where, according to one study, only 6 per cent
of the heads of corporations with more than 10,000 employees are Democrats. Perhaps the best single example of the

pervasiveness of status differences as a factor in American politics is the political allegiances of the chief executives of major American corporations. This study, done in 1955 by the Massachusetts Institute of Technology's Center for International Studies, and based on interviews with a systematic sample of one thousand such men, found that even within this upper economic group, the larger the company of which a man was an officer, the greater the likelihood that he was a Republican (see Table II).

TABLE II

RELATIONSHIP BETWEEN SIZE OF FIRM AND POLITICAL PARTY ALLEGIANCES OF CORPORATION EXECUTIVES—1955*

Size of Firm	Republican	Democratic	Independent
More than 10,000 workers	84%	6%	10%
1,000–9,999	80	8	12
100–999	69	12	19

* Data supplied to author through the courtesy of the Center for International Studies of the Massachusetts Institute of Technology.

Consistent with these findings are the popular images of typical supporters of each party. The Gallup Poll, shortly before the 1958 congressional elections, asked a nation-wide sample what their picture of the typical Democrat was, and received these answers most frequently: "middle class . . . common people . . . a friend . . . an ordinary person . . . works for his wages . . . average person . . . someone who thinks of everybody." The typical Republican, in contrast, is "better class . . . well-to-do . . . big businessman . . . money voter . . . well-off financially . . . wealthy . . . higher class."[2]

All in all, public opinion poll evidence confirms the conclusion reached by the historian Charles Beard in 1917 that "the center of gravity of wealth is on the Republican side

[2] American Institute of Public Opinion news release, November 2, 1958. See Angus Campbell, Gerald Gurin, and Warren Miller, *The Voter Decides* (Evanston: Row, Peterson and Co., 1954), p. 211, for the 1952 electorate's perception of the support of each party.

while the center of gravity of poverty is on the Democratic side."[3] Beard's conclusions were based on an inspection of the characteristics of various geographical areas, and more recent studies using this ecological approach report similar findings. Thus the Harvard political scientist Arthur Holcombe found that among urban congressional districts, "the partisan pattern is the same. The only districts which have been consistently Republican for a considerable period of time are those with the highest rents. . . . The districts which have been most consistently Democratic are those with the lowest rents. . . . The districts with a preponderance of intermediate rents are the districts which have been most doubtful from the viewpoint of the major parties."[4] A detailed survey of party registrations in 1934 in the then strongly Republican Santa Clara County (suburban San Francisco) found a strong correlation between high occupational position and being a registered Republican. About 75 per cent of plant superintendents, bankers, brokers, and managers of business firms identified publicly with the G.O.P., as contrasted with 35 per cent of the cannery and other unskilled workers. Within each broad occupational group, property owners were much more likely to be registered Republicans than those who did not own property.[5]

Although most generalizations about the relationship of American parties to class differences are based on the variations in the backgrounds of their respective electorates, there is some as yet skimpy evidence that the same differences exist on the leadership level, particularly in the local com-

[3] Quote is cited by V. O. Key, Jr., in his *Politics, Parties, and Pressure Groups*, 4th ed. (New York: Crowell, 1958), p. 235.
[4] Arthur Holcombe, *Our More Perfect Union* (Cambridge: Harvard University Press, 1950), p. 135. See also Samuel Lubell, *The Future of American Politics* (New York: Doubleday, Anchor Books, 1956), pp. 51–55, and Duncan MacRae, Jr., "Occupations and the Congressional Vote, 1940–1950," *American Sociological Review*, 20 (1955), pp. 332–40.
[5] Dewey Anderson and Percy E. Davidson, *Ballots and the Democratic Class Struggle* (Stanford: Stanford University Press, 1943), pp. 118–47.

munity. A study of the backgrounds of candidates for nomination for county office in local primaries in three counties in Indiana indicates a close correspondence between the characteristics of leaders and voters. While 76 per cent of those seeking Republican nominations were in professional or business-managerial occupations, 42 per cent of the Democratic aspirants were manual workers (see Table III). In Milwaukee, Wisconsin, 54 per cent of the officers of the local Democratic party were manual workers or in sales and clerical positions. By contrast these groups represented only 10 per cent among the Republicans, whose leaders were largely professionals or ran business firms.[6]

The relationship of socioeconomic position to political behavior in America as elsewhere is reinforced by religious and ethnic factors. Surveys indicate that, among the Chris-

TABLE III

OCCUPATIONAL BACKGROUNDS OF CANDIDATES FOR NOMINATIONS FOR COUNTY OFFICE IN THREE INDIANA COUNTIES—1954*

Occupation	Republican		Democratic	
	Number	Per cent	Number	Per cent
Professional	23	25.8	17	17.7
Managerial	45	50.6	25	26.0
Clerical-sales	8	9.0	10	10.4
Manual workers	11	12.4	40	41.7
Others	2	2.2	4	4.2
Totals	89	100.0	96	100.0

* Frank Munger, *Two-Party Politics in the State of Indiana* (unpublished M.S. thesis, Department of Government, Harvard University, 1955), p. 275; cited in V. O. Key, Jr., *Politics, Parties, and Pressure Groups* (New York: Crowell, 1958), p. 240.

tian denominations, the higher the average income of the membership of a given church group, the more likely its members are to vote Republican. If Christian religious groups in the United States are ranked according to the average

[6] Leon D. Epstein, *Politics in Wisconsin* (Madison: University of Wisconsin Press, 1938), p. 186.

socioeconomic status of their membership, they are, reading
from high to low, Congregational, Presbyterian, Episcopal,
Methodist, Lutheran, Baptist, and Catholic—and this rank
order is identical to the one produced when the denominations are ranked by propensity to vote Republican. This suggests that socioeconomic status, rather than religious ideas,
is the prime determinant of political values among different
denominations. The fact that the Jews, who are one of the
wealthiest religious groups in America, are shown by survey
data to be most Democratic is probably due, as I have suggested earlier, to their sensitivity to ethnic discrimination
and their lack of effective social intercourse with the upper-
status groups in America. But religious beliefs or loyalties,
and the political values associated with them, nevertheless
seem to have some independent effect on voting behavior.
Working-class Protestants belonging to the Congregational
or Presbyterian churches are more likely to be Republicans
than workers who are Baptist or Catholic. Conversely, wealthy
Baptists or Catholics are more apt to be Democrats than
equally rich Congregationalists or Episcopalians are.[7]

---

[7] For a general study of the politics of the Jews, see Lawrence H.
Fuchs, *The Political Behavior of American Jews* (Glencoe: The Free
Press, 1956). See also Werner Cohn, "The Politics of the Jews," in
Marshall Sklare, ed., *The Jews: Social Patterns of an American Group*
(Glencoe: The Free Press, 1958), pp. 614–26. See Wesley and
Beverly Allinsmith, "Religious Affiliation and Political-Economic At-
titudes," *Public Opinion Quarterly*, 12 (1948), pp. 377–89; Paul F.
Lazarsfeld, Bernard Berelson, and Hazel Gaudet, *The People's Choice*
(New York: Columbia University Press, 1948), p. 22; W. F. Ogburn
and N. S. Talbot, "A Measurement of the Factors in the Presidential
Election of 1928," *Social Forces*, 8 (1929), pp. 175–83; H. F. Gos-
nell, *Grass Roots Politics* (Washington: American Council on Public
Affairs, 1942), pp. 17, 33–34, 55, 102; S. J. Korchin, *Psychological
Factors in the Behavior of Voters* (unpublished Ph.D. thesis, Department of Social Relations, Harvard University, 1946), Chap. V; Louis
Harris, *Is There a Republican Majority?* (New York: Harper & Bros.,
1954), p. 87; A. Campbell, G. Gurin, and W. Miller, *op. cit.*, pp.
71, 79; Bernard Berelson, Paul Lazarsfeld, and William McPhee,
Voting (Chicago: University of Chicago Press, 1954), pp. 64–71;
and Oscar Glantz, "Protestant and Catholic Voting Behavior," *Public Opinion Quarterly*, 23 (1959), pp. 73–82.

Roughly speaking, the same differences appear between ethnic groups. Anglo-Saxons are more likely to be Republican than other Americans in the same class position who have a more recent immigrant background. Thus if an individual is middle class, Anglo-Saxon, and Protestant, he is very likely to be a Republican, whereas if he is working class, Catholic, and of recent immigrant stock, he will probably be a Democrat.

Even before the development of the two-party system in its present form, the political issues dividing the society tended to have a class character. Free public schools, for example, did not emerge naturally and logically from the structure and values of American society. Rather, as one historian of American education, Ellwood P. Cubberley, has pointed out: "Excepting for the battle for the abolition of slavery, perhaps no question has ever been before the American people for settlement which caused so much feeling or aroused such bitter antagonism."[8] In large part it was a struggle between liberals and conservatives in the modern sense of the term, although religious issues also played a strong role. "The friends of free schools were at first commonly regarded as fanatics, dangerous to the States, and the opponents of free schools were considered by them as old line conservatives or as selfish members of society."[9] Among the arguments presented for free education was that "a common state school, equally open to all, would prevent that class differentiation so dangerous in a Republic"; while opponents of such schools argued that they "will make education too common, and will educate people out of their proper station in society . . . [and] would break down long-established and very desirable social barriers."[10] On one side of the issue were the poorer classes; on the other, "the old aristocratic class . . . the conservatives of society . . . taxpayers."[11]

[8] Ellwood P. Cubberley, *Public Education in the United States* (Boston: Houghton Mifflin Co., 1954), p. 164.

[9] *Loc. cit.*

[10] *Ibid.*, p. 166.

[11] *Ibid.*, pp. 164–65. "The scheme of Universal Equal Education at the expense of the State is virtually 'Agrarianism.' It would be a

Perhaps no better comment on the meaning of American politics has ever been made than Tocqueville's observation in 1830 about the prominent struggle between aristocracy and democracy:

> To a stranger all the domestic controversies of the Americans at first appear to be incomprehensible or puerile, and he is at a loss whether to pity people who take such arrogant trifles in good earnest or to envy that happiness which enables a community to discuss them. But when he comes to study the secret propensities that govern the factions of America, he easily perceives that the greater part of them are more or less connected with one or the other of those two great divisions which always existed in free communities. *The deeper we penetrate into the inmost thought of these parties, the more we perceive that the object of the one is to limit and that of the other to extend the authority of the people.* I do not assert that the ostensible purpose or even that the secret aim of American parties is to promote the rule of aristocracy in the country; but I affirm that aristocratic or democratic passions may be easily detected at the bottom of all parties, and that, although they escape a superficial observation, they are the main points and soul of every faction in the United States.[12]

---

compulsory application of the means of the richer for the direct use of the poorer classes, and so far an arbitrary division of property among them. . . . Authority—that is, the State—is to force the more eligibly situated citizens to contribute a part of their means for the accommodation of the rest, and this is equivalent to an actual compulsory partition of their substance." Editorial in the *Philadelphia National Gazette* (August 19, 1830), cited in Cubberley, *op. cit.*, p. 182. This indicates that the issue was seen as a left-right one, in the classic economic sense.

[12] Alexis de Tocqueville, *Democracy in America*, Vol. I (New York: Vintage Books, 1955), pp. 185–86 (emphasis added); for similar comments see Harriet Martineau, *Society in America*, Vol. I (London: Saunders and Otley, 1837), pp. 10 ff; and Thomas Hamilton, *Men and Manners in America*, Vol. I (London: T. Cadell, 1833), p. 288.

The relationship between status or class position (as indicated by the three criteria of economic position, religion, and ethnic background) and party loyalty is thus not a new development in American history. Studies of the social bases of the Federalists, America's first conservative party, and the Jeffersonian Democrats in the late eighteenth and early nineteenth centuries indicate that they corresponded closely to the bases of the modern Republicans and Democrats, respectively. The Federalists were backed by the well-to-do farmers, urban merchants, persons of English extraction, and members of such high-status churches as the Congregationalists and the Episcopalians.[13] The Democrats were supported by urban workers, poorer farmers, persons of non-English background such as the Scotch-Irish, and members of the (then) poorer churches like the Presbyterians and the Catholics. The second conservative party, the Whigs, who fought the Democrats from 1836 to 1852, derived their strength from the same group as the Federalists, while the Democrats retained the groups which had backed Jefferson, and added most of the great wave of European immigrants.

Although the Republican party is often thought of as a newly created anti-slavery party, the research on the pre-Civil War period suggests that it inherited both the support and leadership of the northern Whigs. A detailed study of voting behavior in New York State before the Civil War shows that the Democrats kept their urban lower-class, Catholic, and immigrant support.[14]

The evidence compiled by various social scientists indicates that the men of wealth and economic power in America have *never* given more than minority support to the Democrats. Dixon Ryan Fox, an analyst of New York politics in the first half of the nineteenth century, gathered considerable statistical data which show that the upper-class districts of the

[13] Manning Dauer, *The Adams Federalists* (Baltimore: The Johns Hopkins Press, 1953), pp. 24–27, 263.

[14] Research is in process by Lee Benson of the Center for Advanced Study in the Behavioral Sciences.

various cities of the state voted Federalist and Whig.[15] He quotes a biographer of the wealthy merchants of New York who wrote in the 1860s:

> It is a very common fact that for thirty-four years [since the revival of two-party politics in 1828] very few merchants of the first class have been Democrats. The mass of large and little merchants have, like a flock of sheep, gathered either in the Federalist, Whig, Clay, or Republican folds. The Democratic merchants could have easily been stored in a large Eighth Avenue railroad car.[16]

A recent study by Mabel Newcomer of the political views of large business executives in 1900, 1925, and 1950 reports that in all three periods about three quarters of this group were Republicans. Even in 1925, a period not normally considered to be one of political class conflict in America, only 19 per cent of the executives were Democrats. These data certainly underestimate the Republican majority among business executives, since they are based on public party enrollment rather than voting preference and include many registered as southern Democrats who would be Republicans if they were not living in a one-party region.[17]

As a final note on the lack of support for the Democrats among the upper class, the straw votes cast for President by the boys attending St. Paul's School, an upper-class private boarding school, are of some interest. From 1888 to 1932 the Republican candidates consistently received the overwhelming majority (see Table IV). Even the conservative

---

[15] Dixon Ryan Fox, *The Decline of Aristocracy in the Politics of New York* (New York: Columbia University Press, 1919).

[16] W. Barrett, *Old Merchants of New York*, Vol. I, p. 81, cited in Fox, *op. cit.*, p. 426.

[17] Mabel Newcomer, *The Big Business Executive* (New York: Columbia University Press, 1955), p. 49. In 1928 a survey of those listed in *Who's Who* found that 87 per cent favored Herbert Hoover for President. See Jean-Louis Sevrin, *La structure interne des partis politiques Americains* (Paris: Librairie Armand Colin, 1953), p. 58.

TABLE IV*

PER CENT DEMOCRATIC PREFERENCES AMONG
ST. PAUL'S SCHOOL STUDENTS

1888	35
1892	37
1900	19
1904	—
1908	17
1912	37
1916	23
1920	13
1924	16
1928	24
1932	18

* Recomputed from Arthur S. Pier, *St. Paul's School, 1855–1934*
(New York: Charles Scribner's Sons, 1934), p. 181. The original
figures are also to be found in E. Digby Baltzell, *Philadelphia Gentlemen* (Glencoe: The Free Press, 1958), p. 316.

Grover Cleveland only secured 35 per cent of the vote of
these teen-age scions of the upper class.

Party Policies Determined by Party Supporters

This division of Americans into supporters of one of two
parties, one historically based on those who are poorer and
the other on the more well to do, does not mean that the
parties have always divided ideologically along traditional
"left-right" political lines. Such issues did separate the parties
in Jefferson's and Jackson's day, and also—for the most part
—from 1896 to the present, although there were some significant exceptions, like the elections of 1904 and the 1920s.
However, even when the parties did not present opposing
positions on conventional left-right lines, there have almost
always been issues between them which reflected the differences in their social bases. For example, the Federalist-Whig-
Republican party was less receptive to immigration in the
nineteenth century than the Democratic party, and a Republican administration enacted the restrictive immigration legis-

lation of the early 1920s. In general, the various nativist and anti-Catholic movements which have arisen at various periods in American history have been identified with the conservative parties on a local if not a national level.[18]

Even the controversy over slavery reflected differences in class. The Northern urban lower-class groups before the Civil War tended to be anti-Negro and were uninterested in the struggle for abolition. In New York State the conservatives supported the right of free Negroes to vote in the state constitutional conventions of 1820 and 1846, while the major Democratic spokesmen either opposed, or were uninterested in, the extension of the suffrage to Negroes. The free Negroes, in turn, were supporters of the Federalist and Whig parties before 1850, and the freed slaves and their descendants remained loyal backers of the Republican party until the election of Roosevelt produced for the first time a Democratic administration which showed an interest in their problems.[19] The Wilson Administration of 1913–21, although liberal on other issues, reflected southern attitudes in its race-relations policies. The movements reflecting Protestant middle-class morality, such as those designed to prohibit liquor and gambling, or those concerned with the elimination of corruption in government, have also made headway largely through the conservative parties. In the controversies over prohibition in the twentieth century, the Democrats in the North were the "wet" party, while the Republicans were "dry." And in the prosperous 1920s the Democrats as the party of the lower

[18] See Wilfred E. Binkley, *American Political Parties, Their Natural History* (New York: Alfred A. Knopf, 1947), p. 163; a detailed survey of voting in Wisconsin in 1860 based on the exact records of the Wisconsin Domesday Book project reports that five sixths of all Germans and almost all Catholics backed Douglas *against* Lincoln because they identified the Republicans with Know-Nothing nativism. See Joseph Schafer, "Who Elected Lincoln?", *American Historical Review*, 47 (1941), pp. 51–63.

[19] See Dixon Ryan Fox, "The Negro Vote in Old New York," *Political Science Quarterly*, 32 (1917), pp. 252–75; and Marvin Meyers, *The Jacksonian Persuasion: Politics and Beliefs* (Stanford: Stanford University Press, 1957), pp. 189–90.

strata and the Catholics ran the campaign of 1928 largely on the platform of repeal of prohibition.[20]

The differences in the ethnic composition of their social bases have also been reflected in the foreign policy positions of the two parties. The one Democratic administration between 1861 and 1913—that of Grover Cleveland in the 1880s —opposed Great Britain on a number of issues and sympathized with the cause of Irish freedom. A recent study of the British immigrant in America shows that the British, though not viewed as a separate or alien ethnic group like arrivals from other countries, organized British clubs in the late nineteenth century as a means of fighting the political power of the Irish Democrats. These British associations gravitated toward the Republican party.[21] Even during World War I, such differences affected American policy. Although Wilson was personally sympathetic to the cause of Britain and the Allies, the bulk of Americans of non-Anglo-Saxon background were hostile either to Britain or to Czarist Russia, and it was the Republican party, based on middle-class Anglo-Saxons, which advocated greater help to the Allies. Wilson, it should be remembered, fought the election of 1916 on an *anti*-war platform and won or held the support of the Irish, Jews, and Germans for the Democratic party.

The position of the two parties on foreign policy has not only reflected their ethnic bases, but on occasion has alienated part of them. Millions of Americans of Irish and German extraction clearly resented American entry into World

[20] An ecological study of 173 counties in 1928 found that the "wet" counties were consistently more Democratic, even when such otherwise important factors as the number of foreign born and Catholics, and the degree of urbanization were relatively equalized. The authors of the study noted that the ". . . best guess as to the Smith strength in a community is the wetness of the community." "Wetness" was determined by a majority "wet" vote in state elections on some form of the wet-dry issue. See W. F. Ogburn and N. S. Talbot, *op. cit.*, p. 179.

[21] See Rowland T. Berthoff, *British Immigrants in Industrial America, 1790–1950* (Cambridge: Harvard University Press, 1953), pp. 198–205.

War I.[22] The Germans in particular suffered heavily as a result of social and economic discrimination during and after the war. Some analysts have suggested (although the statistical work to prove this has not been done) that the great Republican victory of 1920, in which Harding secured a larger percentage of the vote than any other Republican since the founding of the party, was in part at least a result of a shift away from the Democrats by members of ethnic groups who felt "betrayed" by Wilson's taking the country into war.

It is now largely forgotten that, in his early years of office, Franklin D. Roosevelt was an "isolationist," and that the Democratic party leadership in Congress acted as if it believed that America had been tricked into entering World War I by British propaganda and the manipulation of Wall Street bankers. The neutrality act passed in Roosevelt's first term of office by an overwhelmingly Democratic Congress reflected isolationist and anti-British attitudes. In this respect the Democrats returned to their traditional role of representing the major ethnic groups.[23]

The outbreak of World War II placed Roosevelt in the same dilemma that had faced Wilson earlier. He knew that he had to aid the Allies, but he also wanted to be re-elected.

[22] In Wisconsin, the voters of German and Irish background voted Democratic from 1860 to World War I. See Leon Epstein, *op. cit.*, p. 36; similarly in Missouri, one survey reports that the Democrats dominated in counties with large German populations from the Civil War to the election of 1920, when these counties shifted overwhelmingly to the Republicans. See John H. Fenton, *Politics in the Border States* (New Orleans: The Hauser Press, 1957), pp. 162–63. See also Samuel Lubell, *op. cit.*, Chap. VII, for an attempt to analyze the sources of isolationism in terms of ethnic background and allegiances.

[23] The Spanish Republicans were perhaps the foremost victims of the fact that American foreign policy reflects the social base of the political parties. Although Roosevelt and many of his closest advisers were personally strong supporters of the Loyalists, they felt that it would be politically impossible to antagonize the Catholic Democratic vote by aiding the Loyalists, who were regarded as Communists by the Church.

The fall of France left him with no alternative other than giving "all aid short of war"; but in the 1940 presidential campaign he still promised that the country would *not* go to war. This time, however, unlike 1916, the Republicans took the isolationist and pacifist position, largely as an election maneuver. Wendell Willkie was even more favorable to intervention than Roosevelt, yet he and his advisers apparently felt that their one hope of victory was to entice the Irish, German, and Italian voters, who were against intervention because of their national identification, away from the Democrats. Opinion-poll data for that year show that the Republicans were somewhat successful, since the Democratic vote did drop off greatly among these three groups. It was probably counterbalanced, at least in part, by a swing to Roosevelt among middle-class "Anglo-Saxons."

Ethnic reactions have also affected the handling of the Communist issue in the last decade. It should not be forgotten that Senator McCarthy was Irish and represented a state in which the influence of German-Americans is high. McCarthy, in his charges of Communist infiltration in the State Department, stressed that America was "betrayed" by men of upper-class Anglo-Saxon backgrounds, by the graduates of Harvard and other Ivy League schools. He was saying, in effect, to the isolationist ethnic groups which had been exposed to charges of "disloyalty" in the previous two wars, that the people who had really been disloyal were the upper-class Anglo-Saxons who had manipulated the United States into fighting the wrong enemy, and who had "lost the peace" to the Russians.[24] In 1952 the Republicans made a strong foreign policy appeal to the ethnic groups, especially the

[24] For an attempt to dissect the sources of support of the "radical right" in America, recently centering around McCarthyism, in terms of the politics of status-aspirations in times of prosperity, see S. M. Lipset, "The Sources of the 'Radical Right,' " in Daniel Bell, ed., *The New American Right* (New York: Criterion Books, 1955), pp. 166–235. The social base of this political tendency by no means looks solely to the Republican party as its standard-bearer, and, as the article points out, the attacks by the radical right on "modern Republicanism," combined with the Republican victory in 1952,

Catholics and Germans. Eisenhower, like Willkie before him, allowed electoral expediency to modify his public statements. And the election returns indicate that he made strong headway among middle-class Catholics, Germans, and Irish.[25]

Upper-class Liberalism

Recent research by sociologists and historians has clarified some aspects of American politics which do not seem to fit a "class" interpretation of American history, like the fact, already noted, that the wealthier classes and their parties, the Whigs and Republicans, were more antislavery than the Democrats who were supported by the lower classes. Contemporary studies of political attitudes indicate that it is necessary to distinguish between so-called economic liberalism (issues concerned with the distribution of wealth and power) and noneconomic liberalism (issues concerned with civil liberties, race relations and foreign affairs).[26] The fundamental factor in noneconomic liberalism is not actually class, but education, general sophistication, and probably to a certain extent psychic security. But since these factors are strongly correlated with class, noneconomic liberalism is positively associated with social status (the wealthier are more tolerant), while economic liberalism is inversely correlated with social status (the poor are more leftist on such issues).

Actually within the conservative strata it has not been the wealthier classes in general which have led the political struggle for noneconomic liberalism, but rather those of estab-

---

were important elements leading to the downfall of its McCarthyite expression.

[25] For data on regional and ethnic variations in 1952, from a national cross-sectional poll, see A. Campbell, G. Gurin, and W. Miller, *op. cit.*, pp. 69–83. In a 1952 Roper survey it was found that 85 per cent of the upper-income Irish vote went to Eisenhower, and there was a strong trend at all income levels of the German vote toward Eisenhower. See Louis Harris, *Is There a Republican Majority?* (New York: Harper & Bros., 1954), pp. 87–94.

[26] This distinction is also discussed, in relation to lower-class politics, in Chap. 4, pp. 97–100.

lished "old family" background as differentiated from the *nouveaux riches*. Before the Civil War most abolitionist leaders were, as David Donald has shown in *Lincoln Reconsidered*, "descended from old and socially dominant North-eastern families."[27] Similarly, the leaders of the Progressive movement of the late nineteenth and early twentieth centuries, which arose within the Republican party and resisted the corrupt urban Democratic machines and the growth of big business trusts with their influence over Republican politicians, came from the same strata and family backgrounds as the abolitionists.[28] In a real sense the abolitionists and Progressives have been the American Tory radicals—men of upper-class background and values, who as conservatives helped to democratize the society as part of their struggle against the vulgar *nouveau riche* businessman.

Tory radicalism has always been in difficulty in America since it has rarely dominated its natural outlet, the Republican party. After the broadening of adult suffrage in the 1820s and '30s, American parties came under the control of professional politicians whose major concern was to win elections, secure and retain office, regardless of the means necessary to do so. Such an attitude fitted in well with those elements of the society like the *nouveaux riches* who were also concerned with *ends* (wealth and power) rather than with *means* (honor and status). In the nineteenth century many Americans of well-to-do background objected to both the politics based on the lower classes and immigrants (the Democrats), and the politics drawing its sustenance from the "new money-grubbing class" (the Republicans). As David Donald puts it: "They did not support radical economic reforms because [they] . . . had no serious quarrel with the

[27] David Donald, *Lincoln Reconsidered* (New York: Alfred A. Knopf, 1956), p. 33.

[28] Richard Hofstadter, *The Age of Reform, from Bryan to FDR* (New York: Alfred A. Knopf, 1955). In both periods, the men from old families faced with a rising new commercial and industrial elite had "disdain for the new money-grubbing class . . . were aliens in the new industrial society . . . and agitation allowed the only chance for personal and social fulfillment." D. Donald, *op. cit.*, p. 34.

capitalistic system of private ownership and control of property. What they did question, and what they did rue, was the transfer of leadership to the wrong groups in society, and their appeal for reform was a strident call for their own class to re-exert its former social dominance."[29]

The noneconomic liberalism of this group found its expression in issues like abolition, civil service reform, controlled immigration (so as to reduce urban corruption), and internationalism. In the twentieth century internationalism became the major issue. A large part of the leadership in internationalist local organizations advocating collective security seems to have come from members of old families, usually of Anglo-Saxon origin.

Though linked to the Whig and Republican parties, these upper-class liberals have been ready to help organize "third" parties whenever their issues have become salient. They played a major role in creating the demand for a new antislavery party before the Civil War; they played a dominant role in the effort to create a new Liberal Republican party in the 1870s designed to eliminate governmental corruption and enact civil service reform; they fostered the Progressive party of Theodore Roosevelt; and in the 1940s some of them, including their then leader, Wendell Willkie, seriously considered forming a new party. From the pre-Civil War abolitionist movement to the Committee to Defend America by Aiding the Allies (the William Allen White Committee) in 1940–41, there is a thread of continuity: conservatives who have fought for the "noneconomic" values of honor and freedom, and who have occasionally deserted the traditional party allegiance of their class.

In recent decades the control of large corporations by college-educated men and the scions of established wealth rather

---

[29] *Ibid.*, p. 34; see H. Ludeke, *The "Democracy" of Henry Adams and Other Essays* (Bern: A. Francke Ag. Verlag, 1950), for a discussion of the role of men like Charles Francis Adams, Henry Adams, Henry Cabot Lodge, William Cullen Bryant, and their friends in the reform and third-party movements after the Civil War, esp. pp. 31–41.

than by the relatively uneducated *nouveaux riches* has created
an alliance between economic power and traditional status.
But this alliance has not meant that the Republican party
has easily become the expression of sophisticated conservatism. Rather large sections of it have continued to express the
reactionary sentiments of the small-town provincial middle
classes. Since its centers of electoral strength, particularly
during periods of Democratic dominance, are in the "provinces" rather than the large metropolitan cities, the Republican party can be more properly accused of being the agent of
the small-town *bourgeoisie* than of big business.

The conflict between the values of the established upper
class and sophisticated corporate wealth and those of small
business and self-made wealth has led some observers to suggest that the true party of Tory radicalism in America is the
Democratic party. It has achieved Disraeli's objective of a
party based on the working class but led by the responsible
"squires"—first Roosevelt of Groton and Harvard, and currently "Adlai Stevenson of Choate School and Princeton,
G. Mennen Williams of Salisbury School and Princeton, John
F. Kennedy of Choate and Harvard . . . and Averell Harriman of Groton and Yale."[30] It is more likely, however, that
Nelson Rockefeller, the liberal Republican Governor of New
York, will ultimately prove to be the true representative of
the revived pattern of direct participation in politics by
members of the upper class—participation through their traditional party, the Republican. It is interesting to note in this
connection that Mrs. Nelson Rockefeller, a cousin of Joseph
Sill Clark, Philadelphia Social Registerite and former Democratic Mayor of Philadelphia, now U. S. Senator, was publicly
registered as a member of a third party, New York's Liberal
party, until recently.[31]

The strong strain of Tory radicalism which has reappeared

[30] E. Digby Baltzell, *Philadelphia Gentlemen* (Glencoe: The Free
Press, 1958), pp. 392–94.

[31] This party of left-wing New Dealers is largely dominated by
men whose political views are best described as Social-Democratic in
the European sense of the term.

at crucial points in American history has served to reduce the tensions inherent in class and sectional cleavages. The Tory radicals, to use Richard Hofstadter's words describing the corporation lawyers who became leaders of the Progressive movement, have never wanted "a sharp change in the social structure, but rather the formation of a responsible elite which was to take charge of the popular impulse toward change, and direct it into moderate, and, as they would have said, 'constructive channels,' a leadership occupying, as Brandeis aptly put it, a position of independence between the wealthy [self-interested businessmen] and the people, prepared to curb the excesses of either."[32] From the standpoint of political stability, Tory radicalism has served to retain the loyalties of both the underprivileged out-groups who gain from needed reforms and the conservative strata who are outraged by the same measures. The participation of upper-class persons in liberal politics may also be seen as enlightened self-interest, since they are able to achieve needed reforms, exercise restraint, and, according to E. Digby Baltzell in *Philadelphia Gentlemen*, "perpetuate upper-class influence on the functional class system as a whole by the very fact that they hold important positions within the new avenues to power."[33] At the same time, their presence serves to blur the class lines separating the parties.

The Effect of One-party States

Regionalism—the Democratic control of the South and the traditional Republican domination of many northern states—represents one important deviation, but a disappearing one, from the class basis of American politics.[34] With the exception of the South, it is difficult to estimate how much of the voting behavior of the country remains a reflection of traditional regional attachments to a party which are independent of other factors. Republican regional strength outside of the

[32] R. Hofstadter, *op. cit.*, p. 163.

[33] E. D. Baltzell, *op. cit.*, p. 39.

[34] An excellent discussion of sectionalism in American politics can be found in V. O. Key, Jr., *op. cit.*, pp. 250–79.

South is based mainly on majorities in certain areas who have "Republican" social characteristics: rural and small-town middle-class Protestants. Traditionally Republican New England no longer includes Massachusetts, Connecticut, and Rhode Island, now highly urbanized, in which the Democrats more than hold their own. In Maine, Vermont, and New Hampshire, where rural and small-town votes play a more important role and the proportion of Catholics has grown more slowly, one-party Republican rule characterized state politics until the 1950s and is still far from dead in the last two states, although in 1958 Vermont elected a Democratic congressman for the first time in 106 years. The same pattern is true for a number of Midwest farm states: the absence of major urban centers has meant that many of these states remain Republican. Perhaps the best evidence that Republican strength in predominantly Republican states has not represented a purely regional attachment to a party is the fact that the working class in the cities of these states has been largely Democratic, and that, in fact, the principal urban centers have Democratic majorities. For example, the two largest cities in Vermont and New Hampshire, Burlington and Manchester, are old Democratic strongholds. In one Vermont industrial town, Winooski, the Democrats secure up to 90 per cent of the vote.

But in spite of the fact that the one-party character of many areas in the North may be accounted for by the social traits of the population, the perennial domination of a state by one party reduces the minority party's vote, even among groups one would expect to back it. If a party has no chance of winning, it inevitably reduces the effort it puts into an election. Democratic candidates for state office in predominantly Republican states, or Republican office-seekers in the South, are often individuals who have little political appeal. The national party, or other organizations backing it, like unions or business groups, may feel that money is wasted in such states, and little is therefore spent.[35] In addition, since

[35] For a discussion of the weaknesses of the minority party in one-party states see Warren Miller, "One-Party Politics and the Voter," *American Political Science Review*, 50 (1956), pp. 707–25. For a

the sole road to an effective political career lies in the Republican party in a number of northern states, and in the Democratic party in the South, many ambitious liberals in states like North Dakota or Vermont become active Republicans, while in the South right-wing conservatives choose the Democratic road to office.[36] The fact that the men who might best lead a Republican party in the South are Democrats, and that in some northern states potential Democratic politicians have often been Republicans, is probably one of the major factors serving to perpetuate one-party rule. This also often has the effect of moving the single party farther to the left (or right) than it would "normally" be in a two-party situation, because of the necessity of accommodating the demands of a broader social base.

The Nationalization of Politics

The political pattern in the southern states is a major deviation from the normal picture of political diversity reflecting class, ethnic, and religious differences. With the exception of a brief period in the 1890s when the Populists had strength, the South has been solidly Democratic in presidential elections from the end of Reconstruction down to 1928. Since 1928 some southern states have moved out of the Democratic camp in four elections—1928, 1948, 1952 and 1956—although all of them remained Democratic on the state and local level.[37] The 1928 defection came from the

good discussion of one area see Duane Lockard, *New England State Politics* (Princeton: Princeton University Press, 1959).

[36] V. O. Key, Jr., points out that not only do persons with political ambitions choose the single party in a one-party state, regardless of their political complexion, but that requirements for the maintenance of the one-party system itself are the inclusion of all potentially powerful elements within its ranks, and the existence of sanctions against insurgent individuals or groups. See V. O. Key, Jr., *Southern Politics* (New York: Alfred A. Knopf, 1950), p. 432.

[37] See Samuel Lubell, *op. cit.*, Chap. VI, for a discussion of the conflicts and changes in the South. Key points out that southern unity is based solely on the Negro issue, and that normal class politics, based on the old Populist supporters (the poor white farmers)

resentment of a section of the Protestant, rural and small-town South to the Democratic nomination of a Catholic and antiprohibitionist, Al Smith. The three more recent deviations illustrate the consequences of the nationalization of American politics under Roosevelt and Truman: the more conservative sections of the South are rebelling against the ideological liberalism of the national party, which is for equal rights for Negroes, supports trade-unions, and is hostile to big business.

The nationalization of American politics is one of the major consequences of the New Deal-Fair Deal revolution, and of the urbanization and industrialization of the entire country. Parochial issues which do not involve left-right or foreign policy differences have been reduced in importance. And one finds that the effects of traditional religious, ethnic, and regional factors are also diminishing, although they still play a role when foreign policy issues are salient. In 1952 Eisenhower carried middle-class residential districts in the urban South with about the same majority that he took in comparable districts in northern urban centers.[38] The majority of middle-class Catholics voted Republican in 1952 (a shift facilitated by the foreign policy issues discussed earlier), while the bulk of working-class Catholics, especially those belonging to trade-unions, remained Democratic.[39] Such factors as occupational status, income, and the class character of the district in which people live probably distinguish the support of the two major parties more clearly now than at any other period in American history since the Civil War.[40]

---

against the plantation regions, emerges wherever the Negro issue does not supersede other issues. V. O. Key, Jr., *Southern Politics, op. cit.*, p. 302.

[38] See L. Harris, *op. cit.*, pp. 68–73 and 134–36.

[39] *Ibid.*, pp. 148–49. Sixty-two per cent of the Catholic union members voted Democratic, while 62 per cent of those Catholic families with no union member in the family voted Republican.

[40] This developing pattern of American politics may be compared with that of Britain. As John Bonham puts it, "British politics are almost wholly innocent of those issues which cross the social lines

The importance of class factors should not, however, cause us to overlook the fact that in the United States, as in every other democratic country, a large minority of the workers and a smaller section of the middle classes deviate from the dominant class tendency. One of the necessary conditions for a viable two-party system is that both parties hover around the 50 per cent mark. Hence in every industrialized country the conservative parties must win working-class support; and in the United States and Britain, as was noted in the previous chapter, the Republican and Conservative parties have necessarily accepted many of the reforms enacted by their adversaries.[41] Actually the conservatives' gradual shift to the left is endemic in the sheer demography of democratic politics—the poor will always be in the majority.[42]

The preponderance of "poorer" people also means that the conservatives must always attempt to reduce the saliency of class issues in politics. It is clearly to the advantage of the parties of the left for people to vote consciously in terms of class. Consequently, the Republicans always seek to emphasize nonclass issues, such as military defense, foreign policy, corruption, and so forth.[43]

---

in other lands, for example, race, nationality, religion, town and country interests, regional interest, or the conflict between authoritarian and parliamentary methods." See *The Middle Class Vote* (London: Faber & Faber, 1954), pp. 194–95.

[41] The decline of the Federalists has been explained by their refusal to face the demographic facts. The Hamiltonian wing of the party passed legislation largely concerned with the needs of the urban merchants and industrialists, ignoring the fact that 90 per cent of the electorate were rural farmers. See M. Dauer, *op. cit.*, Chaps. 1 and 2, and Appendix II, especially pp. 6–7.

[42] Bonham details the British Conservatives' acceptance of every piece of labor and socialist legislation, *after* it was enacted, and their claim to have even pioneered some social services. Their "alternative to Socialism" has narrowed to a claim to be more efficient administrators. See John Bonham, *op. cit.*, pp. 185–88. As the satirist Mort Sahl said of the Republican party, conservatives don't want to do anything "for the first time," and "not now."

[43] And, in Britain, the Conservative party "expressly rejects the idea that political parties should seek to serve the interests of named classes." Bonham quotes the 1950 *Campaign Guide* of the party,

The way in which class and nonclass factors operate to affect electoral behavior was shown in a survey of the sources of the Eisenhower appeal. The political sociologist Oscar Glantz found that 1952 Eisenhower voters differed greatly among themselves in their occupational positions and traditional party loyalties. The more well to do a group, the more likely its members were to account for their vote for Eisenhower by identification with the Republican party rather than with Eisenhower; to be strongly favorable to business; and conservative on various domestic political issues. Conversely, the "converts" to Eisenhower from the Democratic ranks who were less well to do than traditional Republicans were less friendly to business and more liberal on domestic matters, and cited factors such as Eisenhower's leadership qualities and their dissatisfaction with the way the Democrats had handled noneconomic issues like the Korean War as their reasons for voting Republican in 1952. Glantz suggests, in line with the analysis here, that the interest basis of political behavior was not weakened by Eisenhower's victory, but rather that 1952 illustrates the way in which loyalties linked to class issues may be suppressed when the stimulus of a noneconomic factor is great.[44]

The current spirit of "moderation" in politics seems at first glance to belie the thesis that class factors have become more significant in distinguishing between the supporters of the two parties, but in reality it does not. There are two basic underlying processes which account for the present shift toward the center on the part of both parties. One, which has been stressed by many political commentators, is the effect of the prolonged period of prosperity the country has enjoyed and the resultant increase in the entire population's standard of living. It has been argued that the lower-class base to which the Democratic party appeals is declining

---

which states that ". . . the strength of the Conservative party lies in its fundamental aim to foster unity among all classes and sections of the people." John Bonham, *op. cit.*, pp. 184–85.

[44] O. Glantz, "Unitary Political Behavior and Differential Political Motivation," *Western Political Quarterly*, 10 (1957), pp. 833–46.

numerically, and therefore the party cannot advocate reform measures if it desires to win. But at least as important as the change in economic conditions is the effect on the ideological "face" of both parties of being in or out of office. The policies of the "out" party are largely set by its representatives in the House and Senate. Thus the Democrats in opposition, as at present, are led by conservative or centrist southerners, while the Republican leadership in Congress veers most sharply to the right when the Democrats hold the presidency.

A Democratic President is invariably to the left of the Democratic congressional leadership, since he is basically elected by the large urban industrial states where trade-unions and minority groups constitute the backbone of the party, while the southerners continue to sway the congressional Democratic contingent. Similarly, a Republican President under current conditions must remain to the left of his congressional supporters, since he, too, must be oriented toward carrying or retaining the support of the industrial, urban, and therefore more liberal sections of the country, while most Republican Congressmen are elected in "safe" conservative districts. So when the Republicans hold the presidency, they move to the left as compared to their position in opposition, while the Democrats, shifting from presidential incumbency to congressional opposition, move to the right. This shift produces a situation in which the policies of the two parties often appear almost indistinguishable.

One result in this century has been that the opposition party often faces an ideological crisis when nominating a President. From 1940 to 1952, every Republican convention witnessed a fight between a right-wing congressional candidate—Taft or Bricker—and a candidate of the liberal Governors—Willkie, Dewey, and Eisenhower. The liberal candidate has always secured the nomination. The Democrats in 1952 and 1956 faced a similar problem, but seemingly resolved it differently by nominating a relatively conservative candidate, Stevenson, and rejecting more outspoken liberals like Kefauver and Harriman, much as in 1944 they chose the then moderate Truman against the liberal Wallace for Vice-

President. In large part the difference in the reaction of the professional politicians in the two parties reflects their judgment of the character of the marginal voters whom they must win to be certain of a majority. The Republicans can be sure of the votes of almost all conservatives outside of the South, particularly the "villagers"; they must increase their vote among the more liberal strata concentrated in the cities. The Democrats have the solid vote of the working class and the liberals; they can easily lose the moderates in the center. The choice of the professionals in both parties is, therefore, a man of the center.

The differences between the social bases of the two major parties which have held up for more than a century and a half suggest that those who believe in the Tweedledee-Tweedledum theory of American politics have been taken in by campaign rhetoric and miss the underlying basis of the cleavage. It is especially ironic that the Marxist critics of American politics who pride themselves on differentiating between substructure and ideology have mistaken the ideology for the substructure.[45] American politicians, particularly the

[45] The conservative strata, on the other hand, have repeatedly recognized that the differences between the parties are fundamental, even though in given historical situations the Republicans may nominate a candidate who is as liberal as, or even more liberal than, his Democratic rival. Thus in 1904 the progressive Republican Theodore Roosevelt ran against the conservative Democrat Alton Parker for the presidency. And the New York *Sun*, the newspaper with closest ties to Wall Street, wrote: "We prefer the impulsive candidate of the party of the conservatives to the conservative candidate of the party which the business interests regard as permanently and dangerously impulsive." Quoted in Malcolm Moos, *The Republicans* (New York: Random House, 1956), p. 247.

It should be remembered that it was a conservative Democrat, Grover Cleveland, who, in 1886, sent the first message to Congress on labor. In it he urged that a commission on labor disputes be set up which could investigate and even arbitrate if so requested by the parties involved or by the state government. In 1888, in his last message to Congress after being defeated for re-election, Cleveland denounced "the communism of combined wealth and capital, the outgrowth of overwhelming cupidity and selfishness . . . not less dangerous than the communism of oppressed poverty and toil. . . ."

conservative ones, have always sought to suppress any overt
emphasis on the real differences between the parties: the
fact that they have been based on and represented different
classes, ethnic groups, and religions. To acknowledge and
accentuate openly these differences would seemingly lose
votes. Each party wants to gain votes from those who belong
to groups linked to the other faction. Hence conservative
party ideologists from Clay to Taft have been denied presidential nominations by the party professionals. The Whig
party could only defeat the party of the "demagogues," as
they described the Democrats, in 1840 and 1848, on both of
which occasions they nominated military heroes whose political opinions were almost unknown. In 1848, Whig leaders
started to nominate Zachary Taylor, the hero of the Mexican
War, before "it was . . . known to what party he professed
to belong," a practice repeated a hundred years later by their
Republican descendants.[46] The Democrats, appealing to the
more numerous lower strata, have been less inhibited about
making explicit appeals to interests, but even for them electoral expediency has often inhibited the expression of class
consciousness. The continuing receptivity of the Democrats
to the lower strata, particularly urban workers, and minority
ethnic groups, explains why all efforts to create a new party
based on these groups has always failed: the Democratic
party has been the expression of the political consciousness
of lower-status groups, much as the Republicans have fulfilled a similar function for the more privileged.[47] The prob-

---

See Samuel Reznick, "Patterns of Thought and Action in American
Depression," *American Historical Review*, 61 (1956), pp. 284–307.
It is important to note that Cleveland was much more conservative
in his second term of office when he no longer had to anticipate
facing the voters than in his first one, and that he was repudiated
by the Democratic party at its next convention in 1896. In fact,
Cleveland was the only President elected in his own right to be repudiated by a convention of his party while still holding office.

[46] Henry R. Mueller, *The Whig Party in Pennsylvania* (New York:
privately printed, 1922), p. 143.

[47] It is now often forgotten that Clement Vallandigham, the leader
of the Democratic "Copperheads" during the Civil War, was in
many ways a precursor of "post-Civil War populism and the Bryan

lem of electoral majorities, which in a two-party system presses both parties to appeal to the center in their electoral tactics, clearly does not negate Tocqueville's still valid observation that the two parties in America reflect the ever-present conflict in all societies between aristocracy and democracy, that is to say, between the more and the less well to do.[48]

Two striking deviations from these generalizations about class and politics in America have been the widespread support which the middle-class intellectual groups—artists, professors, scientists—and the well-to-do southerners have given to the Democratic party. The next two chapters attempt to account for these patterns by dealing with the underlying sources of the politics of American intellectuals, and with the way in which contemporary one-party southern politics emerged out of a deep-rooted *ante bellum* political class struggle.

---

crusade." He argued in 1861 that "The great dividing line was always between capital and labor." See Wilfred Binkley, *op. cit.*, pp. 264–65. He believed that "the monied interest" used sectionalism and anti-slavery as a trick to weaken their opponents. See Charles and Mary Beard, *The Rise of American Civilization*, Vol. I (New York: Macmillan, 1934), pp. 677–78.

[48] As Ralph Waldo Emerson described the differences between the two parties before the slavery issue rose to bedevil the ideologists: "The philosopher, the poet, or the religious man will, of course, wish to cast his vote with the democrat for free trade, for wide suffrage, for the abolition of legal cruelties in the penal code, and for facilitating in every manner the access of the young and the poor to the sources of wealth and power. . . . On the other side, the conservative party, composed of the most moderate, able, and cultivated part of the population, is timid and merely defensive of property." "Politics" in *The Works of Ralph Waldo Emerson*, Vol. I (New York: Hearst's International Library, 1914), pp. 373–74.

CHAPTER 10

American Intellectuals: Their Politics
and Status

AMERICAN INTELLECTUALS have for some time been a source of political controversy. Often during the postwar years, they have been a convenient target for a great number of people who are openly and aggressively anti-intellectual. Conversely, many businessmen and conservatives have felt that American intellectuals are excessively critical of them.[1]

Some intellectuals maintain that their alienation from society, any society, is an inevitable consequence of the basic character of their work and the social environment in which they live. Others regard it as a historical phenomenon which began as opposition to the values and style of life of an emerging capitalist society, and which is now waning as that society changes its character. According to this camp, the reintegration of the intellectual into American society is already well under way.

In this chapter we will attempt to discover how accurate these images of the political role of the American intellectual

---

[1] The identification of the "liberal" who is antagonistic to business with the intellectual is often made by conservatives. In an organ of the Chamber of Commerce of the United States, one finds the following: "The 'liberal' we are told, is cowered into impotence. . . . So far we have not been able to find *one artist or writer or speechmaker or professor* who would admit that he has been slowed down, or that his freedom of speech has been in the slightest impaired." *Economic Intelligence*, June 1954, p. 4 (my emphasis). Herbert Hoover, in discussing the 1928 campaign, comments that "the growing left-wing movement embracing many of the *'intelligentsia'* flocked to Governor Smith's support." See *Memoirs of Herbert Hoover, 1920–1933* (New York: Macmillan, 1952), p. 202.

are, and how the intellectual's political values are changing, if at all, under the impact of the social changes of the last half century.

I have considered as intellectuals all those who create, distribute, and apply *culture*, that is, the symbolic world of man, including art, science, and religion. Within this group there are two main levels: the hard core or creators of culture —scholars, artists, philosophers, authors, some editors, and some journalists; and the distributors—performers in the various arts, most teachers, most reporters. A peripheral group is composed of those who apply culture as part of their jobs— professionals like physicians and lawyers.

When Europeans speak of the *intelligentsia*, they mean all three categories. In America, however, where university educations are much more common, graduates do not constitute a distinct class or community, and it is usual to include only the first two categories, as I do here.

The common definition of intellectuals, especially by their own spokesmen, is that they are critics of society and necessarily detached from it. This avoids some of the knottiest problems about the place of the intellectual in modern society. If intellectuals are by definition alienated, then the problem of what happens when they assume other roles in organizations, or move into the political arena directly, is simply dismissed. But "creators and distributors of culture" who become politicians and administrators may keep their connections with those still principally occupied as intellectuals *per se*, may continue intellectual work themselves, and, being in positions of power, may provide a new sense of identification with politics for intellectuals as a whole. Even though Adlai Stevenson, for example, was not, technically, an intellectual, his identification as such gave many "legitimate" intellectuals the feeling that politicians were not all empty-minded manipulators, and politics itself not alien.

The problem of definition is sharpened by the existence of intellectuals in Nazi Germany and the Soviet Union who used, or still use, the tools and training associated with the *intelligentsia* in the service of anti-intellectual values. Are they really intellectuals? It is too simple an answer merely to write them off as renegades from the cause of reason, the discourse of free men, and creative activity. The participation of intellectuals in politics even in democratic society, even if it marks a victory—the acceptance of the contribution of the intellectual as valuable, or the growing influence of certain groups of intellectuals and their ideas—also marks the increasing commitment of intellectuals to institutions of the *status quo* and their potential transformation into apologists.

Of course, even within totalitarian countries one can still see intellectuals playing a somewhat independent role, and this is often cited as one of the hopes for the evolution of the Soviet Union into something resembling a liberal, democratic state.[2] The existence of a Pasternak, the refusal of a Kapitsa to participate in atomic research, the parading of Georgian students protesting expulsions, and other minute symptoms indicate that there is *something* about the environment of intellectual occupations which preserves the sacred spark of critical detachment.[3]

But the point must be made that, even if they sell their minds completely to antihumanistic values, as the German scientists who experimented on humans and the German historians who glorified the *Volk* did, intellectuals still remain intellectuals—creators and distributors of culture. Only if the possibility of complete commitment is seen, can the conditions which produce dissent, critical rejection, and other traditional hallmarks of the intellectual be evaluated. Those who postulate the eternal isolation of the intellectuals do not see the powerful social forces pulling them toward commitment.

I do not intend this as an entirely negative point, but rather to emphasize that either commitment to and support of existing institutions or a critical detachment from them

[2] For example, Lewis Feuer, "The Politics of the Death Wish," *New Leader*, 41 (1958), pp. 17–19.

[3] See Kathryn Feuer, "Russia's Young Intellectuals," *Encounter*, 8 (February 1957), pp. 10–25; Leopold H. Harrison, "Three Generations of the Soviet Intelligentsia," *Foreign Affairs*, 37 (1959), pp. 235–46.

are equally possible and legitimate positions for the contemporary American intellectual. American intellectuals have not yet been faced with the choice of complete capitulation or total opposition. Any analysis of the politics and status of intellectuals in America must therefore take into account both the forces pulling them into alliance with the major institutions of American society and those maintaining them, or sections of them, in a somewhat isolated, and therefore alienated, position.

The Historic Leftism of American Intellectuals

In the days of McCarthyism, the now defunct journal *Facts Forum* charged intellectuals as a group with being most vulnerable to Communism and described them as "lawyers, doctors, bankers, teachers, professors, preachers, writers, and publishers."[4] Ludicrous as this catalogue of Communist-inclined occupations is, it gives an important clue to the nature of the intellectuals' politics and the sources of political anti-intellectualism in America. *Facts Forum* attacked those occupations whose practitioners are university educated precisely because these professional groups were the most effective opponents of McCarthyism.[5] As we have seen in Chapter 4, a considerable body of evidence shows that the better educated individuals are, the more likely they are to favor all forms of "noneconomic liberalism," including civil liberties for unpopular political minorities. *Facts Forum* and McCarthy were quite right, from their point of view, in attacking "the American respectables, the socially pedigreed, the culturally acceptable, the certified gentlemen and scholars of the day, dripping with college degrees. . . ."[6]

In less extreme circles, many businessmen and other adherents of economic conservatism have sought to reduce the

[4] *Facts Forum Radio Program*, No. 57.

[5] For further discussion of this point see S. M. Lipset, "The Sources of the Radical Right," in Daniel Bell, ed., *The New American Right* (New York: Criterion Books, 1956), pp. 210–12.

[6] *Facts Forum Radio Program*, *op. cit.*

political effectiveness of American intellectuals by ridiculing their supposed lack of practical knowledge or by making scapegoats of them because they have erred in the past. Anti-intellectualism has been a useful, even natural, weapon of conservatives, and to some extent of Republicans, simply because in the twentieth century there have been very few important conservative intellectuals until recently.

During the twentieth century, the great majority of academicians (particularly those in the social sciences), significant literary figures, and leading journals of opinion have been opposed to conservative thought and action in religious and political realms. James Leuba, a psychologist, studied the religious beliefs of the membership of the sociological, psychological, and historical societies and of scientists listed in *American Men of Science*, in 1913–14 and again in 1933. He reported that the majority in each group did not believe in God or immortality, with irreligion stronger in 1933. Although we have no equivalent data on nonacademic occupational groups for the earlier period, studies of American religious behavior suggest that these professors and scientists were far more irreligious than the general population. Actually, about 55 per cent of all persons fourteen years of age and older were affiliated with churches before World War I. Among the members of the American Sociological Society who replied to the questionnaire, the nonacademics among the membership were more likely to have religious beliefs than the faculty members. It is also noteworthy that both in 1913 and 1933 the more distinguished professors were much more irreligious than their less eminent colleagues. In 1935 Leuba continued his investigations into belief in religion by sending questionnaires to samples of bankers, business people, lawyers, and writers listed in *Who's Who*. The replies confirmed the fact that scientists and various professorial groups are much less religious than businessmen, bankers, and lawyers, and also indicated that writers eminent enough to be listed in *Who's Who*, and presumably not as affected by the conflict between science and religion as those in the natural and social sciences, held irreligious views. Sixty-two per cent of the writers did not believe in God, as contrasted with 29 per cent of the bankers, and 40 per cent of the business people and lawyers.[7]

In 1937, a Chicago survey reported pro-New Deal sentiments among 84 per cent of professors of social science and 65 per cent of natural science faculty members, as contrasted with 56 per cent among manual workers, 16 per cent among lawyers, physicians, and dentists, and 13 per cent among engineers. Roughly similar results were obtained on attitudes toward various socioeconomic issues.[8] Almost two decades later, interviews conducted by Paul F. Larzarsfeld and Wagner Thielens, Jr., two Columbia University sociologists, of a systematic national sampling of over 2,000 social scientists teaching in American universities in 1955 revealed that three quarters were Democrats and that two thirds had voted for Stevenson in 1952, a year in which close to half of the manual workers and members of trade-unions swung to Eisenhower. And, like the 1913 and 1933 studies of religious belief, the survey found that the more distinguished professors showed a much higher proportion of liberals.[9]

One interesting indicator of the philosophy of the academic community is the consumer's co-operative movement. Urban co-ops, except for those with strong ethnic links like the many Finnish ones, scarcely exist outside of academic communities, and the prosperity they enjoy there bears witness to the academic world's hostility toward private business. Palo Alto (Sanford University) and Berkeley (University of California) have large co-ops, but efforts to maintain such stores in other parts of metropolitan San Francisco

[7] James H. Leuba, *The Belief in God and Immortality* (Chicago: The Open Court Publishing Company, 1921), pp. 219–87 and *The Reformation of the Churches* (Boston: The Beacon Press, 1950), pp. 50–54. For an analysis of trends in religious belief among the total population see S. M. Lipset, "Religion in America," *Columbia University Forum*, 2 (1958–59), pp. 17–21.

[8] Arthur Kornhauser, "Attitudes of Economic Groups," *Public Opinion Quarterly*, 2 (1938), p. 264.

[9] Paul F. Lazarsfeld and Wagner Thielens, Jr., *The Academic Mind* (Glencoe: The Free Press, 1958), pp. 14–17.

have repeatedly failed. Similarly, Ithaca (Cornell University), Hanover (Dartmouth College), the Morningside-Columbia University area in New York City, and the Hyde Park district in Chicago where the university is located, all have established co-operatives.

Academics are not, of course, the only intellectual group who give heavy support to left-of-center politics. A 1934 study of party registrations in the then strongly Republican Santa Clara County (suburban San Francisco) found that one quarter of the writers living there had registered as members of minority parties, largely Socialist and Communist, while only one third were Republicans. Writers constituted the most markedly left-wing, non-Republican occupation reported in the county.[10] In 1947, a survey conducted by *Time* magazine based on questionnaires returned by over 9,000 university graduates on how they voted in 1944, reported large Democratic majorities among teachers, scientists, and people in the arts.[11] It is significant that while 60 per cent of those who reported their occupation as "scientist" voted Democratic, 80 per cent of those who listed themselves as "engineers" voted Republican.[12] Librarians, whose occupation has close links to the intellectual world, also show strong leftist or liberal propensities. In 1948, 17 per cent of a national sample of librarians listed as their first choice for President third-party candidates—Progressive, Socialist, or

[10] H. D. Anderson and P. E. Davidson, *Ballots and the Democratic Class Struggle* (Stanford: Stanford University Press, 1943), p. 119.

[11] This study is reported in Ernest Havemann and Patricia West, *They Went to College* (New York: Harcourt, Brace & Co., 1952). Occupational analyses of political behavior which are not reported in the book were made from further analyses of the original data. I would like to acknowledge with appreciation the courtesy of the research department of *Time* for permitting such secondary analysis.

[12] Comparable findings concerning the strong conservatism and Republicanism of engineers are reported in A. Kornhauser, *op. cit.*, p. 264, and Arthur Kornhauser, "Analysis of 'Class' Structure of Contemporary American Society," in George W. Hartman and Theodore Newcomb, eds., *Industrial Conflict* (New York: The Cordon Company, 1939), p. 255.

Communist—putting librarians in the forefront among the groups backing such parties.[13]

Journalism also claims a high proportion of members with left-of-center political and economic philosophies. It is one of the few professions which is strongly organized in a trade-union, and that union is one of the more politically active. The American Newspaper Guild is, in fact, one of the few unions in which a Communist-dominated faction has secured considerable support in union elections even after it lost control of the organization. In the New York chapter, the largest local in the Guild, a left-wing slate secured between 20 and 25 per cent of the vote for many years. The political propensities of journalists have also been shown by interview studies. In the mid-thirties, a study of 104 Washington correspondents, a highly paid elite group, reported that 30 per cent had voted Republican in 1936, 6 per cent had supported the Communist or Socialist candidate, and the large majority had backed Roosevelt. Although the average salary of this group was over $6,000—a considerable income for the period —40 per cent favored government operation of mines, public utilities, and railroads, and 56 per cent supported the organization of a reporter's trade-union.[14] Many of these political attitudes reflected depression conditions; but straw votes conducted among reporters on the campaign trains of presidential candidates of both parties in later years suggest that, as a professional group, journalists have remained sympathetic to the Democratic party and to liberal causes. A more recent study of another elite group—foreign correspondents in Western Europe—reported that in the winter of 1953–54,

[13] This study is reported in Alice I. Bryan, *The Public Librarian: A Report of the Public Library Inquiry* (New York: Columbia University Press, 1952). The table dealing with political choice is not included in the printed version of the report, and was secured from a mimeographed version of the same study.

[14] Leo Rosten, *The Washington Correspondents* (New York: Harcourt, Brace & Co., 1937), pp. 342–53. The election in 1936, of course, went heavily Democratic. Poll data show, however, that other middle-class groups earning as much as these journalists gave the Republicans a majority.

58 per cent of those interviewed favored Stevenson, while 36 per cent supported Eisenhower for re-election.[15]

The arts also contribute heavily to Democratic and left-of-center support. The radical propensities of writers living in Santa Clara County during the Depression have already been noted. Although only sixteen people were classified as being employed in "the arts" in the *Time* study of college graduates, this group was overwhelmingly for Roosevelt. Like journalists, employed creative artists are almost entirely organized within trade-unions which have shown a strong liberal and left-wing political slant. Actors Equity has had a strong Communist faction, and the Radio Writers Guild has been controlled by Communists. The Democratic party has also received heavy financial backing from those employed in the motion-picture industry,[16] and it is no secret that Hollywood was a major source of Communist party funds in this country.[17]

While the Communists and their fellow travelers were never more than a minority among American intellectuals (no matter who defines them), they did constitute an influential minority at times during the thirties and forties.[18] In the debates over the validity of the Moscow trials, which went on among American Communist and anti-Communist

[15] Theodore E. Kruglak, *The Foreign Correspondents: A Study of the Men and Women Reporting for the American Information Media in Western Europe* (Geneva: Librairie E. Droz, 1955), pp. 87–89.

[16] Louise Overacker, "Presidential Campaign Funds in 1936," *American Political Science Review*, 31 (1937), p. 485; and "Presidential Campaign Funds in 1944," *American Political Science Review*, 39 (1945), p. 916.

[17] John Cogley, *Report on Blacklisting*, Vol. I, *Movies* (New York: Fund for the Republic, 1956), pp. 24–46; and Vol. II, *Radio and Television*, pp. 142–62.

[18] For a detailed discussion of Communist influence among American intellectuals, see Irving Howe and Lewis Coser, "The Intellectuals Turn Left," *The American Communist Party: A Critical History* (Boston: The Beacon Press, 1957), pp. 273–318; see also Daniel Bell, "Marxian Socialism in the United States," in Donald Egbert, *et al.*, eds., *Socialism and American Life* (Princeton: Princeton University Press, 1952), pp. 351–65.

intellectuals during the late thirties, the Communists were able to secure a larger and more eminent group of signers for public statements defending the trials than the anti-Communists could for statements attacking them. And the fact that most intellectual groups organized to combat Communist influence have invariably been led by Socialists and fairly left-wing liberals is perhaps even more indicative of the intellectuals' general left-wing bent. The most important such group recently, the American Committee for Cultural Freedom, has been under the leadership of Socialists—Sidney Hook and Norman Thomas—and men active in the New York Liberal party—George Counts and James T. Farrell, among others. In general, a wide variety of evidence shows that the intellectual sectors of the middle class—writers, persons in the arts, journalists, librarians, scientists, and university professors—have given more support to the Democratic party, and to small left-wing parties, than has any other stratum of the population in proportion to its size.

Sources of Liberalism

Analyzing the sources of the American intellectuals' leftism is a more complex problem than documenting the phenomenon. Part of the answer lies in the conditions which are general to the life of segments of the intellectuals in most societies and which account for patterns of left-wing support by such groups in other countries. Bertrand de Jouvenal, the French political theorist, has pointed out that there is an inevitable conflict between the values of the business classes and creative artists. Business is institutionally committed to giving its clientele what they want—the customer is always right. In contrast, the creative artist views the worth of his products independently of their immediate market value.[19]

[19] Bertrand de Jouvenal, "The Treatment of Capitalism by Continental Historians," in F. A. Hayek, ed., *Capitalism and the Historians* (Chicago: University of Chicago Press, 1954), pp. 118–20. Talcott Parsons has urged the view that there is a basic conflict between the values of business and that of all *professions*, e.g., law, architecture, medicine, and so forth: ". . . the dominant keynote of

Since in modern capitalist society rewards for cultural products increasingly depend on a market organized around business norms, the divergent views of the middleman or employer of creative talent (e.g., Hollywood executives, newspaper publishers, and so forth) and the professional norms of the artist are bound to lead the artist who cannot or will not create what will sell either to hostility toward the businessman, or to feelings of self-deprecation; while those who successfully adapt to the market tend to feel they have surrendered their personal integrity.[20]

The German sociologist, Theodore Geiger, attempted to account for the general propensity of social scientists to support the left in these terms:

> Of all groups in the *intelligentsia*, the social scientists are most sensitive to the power dimension in society, and also the most exposed to the attacks on

---

the modern economic system is almost universally held to be the high degree of free play which it gives to the pursuit of self-interest. . . . But by contrast with business in this interpretation the professions are marked by 'disinterestedness.' The professional man is not thought of as engaging in the pursuit of his personal profit, but in performing services to his patients or clients, or to impersonal values like the advancement of science." Talcott Parsons, *Essays in Sociological Theory* (Glencoe: The Free Press, 1949), p. 186. It should be noted that Parsons does not relate this conflict to any specific political consequences.

[20] The two studies of journalists cited earlier both call attention to the fact that the majority of reporters interviewed disagreed with policies of their newspapers, and felt it necessary to slant their news stories to reflect the wishes of their superiors. L. Rosten, *op. cit.*, p. 351. T. E. Kruglak, *op. cit.*, pp. 100, 102. An English study reports that the pressures for a Royal Commission on the Press after 1945 "arose from a desire to protect the intellectual freedom and integrity of journalists from the assaults of their employers." Roy Lewis and Angus Maude, *The English Middle Classes* (London: Phoenix House, 1949), p. 179.

"Great commercial success, especially in marginal fields like Hollywood, advertising, and publicity, tend in contemporary America to give a bad conscience to the successful writer, and drive him leftward." Crane Brinton, *Ideas and Men: The Story of Western Thought* (Englewood Cliffs: Prentice-Hall, 1950), p. 449.

intellectual freedom by those in power. The loss of intellectual autonomy and freedom also endangers their professional work and calling. Therefore, we can expect that in a social order in which capitalist business enjoys a great amount of power and has or could use pressure of one kind or another against criticism coming from academics . . . a significant number of social scientists—defined in the broadest sense possible—would be attracted to the left in one or another of its forms.[21]

Some analysts of intellectual life such as Helmut Plessner, a German scholar, have even posited "a general connection between the exact sciences and a leaning towards left-wing ideas." He suggests that the very concepts which scientists use in their work influence them toward the left:

For those engaged in the exact sciences, where ideas are mainly framed in a mathematical form, and where the progress of knowledge is based on controlled experiments and on the different applications of theoretical results to objective experience, there is a strong attraction in the doctrines of enlightened positivism. The clearest reflection of this type of approach in the sphere of political ideology is to be found in the doctrines of Marxism. The close connection established by Marx between the exact sciences and the techniques of industry on the one hand, and the structure of political power on the other, has a special appeal for the scientist who sees in it the key to the truly rational world community of the future.[22]

[21] Theodore Geiger, *Aufgabe und Stellung der Intelligenz in der Gesellschaft* (Stuttgart: Ferdinand Enke, 1949), p. 124.
[22] Helmut Plessner, "Ideological Tendencies among Academic Thinkers," Congress for Cultural Freedom, *Science and Freedom* (London: Secker and Warburg, Ltd., 1955), p. 178. It should be noted that Plessner believes that the work of historians makes them conservative since their assumptions are "rooted in the soils and traditions of their homeland." This view of historical sciences as conservative and the exact ones as leftist may be found summarized by Michels in 1911 in his *Political Parties* (New York: Hearst's In-

There are other factors, too, intrinsic to different intellectual occupations which probably affect the political values of intellectuals everywhere, but the liberalism of American intellectuals also has sources which are specific to this country and its history. Two factors, both resulting from our equalitarian ideology, have been important. First, the historic ideology of the United States has been the equalitarian dogmas of the Declaration of Independence which are fundamentally the values of the democratic left everywhere. Second, the very intellectuals who completely accept the equalitarian implications of the American Creed have felt themselves underprivileged, as a group, because they have not been accorded the symbols of high status which their counterparts in Europe receive. Ironically some of the reasons why American intellectuals do not get the signs of respect which they crave spring from the strength of the egalitarian standards which they espouse.

On the first point, there is no really conservative tradition in America, a condition common to many former colonies.[23] American democracy was born in a revolution against a foreign oppressor and rejected the claims of inherited privilege. And Americans, regardless of party, class, or religious per-

---

ternational Library, 1915), pp. 256–57, and with regard to the historian in Karl Mannheim, *Ideology and Utopia* (New York: Harcourt, Brace & Co., 1936), pp. 119–22. Michels summarizes hypotheses which contrast "the speculative sciences . . . such as philosophy, history, political economy, theology, and jurisprudence . . . so profoundly imbued with the spirit of the past . . . [with] the study of the experimental and inductive sciences . . . easy to win over to the cause of progress."

[23] See Louis Hartz, *Liberal Political Tradition in America* (New York: Harcourt, Brace & Co., 1955). "The ironic flaw in American liberalism lies in the fact that we have never had a real conservative tradition," *ibid.*, p. 57. "With high [intellectual] conservatism . . . excluded by [American] history, all we have left is practical conservatism—the conservatism, not of the professors, but of the industrialists, the financiers, and the politician." Arthur Schlesinger, Jr., "Burke in America," *Encounter*, 5 (October 1955), p. 79. See also Herbert McCloskey, "Conservatism and Personality," *American Political Science Review*, 52 (1958), p. 39, and Clinton Rossiter, *Conservatism in America* (New York: Alfred A. Knopf, 1955), p. 68.

suasion, believe in their revolutionary creed—unlike those Europeans who live in societies with ancient aristocratic class structures and established churches, where the forces of conservatism never really accepted the legitimacy of equalitarian democracy even when imposed by revolutions.

This means that conservative ideologies that look back to a golden age have never held sway in this country (except to some degree in the South and among some nineteenth-century "old family" New Englanders). No conservative utopia has ever been counterposed to the equalitarian utopias that have guided our political struggles. The political intellectual, the man of ideas, is nowhere very interested in defending inconsistencies, and every *status quo* is full of inconsistencies. Only by attacking the limitations of his political and social order can he feel he is playing a fruitful creative role. In Europe, he has been able to do this either by supporting a reformist utopia—an image of the good society of the future—or by advocating a conservative utopia, usually in the image of a society with traditional values—an Establishment and a creative aristocratic elite uninhibited by the need to flatter the uncreative masses. In either case he can criticize the present from the vantage point of an image of one or the other of these "good" societies.[24] And, quite often, both reformers and traditionalists dislike the same features of the present, like the nature of popular culture, which the leftist blames on the institutions of a business society, and the conservative sees as the necessary outcome of democracy's giving the masses power over taste.[25]

[24] "Almost all the men we now study as part of our heritage, almost all the great writers . . . attacked things as they were. . . . Now with the nineteenth century the creative intellectuals are still in rebellion, but . . . some have moved in ideal toward the right, toward the old religion, toward the old, or a rejuvenated aristocracy. . . . Some have moved left, toward some form of what now begins to be a word of fright to the conventional man of property—socialism." Crane Brinton, *op. cit.*, pp. 449–52.
[25] See Gertrude Himmelfarb, "American Democracy and European Critics," *The Twentieth Century*, 151 (1952), pp. 320–27, for a critique of the viewpoint of socialist intellectuals concerning popular culture.

The restriction of possible ideological choices for American intellectuals has meant that even the conservatively disposed have defined their political ideals in terms of the only available doctrines—those of the nation's revolutionary past, which true European conservatives abhor as the rankest radicalism. (In an unfortunately almost unknown book, written in the early 1930s, Leon Samson, a Socialist writer, pointed up the amazing parallels between the language used by certain important American businessmen and Republican leaders to describe the nature and objectives of American society with the statements of various Socialist and Communist leaders from Marx to Stalin. Samson argued that a principal cause for the failure of Socialist ideology in America has been the fact that the symbolic goals of Socialism are identical with those of Americanism.) [26]

American conservative politicians, lacking an ideology, have simply attempted to prevent change, or, like the present-day modern Republicans, competed with liberals in seeking equalitarian reforms which they could espouse. As I pointed out in the preceding chapter, American conservative parties have, in fact, demonstrated their own liberalism in noneconomic spheres by waging a more consistent fight for Negro rights than did the pre-Roosevelt Democrats. [27]

The second major source of American intellectuals' political leftism derives from their seemingly almost universal feeling that they are an underprivileged group, low on the ladder of social recognition (prestige), income, and power, as compared with businessmen and professionals. [28] In a recent study, so-

[26] Leon Samson, *Towards a United Front* (New York: Farrar and Rinehart, 1933).

[27] See Chap. 9, p. 303.

[28] Melvin Seeman reports in a study based on intensive and unstructured interviews with 40 assistant professors in the social sciences and the humanities that "these intellectuals use the language and mechanisms of minority status to describe themselves and their situation." "The Intellectual and the Language of Minorities," *American Journal of Sociology*, 64 (1958), p. 27. And David Riesman has pointed out that "intellectuals who, for whatever reason, choose to regard themselves as victimized contribute to the very pressures they deplore. These pressures are not so strong as alleged; thinking them

cial scientists teaching in universities were asked how typical businessmen, congressmen, or college trustees would rank professors in relation to "the manager of a branch bank, an account executive in an advertising agency, and a lawyer." The majority of those answering thought that businessmen and congressmen would put them in the last place. They were most confident about where they stood with college trustees, but even here almost half said that the "average" trustee would rank them either third or fourth. This low self-image encourages professors and, I would suggest, other intellectuals as well to pursue the same political path as other "deprived" groups the world over—to support those political parties that attack the existing distribution of privilege. The data clearly show that feelings of low status are closely correlated with liberal politics. "The Democratic voters [among these social scientists] are consistently more inclined to think that nobody loves the professor."[29]

The Real Status of the Intellectuals

It is a surprising fact that the image of the American intellectual held by his fellow-citizens is quite different from that he himself holds. While *he* may feel neglected and scorned, the community places him fairly high when it is polled on the relative status of occupations. In one such study of ninety-six occupations, conducted by the National Opinion Research Center of the University of Chicago, college professors rank above every nonpolitical position except that of physicians. Artists, musicians in a symphony orchestra, and authors rank almost as high.[30] Essentially, this study suggests that those in intellectual occupations have about the same prestige in America as important businessmen, bankers,

---

strong helps make them become so." David Riesman, "Some Observations on Intellectual Freedom," *American Scholar*, 23 (1953–54), p. 14.

[29] P. F. Lazarsfeld and W. Thielens, Jr., *op. cit.*, pp. 11–17.

[30] National Opinion Research Center, "Jobs and Occupations," in R. Bendix and S. M. Lipset, eds., *Class, Status, and Power* (Glencoe: The Free Press, 1953), pp. 412–14.

and corporation directors.[31] In 1950 a second national opinion survey reported similar results. That study asked people to place various jobs in the "upper, middle, working, or lower classes." Professors were fourth among twenty-four categories, and 38 per cent of the people polled actually placed them in the upper class.[32]

It may be argued that national surveys are not significant in this regard since what counts is elite opinion—the social science professors interviewed in the earlier study mentioned that big businessmen and high government officials do not respect intellectuals. Yet studies which have compared the ratings made by people from different classes indicate that those in high social and economic positions actually think far better of intellectual pursuits than do those in the working and lower classes.[33]

Perhaps the best evidence that intellectual occupations, particularly college teaching, enjoy high status in America comes paradoxically from the same professors interviewed by

[31] It is interesting to note that studies made in different countries and at different times indicate that the relative prestige of occupations is everywhere similar. Two sociologists, Alex Inkeles and Peter Rossi, have compared the results of surveys completed in Japan, Great Britain, the United States, Germany, Australia, and among a sample of Russian "defectors," and they concluded that occupations receive approximately the same rank in each country! Inkeles and Rossi, "National Comparisons of Occupational Prestige," *American Journal of Sociology*, 61 (1956), p. 339. Later studies completed in Brazil, the Philippines, Denmark, and the Netherlands show similar results. Two comparable American studies of the prestige of twenty-five different occupations, one completed in the mid-twenties and the other in 1947, found almost identical rankings at both times. Essentially all these studies indicate that occupations which require high levels of educational attainment (intellectuals and professionals) or which command considerable power (business elite and politics) are ranked high everywhere. For discussion and references see S. M. Lipset and R. Bendix, *Social Mobility in Industrial Society* (Berkeley: University of California Press, 1959), pp. 14, 111.

[32] Richard Centers, "Social Class, Occupation, and Imputed Belief," *American Journal of Sociology*, 58 (1953), p. 546.

[33] See John D. Campbell, *Subjective Aspects of Occupational Status* (unpublished Ph.D. thesis, Department of Social Relations, Harvard University, 1952).

Lazarsfeld who thought that their occupation would be ranked relatively low by businessmen and politicians. These professors, who constitute a good sample of university social scientists, turn out to come from "relatively high-status . . . family backgrounds," as Table I indicates.

Though professors prefer to believe that they are undervalued by people outside of the intellectual fraternity, the fact that they are able to attract into their ranks men from relatively privileged origins suggests that their occupation is actually highly valued. Almost half the respondents have fathers who are in managerial posts or in professions other than teaching. Only 15 per cent are the children of manual workers. A comparison of these data with those on different samples of the American business elite, like the heads of the largest corporations, indicates that the origins of both groups are roughly similar.[34] Actually the comparison may be unfair to the academic profession since the sample of college professors is drawn from all institutions of higher learning in the United States, and professors at the better institutions (which are on the average the largest schools) come from

TABLE I

SOCIAL ORIGINS OF UNIVERSITY SOCIAL SCIENTISTS*

Father's Occupation	Per Cent
Teacher (largely college professors)	8
Other professional	23
Managerial	25
White-collar and small business	15
Farmer	13
Manual labor	15
No information given	1
Total	100% (2,451)

* P. F. Lazarsfeld and W. Thielens, Jr., *The Academic Mind* (Glencoe: The Free Press, 1958), p. 7.

[34] See S. M. Lipset and R. Bendix, *op. cit.*, pp. 128–37, for a summary of the various business elite studies.

higher socioeconomic backgrounds: 62 per cent of those at very large schools (above 9,000 students) are from managerial or professional families, as contrasted with 49 per cent at very small ones (700 and below); two thirds of the social scientists at private nondenominational schools are from high-status backgrounds, as compared with 44 per cent at institutions with a religious affiliation or at teachers' colleges.[35] Since the social sciences do not carry the highest prestige within the university, it is possible that the social origins of humanists and natural scientists are even higher.

Coming from similar social origins does not mean, of course, that the differences in the attitudes and behavior of academic men and business executives are largely a result of differences in their occupational environment and status. Studies of the values of college students pursuing different vocational goals indicate that values, including political beliefs, may determine, as well as flow from, occupational position. For example, one study of university students (first as freshmen or sophomores, and two years later as juniors or seniors) reported that among students originally planning to major in business, political liberals tended to change their major, while conservatives remained in the business school. Similarly, when the values of students aspiring to different occupations were compared, it was found that men seeking sales, medical, or business careers exhibited low interest in personal creativity, and great concern with "money, status and security," while the reverse was true for the aspirants to scientific and teaching jobs. So some of the characteristics associated with different professions may be due to the fact that they recruit different kinds of people.[36]

[35] P. F. Lazarsfeld and W. Thielens, Jr., *op. cit.*, pp. 23, 26.

[36] In this regard, it would be intriguing to find out more about the causes and consequences of the fact that (as this and other studies show) the medical profession seems to attract the same type of individual as do the highly competitive and manipulative business occupations—men whose foremost objective seems to be to make money and get ahead. See Morris Rosenberg, *Occupations and Values* (Glencoe: The Free Press, 1957), pp. 16–19, 82.

Intellectuals vs. an Intelligentsia

Since the American intellectual's self-image as a man of low status seems to be one major source of his leftism, and since the facts contradict this appraisal, the question naturally follows: Why does the intellectual feel that he is looked down upon?

I suspect that, in large measure, his feelings of inferiority derive from his glorified concept of the European intellectual's status, and from using the European situation as a point of reference and comparison.[37] Anyone who has ever been in a discussion about the life of the intellectual in this

[37] "In Emerson's day professors and their fellow intellectuals had not come to be regarded as a special group; they were not then, nor have they ever come to be, looked up to, rewarded, and honored as in Europe." Merle Curti, "Intellectuals and Other People," *The American Historical Review*, 60 (1955), p. 260.

It may be that the grass always looks greener elsewhere, particularly to intellectuals who want to prove that it *is* better elsewhere, and who as important foreign travelers are often involved in exchanges with many sections of the native elite whom they rarely meet regularly at home. Thus, writing in the 1880s, James Bryce tells us that intellectual eminence in America "receives, I think, more respect than anywhere in Europe, except possibly in Italy, where the interest in learned men, or poets, or artists, seems to be greater than anywhere else in Europe. A famous writer or divine is known by name to a far greater number of persons in America than would know a similar person in any European country. He is one of the glories of the country." James Bryce, *The American Commonwealth*, Vol. II (Toronto: The Copp Clark Pub. Co., Ltd., 1891), p. 621.

More recently Raymond Aron, who believes that, all things considered, the position of the British intellectual is superior to that of the French, nevertheless states: "English writers of the *avant-garde* . . . are overcome with rapture when they come to Paris. . . . They at once develop a passionate interest in politics. . . . The last article of Jean-Paul Sartre is a political event, or at least it is greeted as such by a circle of people which, though narrow, is convinced of its own importance." This impression which the English and—need it be added—American intellectuals have of the political influence of their French brethren is, according to Aron, superficial and wrong. Raymond Aron, *The Opium of the Intellectuals* (New York: Doubleday & Co., Inc., 1957), p. 218.

country knows that sooner or later someone will remark that in England, Germany, France, or Italy, a writer, painter, composer, or professor *really* counts. *There* he is recognized by both the public and the political and economic elites.[38]

It is certainly true that there is a difference between the European and American treatment of the intellectual. This difference is no more or less than the difference between a fairly rigid class society and a society which emphasizes equality. In Europe, open deference is given to *all* those with higher status, whether engineers, factory owners, or professors, while in this country it is not given to *any* to the degree that it is abroad.[39]

An English writer, A. G. Nicholas, has pointed out, comparing the situation of the American and the British intellectual, that the latter "has been in some degree sheltered by his very position in what Bagehot called a 'deferential society.' Not *very* deferential to him, perhaps; less deferential than to the landowner, the administrator, the soldier, the clergyman or the lawyer, over all of whom the protective gabardine of the appellation 'gentleman' has fallen more inclusively, with fewer loose ends sticking out. Nevertheless the [Brit-

[38] A French analyst of American intellectuals has recently written: "It seems to me that the attitude of the American intellectual in comparison with his European counterpart is based on frustration and an inferiority complex. I am continually meeting people who tell me that the intellectual in Europe enjoys a position which, if not happier, is at least more dignified than that of the intellectual in America." R. L. Bruckberger, "An Assignment for Intellectuals," *Harper's*, 212 (February 1956), p. 69.

[39] "One thing and perhaps one thing only, may be asserted with confidence. There is no rank in America, that is to say, no external and recognized stamp, marking one man as entitled to any social privileges, or to deference and respect from others. No man is entitled to think himself better than his fellows, or to expect any exceptional consideration to be shown by them to him." James Bryce, *op. cit.*, p. 618. For an elaboration of these ideas, which attempts to show how the efforts of upper-status Americans to establish distinctions of family rank are a consequence of the strength of the equalitarian ideology, see S. M. Lipset, "Social Trends in America," in Lyman Bryson, ed., *A Guide to Knowledge* (New York: McGraw-Hill Book Co., 1960).

ish] intellectual has shared in it too, whether he was behaving as a rebel or as a hired apologist."[40]

Within most European factories there are rigid status lines drawn between occupations. I have heard American workers and engineers, temporarily employed in Europe, complain about the "silly" differences between social relations in these factories and our own. One oil refinery foreman working in Belgium once told me that he was in charge of a company Volkswagen bus, and after realizing that most workers on the project—which was outside the city—bicycled to work, he invited a number of them to travel with him on the bus. He asked both manual and white-collar workers. After the first day, the white-collar workers came to him and said that they could not ride in a car with manual workers, that he should realize this was not the custom in Belgium.

Similarly, a German Socialist professor told me of the difficulty sometimes experienced because of the use in German of two forms of "you," *Sie* and *du* (familiar). The latter is supposed to be used only among intimates and status equals, but the Social Democratic party decades ago institutionalized the *du* form among party comrades. Workers who do not know each other will use it immediately at a party meeting, but when faced with a Herr Professor Doktor they become embarrassed and attempt to avoid using any form.

[40] A. G. Nicholas, "Intellectuals and Politics in U.S.A.," *Occidente*, 10 (1954), p. 47. Another source of variation in the status accorded intellectuals in Europe and America flows from the difference in numbers. The title "professor" is held by close to 200,000 people in the United States and by a few thousand at most in the larger European states. This is partially because there are fewer universities in Europe, a point to be discussed later, and partially because Europeans limit the title, professor, to a few men in each field in each university, often just one. As John D. Hicks has pointed out: "In this country we have gradations—assistant professors, associate professors, full professors—and they are all professors. . . . But in the Old World it is different. There one finds no gradations. A man is a professor, or he is not a professor; and if he is a professor, that puts him on a pedestal of some eminence. Most of the teaching staff of an Old World university are not professors at all, and can never hope to become professors." John D. Hicks, "The American Professor in Europe," *Pacific Spectator*, 6 (1952), p. 432.

Intellectuals obviously receive gratifying social deference in many parts of Europe—*but so do all positions of high status.* What the American intellectual who envies his European brother fails to see is that he is really objecting to the equalitarianism of the United States, not to a lower evaluation of his occupation by its citizens. In this country, a worker will correct the judgment of engineers, and a worker's son will "tell off" his professor at a university if he disagrees with him. American employers and engineers find this code of manners natural, but intellectuals object to it. Unconsciously they think in European terms, much as do the various European middle-class *émigrés* from Nazism and Communism who have felt themselves reduced in status in America even when they hold comparable positions to those which they held in Europe:

> With his deep sense of class and status, integration in American society is not easy for the *émigré.* The skilled engineers or physician who, after long years of interneship, flunking license exams, washing dishes or laboratory floors, finally establishes himself in his profession, discovers that he does not enjoy the same exalted status that he would have had in the old country. I met several young Croatian doctors in the Los Angeles area who were earning $25,000 to $35,000 a year, but still felt *declassed.*[41]

Many American intellectuals see in the supposedly great dominance of "low-brow" popular culture in America, as compared to Europe, further evidence of the lower prestige of genuinely creative endeavor in this country. Yet in recent years, as Europe has become more like America in its economic and class structure, many European intellectuals have been in despair at the rapid increase of similar patterns of culture in their own countries. Perhaps the growth of mass culture in Europe is a result of the fact that, for the first time, the lower classes have enough money and time to make their demands in the culture market felt. Perhaps "Ameri-

[41] Bogdan Raditsa, "Clash of Two Immigrant Generations," *Commentary*, 25 (January 1958), p. 12.

canization" is merely a rise in the standard of living of the masses and a narrowing of the gap between the classes. The problem does not lie in popular dislike of "high-brow" activities or of intellectuals, but rather in the relationship between the degree of democracy and the level of culture of the average man.

David Riesman, one of the few American intellectuals to argue that "in the much more fluid and amorphous America of our time, *the writer, the artist, the scientist have become figures of glamour,* if not of power," has suggested an intriguing theory to explain why these men are so sensitive to criticism.[42] He points out that intellectually oriented students are usually in a small minority in American public high schools. As deviants from the school norms, which emphasize nonintellectual concerns, budding intellectuals are often ridiculed and isolated. This early school experience remains with them in later life, and any subsequent criticism of their intellectuality reminds them of their high school experience. If this is true, those intellectuals in this country and elsewhere who studied in schools designed to train an elite should be much less worried about anti-intellectualism.

The Problem of Numbers

Two other sources of the American intellectual's leftist tendencies, which do not follow as directly from America's equalitarian values, are the intellectual's seeming isolation from other sections of the elite—particularly his lack of direct contact with political power as compared to the European intellectual—and his income, as contrasted with that of business executives and professionals.

Why does the *average* American intellectual have less di-

[42] David Riesman, *op. cit.*, p. 15; Lionel Trilling and Saul Padover also have called attention to the high status of American intellectuals. See Lionel Trilling, "Mind and Market in Academic Life," *The New Leader* (February 9, 1959), pp. 19–23 and Saul Padover, "Kissinger and the Egghead," *The Reporter* (April 30, 1959), pp. 7–8. For discussion of the effects of school experience see David Riesman, "Comments," *Daedalus* 88 (1959), pp. 491–93.

rect contact with other sections of the elite, particularly with the men who wield political power, than the *average* European intellectual? Quite simply because there are, in absolute as well as proportionate terms, more intellectuals in America and they are more widely dispersed geographically than in any other country. In 1929 all *ten* professors of economics in Australia met and told the government they believed it would be disastrous for the country to go off the gold standard. The Labor government of the day was not happy about this, but it felt it should not move against the "experts." How could the thousands of American economics professors possibly exert such a corporate influence? There are more than 1,800 colleges and universities in this country, while Great Britain has about 15, West Germany has less than 20, Norway has one, Denmark, two, Sweden, four, and so forth. In greater New York alone there are over 20,000 people teaching in about forty institutions of higher learning. The Boston area has about 9,000 college and university teachers, 3,000 of whom are on the Harvard faculty. The northern California area of which San Francisco is the center has 14,000. There are now over 1,100 community-sponsored symphony orchestras in the country. And as the *Times Literary Supplement* pointed out in its issue on American writing, there are well over a hundred literary magazines in the United States as compared to less than a handful in Great Britain.

No urban center in the democratic world approaches New York City in the number of intellectuals employed in universities, magazines, publishing houses, and other "intellectual" industries. Yet while New York may be said to be the intellectual capital of the United States, there are important groups of intellectuals scattered around the country whose combined number is far greater than that of those in or adjacent to New York. (New York has but one major school— Columbia—and it places third in national rankings based on faculty caliber, after Harvard and the University of California at Berkeley.)[43] Important schools of painters and writers ex-

[43] The President's Committee, *The Educational Future of Columbia University* (New York: Columbia University Press, 1957), p. 13.

ist in various parts of the country from Seattle and Los Angeles on the West Coast to New Mexico, New Orleans, Chicago, Boston, and so on. As Nicholas has observed, "Broadway must never relax for a moment against the ambitions of Hollywood. . . . Boston has not given up the hope of wresting back its literary pre-eminence, or San Francisco the conviction that the course of cultural empire will take a westward way."[44]

The sheer number of intellectuals in the metropolitan centers, as well as the enormous size of the country, necessarily limits the extent to which intellectuals are acquainted with one another, let alone with those in other fields, such as politics or business. Academicians in large cities often know well only people within their own disciplines, and I can testify from direct experience that social relations among people in the same specialty in different universities in the same community are rare. There are over sixty historians employed full time on the faculty of Columbia University. The Berkeley faculty harbors more than thirty sociologists—more than are employed by *all* the British or Canadian universities. Groups of artists, *avant-garde* writers, writers employed in the publishing industry, exist in many cities, but their membership is often too large to permit much contact with other groups.[45]

It is worth noting that Columbia, though located in New York, has declined in the social sciences, rating first in 1925, but third in 1957, *loc. cit.*

[44] A. G. Nicholas, *op. cit.*, p. 45. "In the U.S., the political people are in Washington, the publishing and theatre people in New York, the movie people in Los Angeles, while the professors and the press are everywhere. (Most Englishmen I have met are not *really* aware that America has no national press, and that the overwhelming majority of university professors live in small towns.) It is quite possible for a man to edit a magazine with over a half-million readers, and never to have met anyone of distinction in politics, the drama, or music." Irving Kristol, "Table Talk," *Encounter*, 5 (October 1955), p. 60. (Emphasis in original.)

[45] The city of Oakland, California, which has 400,000 population and is basically an industrial and working-class city could claim in 1958 that "the number of working artists in Oakland is amazing. Nearly 1,000 men and women can be found painting for pay. Two of America's 17 painters at the Brussels Fair were from Oakland." Ed Schoenfeld, "Oakland and the Arts," Oakland *Tribune* (December 28, 1958), p. M-3.

The relative isolation of American college professors from all groups, intellectual or other, is borne out by the Lazarsfeld-Thielens study of social scientists. Over three fifths of the respondents (62 per cent) reported that "their main social contacts are confined to the university," a figure which rises to above 70 per cent among those at the more distinguished colleges and universities.[46] In countries with smaller elites, there is necessarily much more intermingling. Irving Kristol, who has edited magazines in New York and London, once observed: "What has astonished me, and what astonishes any American, is the extent to which almost all British intellectuals are cousins. . . . In America it is otherwise, to put it mildly. . . . It is by no means unimaginable that the senior editors of *The New Yorker* should never have met the senior editors of *Time*."[47] Dwight Macdonald, whose writing experience also covers both cities, commented: "As an alumnus of both of these magazines, I can testify this is accurate; intellectual circles in New York are neither concentric, interlocking, nor tangential, and one knows 'personally' . . . only a small proportion of the authors whose books and articles one reads. The London intellectual community is much broader, including businessmen, lawyers, and even publishers, even Members of Parliament."[48]

American professors teaching in Canada report similar experiences. They soon know the leading figures in a number of fields, since there is a relatively small group in each. The Canadian Broadcasting Corporation makes use of a large proportion of Canadian intellectuals. Government bureaus and politicians consult a fair proportion of the social science specialists in the country. The political parties will make use of any sympathetic intellectual who is willing to participate in politics.

[46] P. F. Lazarsfeld and W. Thielens, Jr., *op. cit.*, pp. 31–32.

[47] I. Kristol, *op. cit.*, pp. 60–61. Kristol has edited *Encounter* in London and *Commentary* and *The Reporter* in New York.

[48] Dwight Macdonald, "Amateur Journalism," *Encounter*, 7 (November 1956), p. 19; for later comments by Macdonald on the same subject, see his letter "Politics and Partisans," *Columbia University Forum*, 2 (1958), p. 3.

The government of the United States, even when the Republicans are in office, also employs and consults professors and other intellectuals. According to John Fischer, the editor of *Harper's* magazine, "The Eisenhower administration employs more professors than the New Deal ever did."[49] (The Republican need for intellectuals can be seen in the fact that the two professors who wrote sympathetic appraisals of the party, Arthur Larson and Malcolm Moos, were later employed as presidential aides in the White House.) The great majority, of course—over 90 per cent—must be left out of the picture, but I would guess that as many, if not more, professors and other intellectuals are employed and consulted at high levels by the state and federal governments as in most European nations.[50] It is only when the comparison is made in terms of proportion of intellectuals that America is lower—because there are so many more of them.[51]

[49] John Fischer, "The Editor's Easy Chair," *Harper's*, 216 (March 1958), p. 18.

[50] It has been suggested that the separation of the political capital, Washington, from the intellectual capital, New York, also contributes to the feelings of isolation from political power of many intellectuals. "The only type of intellectual who is likely to congregate in Washington is . . . one who has decided to make politics his full time business." A. G. Nicholas, *op. cit.*, p. 44. Not only is Washington separated from the intellectual activities of New York, but, curiously, it is one of the very few major American cities which lacks an important secular university. In this respect it is comparable to many state capital cities like Albany, New York; Sacramento, California; Harrisburg, Pennsylvania; and Springfield, Illinois. It would be interesting to compare the political role and subjective feelings about power of social scientists at universities located in state capitals with those elsewhere. Richard Hofstadter has pointed out that in one state, Wisconsin, where the capital and university coincide "even before the turn of the century there was an intimate union between the La Follette regime and the state university at Madison that foreshadowed all later brain trusts." *The Age of Reform* (New York: Alfred A. Knopf, 1955), p. 149. Minnesota is another state in which university and capital are located in the same urban area, and in which there is close co-operation and social relations between social scientists and politicans.

[51] It is interesting to note in this connection that the French sociologist, Raymond Aron, attempting to explain the allegiance of

Another point, and a very sore one, in the negative image the American intellectual presents of himself is his income. Compared to businessmen and independent professionals, he is threadbare.[52] His argument goes like this: People are paid according to what they are worth; consequently, lower pay implies that one's value is low. This syllogism omits the important fact that there are really two income structures in modern Western countries—the private one and the public one. A high-status public position is always more poorly paid than a corresponding private one. A lawyer at the peak of his profession, that is, as a justice of the Supreme Court of the United States, earns a good deal less than many a corporation lawyer in private practice. When they left private employment, Eisenhower's cabinet members had to take considerable cuts in salary. To consider a comparable group

a large section of the French intellectuals to Communism in spite of their high status, argues that they feel isolated from power, and legitimately so. "Most of the [French] intellectuals who take an interest in politics are embittered because they feel they have been defrauded of what was their due. Whether docile or rebellious, they seem to be preaching in the wilderness. . . . In the United States, in Great Britain, even in Germany, ideas and personnel never cease to circulate between the economists and the managerial circles of banking and industry, between these and the higher ranks of the civil service, between the serious press, the universities and the government. Most French businessmen have never met an economist, and until recently they tended—confidentially—to despise the species. French civil servants are totally indifferent to the advice of scholars, and journalists have few contacts with either. . . . In this respect no other ruling class is as badly organized as the French." R. Aron, *op. cit.*, pp. 220–21.

[52] "Writers occupy a peculiar position in the class structure of American society: they compose what sociologists would call an out-group or rather a collection of such groups. . . . Their incomes are smaller on the average than those of doctors and attorneys, larger than those of clergymen, and roughly equal to those of college professors." "Prophets Without Honour? The Public Status of American Writers," *Times Literary Supplement* (Sept. 17, 1954), p. liv. But Raymond Aron tells us that in France, some intellectuals "cast their eyes longingly across the Atlantic, where certain specialists of the written word, whom one would hesitate to call intellectuals, achieve considerable incomes." R. Aron, *op. cit.*, p. 219.

among intellectuals, leading professors at major American universities earn salaries which compare favorably with those paid in all but the very summit of high-level posts in government, or other nonprofit institutions. The *minimum* salary for full professors at certain good colleges at present is $11,000 for the academic year, and some have fairly automatic raises to higher stipends. Many professors make considerably more money on the side, in consulting fees from corporations and governments, in fees for articles, lectures, and books. Data in the study of social science professors previously cited show that 62 per cent of the people in this field have outside sources of income, and that the more productive faculty members, presumably earning the highest regular salaries, are the most likely to make extra money.[53] It is, of course, true that many professors could earn more in private industry, but this very fact disproves the contention that their talents are undervalued. The truth of the matter is that professors, like the lawyers who become judges or elective officials rather than corporation counsels, really believe that the noneconomic rewards of the job are better than monetary gains.[54]

Intellectuals in Politics

The two defeats of Adlai Stevenson have been taken by many intellectuals as an indication of the inability of American intellectuals to play an effective role in politics.[55] But

[53] P. F. Lazarsfeld and W. Thielens, Jr., *op. cit.*, p. 241. The authors divided their sample into five groups on a "productivity" scale. Of those who fall in the lowest group, and are presumably least eminent and earn the lowest pay, only 47 per cent have outside income sources, while among those in the "most productive" category, 76 per cent earn funds in addition to their university salaries.

[54] There can be no question that the average salary of college faculty is low, and that many full professors earn inadequate salaries. But young university scholars and civil servants are paid extremely low salaries everywhere, and the large number of mediocre colleges with inadequate endowments pull down the average.

[55] "Authors as a class had little or no political power. What some of them wrote might influence voters in ten or twenty years, but they were seldom able to help their candidates in a given election. It is

it is doubtful whether his defeats by the charismatic personality of Eisenhower prove any more about the effectiveness of an "intellectual" approach to campaigning than did Stevenson's success in his 1948 race for Governor of Illinois when he ran 400,000 votes ahead of the "man of the people," Harry Truman. Actually, on the level of party politics and electoral office, intellectuals do amazingly well. In the United States Senate, there are fourteen former members of college faculties (eleven Democrats and three Republicans) and "more than half of the remaining Senators have *earned* advanced degrees."[56] The first Democrat elected to the Senate from Oregon in over forty years, Richard Neuberger, is a professional writer, as is Ernest Gruening, elected to the Senate from Alaska in the forty-ninth state's first election. John Kennedy, re-elected in 1958 as Senator from Massachusetts with an all-time record of over 75 per cent of the total vote, has published two books, one an academic thesis written before he entered politics; he is a Harvard *cum laude* graduate; and he won a Pulitzer prize.

The ability of American intellectuals to win office is especially striking, given the fact that the American electoral and party system with its lack of central party control of candidates makes it difficult for men to obtain party nominations unless they come up via the machine-politics road and enjoy the backing of local party officials. In much of Europe,

---

even a serious question whether their almost unanimous support of Mr. Stevenson in 1952 added to or subtracted from his total vote; other groups may have decided to vote against anyone who aroused such enthusiasm among the 'eggheads.' " *Times Literary Supplement* (Sept. 17, 1954), p. liv.

[56] The quote is from John Fischer, *op. cit.*, p. 18, who also points out that "Lyndon Johnson . . . the second most powerful politician in the country, once taught school. His assistant leader of the Senate majority is an ex-college teacher." The statistics on the composition of the present Senate are from the *New York Times* (November 9, 1958), p. 65, "Cap and Gown Win Favor of Voter—3 Newly Elected College Professors to Join Faculty of 11 Current Senators." This article also points out that seven other Senators (six of them Democrats) are members of Phi Beta Kappa, the national scholastic honor society.

on the other hand, the officers of centralized parties can confer nominations on party intellectuals. Few American intellectuals are prepared to follow the path of direct participation in local politics as Paul Douglas, Ernest Gruening, Richard Neuberger, and Hubert Humphrey have.

Anti-intellectualism and American Values

Although much of the self-deprecating image which the American intellectual projects to justify his feelings of alienation from his society turns out to be invalid, there have been strong anti-intellectual tendencies in this country; and these further account for the historic lack of a sizable group of politically conservative intellectuals. Anti-intellectualism in this sense does not imply that intellectuals are or have been a low-status group in America, but stems in part from the lack of a hereditary aristocracy to lay down certain basic norms of upper-class behavior, and from the early history of adult suffrage in this country.

The absence of an aristocratic class in America has meant that for a long period the nation lacked the respect for cultural activities which traditional aristocracies developed as part of their way of life, and which were taken over by much of the European *bourgeoisie* as they sought to imitate the style of the class which they replaced. For much of the nineteenth century, particularly the second half, the rise of literally hundreds of self-made American millionaires brought into prominence and civic power men who lacked the social graces and cultural interests of established upper classes. The self-made man tends to emphasize the worth of material success and conspicuous consumption and to deprecate seemingly nonproductive activities. He takes pride in economic and technological advancement, and it is no accident that one of the first arts to flourish in this country was architecture. During the latter part of the nineteenth century, many American intellectuals like Henry Adams felt themselves outcasts in a world dominated by such men.

(Parenthetically, it should be pointed out, however, that no upper class of modern times has ever made so many funds available for intellectual activity. Men like Carnegie, Rockefeller, Stanford, Guggenheim, Ford, and others, set new standards through their gifts to universities or through the establishment of foundations. Veblen and others have pointed to these munificent contributions as examples of conspicuous consumption. What is left out of this analysis is the implication of the fact that the support of intellectual activities is assumed to bestow prestige on American men of wealth. In his last years, Andrew Carnegie surrounded himself with intellectuals and artists and concerned himself with their economic problems. In his letter of gift establishing the Carnegie Foundation, he stated that among its purposes was to "do and perform all things necessary to encourage, uphold, and dignify the profession of the teacher and the cause of higher education."[57] This pattern of large donations to intellectual activities has few counterparts in other parts of the world. With rare exceptions, wealthy Frenchmen, Britons, or Germans, have not felt the need to support intellectual endeavors on a large scale.)

During the twentieth century the vulgarities in taste introduced by the so-called "robber barons" began to decline. Their scions established the Social Register and attempted to create an American aristocracy. E. Digby Baltzell has well described, in a recently published study of the Philadelphia upper class, the emergence in this century of elite private schools like Groton which have come to play a part comparable to Eton and Harrow in Britain, the gradual centralization of upper-class education in a few universities, the codification of upper-class membership in the Social Register, and the conversion of high-status families to Episcopalian-

[57] Claude C. Bowman, *The College Professor in America* (Philadelphia: privately printed, 1938), p. 57. In 1919 John D. Rockefeller followed in Carnegie's footsteps by giving "$50,000,000 toward a nation-wide movement to pay college teachers more adequately." *Ibid.*, p. 43. And in 1955 the Ford Foundation, in which the Ford family retains considerable influence, contributed $500,000,000 for salary increases in universities.

ism.[58] All these trends have served to reduce, if not to eliminate, the type of materialistic anti-intellectualism which disturbed Henry Adams.

But as overt anti-intellectualism stemming from the social situation of the *nouveaux riches* declined, a new source emerged. The antagonism to the American business-dominated culture which had led many nineteenth-century intellectuals to withdraw completely from any concern with politics or public affairs turned, in the twentieth century, to support of liberal and left-wing politics—first, Progressivism and Wilson's New Freedom; later, as we have seen, Marxism and the New Deal.[59] And Marcus Cunliffe, an English student of American history, suggests, World War I, "along with the Russian Revolution . . . finally proved to the American *avant-garde* that they knew better than their society. It is not too wild to say that 1917, the year of revolution and mutiny, also marked a cultural revolution in America—a movement that was to adopt the vocabulary of Marx together with that of Freud."[60]

This emergence of the intellectual into the political battle as an active partisan brought with it anti-intellectualism as a line of counterattack by the harassed political and religious conservatives. McCarthyism is but the latest example of an attack on intellectuals by politicians. Comparable attacks have a particularly long history in America, as the historian Merle Curti has documented.[61] But the length of this history is

[58] E. Digby Baltzell, *Philadelphia Gentlemen* (Glencoe: The Free Press, 1958).

[59] R. Hofstadter has perceptively analyzed some of the sources of the leftward drift of the American *intelligentsia* in which "beginning slowly in the 1890's and increasingly in the next two decades, members of these professions deserted the standpat conservatism of the post-Civil War era to join the main stream of liberal dissent and to give it both moral and intellectual leadership." See *The Age of Reform, op. cit.,* p. 149; see also pp. 148–63. See also William E. Leuchtenburg, "Anti-Intellectualism: An Historical Perspective," *Journal of Social Issues,* 9 (1955), pp. 8–17.

[60] Marcus Cunliffe, "The Intellectuals II. The United States," *Encounter,* 6 (May 1955), p. 29.

[61] Merle Curti, *American Paradox* (New Brunswick, New Jersey: Rutgers University Press, 1956).

largely due to the fact that the United States has the longest continuous history of democratic politics and adult suffrage in the world. It is clearly necessary for men in politics to try to demolish the strength of opposition views, and the very fact that the intellectuals have always claimed that their superior education and intelligence make their views important has tempted those who have disagreed with them, in both Europe and America, to resort to anti-intellectualism.[62] The masses nowhere have real understanding of or sympathy for the problems of intellectual life, and they can be aroused against the intellectuals as part of their general resentment against the advantages of the more privileged and powerful. Engels noted how, in the early days of the European Socialist movement, it was possible for anarchist and other left-wing opponents of Marx to foster among Communist workers "ineradicable suspicion against any schoolmaster, journalist, and any man generally who was not a manual worker as being an 'erudite' who was out to exploit them."[63]

[62] The British socialists were attacked for following the theories of the impractical Fabian intellectuals, and the German Right has always been hostile to *Kathedersozialismus*. There is, however, one important difference between the United States and much of Europe during most of the twentieth century: we have not had many conservative intellectuals. Anti-intellectualism has thus been a natural weapon of the conservatives.

But Richard Hofstadter reminds us correctly that American liberal politicians, like the radical opponents of Marx, can be equally intolerant of intellectual opposition. "Our history books tell us . . . that during the Populist-Bryan period the university professors who failed to accept the gold standard economics of the well-to-do classes were often victims of outrageous interference; they do not usually trouble to tell us that when the Populists captured Kansas they raised hob with the University of Kansas in much the same way that they complained of so bitterly when the shoe was on the other foot." Richard Hofstadter, "Democracy and Anti-intellectualism in America," *Michigan Alumnus Quarterly Review*, 59 (1953), p. 288.

[63] Friedrich Engels, "On History of Early Christianity," in Karl Marx and Friedrich Engels, *On Religion* (Moscow: Foreign Languages Publishing House, 1957), p. 319. A more detailed account of anti-intellectual episodes within the European socialist movement may be found in John Spargo, "Anti-Intellectualism in the Socialist Movement: A Historical Survey," in *Sidelights on Contemporary Socialism* (New York: B. W. Huebsch, 1911), pp. 67–106.

And David Riesman has correctly observed that political anti-intellectualism may be regarded as a form of the "class struggle" reflecting the fact that various groups "feel threatened by . . . the growth of intellectualism," and the powerful enemy is "no longer only bankers, lawyers, drummers . . . [but also] professors, teachers, writers, and artists."[64]

This is another proof that the left politics of intellectuals in America does not arise from low status. *If political anti-intellectualism is evidence that intellectuals have low status, then the persistent attacks on bankers, Wall Street brokers, and railroad magnates in American history would be evidence that they also are low-status groups, and this is clearly not the case.* Attacks upon any group frequently indicate their visibility as high-status groups, and reflect a kind of populist antagonism to any elite.[65]

The Move to the Right

This analysis of the sources of contemporary anti-intellectualism, and of the dominant politics of American intellectuals, has produced some curious paradoxes. I have argued that anti-intellectualism has been particularly widespread among conservatives because intellectuals have not been distributed more or less equally among the different political parties and tendencies. American intellectuals have accepted the equalitarian ideology of the United States, and this has both eliminated conservatism as a real alternative for them and also led many of them to regard themselves as underprivileged because they do not receive the overt deference that the more class-bound European societies give their Continental colleagues. The very success of the liberal ideology which most American intellectuals espouse reinforces their feelings of deprivation, which then become an additional source of their reformist zeal; and that zeal in turn stimulates political attacks on intellectuals by conservatives, and furnishes further

[64] D. Riesman, "Some Observations on Intellectual Freedom," *op. cit.*, p. 15.

[65] Of course, attacks do not always imply high status, as shown by the case of the Jews and anti-Semitism.

support for the intellectuals' left-of-center political tendencies.[66]

However, this self-supporting cycle, which would keep American intellectuals on the left and right-wing groups on the offensive against them indefinitely, has shown some signs of breaking down in the last few years. American intellectuals as a group seem to have shifted toward the center, although most of them probably remain to the left of that imaginary line; and a significant minority have become conservative in their thinking. Many circumstances underlie this shift. Clearly one of the most important is the social consequences of prolonged postwar prosperity. Another is the reaction of liberal leftist intellectuals in America, as elsewhere, to the rise of Communism as the main threat to freedom. Faced with a society far worse than the one which now exists in the West but one which claims to be fulfilling the values of the American and French revolutions, such intellectuals, including many of the socialists among them, now have for the first time in history a conservative ideology which allows them to defend an existing or past society against those who argue for a future utopia. Like Burke, they have come to look for sources of stability rather than of change. The very social classes which the intellectual reformer saw as the carriers of the good society—the lower classes, especially the workers—back the new despotism, and not only the despotism of the left, but, as McCarthyism and Peronism showed, often of the "radical right."[67] Furthermore, the very success of

---

[66] The French writer R. L. Bruckberger has argued that "the American intellectual often tends to say that his country has failed him, that she will not give him the honor which is his due, and that he feels like a spiritual exile. *I wonder if the contrary is not true.* Perhaps the American intellectual has failed his country, and perhaps he is more deeply missed than is first apparent. . . . This misunderstanding would indeed be comic if a nation could get along without intellectuals. Yes, the American intellectuals should stop complaining about America. It would be more in order for America to complain about them. All too often, it seems as if their country were of no interest to them." R. L. Bruckberger, *op. cit.*, p. 70. (Emphasis in original.)

[67] An earlier alliance between the intellectuals and the lower-class based Democratic party broke down in the 1840s because a

moderate forms of leftism—the New Deal in this country, democratic Socialism in the British Commonwealth and Scandinavia—has removed programs for economic reform from the category of a utopia to that of a reality with imperfections and inconsistencies.

And while changing political events have everywhere destroyed the utopias of the democratic left, prolonged prosperity, with its concomitant improvement of the relative positions of workers and intellectuals, has reduced the visible reasons for an intense concern with economic reform. The political issue of the 1950s has become freedom versus Communism, and in that struggle many socialist and liberal intellectuals find themselves identifying with established institutions. This identification comes hard to intellectuals who feel called upon to reject conventional stupidities, and results in a feeling of malaise which takes the form of complaining that everyone, including the intellectuals, is too conformist. Many American liberal intellectuals in the 1950s know that they should like and defend their society, but they still have the uneasy feeling that they are betraying their obligation as intellectuals to attack and criticize. Their solution to this dilemma is to continue to feel allied with the left, but to vote Democratic; to think of themselves as liberals—and often even as socialists—but to withdraw from active involvement or interest in politics and to concentrate on their work, whether it be writing poetry or scholarly articles.

It is important to emphasize that this evidence on the changes in many intellectuals' attitudes does not support the assumption, thrown out by the few who still remain in the extreme left, that McCarthyism or other forms of intimidation have silenced the radicals and created a frightened or bought group of conformists. An opinion survey of the atti-

---

noneconomic issue, slavery, became the principal liberal intellectual cause, and the masses and the Democrats were on the wrong side. Many political intellectuals allied themselves with the "upper class" or Republican Tory liberalism discussed in the previous chapter, or with small left-wing parties. They began their return to the Democrats with Wilson's New Freedom and completed it with the New Deal.

tudes of American social scientists supplies strong evidence that those who thought the spirit of the academic profession was crushed by McCarthyism were wrong. In general, the liberals among them stood up for the rights of unpopular minorities and continued to exercise their own right of free expression, even though they felt apprehensive about the threats to intellectual activity. As Lazarsfeld and Thielens remark about the behavior of the social science professors they interviewed: "There is indeed widespread apprehension among these social science teachers, but in general it is hardly of a paralyzing nature; the heads of these men and women are 'bloody but unbowed.' "[68]

The courage and liberalism of the university professor is actually constantly reinforced by his relations with his confreres. "While outside forces such as legislative committees may have harsh and definite means to do him damage, he cannot underestimate the subtle deprivations to which his immediate professional environment could subject him."[69] Men live in small communities, not simply in the great society, and the small community both reinforces its own attitudes to and punishes deviations from group norms. Thus the liberal consensus within the intellectual community has served to intimidate conservatives much more than outside prying and criticism has inhibited those left-of-center.[70] Today the larger social forces pushing the intellectual community as a whole in a conservative direction may also reduce this internal consensus on liberal political values and allow the release of more latent conservatism than has yet been apparent.

Even more significant evidence that the decline of intellectual leftist sentiment in America is not primarily a result of coercion is that a similar reconciliation between imperfect democratic society and leftist intellectuals has lately taken place in a number of other Western countries, where the

[68] P. F. Lazarsfeld and W. Thielens, Jr., *op. cit.*, p. 95.

[69] *Ibid.*, p. 104.

[70] Morris Freedman, "The Dangers of Nonconformism," *American Scholar*, 28 (1958–59), pp. 25–32.

pressures linked to internal security programs and anti-Communism have been much less. In Britain, the London School of Economics, once regarded as a stronghold of the Labor party, now contains a Conservative voting majority among its faculty, according to a number of reports.[71] In Canada, the *Canadian Forum,* the organ of Socialist writers and academics for three decades, ceased being a Socialist magazine within the past five years. One can point to similar changes in Scandinavia. And in France and Italy many intellectuals have moved from Communism to Socialism.

Only time will tell whether a permanent change in the relation of the American intellectual to his society is in process. In spite of the powerful conservatizing forces, the inherent tendency to oppose the *status quo* will still remain. As Edward Shils, a Chicago sociologist, has written: "In all societies, even those in which the intellectuals are notable for their conservatism, the diverse paths of creativity, as well as an inevitable tendency toward negativism, impel a partial rejection of the prevailing system of cultural values. The very process of elaboration and development . . . of the potentialities inherent in a 'system' of cultural values . . . involves a measure of rejection."[72] Any *status quo* embodies rigidities and dogmatisms which it is the inalienable right of intellectuals to attack, whether from the standpoint of moving back to traditional values or forward toward the achievement of the equalitarian dream. And in so doing the intellectual helps to maintain the conflict which is the lifeblood of the democratic system.

[71] See William C. Harvard, "The London School of Economics Revisited," *South Atlantic Quarterly,* 58 (1959), pp. 108–23.

[72] Edward Shils, "The Intellectuals and the Powers: Some Perspectives for Comparative Analysis," *Comparative Studies in Society and History,* 1 (1958), p. 8.

CHAPTER 11

The Emergence of the One-party South—The Election of 1860

THE CONTINUED allegiance of the South to the Democratic party stands out as the largest single deviation from a class conflict view of the American party struggle. Though some suggest that the Democratic loyalties of the South are reinforced by its position as an economically relatively depressed section of the country, it seems somewhat preposterous to view the southern planters and small-town businessmen as a depressed stratum. But there is no denying that some of the most conservative, if not reactionary, segments of the American body politic are southern Democrats. Some of the variables underlying this fact have already been discussed in previous chapters, and a thorough analysis will not be attempted here.[1] However, an analysis of the link between the post-Civil War identification with the Democratic party and class cleavage within the *ante bellum* South may illustrate how the diverse interests and values of different strata are affected by such confusing and emotion-laden issues as slavery and Negro rights, and supply some of the reasons for the long-term continuation of a seemingly nonlogical pattern. This chapter deals briefly with these issues by a survey of the last real two-party election in the South—that of 1860.

The election of 1860 stands out decisively as the presidential election which most affected American life. Its controversies culminated in the Civil War. The formal party

[1] For detailed analyses of the one-party South, see V. O. Key, Jr., *Southern Politics* (New York: Alfred A. Knopf, 1949); Alexander Heard, *A Two-Party South* (Chapel Hill: University of North Carolina Press, 1952); and J. B. Shannon, *Towards a New Politics in the South* (Knoxville: University of Tennessee Press, 1949).

system has not changed much since then, and the regional loyalties and antagonisms formed in that period have continued to affect party allegiances down to the present day. The election itself took place as the end to a great national debate on the place of slavery in American life—a debate which had grown in intensity during the entire first half of the nineteenth century. As one reads over the story of the period, it is difficult to avoid the feeling that if there was ever an election with a salient issue, in which voters made a fundamental choice, it was this one.

However, an examination of the sources of support of the four presidential candidates in this election suggests that issues associated with slavery or the rise of the Republican party were not the decisive ones affecting the vote of *most* Americans, although they may have changed the vote of important minorities. There were four candidates: Lincoln representing the Republicans; Douglas, the northern Democrats; Breckenridge, the southern Democrats; and Bell, the Constitutional Union party. Lincoln and Bell, seemingly, were nominees of new parties, but in fact they represented the northern and southern Whig parties, which had split along regional lines earlier than the Democrats. Although there were four candidates in the race, the contest in each region of the country was largely a two-party affair. In the southern states it was a contest between the secessionist Democrats supporting Breckenridge and the Old Whig Constitutional Unionists who advocated remaining in the Union. In the North it was the Democrat, Douglas, who opposed slavery but favored saving the Union by giving the southern states various guarantees for their "peculiar institution." The northern Whig-Republicans under Lincoln also hoped to save the Union but vigorously opposed the extension of slavery in the territories or new states and included a number of prominent abolitionists in their ranks. Thus the northern Whig-Republicans and the southern Democrats represented the two extremes, while the northern Democrats and the southern Whig-Constitutional Unionists represented the groups in each section of the country who were seeking to compromise the cleavage.

The four-candidate race of 1860 succeeded a three-party fight in 1856, when the American, or Know-Nothing, party contested the election against the Democrats and Republicans. Any attempt to understand the results of the 1860 election must begin with an examination of the social composition and ultimate political destination of the Know-Nothing voters. Both their leadership and voting strength suggest that the bulk of their vote came from former Whigs. This was particularly true in the South where their presidential candidate, Millard Fillmore, secured 45 per cent of the vote in 1856, essentially the strength of the Whig party. In the North, most former Whigs voted for the Republican party, which won 45 per cent of the total sectional vote, while Fillmore secured only 13 per cent of the votes of the northern electorate.

In 1860, the now divided Democrats increased their vote in both the North and the South, but the Republicans, absorbing the bulk of Fillmore's vote in the North, obtained approximately 54 per cent of the vote in that section and a majority in the Electoral College. The Republican victory in 1860 cannot be credited to any drastic shift away from the Democrats, but rather to the fact that all northern anti-Democratic votes were gathered together under one party for the first time since the Whig victory of 1848. As a matter of fact the Democrats actually *gained* five congressional seats in the North in 1860. In the South, the Constitutional Unionist and former Whig, Bell, secured 41 per cent of the vote, only 4 per cent less than the 1856 vote of the candidate of the Know-Nothing party, the former Whig, Fillmore.

A cursory analysis of the county election returns, North and South, indicates that for the most part men continued to vote in 1860 for the same party they had always voted for, although a shift to the Democrats in the South and to the Whig-Republicans in the North continued. If one compares the results of the elections from 1840 to 1860, one finds that in each of them, in both North and South, the Democrats were disproportionately backed by the lower strata —the poorer farmers, the foreign born, the non-Anglo-Saxons, the Catholics, and the nonslaveholders in the South; while the Whigs were based on the more privileged classes—the merchants, the more well-to-do farmers, the native-born Protestants of Anglo-Saxon ancestry, and the large slave-holding plantation owners.[2] These relationships obtained during this entire period, although, as indicated above, the southern Democrats gained considerably in Whig areas, while the Republicans absorbed a group of Free Soil (Van Buren) Democrats as well as some anti-Catholic groups who had supported the American party.

These results—particularly in the South—present some interesting problems for the student of elections. It is clear that Bell, the southern candidate opposing secession and seeking to keep the South in the Union even under Republican control, was disproportionately backed by slaveowners, while Breckenridge, the candidate of the "red-hots" who saw little future for the South and its institutions in the Union, received the bulk of the votes of the men who did not own slaves and who had often opposed the conservative well-to-do plantation owners in intrastate political controversies.

The correlations between party vote and various social characteristics in 1860 are understandable only if we make the assumption that most voters in that year voted along traditional lines. The more deprived social groups remained loyal to their regional Democratic candidates, Breckenridge and Douglas, while the more privileged voted for the regional candidates of the old Whig party, Bell and Lincoln. For example, the straw votes cast for President in 1860 at St. Paul's School were divided almost entirely between the two Whig candidates, with Bell receiving 46 per cent and Lincoln 37 per cent.[3] The election of 1860, like every election since

[2] The basic research to demonstrate the continuity of voting choices within the Whig-Democratic framework has not been fully done although there are a number of local studies which indicate that the Whigs, Americans, and Republicans drew their votes from the same sources, while the Democrats, united or cleaved, retained the loyalties of the strata and sections which had backed Jackson and Van Buren from 1828–1840.

[3] Arthur Stanwood Pier, *St. Paul's School* (New York: Charles Scribner's Sons, 1934), p. 60; also quoted in E. Digby Baltzell, *Philadelphia Gentlemen* (Glencoe: The Free Press, 1958), p. 316.

1828, was fought out between the supporters and opponents of Andrew Jackson. Table I, which shows the variation in

TABLE I

PROPORTION OF COUNTIES VOTING FOR BRECKENRIDGE IN SEVEN SOUTHERN STATES—VIRGINIA, ALABAMA, GEORGIA, MISSISSIPPI, NORTH CAROLINA, TENNESSEE AND LOUISIANA*

Relative Position of County in Proportion of Slaves within Its State	Total	Number for Breckenridge	Per cent for Breckenridge
High	181	94	52%
Medium	153	87	56
Low	203	130	64

* Douglas, the northern Democrat, secured 13 per cent of the southern vote. Since he, like Bell, supported the Union his votes have been considered together with Bell's as anti-Breckenridge. In locating counties as high, medium, or low in proportion of slaves, it was necessary to use different classifications for each state. This was done in part because the sources employed to secure the data differed among themselves in the way in which they reported percentage of slaves in the population. More important than this reason, however, was the fact that states varied greatly in the proportion of slaves so that the plantation states had many slaves in most counties, while some of the border states had few counties in which slaves were a majority. In all the southern states, however, the proportion of slaves in the population served to differentiate the wealthier from the poorer counties, and in general, whether a county was high or low in proportion of slaves within a state was highly correlated with its voting patterns.

The data for this and succeeding tables have been calculated from information reported in the following works: Joseph Carlyle Sitterson, *The Secession Movement in North Carolina* (Chapel Hill: University of North Carolina Press, 1939); Henry T. Shanks, *The Secession Movement in Virginia, 1847–1861* (Richmond: Garrett and Massie, 1934); Lewy Dorman, *Party Politics in Alabama from 1850–1860* (Augusta: Alabama State Department of Archives and History, 1935); Percy Lee Rainwater, *Mississippi Storm Center of Secession, 1856–1861* (Baton Rouge, La.: Otto Claitor, 1938); Thomas P. Abernethy, *From Frontier to Plantation in Tennessee* (Chapel Hill: University of North Carolina Press, 1932); and Ulrich B. Phillips, *Georgia and State Rights* (Washington: Government Printing Office, 1902).

voting patterns of southern counties according to the ratio of slaves in the county, clearly demonstrates that the strength of the secessionist Democrat Breckenridge lay with the whites living in areas in which there were few slaves. The table seems to suggest that the fewer the slaves in a county, the greater the support for secession, since Breckenridge carried almost two thirds of the counties which were low in slaves, while almost half the counties that were high in slaves voted against him.

Whether a Breckenridge vote actually meant a vote for secession, however, was tested directly three to six months after the presidential election when the same states held referenda (or elections to conventions) in which voters were called upon to express directly their sentiments for or against secession from the Union. The situation had changed, of course, since Lincoln had been elected President, and it was clear that a large group in the South had decided on secession. These convention-delegate elections were hotly contested in most southern states, and the results were closer than many realize, with the Union forces getting over 40 per cent of the vote in many states. Although no one has done a detailed study of the leaders of the secession and Union forces in these elections, historical works on the struggle in different states indicate that most of the antisecession leaders had been leaders of the Whig and Constitutional Union parties, while the secessionist leadership was largely, though far from exclusively, in the hands of Democrats. This fact, together with the results of the presidential election presented in Table I, might lead one to expect that the Whig slaveholders who backed Bell in the presidential election would be the principal source of Unionist sentiment, while the low-slave counties would back secession, following up their vote for Breckenridge.

In fact, however, the relationship between slave-ownership and voting Unionist shown in the presidential election was completely reversed in the referenda. In these elections, the counties with many slaves supported secession, and those with few slaves backed the Union.

TABLE II

PROPORTION OF COUNTIES WITH DIFFERENT RATIOS OF SLAVES
VOTING FOR SECESSION IN SEVEN SOUTHERN STATES

Relative Position of County in Proportion of Slaves within Its State	Secession	Union		(N)
High	72	28	100%	(181)
Medium	60	40	100%	(153)
Low	37	63	100%	(203)

A comparison of Table I and Table II reveals about as drastic a shift in identification with an issue as it is possible to imagine in elections occurring within a three- to six-month period. A majority of the voters in 64 per cent of the counties having few or no slaves voted for the secessionist Democrat Breckenridge in the fall of 1860, and a majority in 63 per cent of these same counties voted for the Union in the subsequent referenda held in the winter of 1860–61. Conversely, a majority of the voters in almost half the counties with plantation farming and many slaves voted against Breckenridge in the election, but the secessionist position carried 72 per cent of them a short time later. The factors underlying this astonishing change can be partially clarified by looking at the vote of counties in the same way that panel studies of voting analyze changes of decision in individuals who are reinterviewed over a period of time. That is, we can differentiate among these counties in terms of the shifts in the two votes, and see where the shifts took place.

The data in Table III make clear what happened in 1860–61. In the presidential election, men continued to vote along traditional party lines. When, however, party labels vanished and the issue became one of secession versus Union, the class or economic factors previously inhibited by party loyalties broke through. The slaveholders voted for secession in the referenda, while those living in areas with few slaves voted

TABLE III

RELATIONSHIP BETWEEN VOTE IN PRESIDENTIAL ELECTIONS IN 1860 AND SUBSEQUENT VOTE FOR SECESSION OR UNION IN SEVEN SOUTHERN STATES IN COUNTIES WITH DIFFERENT PROPORTIONS OF SLAVES

Relative Proportion of Slaves in County

	High		Medium		Low	
	Presidential Vote—1860					
	Breckenridge	Bell-Douglas	Breckenridge	Bell-Douglas	Breckenridge	Bell-Douglas
Vote on Secession						
Pro-Secession	82%	61%	82%	30%	50%	14%
Pro-Union	18	39	18	70	50	86
(N)	(94)	(87)	(87)	(66)	(130)	(73)

for the Union.[4] Party loyalties and issues linked to parties did, however, continue to have some effect on voting behavior and attitudes toward secession in the referenda. This is clear from the fact that two fifths of the high slave counties which were predominantly Whig in their presidential voting followed Whig policy and the advice of many of their leaders by voting to remain in the Union. Among low-slave counties, half of those which had voted for Breckenridge shifted to vote for the Union, while over four fifths of the low-slave counties which opposed Breckenridge voted for the Union. Party tradition was most decisive among the group of counties which were in the middle group in the proportion of slaves in the population. On the whole, they voted in the referenda as they had voted in the election. If they were Democratic, they went for secession; if Whig, they were for the Union.

Thus the heavily Democratic counties which had a large slave population were much more likely to support secession. A tradition of Whig voting and the presence of few or no slaves increased support for the Union. The Democratic party, however, received its support from the group which was most predisposed to favor the Union—the voters in non-slave areas—while the pro-Unionist Whigs were backed by whites living in plantation areas with many slaves.

It must, of course, be kept in mind that the conclusions presented here are subject to all the pitfalls of ecological analysis, particularly the fact that the imputation from the voting of areas to the voting of individuals within those areas

[4] A study of German settlements in Texas suggests that some of the non-Anglo-Saxon minority ethnic groups among the whites may have followed similar patterns to those of the poor white farmers. Analysis of voting patterns of German towns in Texas before 1860 indicates that most of them voted overwhelmingly for the Democratic party, although their organizations and publications were antislavery. This pattern of loyalty to the Democratic party continued in the election of 1860 when they voted for Breckenridge. In the secession referendum in 1861 they voted against secession. See Rudolph L. Biesele, *The History of German Settlements in Texas* (Austin: Von Boechmann-Jones Co., 1930).

does not necessarily follow.[5] It is possible, though not likely, that the vote of the high slave areas for the Unionist candidate in 1860 came from the nonslaveowners in plantation districts and that the slaveholders actually voted for Breckenridge. Many variables besides traditional party loyalty and the proportion of slaves in a given area affected the voting picture.

Nevertheless, viewing the 1860–61 elections and referenda in the South in terms of the characteristics of the counties which changed their votes sharply illuminates what occurred in that crucial year among the southern electorate. The old well-to-do Whig slaveowners and their followers continued in 1860 to oppose the southern demagogues from the lower nonslave-owning strata of the white population, and the latter remained loyal to the party of Jackson even after it became the party of slavery and secession. But once the die was cast and the vote represented an issue rather than a party, enough of the Breckenridge supporters opposed secession and enough backers of Bell, the Constitutional Unionist, supported it to make it accurate to say that, in proportionate terms, the slaveowners voted for secession and the nonslave-owning whites opposed it.

Although the data are unsystematic and incomplete, an examination of election returns by county for the South suggests that the two major parties, Whig and Democratic, divided the electorate more or less along economic and status lines from the 1830s on.[6] The major deviation from this

[5] For discussions of the limitations of the application of ecological correlations to individual attributes, see W. S. Robinson, "Ecological Correlations and the Behavior of Individuals," *American Sociological Review*, 15 (1956), pp. 351–57; Leo A. Goodman, "Ecological Regressions and Behavior of Individuals," *American Sociological Review*, 18 (1953), pp. 663–64; and O. D. Duncan, "An Alternative to Ecological Correlation," *American Sociological Review*, 18 (1953), pp. 665–66.

[6] "The line of social cleavage that separated the Whig planters from the toiling but prosperous hill farmers and from the indolent 'poor whites' was a severely distinct one, enough to engender political antagonism. In their stately mansions, surrounded with almost every comfort of the day and with many luxuries, and educated in the

tendency occurred in mountain areas, where poor nonslave-owning white farmers voted for the Whigs, reputedly because the party supported government payment for internal improvements such as roads. The Democrats were traditionally opposed to internal improvements on the grounds that these benefited the mercantile classes of the cities who should properly pay for them.

With the rise of the slavery issue, the Whigs lost some strength in the plantation areas but still remained the domi-

---

polished manners of their class, the planters regarded as social necessities what to others were symbols of effeminacy and dandyism, or at least of foolish extravagance. . . .

"The origin of this social line which so nearly coincided with the party line can be traced, in the southern Atlantic states at least, well back into the eighteenth century. But it was in connection with the developments which culminated in the triumph of Jacksonian Democracy that the real tightening of these lines was begun . . . the Jackson party was met by a powerful opposition in which the southern planters played a conspicuous part. Social distinctions between the people of the black belt and the people of the back country were then able to reassert themselves and the social unity of each class had the inevitable effect of furthering and cementing their political unity.

"The Whig party in the South, then, contrary to the prevailing notion that it drew its chief support from the non-slave-holding whites above the 'mean-white' class was from its origin, and continued to be through-out its history, the party of the planter and the slave-holder—the aristocrat of the fertile black belt. The Democratic party, on the other hand, drew upon the opposite side of the social scale—especially upon the small farmer of the back hill-country who could always be reached by the party's appeal to the agrarian spirit." A. C. Cole, *The Whig Party in the South* (Washington: The American Historical Society, 1913), pp. 69–72; an important addition to this generally held view has been presented by the historian Charles Sellers, who points out that the southern Whigs were formed and led by "business and professional men of the towns," that 74 per cent of their Congressional representatives were lawyers, that almost all southern bankers were Whigs. "The Whig party in the South was controlled by urban commercial and banking interests, supported by a majority of the planters, who were economically dependent on banking and commercial facilities." Charles G. Sellers, "Who Were the Southern Whigs?", *American Historical Review*, 59 (1954), pp. 335–46.

nant party there. The fact that the northern Whigs, who were predominantly middle-class Protestants, were the strongest antislavery group in either major party made the existence of the Whigs as a national party impossible, and the southern Whigs floundered while their northern compatriots formed the Republican party.

After the Civil War and the end of Reconstruction, the Democratic party retained the old centers of Jacksonianism—the areas which did not have a plantation economy and which were low in Negro population—and also gained the support of, was in fact captured by, the old Whig-supporting plantation owners and businessmen of the cities. The Republican party maintained some continuity with the old southern Whigs by retaining the votes of the poor whites in the mountains who backed the Whigs in the '30s and '40s because they wanted roads. It was this group which voted Constitutional Union in 1860, for the Union in the referenda of 1860–61, fought in the Union army against the Confederacy, and remained loyal to the Republican party all during Reconstruction, the later era of white supremacy, and the age of Roosevelt and Truman.

An ecological panel analysis among southern whites which focused on the shifting counties and areas over a long period would probably show that the two groups which were unstable in 1860–61 have been a potential source of change in the one-party South ever since Reconstruction. The old Whig classes became Democratic as a result of the Civil War, but they are miscast outside of the legitimate inheritor of the Whig tradition, the Republican party. The well-to-do strata and areas which were most loyal to the Constitutional Unionists in the election and to the Union in the referendum seem to be the same ones that today have a propensity to shift to the Republicans. On the other side, the counties which were traditionally nonplantation Democratic and which shifted to vote for the Union in 1860–61, appear to be the same counties which, after the Civil War, backed agrarian third parties or "populist" factions within the Democratic party, and which

remain in the party now while the old Whig strata bolt to
the Republicans as a reaction to the restored liberalism of
the national Democratic party.[7]

[7] A recently published study of Louisiana elections from the
beginning of statehood to the present suggests some of the potential
untapped resources for a study of electoral continuity and discontinuity. It clearly indicates continuities in Louisiana politics from
the pre-Civil War period down to the present. See Perry H.
Howard, *Political Tendencies in Louisiana, 1812–1952* (Baton Rouge:
Louisiana State University Press, 1957); see also Allan P. Sindler,
Huey Long's Louisiana (Baltimore: The Johns Hopkins Press, 1956).

PART IV

THE POLITICS OF PRIVATE GOVERNMENT: A CASE STUDY

CHAPTER 12

The Political Process in Trade-unions

THE CONDITIONS of democracy within various countries have been the basic problem of this book. But the problem of politics does not simply concern nation-states, since every group within a nation must also find mechanisms which make decisions for the group and distribute power within it. All organizations, be they athletic clubs, men's fraternal lodges, the National League, the American Legion, or the Teamsters Union, have formal constitutions which define the political process within the organization. Study of these private governments can teach us much about the ways in which political life in the national society may be organized, since there is a great range of political forms among them, running the gamut from semi-anarchistic communes to one-party absolutist dictatorships.

Private governments, of course, lack the sovereignty and control over the use of legitimate force which define the unique character of public government, but many of them acquire the right to act for the state in specific areas, or are assigned actual monopolies. The real powers of many private governments—the associations which control licensing and admission to a profession, the unions which acquire dominant representation rights, the veterans and farm organizations which practically control access to state aid—illustrate the difficulty of maintaining the separation between public and private government.

In this final section I want to illustrate the importance of private government for the student of democratic politics by looking at some of the conditions which govern the internal political life of one major type of private government:

the trade-unions. They have been scrutinized more than any other type of private government, and this permits some effort at systematization.

Observers have called attention to the fact that in their internal organization and operation most labor unions more closely resemble one-party states than they do democratic organizations with legitimate and organized oppositions and turnover in office. This pattern is so common in the labor movement that one defender of the Soviet Union has pointed to it as a justification of the one-party regime in that country. At the 1947 convention of the International Longshoremen's and Warehousemen's Union, Harry Bridges stated:

> What is totalitarianism? *A country that has a totalitarian government operates like our union operates.* There are no political parties. People are elected to govern the country based upon their records. . . . That is totalitarianism . . . if we started to divide up and run a Republican set of officers, a Democratic set, a Communist set and something else, we would have one hell of a time. . . .[1]

In large part, however, the literature which deals with the problem of bureaucracy and oligarchy in trade-unions either

[1] Quoted in *Proceedings of the Seventh Biennial Convention, I.L.W.U., April 7–11, 1947* (San Francisco, 1947), p. 178. (My emphasis.)
Bridges' frankness is matched by an earlier statement by John L. Lewis made at the 1933 convention of the A. F. of L. in reply to an attack on him as a "dictator" by Daniel Tobin, then president of the Teamsters Union. Lewis stated, "The United Mine Workers are not apologizing for the provisions of their constitution. . . . *We give Tobin the right to interpret his own constitution in the Teamsters Union and to run his organization any way he wants to run it—and we understand he runs it. Frankly and confidentially we do the same.*" Quoted in Eric Hass, *John L. Lewis Exposed* (New York Labor News Company, 1937), p. 50.
Philip Taft, in a study of union political systems, has pointed out that "opposition in union elections is the exception, rather than the rule." "Opposition to Union Officials in Elections," *Quarterly Journal of Economics*, 58 (1944), p. 247.

simply documents this fact in one or more unions, or reworks Michels' classic analysis of the conditions which breed oligarchy or dictatorship in parties and unions.[2] Little work in the field is aimed at developing a set of propositions which can be tested by research.

This chapter is an attempt to specify at least some of the factors which must be considered in the analysis of one aspect of trade-union behavior, that of internal political organization. Each section contains a number of hypotheses about the functional relationship between different aspects of the social structure and the conditions for democracy or dictatorship in trade-unions. It will be evident to any student of the trade-union movement that the list is not exhaustive.

Hypotheses that bear on the probabilities of oligarchy in trade-unions can be drawn from analyses of (1) factors endemic in the structure of large-scale organization, (2) attributes of the members of trade-unions, and (3) the necessary functional adaptations to other structures and groups that trade-unions must make to achieve organizational stability.

The Need for Bureaucracy

Unions, like all other large-scale organizations, are constrained to develop bureaucratic structures, that is, a system of rational (predictable) administration. The need for bureaucracy comes from both internal and external sources. In dealing with their members or locals, unions must set up administrative systems with defined patterns of responsibility and authority. Subordinate officials and administrators must operate within the given rules for dealing with commonly

[2] Robert Michels, *Political Parties* (Glencoe: The Free Press, 1949). Two books which summarize and illustrate Michels in terms of the American labor movement are Sylvia Kopald, *Rebellion in Labor Unions* (New York: Boni and Liveright, 1924), and James Burnham, *The Machiavellians* (New York: John Day, 1943). An excellent general discussion of the problem of union government will be found in A. J. Muste, "Factional Fights in Trade Unions," in J. B. S. Hardman, ed., *American Labor Dynamics* (New York: Harcourt, Brace & Co., 1928), pp. 332–48.

met situations. The larger the size of a local union, or an international, the greater the need to establish a bureaucratic hierarchy. A large local, for example, may be involved in handling workmen's compensation, apprentice schools, pension plans, hospitalization, insurance, and assignment of workers to jobs, besides the usual trade-union tasks of collective bargaining, handling of workers' grievances, and keeping basic records on all members.

On the international level these problems are often magnified by the increased size and complexity of operations and require the creation of a specialized staff which is appointed by and under the control of the officials. And so the knowledge and skill of union operation gradually become available only to members of the administrative elite.

In addition to the need for bureaucracy inherent in the sheer problem of administration—a determinant largely related to the size of the organization—the degree of bureaucratic centralization in unions is influenced by the extent of centralization in the outside groups with which they must deal. I would suggest as a research hypothesis that the more centralized an industry, the more need for a union to be bureaucratic. A union like the steelworkers', which bargains with a few gigantic corporations, must set up a union authority-structure which parallels that of the corporations. Grievance procedures or wage rates must be comparable in every part of the industry. The union cannot permit a local leader in one plant to reach an agreement that may be used as a precedent for the handling of grievances in other parts of the country.[3]

Management bureaucracies usually require "responsible union leadership" as their price for recognizing the union's position. "Quickie" or wildcat strikes over grievances, jurisdictional or factional fights, militant demands by a membership in excess of those agreed upon by the union officials, and all other kinds of action outside the control of the union

[3] See Joseph Shister, "The Locus of Union Control in Collective Bargaining," *Quarterly Journal of Economics*, 60 (1946), pp. 513–45.

officers upset the routine of production or profit making, and management demands their elimination. This insistent cry for union "responsibility" often leads to undemocratic unionism since it sometimes becomes a demand that unions coerce their members.

There is a basic conflict between democratic unionism and "responsible" unionism which many conservatives and business leaders do not recognize, at least in their public pronouncements. The dictatorial mechanisms found in many unions are an adaptation to management's insistence that its yielding on union security issues must be followed by union responsibility.

At least one major industrial union has openly acknowledged this problem. In *The Dynamics of Industrial Democracy*, Clinton Golden and Harold Ruttenberg, then officials of the United Steelworkers, pointed out that this union has consciously developed a number of mechanisms, partly educational and ideological and partly formal control devices, to prevent variations in local practices. They describe a case in which a militant and loyal local union officer was expelled from the union because he refused to recognize that he could not set local policies which violated national agreements. The problem of the local leader under a national bureaucracy was well put by this expelled leader: "Being a good union man is agitating—that's what I always knew as a union man—and I got fired for agitating. . . . The company has had it in for me since 1933. I'm a thorn in the flesh to it. Now the union sides with the company and I am out."[4]

---

[4] See Clinton S. Golden and Harold J. Ruttenberg, *The Dynamics of Industrial Democracy* (New York: Harper & Bros., 1942), pp. 60–61. Recently in one major industry, management officials complained to the union heads about the propaganda against monopolies and large profits that the union was sponsoring. These industrial executives pointed out that the continued union criticism, charging management with lack of good faith and of legitimate functions stimulated attitudes among the members that made them responsive to agitation for wildcat strikes, and encouraged them to refuse to co-operate with management production objectives. Union officers, who were themselves sympathetic to socialist objectives, were forced

Adaptations to the need to adjust to bureaucratic industry which preserve union organizational stability also serve the interests of the leaders of trade-unions by reducing the hazards to their permanent tenure of office. By increasing the power of the administration over local units, the officials reduce the sources of organized opposition. The United Automobile Workers has given its international executive board the right to suspend the officials of local unions for violating international policies. This modification in the union's constitution was defended as necessary for contract negotiations, but it also enabled the international officials to eliminate potential rivals. In both their conciliatory tone—as when they call for intra-union discipline and responsibility—and in their militant tone—as when they call for union solidarity in a dispute with management—union leaders strengthen their own hands and justify their monopolization of internal power in the course of articulating organizational needs and purposes.

Unions which are small or which do not deal with large centralized industries may permit local units a great deal of autonomy. The International Typographical Union, for example, permits its locals considerable freedom in negotiations. It is, however, operating in an industry which does not have large national companies and which is in part noncompetitive from one section of the country to another. But even this union limits its locals' freedom to strike or to make concessions to management on issues involving union security, or jurisdiction over various mechanical processes. The I.T.U., like many other unions, is faced with the problem that a prolonged series of strikes in different parts of the country could bankrupt the union's strike funds.

A somewhat different situation giving rise to increased bureaucratization is found in industries which are highly competitive. Here the pressure for bureaucratization may come from the union; large unions are often unable to stabilize their own position unless the industry becomes less competitive, and therefore more predictable, in character. Unions

to agree that a long-term contract and continued stimulation of antagonistic attitudes toward large-scale capitalism were incompatible.

like the garment unions have developed highly centralized structures so as to be able to force employers to develop similar collective-bargaining practices. In some cases the unions have been able to force bureaucratic structures on employers by forcing them to join industrial associations and set up codes of business practice. In such industries unions are as constrained to prevent their local units from violating standard policy as are unions operating within highly bureaucratized industries.

The participation of government boards in collective bargaining may also increase trade-union bureaucracy. Local unions yield powers they once possessed to their international as the locus of decision shifts from a local to a national governmental level. This phenomenon is an illustration of the functional interrelationship between patterns of social organization. The reaction to increased bureaucracy in one institutional area—in this case government—increases the need for bureaucratization of other institutions like trade-unions, which interact with it.

As control over decisions shifts away from the local levels, there is a decrease in membership participation and interest in local affairs. Similarly, disagreements over policy are increasingly limited to conflicts over national policies, knowledge about which is limited to members of the bureaucracy itself. Thus conflicts occur more and more as administrative fights at international headquarters and less and less as political struggles between groups in the locals. The implications of this shift were once graphically expressed to a friend of mine by a steelworker who said, explaining his lack of interest in the local union: "We don't have a union any more, we have a contract. The economists and statisticians negotiate contracts—all we can do is vote yes or no to them."

Increased bureaucratization within the union does, of course, help protect the rights of the workers as well as reinforce the position of the leadership. In so far as unions operate to protect their members from management arbitrariness and caprice in hiring and promotion, they emphasize rational and impersonal norms and standards like seniority and "equal pay for equal work." These standards, systematized, standard-ized, and administered, are a bulwark of the workers' se-curity and freedom.

Bureaucracy as an organizational pattern which effectively meets so many and varied needs—of the organization, of the leadership, of the members—has deep roots in the trade-union movement. It may be stated as a general proposition, how-ever, that the greater the bureaucratization of an organiza-tion, the less the potential for membership influence over policy.

Communications within Unions

One major source of administrative power which is ex-clusively available to the incumbent bureaucratic hierarchy is control over the formal means of communication within the organization. The right of free speech of individual mem-bers means little as an effective check on administrative power if the union leaders control all public statements made by members of the administrative or field staff, the union newspaper, and the expense account which enables officials to travel around the country to see and talk to local members and leaders. The monopolization of the channels of commu-nication is one of the basic conditions for shaping attitudes and behavior by propaganda.[5] This condition is indigenous to the structure of totalitarian states; it is also characteristic of the one-party structure of most labor unions.

This particular form of control has a number of conse-quences for the power structure of a union. The only view-points about union matters that are widely available to the membership under such conditions are those of the admin-istration. Official policy is justified, opposing proposals or programs discredited if mentioned at all, and the only infor-mation concerning union affairs which reaches the general

[5] See R. K. Merton and P. F. Lazarsfeld, "Mass Communications, Popular Taste and Organized Social Action," in Lyman Bryson, ed., *The Communication of Ideas* (New York: Harper & Bros., 1948), pp. 95–118.

membership is that which officialdom wishes it to hear. Secondly, this control obstructs the crystallization and organization of opposition. Even if the membership is not thoroughly convinced of the correctness and efficiency of administration policies and there is widespread discontent, organizing active opposition presupposes a means of "getting together," of communicating. The reduction of "collective ignorance" is impossible without widespread contact and information.

No administration group can, to be sure, exercise a total control over the flow of communications within its organization. And different organizations vary in the degree to which the administration "party" approaches a monopoly. Any attempt to analyze the factors which differentiate democratic from nondemocratic organizations must consider the determinants of such variations. A few are suggested here:

Communications reaching the membership from sources outside the organization may weaken administrative control. Political parties, for example, do not, in the United States at least, control the newspapers which their members read. Such newspapers, by criticizing acts of party leaders, can help create the basis for factional opposition. In the labor and Socialist parties of Europe the party usually owns or controls the newspapers which support it, and this facilitates continued domination by party leaders.

The internal structure or political processes in trade-unions are not usually exposed in the press. There have, however, been a number of cases in which outside media have attempted to reach trade-union members. In New York, the Yiddish press, especially the *Forward*, a Socialist paper, played a major role in the life of the garment unions for a long period. The *Forward*, which was widely read by immigrant Jewish garment workers, criticized union policies and often acted as the organ of groups within the union. As might be expected, the union leadership resented its independence. In many unions today, the press of the Catholic Church reaches Catholic workers with propaganda about internal union issues, and it has played an important role in factional situations. Radical political groups have played a similar role in furnishing union members with information and propaganda about their union.

Certain occupational groups have supported newspapers or magazines devoted to news of the trade but independent of union control. This has been true in the entertainment and printing fields, whose unions have significantly more internal democracy than most trade-unions.

In small union locals personal contacts or oratorical communication may be effective in reaching the members, and control of the organizational machinery is not an important communications asset. But in larger one-party organizations, the effective monopolization of communications varies inversely with the extent to which communications media stemming from extra-organizational sources are directed to the members of the organization. Such independent organs can be based on an ethnic community or religious group which overlaps with an occupation, on political groups that are concerned with the internal policies of trade-unions, and, in a few special cases, on interest in occupational affairs.

The Monopoly on Political Skills

In most unions one of the principal factors which perpetuate incumbent power is the administration's almost complete monopoly of the chances for learning political skills. One of the few roles open to a manual worker in which he can learn such skills is that of union leader. In the political life of the nation as a whole, as already discussed in Chapter 6, pp. 203–7, leaders are recruited mainly from occupations which themselves require political skills—largely those of organization and communication. The legal profession is, of course, the one which best trains its members in such skills. But many business executive positions run law a close second, since the successful executive must be able to make speeches, secure assent, mediate conflict, and so forth. Anyone who has been concerned with public relations work must also learn these skills, and so must the leaders of mass organizations—trade-unions, farm groups, professional societies, and so forth.

In large measure, the existence in the society at large of many and diverse "political" leadership roles means that almost every group can find politically trained people to present and organize support for its viewpoints.

The average worker has little opportunity or need to learn political skills. He is rarely, if ever, called upon to make a speech before a large group, to put his thoughts down in writing, or to organize a group's activities. The officers' monopoly of political skills within the union may therefore be suggested as one of the major factors which prevent the effective organization of opposition sentiment in labor organizations, and which enable an incumbent administration to use its superior communicative skills to subdue or divert discontent.

The one-party union organization may offer office-seeking union members the opportunity to learn organizational skills through formal educational programs or through participation in unpaid voluntary positions. Such aspiring members are, however, usually subjected to a barrage of administration views on economics, politics, and union organization. Mobility within the union structure requires that the aspirant take over the norms and orientations dominant in the organization—that is, those held by the leaders. It is also likely that active members, the potential leaders, will be receptive to the viewpoint—broad or narrow—of the administration and develop a loyalty to it as the source of a more interesting and rewarding pattern of life activity than they have formerly experienced. In this sense a union organization provides ambitious workers who are confined to their occupation opportunities that few other agencies in society do.

Aside from education or indoctrination, the aspiring leader has literally one place to go if he is to go anywhere—into the administration. Unless some opposition group exists, his political activity has to be within the bounds set by the incumbents. Union officers, who are often faced with a paucity of skilled prospective subordinate officials and the lack of any means to train them, are usually willing and even anxious to recruit capable union activists into the administrative structure.

The major advantage accruing to union officers from their possession of the skills of politics may, however, be lessened and even eliminated if the members of their union have other extraorganizational sources of developing these skills. For example, actors must learn to deliver speeches effectively, and observers of the membership meetings of Actors Equity report that there is a high degree of membership participation in discussion, as well as a long history of internal factional politics.

But most workers who belong to unions do not gain these abilities through their jobs, and research studies indicate that they do not usually belong to formal organizations outside the union either. There are, however, at least two organizations which have contributed to the training of workers in political skills—churches and radical political parties. In the United States and Great Britain many workers belong to churches whose membership is predominantly working class and whose lay leaders or ministers are themselves workers. As was noted earlier, a great many of the early leaders of British trade-unions and labor political groups were men who first served as officers or Sunday school teachers in the Methodist or other nonconformist churches.[6] In the United States many of the early leaders of the United Automobile Workers, which had a large membership from the South, were men who had been active in southern sects. Today the Catholic Church, through the Association of Catholic Trade Unionists and Catholic Labor Schools, seeks to train Catholic workers

[6] "The training in self-expression and in the filling of offices and the control of public affairs which these [Methodist] Societies provided for a great host of working men and women was invaluable as a preparation for industrial combination and for the future work of Trade-Unionism. The Dissenting Chapel and the Methodist Society were the pioneer forms of the latter self-governing labour organizations, and they became the nurseries of popular aspirations after place and power in civic and national government." A. D. Belden, *George Whitefield, the Awakener* (London: S. Low, Marston and Co., Ltd., 1930), pp. 247 ff.

in the skills of oratory, parliamentary procedure, organization, and administration. In situations in which Catholics as a group wish to fight the incumbent leadership, Catholics trained in these church groups often form the active core of opposition groups.

On the other side, left-wing political parties like the Communists and Socialists have contributed a large number of the labor leaders of America. Workers who join such parties are trained, formally or informally, in the skills of organization and communication and become potential union leaders. During the late thirties, John L. Lewis, though a political conservative, was forced to hire many Socialists and Communists as C.I.O. organizers because these parties were the only reservoirs of organizing talent and skill that were friendly to the labor movement. One of the things that has enabled Communists to gain support from non-Communists within the labor movement is the fact that in many unions Communists, although they are a small minority, are the only persons not in the union administration who know how to organize an effective opposition.

The Social Status of Union Leaders

It has been noted frequently that labor-union officials become set apart from the rank and file in both their styles of life and their perspectives and modes of thought. This cleavage is most clearly visible in the upper rungs of union administrative hierarchies, where the income differential between union officials and working members is sizable, and where the more or less permanent tenure of most national officials makes their higher income more secure and more regular than many workers can ordinarily expect. This higher, more secure income, together with the different range of experience that is involved in being a union official—desk-work, travel, association with business, government, and other union leaders—provides the basis and substance for a style of life markedly different from that of the men in the shop. At the local level there is generally not a large difference between the official's income and the worker's pay, but the local officer still has an advantage in the security of his income, the greater chances he has to rise within the union structure, and (by no means least important) the fact that the union job gets him out of the shop into a much pleasanter, more varied, and more rewarding type of work.

The special interests and kinds of activity union officials experience, both on and off the job, create bonds of sentiment and a common orientation and perspective which, while sharpening the cleavage between officials and rank and file, serve as important cohesive elements within the leadership group. The members of a union officialdom, who share far more in common with each other than they do with the rank and file, develop a self-consciousness about their common interests which finds expression in their use of the organization machinery for the defense of their individual tenures and group retention of power.

If a trade-union structure is further viewed as part of the total system of social stratification, other factors which contribute to the tendency toward oligarchy and undemocratic behavior on the part of labor officials become clear. Status— the honor and deference accorded individuals by certain others—has no meaning except as it locates an individual, group, or stratum relative to others in the same frame of reference. Psychiatrists and social psychologists have indicated the tremendous importance to an individual of the position accorded him by those from whom he claims a given status. In American society an individual's status is most closely related to his occupation, but it is also influenced in some contexts by such attributes as kinship, power, length of residence, and other factors. A look at the status of the working members of a union compared to that of their officers may suggest how these relative positions affect the degree and nature of the two groups' participation in union affairs.

In general, the officers of local and international unions do not appear to be accorded status by virtue of their association with their particular trade or industry, but rather in regard to the quite different roles they play in their occupation of "trade-union official." That this status is very much higher, in the eyes of both the general public and their own rank and file, than the status of almost all working-class occupations can hardly be doubted. A study of the relative job prestige of different occupations (as ranked by a national cross-section of the population) indicated that an "official of an international union" ranks about the same as "proprietors, managers, and officials."[7] The following comment by the authors of an evaluation of the United Auto Workers, Irving Howe and B. J. Widick, gives strong evidence that workers themselves generally accord higher status to their officers than to their fellow workers.

The status of the union official can be very high; . . . he is usually highly respected by the workers for his presumed superior knowledge and greater articulateness; he earns a larger and more steady income than they do; he does not have to submit to factory discipline and can keep comparatively flexible hours; and he enjoys what is for most Americans a very great privilege and mark of social authority: he can wear "white collar" clothes rather than work clothes.[8]

Each of the grounds on which this deference is accorded—knowledge, skills, income, job control, head instead of hand work—separates the official from the ranks in terms of style of life, perspectives, and so forth. Taken together they support a status differential which tends to *justify* the leader's monopolization of union functions and important activities which his position in the union hierarchy only makes *possible*. He not only wields his power and makes his decisions by virtue of his office, but, equally important, the high status

[7] Cecil C. North and Paul K. Hatt, "Jobs and Occupations: A Popular Evaluation," in Logan Wilson and William A. Kolb, eds., *Sociological Analysis* (New York: Harcourt, Brace & Co., 1949), pp. 464–73.

[8] Irving Howe and B. J. Widick, *The U. A. W. and Walter Reuther* (New York: Random House, 1949), p. 257.

accorded him by the members serves to make his authority legitimate in a familiar self-reinforcing pattern of power and status: union office carries with it power, develops skills, supports a middle-class style of life, and is in fact a middle-class occupation. All of these, together with the position itself, are accorded relatively high status by the rank and file—a status which makes the entire role and the actions of its incumbent legitimate.

There is a basic strain between the democratic values of the trade-union movement and this system of status placement. With few significant exceptions, every trade-union official has moved up in the hierarchy through his own achievements. The occupation is one of the few high-status ones in which status is secured almost entirely by achievement rather than ascription. Most high-status positions necessarily carry with them some security of tenure once a given position is reached. Democracy, however, implies permanent insecurity for those in governing positions—the more truly democratic the governing system, the greater the insecurity. Turnover in office is inherent in the democratic value that demands equal access by all members of the system to positions of power. Thus every incumbent of a high-status position of power within a democratic system must, of necessity, anticipate a loss of position if democratic values are accepted.

It is not in harmony with what is known of the psychological needs of individuals to expect people in such positions to accept this insecurity with equanimity. Once high status is achieved, there is usually a pressing need to retain and protect it. This is particularly true if the discrepancy between the status and the position that one is apt to be relegated to upon losing it is very great. In other words, if the social distance between the trade-union leader's position as an official and as an ordinary member is great, his need to retain the former will be correspondingly greater.

It is quite true that this insecurity is faced by holders of public office in any democratic society, but there are important differences. Politicans in the larger society are more than likely to be drawn from what Weber so perceptively termed the "dispensable" occupations like those of law and journalism.[9] These occupations are dispensable in the sense that the practitioner is able to leave them for extended periods and enter politics without any loss of skill during his period of absence (perhaps the opposite is true in the case of the lawyer) and return to the practice of his profession without too great a financial loss or dislocation. Actually, former public officials, whether lawyers or not, are usually able to capitalize on the skills and informal relations they have established while in office. A defeated politician is often in a better financial and status position after leaving office than while he was a public official. And, significantly for the democratic process, he may continue to play the role of political leader outside of office and be of use to his party in opposition.

The trade-union leader, on the other hand, if he is one of the relatively few who are defeated after serving in high union office, cannot find a position which will enable him to both maintain his high-status position *and continue to take part in the union's political system*. This may explain why so many union leaders who lose office for one reason or another do not return to the shops but leave the occupation entirely, or secure an appointive office in some other union hierarchy. The absence of an experienced and trained cadre of leaders in the ranks, which defeated officeholders could provide, makes very much more difficult, if not impossible, the maintenance of an active opposition which could present alternative sets of leaders and policies at union elections. When all the men of experience in union affairs are either in the administration or out of the union, there is no nucleus of skills, ideas, and reputations around which an opposition can crystallize. The history of the United Automobile Workers is a good example: three former presidents and the former international secretary-treasurer, as well as a number of past vice-presidents and other high officials, have left the union for jobs in private industry or other unions.

[9] Max Weber, *Essays in Sociology*, translated and edited by C. Wright Mills and Hans Gerth (New York: Oxford University Press, 1946), p. 85.

The alternative to leaving the union for a defeated leader is a return to the assembly line or the mine pit. It has been impossible for a number of decades to imagine John L. Lewis digging coal after defeat by the miners' convention.[10] Return to the shop, even by local leaders, in addition to making for a sharp reduction in their style of life, is often regarded as humiliation and failure, both by the defeated leader and by his fellow workers.

The strenuous efforts on the part of many trade-union leaders to eliminate democracy (the possibility of defeat) from their unions are, for them, necessary adaptive mechanisms. The insecurity of leadership status (endemic in democracy), the pressures on leaders to retain their high-status achievement, their control over the organizational structure, the differential skills that leaders possess vis-à-vis other union members are all strong factors in the creation of dictatorial oligarchies.

The relation of a leader's status to his efforts to minimize democracy in a union is quite direct. The hold of a union machine on officials does not lie simply in the fact that lower- and middle-level leaders retain their jobs at the pleasure of the top administrative leaders. It is primarily the attractiveness and status of these positions compared to work in the shops that gives union officeholders their huge stake in their positions and, depending on their rank, makes them dictatorial (if they hold high rank) or subservient to their union superiors (if they hold a low or intermediate position).

The effect of high but insecure achieved status becomes clear if we examine the consequences for the union structure of an occupation which gives status to the worker equivalent or superior to that of union official. Under these conditions, union machines cannot be as strong and cohesive, or demand and receive complete devotion and obedience from subordinate officials. The lack of a clear and significant differential of

[10] See Bernard Barber, "Participation and Mass Apathy in Associations," in A. W. Gouldner, ed., *Studies in Leadership* (New York: Harper & Bros., 1950), pp. 493–94, and A. J. Muste, *op. cit.*, p. 341.

privilege (and style of life) between the officers and the rank and file will mean that the elected leader is not under as great a strain to eliminate democratic procedures and the possibility of turnover.

Actors Equity and the American Newspaper Guild are trade-unions whose members may aspire to higher income and status than their officials. Far from suffering from entrenched oligarchies, these two unions have had difficulty recruiting members to serve as full-time officials. Their solution has been to create a number of unpaid policy-making positions, so that members may continue their occupational careers while serving as union officials. In Actors Equity, few members of the executive council ever run for re-election. In the Guild, many of the officers come from the lower-status non-journalist occupations which the union has organized. Recently the highest full-time official of the Guild, who previously had not been a journalist, resigned to become editor of a labor newspaper. This conforms to the value system of the craft which ranks the occupation of journalist higher than that of union officer. Another union with a history of continuous opposition to administrations and frequent turnover in officialdom is the International Typographical Union. The members of this union are among the best paid, highest-status groups of American workers. This may help account for the fact that in the I.T.U. defeated union leaders return to the printshop after losing office. Interviews with members and leaders of this union suggest that they have a strong attachment to their craft, and also look upon it as an important high-status job.[11]

Membership Participation

American workers especially, but members of other social classes as well, do not have the integrative participation that individuals in nonindustrial societies experience. In our so-

[11] For an analysis of this and other factors which are related to the high level of democracy in the I.T.U., see S. M. Lipset, M. Trow, and J. S. Coleman, *Union Democracy* (Glencoe: The Free Press, 1956).

ciety work, leisure, family relations, politics, and many other aspects of life are organized or insulated within the social structure. The two roles our society defines as most salient and significant are the occupational role and the family role. All others—for example, the role an individual plays as a member of a voluntary association—are more or less subsidiary and peripheral.[12] Although there is a great proliferation of voluntary associations in the United States, a large proportion of the population, especially manual workers, is not involved in them, and a much greater proportion does not actively participate in them. As has been indicated earlier, most of these organizations are essentially one-party systems with an active controlling elite and an inactive mass membership. Most of them serve social needs separate from the occupational and family roles—needs socially defined as of secondary importance. When the membership of such political, fraternal, charitable, or other leisure-time organizations shows a lack of interest in their internal operation or control, this is called "apathy" and is ritually deplored. Even in trade-unions and professional associations which vitally affect the individual's occupational role, such membership apathy is the usual state of affairs.

When members are not impelled to action by organizational crisis, the outcome of which may directly affect them, various forces draw them away from active participation. It seems to be generally true that large numbers of men in a union cannot be organized for any considerable length of time solely on the issues of political struggles for organizational power. A naked struggle for power in a union is apparently too corrosive of personal relations, too removed from the deepest, most enduring concerns of the members, and holds too little promise of ultimate reward to those not anticipating jobs to be able to sustain mass interest. Of course, factional fights are rarely presented as naked power struggles but are almost always focused around contracts or other union issues, and sometimes, as in the early period of the U.A.W.,

12 See Bernard Barber, *op. cit.*, pp. 477–504.

these economic struggles for union recognition and security are sufficiently moving to sustain widespread, although intermittent, interest in factional fights for periods of several years. But sooner or later, as external conditions become stabilized, the deep and enduring concerns of job, family, recreation, and friends pull the ordinary member out of the disputatious and time-consuming arena of factional struggle back to the normal and routine rhythms of life. Only a small minority find the rewards for participation in union affairs and politics great enough to sustain a high level of interest and activity.

There is, of course, considerable variation in the level of membership participation in different kinds of groups and organizations, and since we are concerned with the possibilities of democracy in private organizations, it is important to explore some of the sources of these variations.

Participation in any organization appears to be related to the number and saliency of the functions which it performs for its members and the extent to which they require personal involvement. In most cases, trade-unions perform only one major function for their members—collective bargaining, which can be handled by a more or less efficient union administration without requiring any membership participation, except during major conflicts. In such unions one would not expect continuous participation by more than the handful of members who are involved in administration.

But there are a number of important exceptions to the usual situation. In some occupations and unions participation in union affairs affords additional rewards in the form of higher status, improved job opportunities, or valued social relations. Under certain conditions, unions do not merely perform the protective and acquisitive functions of collective bargaining, but, as discussed in Chapter 6, become part of an "occupational community," or broad network of social relations among their members. Participation in the occupational community is not focused exclusively on the union's economic functions or internal politics, but is sustained by just that wide variety of motives and interests that are not involved in membership in the average union.

One source of an occupational community is the geographical isolation of a given job. In the small mining towns of the United States, workers meet with each other constantly in all their social roles, and in their religious, leisure, and informal organizations as well as their union. Similar conditions exist for sailors and longshoremen. This frequent interaction of union members in all spheres of life appears to make for a high level of interest in the affairs of their unions, which translates itself into high participation in local organizations and a greater potential for democracy and membership influence. To be sure, most of the unions in this category are oligarchic and dictatorial on the international level, but the high level of local membership participation may be one of the major reasons for the militant tactics pursued by the oligarchs in these unions. It is also true that these unions appear to have more frequent rank-and-file upheavals than other similar low-status, oligarchic unions.

An occupational community may also occur in large communities in which members are not physically isolated from other workers but have "deviant" work schedules—e.g., nights and/or week ends. These schedules cut the workers off from normal social contacts with their neighbors, friends, or relatives. As a result, they spend more free time with their fellow workers. Such leisure relationships often result in the formation of formal organizations like sports clubs, veterans' posts, religious organizations, and others, whose members are limited to those working in the same occupation.

A related factor which may operate independently in a similar way is the extent to which workers are involved in their jobs. In certain fields, like journalism or acting, the workers view the judgment of their co-workers as the principal measure of professional esteem. These occupations are, of course, atypical for the trade-union movement, but they illustrate the relationship between participation in a group and its function as a status-reference group.

In the majority of manual occupations, workers perceive each other almost exclusively in their occupational roles. But where occupational communities exist, the union organizes relations among its members in a variety of their social roles, with direct consequences for union politics. The component groups of the occupational community, especially if they are independent of union-leadership control, serve to keep union issues alive. In providing regular opportunities for union members to meet frequently outside working hours, they also provide opportunities for informal discussion of current union controversies and of the relative merits of candidates; thus they serve as auxiliary sources of information and opinion which are not under the control of the incumbent administration. And it is in the occupational community that prospective opposition leaders can learn the skills of politics and find independent sources of status and power on which to base a challenge to the incumbents and so increase the influence of the rank and file.

A number of "progressive" trade-unions have attempted to increase membership participation by using their educational departments to create leisure-time organizations for their members. However, attempts to impose extra-vocational activities artificially usually fail. The International Ladies Garment Workers and the United Automobile Workers have made valiant efforts in these directions with comparatively little success. The workers in these industries apparently have other sources of leisure activities, and the opportunity to use union facilities does not affect their behavior. In the I.L.G.W.U., studies of participants in such union organizations have revealed that they are mostly women who, for a variety of reasons, have been forced to search out formal leisure groups. These women are usually widows, divorcees, or unmarried women who have reached an age when most of their friends are married, plus another group of married women whose children have grown up.

A number of factors which appear to be correlated with the status level of given occupations also affect the level of participation in a union. In general, the degree to which workers identify with a given occupation and its union is related to the status of the occupation. The higher the occupation's status, the higher the level of union participation.

Studies of participation in politics and other voluntary associations have shown that the higher the status of the group in question, the more likely they are to be active in such matters. Therefore it follows that the closer a working-class group approximates a middle-class way of life and orientation, the more likely it is to show a high level of union participation. This may be, as was suggested earlier, partly the result of the fact that, in a high-status occupation, the narrower gap in status between the rank and file and the leadership reduces the pressures on the latter to keep a tight oligarchic grip on union affairs. But, in addition, the higher education and status aspirations of workers in "middle-class" occupations like journalism, the entertainment field, and printing, apparently lead them to use their unions more freely for more purposes, and participate in them more widely than do workers in low-status occupations. Some work has been done on the connections between social class and participation in voluntary associations other than trade-unions.[13] Similar investigations can be carried through between and within given trade-unions.[14]

[13] See Herbert Goldhamer, "Some Factors Affecting Participation in Voluntary Associations" (Ph.D. thesis, Department of Sociology, University of Chicago, 1943); Mirra Komarovsky, "The Voluntary Associations of Urban Dwellers," *American Sociological Review*, 9 (1946), pp. 686–98; Bernard Barber, "Mass Apathy and Voluntary Social Participation in the United States" (Ph.D. thesis, Department of Social Relations, Harvard University, 1949). See also pp. 52–53, 101–2, 200–7 of this book.

[14] A. W. Gouldner, "The Attitudes of 'Progressive' Trade Union Leaders," *American Journal of Sociology*, 52 (1947), p. 389. Ely Chinoy, "Local Union Leadership," in A. W. Gouldner, *Studies in Leadership* (New York: Harper & Bros., 1950). Herbert A. Shepard, "Democratic Control in a Labor Union," *The American Journal of Sociology*, 54 (1949), pp. 311–16. It should be emphasized, however, that the sheer increase in the income of workers in a given occupation may actually have the opposite effect of reducing participation in union affairs. If the higher income permits workers to approach middle-class income status, while the occupation itself remains low status, they may attempt to disassociate themselves from the occupation. For example, a study of the members of the San Francisco Longshoremen's Union indicated that many unionized longshoremen

Time-line Factors

The preceding sections have discussed the consequences of different aspects of trade-union structure and the attributes of the members (those derived from their position in the larger social structure) for the possibilities for democratic government in trade-unions. There are also a number of other conditions which can influence the degree of democracy in organizations. These we may call "time-line factors," since they are in large measure related to conditions which occur only at specific periods in an organization's history.

PATTERNS OF ORGANIZATION

There are two general processes through which organizations are created. One is organization from the top down, where the group which originally starts the association organizes other individuals or branches into a larger structure. In such a situation a formal bureaucratic structure exists from the start, with the new subordinate officials deriving their authority from the summits of the organization.

A large national organization may also come into existence as a federation, either through the successive but autonomous formation of one group after another, or by the comparatively simultaneous formation of a number of unconnected groups which later unite. In both cases a ready-made opposition is built into the organization. In such federations the creation of a "one-party" bureaucratic hierarchy would require the reduction of once-independent groups or leaders to subordinate status and power positions. Moves in this direction often meet strong resistance from the autonomous leaders of component units. Instead of a clear hierarchy of leadership, there is considerable competition for leadership among those who

moved away from the waterfront after receiving large wage increases, and became less active in the union. It is only when high status is linked to the occupation that we should expect to find greater participation. The study referred to above is an unpublished one by Joseph Aymes, formerly a graduate student in the Department of Psychology at the University of California.

were at the top of comparatively independent units before real amalgamation occurred. The current struggles within the newly merged A.F.L.-C.I.O. are a good example of this phenomenon.

The varying political histories of different unions may be related to the different ways in which they were first organized. The United Steelworkers of America, for example, was originally formed by the Steelworkers Organizing Committee under Philip Murray. With few exceptions, almost every local of this union was created after the initial power structure was established. From its inception until 1950, when the problem of succession of leadership first arose, there were no serious factional disputes in the union. Any local center of disturbance was eliminated by Murray. On the other hand, the United Automobile Workers, which parallels the Steelworkers in age, size, and centralization of industry, was formed out of the amalgamation of a number of existing automobile unions, and many of its other local units were organized independently with relatively little help from the national body. The subsequent bitter factional fights in this union resulted, at least in part, from the attempt of various national administrations to set up a single bureaucratic hierarchy. Most of the factional leaders in the U.A.W. were leaders in the early organizing period of the union, and the different factions have mostly been coalitions of the groups headed by these different leaders jointly resisting attempts to subordinate them to the national organization. In spite of the fact that the structural conditions in a large industrial union like the U.A.W. are not favorable to internal democracy and large-scale rank-and-file participation, it has taken more than two decades to approach a one-party structure, and the process is still not completed.

THE PROBLEM OF SUCCESSION

In any organization which does not have a democratic system for replacing leaders, or in which there is no formally prescribed system of promotion or selection, the problem of succession often precipitates a crisis. The death of the leader of a one-party structure necessarily upsets the power equilibrium. The more the power structure was organized around personal allegiance to the "leader," the more likely it is that his death or retirement will result in major internal conflict.[15]

In large measure, the passing of a dictatorial union leader creates or re-creates the situation that exists in a union which has been formed from a merger of existing autonomous groups. With the elimination of the person at the top of the pyramid, each leader immediately below him may claim some rights of succession. As in the earlier case, the union may be faced with the problem of creating a power hierarchy out of equals. Each of the claimants has reputation, skill in union politics, and the resources of control of a segment of the organization.

A recent situation which illustrates this pattern occurred in the United Steelworkers. Philip Murray became seriously ill during 1950 and was not expected to live. During his long stay in the hospital, several members of the International Executive Board began preparing for the struggle to succeed him. The apparent monolithic character of the union broke down. Murray, upon recovering, learned of this struggle and, according to reports, attempted to rearrange the internal power hierarchy so as to prevent a succession conflict. It is clear that Murray died before he was able to complete his internal rearrangements. No open conflict developed immediately as David McDonald, the secretary-treasurer, stepped into the presidency before his opponents could successfully organize against him. However, a number of top Steelworkers' leaders resented McDonald's succession, and close observers of the union predicted that open factional conflict would develop—a prediction which has been borne out.[16]

There is an interesting similarity between the succession

[15] See A. W. Gouldner, *Patterns of Industrial Bureaucracy* (Glencoe: The Free Press, 1954), for an excellent empirical study of the consequences of a succession crisis in a factory.

[16] See Daniel Bell, "The Next American Labor Movement," *Fortune*, April 1953, pp. 120–23, 201–6; and "Labor's New Men of

problem of the Steelworkers and that which developed in the Soviet Union in 1923–24 around the illness and subsequent death of Lenin. Like Murray, Lenin was taken ill, and several members of the Central Committee began immediately to struggle over succession. Lenin was aware of this and attempted to eliminate Stalin as a candidate, but, as history has recorded, failed. Lenin's death brought about a bitter internal fight for succession in which at least five members of the Central Committee attempted to succeed to his mantle.

Within the trade-union movement there have been situations in which the death of a strong dictatorial leader did not result in a succession crisis. The death of Sidney Hillman, the president of the Amalgamated Clothing Workers, for example, was not followed by any open internal cleavage. This seeming exception to the succession crisis was not, however, due to a lack of conflict among Hillman's lieutenants. Two major groupings exist within the union, led by Hyman Blumberg and Frank Rosenblum. Each is very powerful in his own right, based largely on different regions of the country. Blumberg's power rests in the East, Rosenblum's in the Midwest and other sections of the country. Instead of an open conflict developing over control of the entire union, the previous secretary-treasurer, Jacob Potofsky, was made president, even though he had little backing of his own. It is significant that in this union, in which a strong leader did not succeed a powerful president, the old leader, Hillman, has been deified. The union constantly erects monuments of various kinds to him, and his name is used to give legitimacy to all present actions. Here the existence of regional blocs may lead to a permanent division of power, as has occurred at times in nations. Such a distribution of power contains within it the seeds of a secession movement.

Max Weber, in dealing with the succession problem in one specific context, has pointed out that the death of a charismatic leader (one to whom his followers impute ex-

Power," *Fortune*, June 1953, pp. 148–52, 155–62, for analysis of problems of succession in the Steelworkers' and other unions.

traordinary personal qualities) may cause his staff and followers, whose power does not rest on any traditional or legitimate basis, to experience tremendous insecurity about the consequences of succession.[17] He considered that one solution was the bureaucratization of the structure, but his formulation of the problem did not clearly indicate the manner in which succession would bring about increased bureaucratization. More recent investigators have extended his analysis, pointing out that resistance to the authority of a new leader by the remaining staff of the old one leads him to institute allegiance to rationalized rules—that is, to increased bureaucratization. One might hypothesize on the basis of this that when a trade-union leader with charismatic attributes is succeeded without conflict, as in the case of Hillman, the union will become more bureaucratic; and there is evidence to suggest that this has been the case in the Amalgamated Clothing Workers. In this case the potentialities for democracy will be reduced rather than increased. But there is as yet little definitive evidence for this hypothesis.

There appear to be trade-unions in which the process of bureaucratization has reduced the problem of succession to one of moving up a recognized ladder. It is possible to raise, if not answer on the basis of existing evidence, a number of questions which relate aspects of organizational structure to the process of leadership succession. Under what conditions will succession crises occur so as to give the membership some voice in the choice of a new leader? Under what conditions do the leaders of a union hierarchy feel constrained to keep the struggle within the hierarchy itself? When does a succession crisis open the door for new and independent groups to contest for union leadership? Under what conditions does the process become one of moving up within the hierarchy?

The succession crisis actually may give students of union organizations the opportunity to test many of the hypotheses

---

[17] Max Weber, *The Theory of Social and Economic Organization*, trans. by A. M. Henderson and Talcott Parsons (New York: Oxford University Press, 1947), pp. 363–73.

in this chapter. The conditions which determine variations
in patterns of succession should be the same ones that have
been suggested here as determining variations in union political structure. A study of a large number of cases of succession
should enable us not only to shed more light on the process
of succession itself, but may be the best way to test hypotheses bearing on the factors making for different degrees of
leadership control and oligarchy.

<h2 style="text-align:center">CRISIS SITUATIONS</h2>

Unions, like most human groupings, occasionally undergo
changes or meet threats that disturb the stability of the going
structure. Such crisis situations often upset some of the
sources of control and open the way to the organization of
political differences. It is impossible to list all the sources
of crisis which may upset a union's stability but some of
the most important are the succession crisis, already touched
on; shifts in the business cycle resulting in a reduction in
wages and weakening the organization through the unemployment of many members; strikes or lockouts, especially
prolonged and defeated ones; new technological devices which
result in a reduced need for the skills of the members; changes
in legislation which weaken the bargaining position of a union; jurisdictional rivalry with another union.

Any of these situations may require a union leadership to
make major policy decisions and reverse traditional practices.
The consequence may be the loss of relative position or
privilege by one section of the union as compared to another,
or perhaps a loss in economic position for the entire union.
A major shift in policy may upset the support for a given
leader among the rank and file or among sections of the
union officialdom.

Any disruption of stable internal relations and of the basis
for membership support may give subordinate leaders the
hope that they can take over the organization and solve the
crisis through new methods. Such factional fights, the most
common form of organized intra-union opposition, are the
characteristic mode of conflict when leaders and groups of

leaders, who have arisen out of the power sources opened up during crisis situations, challenge the incumbent administration or each other. Their sources of power and status, while strong and spontaneous, and based on the rank and file rather than on organizational machinery, are linked to the specific crisis situation, and are transient. If a would-be leader is not able to institutionalize his power and status by hooking it to the one enduring source of power and status in the union—the administrative hierarchy itself—he is likely to find that his strength in the ranks does not outlive the crisis in which it was born.

The specific effects of crisis on trade-unions or other organizations cannot, however, be predicted simply from the knowledge that a given equilibrium has been upset. A crisis may result in a major split among the top leaders of an organization, or it may appear to have the exact opposite result by giving a leader the opportunity to tighten his control. An anxious membership faced with grave and vital problems and wanting to get things "done and done fast" may agree to give considerable power to the man or group who appears ready and able to do the job. Union leadership has often secured consent to the growth of secrecy in policy formation, or in dispersal of funds, as a means of strengthening the union against the employer during crises. And these measures may in turn become a means of strengthening the internal power of the incumbent administration.

The specific determinants of different responses by trade-unions to organizational crises can be identified only through an analysis of variations in organizational structures and types of crises. Although I cannot undertake this type of analysis here, it is important to recognize that in any specific case external factors may modify the pattern of behavior expected on the basis of the internal analysis.

THE CHARACTER OF THE LEADER

So far we have not considered the characteristics and values of the leaders themselves. Although the personal attributes of the men who guide and control trade-unions are not the major causal factors in union activities and structure that some observers would make them out to be, they can still be examined fruitfully without subscribing to the "great man" theory of history. Examining the behavior of different trade-union leaders who are in roughly the same structural position reveals considerable variation in their behavior in terms of personal integrity and commitment to democratic values.

People familiar with the personal characteristics of large numbers of labor leaders have pointed to men like Philip Murray, David Dubinsky, and Walter Reuther as individuals who have made special efforts to minimize the more obvious negative consequences of bureaucratization and oligarchy in their unions. It is difficult to specify clearly the differences between these leaders and others, but the distinction which appears most appropriate is between those officials to whom the occupation of union leader has some component of a "calling" and those for whom it is primarily a livelihood and a means for the achievement of personal goals. The former is the leader who sees in the union something to which he can dedicate himself. His motivation in this direction usually stems from some ideological base, although it need not have any particular salient political content: the union itself and the welfare of the workers may be his main concern rather than a more far-reaching political goal. For this type of man the material rewards of the position, initially at least, are overshadowed by idealism. Such men are characterized by strong convictions and a sense of responsibility.

At the other extreme is the leader who looks upon his union office as a job with mobility potential. In the extreme case, he is an individual who may have had other avenues of mobility blocked to him, and who has planned to enter the union hierarchy with the express intention of raising his status and standard of living. These "career" or bureaucratic leaders may include what one observer of the trade-union movement has called the "accidental" leader. He is often a man who is fairly fluent and personable, who speaks up at meetings or is chosen by his work-mates for some minor position in the shop, is recognized by the union leadership as a potential asset, and is co-opted into office. An apprenticeship in the lower rungs of the union hierarchy may not seem rewarding to many such individuals, but those who find it so may soon be in the position of the consciously motivated union "careerist." For these men, the rewards that go with status and office within the union create a continuing motivation to retain and increase them.

This classification of leaders is, of course, an abstraction from a far more complex reality, as all conceptualizations are. Although no one leader completely exemplifies any one type, the supposition is that any given leader can be located on the continuum of "committed-careerist" orientation.[18]

This raises the questions: Under what conditions is one or the other type more likely to be found, and what are the consequences for union behavior when such variation exists? These conditions seem to be related to time-line factors, rather like the situations discussed above. Leaders characterized by a calling are usually men who have helped to organize their union from the start, have come to power as a result of taking part in an internal "revolution" against an entrenched dictatorial oligarchy, or have entered the labor movement as a result of a commitment to a political ideology which views the labor movement as an instrument to be used to gain a desired social goal. In the formation of a new union or participation in a "revolt" against entrenched leadership, the new leaders have historically faced great difficulties. The organizers of new unions have often risked loss of job and blacklisting in their industry, and sometimes imprisonment and physical injury. The monetary rewards have usually been slight or nothing at the beginning. The new leader may be accorded status by his fellow workers but, if he is organizing a new group, may be subject to personal attacks on his character and is frowned upon by those with status in the larger community and in the industry. Men who are willing to take

18 The "committed" orientation probably plays a part in the motivation of all union leaders. To carry out their role of workers' leader effectively they must to some extent believe that they are serving the workers' interests. See Ely Chinoy, *op. cit.*

such risks must be motivated by more than a desire to make a higher salary or gain a white-collar position. In many initial organizing situations there is little assurance that these rewards will be forthcoming even if organizational success is attained. Participation in a revolt against an entrenched oligarchy often carries with it the same chances as an initial organizing situation.

The leaders of new unions or internal political groups, therefore, are apt to be men who have a calling. Without such men, revolutionary movements (and union organization often resembles revolutionary activity) cannot be started. Only a strong commitment can outweigh the sanctions attendant on activity in such a group, and for this reason Communists and Socialists played a disproportionate role in the creation of many if not most American trade-unions. As mentioned earlier, John L. Lewis was forced to employ many young Communists as organizers for the C.I.O. when it first started, because they were the only people with the necessary skills who were willing to take the risks involved for low pay. Two of the three major unions in the old C.I.O. —the U.A.W. and the United Electrical Workers—as well as most of the smaller ones, were organized largely by Communists or democratic leftists. The one major exception, the United Steelworkers, was organized by professional organizers from the Mine Workers Union, but even there Lewis employed many who had been in the left-wing opposition to him in the U.M.W. The opposition to Joseph Ryan's control over the Longshoremen's Union, which eventually culminated in the formation of an independent West Coast union, was led in large part by Communists. Men like Samuel Gompers, Sidney Hillman, David Dubinsky, John Mitchell, and many others, all had some relation to the Socialist movement when they helped form their unions.

The strong commitment which presumably many of these men had when they first became union leaders was in large measure vitiated by the pressures of office. However, the later actions of such once-committed union leaders which seem to demonstrate that they no longer operate in terms of their original value goals may obscure the fact that, for the leader himself, the commitment and calling may still exist. It is not the personal weakness of the individual or his conscious rejection of past commitments that is involved, but rather the constraints of the structure within which he operates that bring about actions which appear to be oriented to the simple maintenance of office, or which may be undemocratic and at odds with what can be objectively described as the goals of the union. As Michels pointed out, in a great number of cases, regardless of the leader's original commitment or sense of calling, there are pressures—some of which we have been attempting to examine—which result in the leader's equating the security of his own position with the best means of achieving union goals.

The "career" union leader is more likely to be found in long-established unions. Entering the hierarchy of a stabilized bureaucratic union carries with it many advantages and few liabilities. Persons with ideological commitments are likely to be at a disadvantage rather than an advantage in seeking office in a stable organization. Their adherence to utopian or ideologically prescribed ends will bring them into conflict with the day-to-day pragmatic policies of the union—even of unions led by men who still think they adhere to these values. Men with a "calling" are likely to be viewed as irresponsible by the heads of bureaucracies who prefer to select persons who will work within the framework of the organization's goals as defined by the leaders. Weber's discussion of the bureaucratization of charisma is relevant to the situation in the trade-union movement as men with a "calling" are replaced by "bureaucrats."

The change from a "calling" to "bureaucracy" is not a direct time relationship. Holding all other factors constant, one would expect that the older a union is, the more likely its leaders are to be people who have come up the bureaucratic route to power. But this process may be reversed or slowed by crises in which an incumbent leadership is overthrown. It may also be affected if the union leaders remain organizationally affiliated with an outside group like the Communist or Socialist parties, and recruit their successors from the external organization. Continued affiliation with such groups in the context of the American labor movement, however, has meant the continual creation of elements of strain. The policies of such external groups and parties have been considerably at variance with those prescribed by the trade-union situation. The leaders therefore have been under pressure to leave the parties when the parties demanded that the trade-unions follow policies which might disrupt their internal equilibrium or stability or affect the leaders' chances for re-election. The Communist party has, in part, been able to prevent this situation from occurring in some unions where it has maintained factions whose loyalty was to the party and not to the particular union leaders.

Another factor which enters into the difference in behavior between the originally "committed" leader and the "bureaucratic" one is the possible variation in the groups of "significant others" whose esteem they value.[19] While individuals who become union leaders change their status and slough off many of their old friends and associates, few men can escape completely from their past. Men who entered the union movement to serve a cause are more likely than persons who moved up a bureaucratic hierarchy to have as a frame of reference for their own achievements the judgments of other people who also believed in the cause. Many former Socialists who are now trade-union leaders still attempt to explain and justify many of their actions as being consistent with a Socialist or left-democratic goal, and this orientation influences their behavior in ways that cannot be understood solely in terms of their unions' objective situations.

Some of the differences between seemingly similar large oligarchic and bureaucratized unions lie in the fact that some are led by men who still view their positions as a calling,

[19] For a fuller discussion of the relationship between trade-union behavior and the reference groups of members and leaders, see S. M. Lipset and Martin Trow, "Reference Group Analysis and Trade Union Wage Policy," in Mirra Komarovsky, ed., *Common Frontiers in the Social Sciences* (Glencoe: The Free Press, 1957), pp. 391–411.

whereas others are led by careerists. The first group may be no more democratic in practice, but they are often more accessible to the membership, more aggressive in their tactics, more concerned with violations of a union ethic of service to the membership, and have greater personal integrity. A Socialist or other radical past is obviously more likely to be related to such behavior than a Communist past. The "called" leader whose values are democratic is also more likely to be concerned with the forms of democracy than is the "bureaucratic" leader.

It is, again, difficult to posit hypotheses about the relationship between "calling" as a leadership orientation and the conditions making for significant internal democracy within a trade-union. It is probable that the different "calls" that have led people into the labor movement make for significantly different types of behavior. A former Communist, for example, may continue to operate an effective dictatorial machine after leaving the party, and while his behavior may differ in terms of more militancy and integrity as compared with leaders who have come up the "bureaucratic" path, he may be far more ruthless in using the organizational machinery to maintain power. A "calling" may also be related to ruthlessness in the maintenance of power by "democratic" labor leaders. The sense of righteousness and devotion to a "cause" that is usually associated with a political or religious calling often leads to actions which might strike observers as being at considerable variance with their doer's presumed values and goals. The "committed" leader who "knows" that he is serving the "right" cause sees opponents as witting or unwitting agents of the enemy, whether the enemy is defined as the employers, the capitalist system, or the Communist party.

On the other hand, "committed" leaders, although often ruthless in dealing with opposition, appear to have a need, flowing from their commitment, to believe that the membership approves their actions, and they attempt to convert as many as possible to their approach. Concern with the "education" of the rank and file is more likely to be found in unions led by "calling" leaders than in those led by "careerists." However, the effort to build a trade-union machine on a consistent ideology as well as on the more typical basis of mutual reward and obligation often threatens the stability of the bureaucracy. New situations which require the establishment of new policies may lead men who take their ideologies seriously to disagree. The fairly common pattern of factional disagreements and cleavages in leftist political groups appears to reflect the greater sense of serving the righteous cause that these movements require from their leaders and members, as compared with more conservative groups. Unions in which leftists have held power in the United States have had more frequent internal differences than those which followed the Gompers' nonpartisan policies.

Value Systems

This analysis has thus far ignored in large part the effect on union organization of the value system of the total society and, more specifically, the value systems of the different strata of workers who belong to unions, as well as the manifest goals of different unions.

One would expect that (if structural and time-line factors are constant) trade-unionists, whether leaders or members, would behave differently within the different value systems which characterize different social structures. An American trade-union operating within the American social structure, with its emphasis on individual achievement, the right of each individual to equality with others, and the norm of democracy, should behave differently from a German union working within the context of a more rigid status system, with greater emphasis on ascription than achievement, with greater acceptance of the leadership role, with less concern for the right of the individual compared to the group, and with presumed less emphasis on the norm of democratic control. Similarly, the behavior of two American trade-unions should vary with the composition of their memberships, in so far as the difference in membership is reflected in different weights and distributions of the crucial norms regarding authority and democracy.

The more a given group holds a democratic, anti-elitist value system, the more difficult it should be to institutionalize oligarchy. On a comparative social structure basis, German union leaders should be able to maintain an oligarchic structure more easily than leaders of American unions can. German workers should accept more easily the permanent tenure of leadership, the lack of discussion of policies, and the absence of opposition. American workers, all other things being equal, would presumably be more likely to resist hierarchical control. Assuming that leaders in both countries seek to make their tenure secure, American labor leaders are then under greater pressure to formalize dictatorial mechanisms so as to prevent the possibility of their being overthrown. Or, to put it another way, since the values inherent in American society make American union officers more vulnerable than their German counterparts, they must act more vigorously and decisively and dictatorially to stabilize their status.

Within the American labor movement itself somewhat similar variations exist. Some American unions have memberships which put a high premium on rank-and-file participation and control; other memberships hold these values less strongly. It has often been observed that participation in national politics varies with position in the society; it has similarly been suggested here that the higher the status of the worker, the more likely he is to claim a right in decision making. Such values, combined with the greater resources of high-status workers for political participation, would, if our assumptions are empirically valid, add to the possibilities for democracy in a union. There are two organizational responses to this condition. One is the pattern of institutionalized democracy found in the I.T.U., Actors Equity, and similar unions. The other is a more rigorous use of dictatorial mechanisms by leaders whose position is vulnerable. One union which illustrates both of these tendencies is the Musicians' Union, some locals of which are as democratic as

Equity, while other locals and the International itself are dictatorially oligarchic.

Another adaptive mechanism which operates to make oligarchy and American democratic values compatible is an ideology that emphasizes the union's specific functions. The more narrowly an organization defines its functions as fulfilling limited and specific needs, the less likely a member is to feel the need to participate in and influence its policies. People may belong to many organizations, like an American Automobile Association, a local consumer's co-operative, a medical plan, a bowling group, a national stamp club, without feeling any obligation to participate actively in the internal operation of the group and without feeling coerced by the fact that decisions are made without their having been consulted. In large measure, people judge each of the various voluntary associations to which they belong on the basis of its ability to satisfy a limited need. Conversely, the more diffuse the functions of a group or organization, the more likely an individual is to find sources of disagreement with it and to desire to participate actively in its operation.

The union which simply operates as a "business union" is in the category of specific, one-function organizations. Outside of the shop organization where there is normally the largest participation by workers, the single major task of the "business union"—collective bargaining—does not take place more than once a year, and in many unions only once every two or three years. The day-to-day administration of union affairs need not concern the average member any more than do the day-to-day activities that go into running a medical plan. It is of course true that a union deals with the individual in his occupational role, and we might expect it to call forth more of his interest and concern than other voluntary organizations which are concerned with his less important roles. But the generalization still holds on a comparative basis. Such unions as the I.T.U. and Actors Equity, which fulfill many functions related to the status and leisure time of their members, have high membership participation and involvement.

Thus the most appropriate ideology for a union seeking to limit its functions is business unionism, the most common ideology in American unions. By stating that a union should not be concerned with other than the traditional trade-union activities of collective bargaining, worker defense, and membership welfare, union leaders are also declaring that they do not want other values deriving from various extra-union interests to affect them.

"Business unionism" as a set of ideas justifying the narrowest definition of a union's role in society and area of service to its members discourages widespread membership participation and legitimates oligarchic leadership. However, the congruence of business unionism as an ideology with oligarchy as a power structure by no means fully explains the widespread adoption of business unionism. The point here is merely that whatever other factors may be related to the acceptance of the ideology, one of its consequences is to reduce some of the strains of perpetuating an oligarchy in an organization whose membership holds democratic values.

No one has attempted either a qualitative or quantitative analysis of the relationship between diffuse political or specific "business union" ideologies and the presence or absence of political conflict within trade-unions. But the general proposition may be suggested that the more diffuse the ideology of a trade-union, the greater the likelihood of internal factionalism. European trade-unions, which are much more political than American ones, have been much more prone to internal cleavage. But American observers of European unionism have called attention to the fact that a secular tendency in the direction of business unionism exists in Europe. This fact has been used as validation for the hypothesis that the normal function of trade-unions is business unionism, and that labor unions as they become established tend to shed superfluous political ideologies. Selig Perlman, the Wisconsin labor economist, has presented the case for this thesis most brilliantly in his *Theory of the Labor Movement*.

Such analysis, which treats trade-unions as collective bodies and does not differentiate between the needs of the bureaucracy and those of the membership, tends to ignore the possibility that the drive to limit the functions and goals of unions may be primarily the adaptive mechanism of a security-seeking leadership rather than (as Perlman suggests) a result of the social situation of workers. The commitment, for example, to support a Socialist party or general Socialist objectives necessarily involves acceptance of discussion of differences in politics. Many British trade-union conventions in the past have spent considerable time discussing the split between Aneurin Bevan and the leadership of the Labor party and the Trades Union Congress.

To suggest that limiting the functions of trade-unions promotes the stability of the bureaucracy does not imply that the members of most or any trade-unions are prone to support broad definitions of union goals. In fact, as much of the earlier analysis suggests, the majority are apathetic and probably more conservative than their union officers. However, this fact does not negate the generalization that any factor, such as a "business union" ideology, which serves to reduce the possibility for internal cleavage also operates to lower the potential influence which a membership may have on the policies of the organization.

Conclusions

The analysis developed in this chapter obviously implies some pessimistic conclusions about the long-term chances for democracy in trade-unions. To recapitulate the major points:

1. The structure of large-scale organization inherently requires the development of bureaucratic patterns of behavior. The conditions making for the institutionalization of bureaucracy and those making for democratic turnover in office are largely incompatible; and the degree of incompatibility varies with the degree of bureaucratization imposed by the need to come to stable terms with other bureaucratized institutions in the union's environment.

2. The structure of large-scale organization gives an incumbent administration very great power and advantage over

the rank and file, or even over an organized opposition. This advantage takes such forms as control over financial resources and internal communications, a large permanently organized political machine, a claim to legitimacy, and a monopoly of political skills.

3. The ease with which an oligarchy can control a large organization varies with the degree to which the members are involved in the organization. The more important membership is considered, and the more participation in it there is, the more difficult it will be for an oligarchy to enforce policies and actions which conflict with the values or needs of the members. The concept of "business unionism," which assumes that a union performs only the one major function of securing the best possible contracts for its members helps prevent internal politics and conflict and encourages only limited participation on the part of the members. Any conception of trade-union functions which increases the involvement of the members in the organization increases the potentialities for democratic conflict.

4. The inherent instability of democracy in trade-unions is revealed by the implications of a trade-union as a status-placing mechanism.

    a. A functional requirement of the leadership role is that it be assigned higher status, that is, be a higher achievement, than the follower role.

    b. A dominant value of achievement is that upward mobility is a cultural goal.

    c. One key attribute of a democratic political structure is the possibility of the circulation or rotation of leadership. This means that oligarchy can be avoided only if a mechanism exists by which leaders can be retired from office.

    d. In society at large, political leaders may leave office and assume positions of equivalent or higher status. In the trade-union movement, the defeated leader moves from a high-status to a low-status position if he remains within the union.

    e. The institutionalization of movement from high to low status, which is what democracy in trade-unions would mean for the leaders, would be a major deviation from the dominant value of achievement.

f. Fulfillment of these contradictory norms would result in *anomie* for the leaders and is a psychologically impossible situation.

The obvious conclusions of this analysis are that the functional requirements for democracy cannot be met most of the time in most unions. For example, the conflict between democratic and achievement norms means that democracy can exist as a stable system in unions only where the status differentiation between leaders and followers is very small. This may help account for the fact that democracy is found mostly in high-status unions and in local unions. Instead of suggesting that power corrupts in all situations, this analysis suggests that such "corruption" is a consequence of specific social structures *where conformity to one norm necessarily involves violation of another norm.*

Nevertheless, the general proposition that trade-unions, like many other internally oligarchic organizations, help sustain political democracy in the larger body politic still holds. As Franz Neumann, the American political scientist, among others, has made clear, many internally dictatorial associations operate to protect the interests of their members by checking the encroachments of other groups.[20] Even the most dictatorial union is a better protector of workers' economic interests, and of political democracy within the larger society, than no union, provided that the union is not a tool of either the state or the employer. In large measure, the chance that the collectivist society which is developing in most countries will be democratic rests on the possibility that trade-unions, although supporters of Socialist objectives, will maintain their independence of the state. The behavior of the trade-unions in the British Commonwealth and the Scandinavian countries furnishes real evidence that such a pattern is possible.

[20] Franz L. Neumann, "Approaches to the Study of Political Power," *Political Science Quarterly*, 65 (1950), pp. 161–80.

It is also necessary to remember that even the most dictatorial trade-union leaders must be somewhat responsive to the economic needs of their members. A union oligarchy which does not defend the economic interests of the rank and file may find its membership disappearing, as John L. Lewis did in the twenties. Lewis, then a trade-union as well as a political conservative, almost lost the United Mine Workers. Only after adopting the militant tactics for which he is now famous was he able to rebuild the union. A trade-union which is not an economic defense organization has no function and will not long remain on the scene. But the fact that most unions do represent their members' interests must not be confused with the problem of internal democracy, for as Howe and Widick have pointed out:

> There is one decisive proof of democracy in a union (or any other institution): oppositionists have the right to organize freely into "parties," to set up factional machines, to circulate publicity and to propagandize among the members. . . . The presence of an opposition . . . is the best way of insuring that a union's democratic structure will be preserved. . . . To defend the right of factions to exist is not at all to applaud this or that faction. But this is the overhead (well worth paying!) of democracy: groups one considers detrimental to the union's interest will be formed. The alternative is dictatorship.[21]

A final note: institutionalized democracy within private governments is not a necessary condition for democracy in the larger society, and may in fact at times weaken the democratic process of civil society. The various secondary associations independent of the state which Tocqueville saw as necessary conditions of a democratic nation have been in both his day and ours largely one-party oligarchies. In spite

[21] Irving Howe and B. J. Widick, op. cit., pp. 262–63. Some more recent research and a detailed bibliography on this topic are reported in a special issue of the American Journal of Sociology devoted to "democracy and bureaucracy in labor unions" 61 (May 1956).

of this, they have facilitated political education and opposition by training new leaders, organizing and communicating opinions, and representing their members to other groups and the state. Many such groups acquire trained leaders who are better informed, even when not full-time officials, concerning the problems of the organization and ways to serve its members than are the less educated and less aware rank-and-file members.

An organization under direct membership control may become irresponsible from either the vantage point of its needs or those of the society. The members may want their "selfish" objectives pursued even if achieving them will hurt others or endanger the organization. Employers know well that the more democratic a union—that is, the more opposition in it to the incumbent leadership, the more factions, the more turnover in office—the more irresponsible the union will be. And a study of the attitudes on civil liberties of a sample of Americans found that even leaders of organizations like the Daughters of the American Revolution or the American Legion were much more likely to believe in civil liberties for Communists and other unpopular political deviants than were the rank-and-file members of their organizations.[22]

It is noteworthy that the conditions which seem most plausibly related to membership participation and hence to internal democracy in trade-unions and other voluntary associations discussed on pages 407 to 409 are the same conditions which seemingly weaken democracy within the larger society. That is, to the extent that members of an association have a diffuse set of relationships with the organization, to the extent that a large part of their lives is lived within its influence, to the extent that its members interact with each other, to that degree are the chances for a high level of concern and participation increased. But these same factors isolate the members of the group from cross-pressures and exposure to diverse values and influences, and, as we have seen in the

[22] Samuel A. Stouffer, *Communism, Conformity and Civil Liberties* (New York: Doubleday & Co., Inc., 1955), pp. 26–46.

case of those in "isolated" industries like miners or longshore-men, heighten the intensity of their political beliefs. This again poses a dilemma for us. Integration of members within a trade-union, a political party, a farm organization, a professional society, may increase the chances that members of such organizations will be active in the group and have more control over its policies. But extending the functions of such organizations so as to integrate their members may threaten the larger political system because it reduces the forces making for compromise and understanding among conflicting groups. Trade-unions like those of the miners or the printers, which are characterized by high membership involvement and loyalty deriving largely from the existence of an "occupational" community, exhibit less concern for the values of other parts of the community than do unions whose members are less isolated and hence less committed.

It should be obvious that I do not advocate dictatorship in private organizations. But it is necessary to recognize that many organizations may never fulfill the conditions for a stable internal democracy and still contribute in important ways to the democratic process in the total society, by providing a secure base for factionalism and real vested interests at the same time that they limit individual freedom within the organization and allow a degree of autonomy of action for both the leaders and the organization which may undermine other social values. This is another case of the incompatability of values where they have contradictory consequences. There is no simple answer which can resolve these problems of democracy in modern society.

Methodological Appendix

Students of the labor movement will be able to point to major exceptions to each proposition suggested in this chapter. Clearly it is impossible in the case of given organizations or individuals to abstract any one variable and make it the sole or even primary determinant of a given behavior pattern. The problem of how to deal with many-sided determinants of specific behavior patterns is a basic one in the social sciences. When dealing with individuals, analysts may partially escape this difficulty by collecting data on a large number of cases, so that they can isolate the influence of specific factors through use of quantitative techniques. The analysis of organizations is hampered, however, by the fact that comparable data are rarely collected for more than a few cases. The cost of studying intensively even one large organization may be as much as that of gathering survey data from a large sample of individuals.

The procedure followed by most analysts in searching out the determinants of a given pattern of behavior, such as oligarchy or rank-and-file militancy within a given union, is to cite those factors in the organization which seem to be related to the behavioral item in question. Such a procedure is essentially *post factum*, if the only case in which the given pattern of significant variables is observed is the one under observation. The analyst rarely has the opportunity of establishing any controls or comparisons. Often an attempt is made to escape this dilemma by citing illustrative materials from other cases, which appear to validate the hypothesis. Such illustrative data do not solve the methodological problem of validation, and usually only serve to give the reader a false sense of the general validity of the interpretation.

It is of crucial importance, therefore, that students of organizational behavior address themselves to the problem of verification of hypotheses. At present one may spend a great deal of time examining the large number of studies of individual trade-unions or other large-scale organizations without being able to validate a single proposition about organizational behavior. The data collected in such case studies do not lend themselves to re-analysis to test hypotheses, since the researchers rarely focused their observations in terms of any set of explicit hypotheses.

Three methods may be tentatively suggested as ways through which greater progress can be made in this area: the gathering of quantitative data from a large number of organizations, clinical case studies, and deviant case analyses. The following example illustrates the first method, quantification. To test the proposition that the greater the status differentiation between the officers and members of a trade-union, the more likely such an organization is to have a dictatorial political structure, data could be collected from a large number of international and local unions. Such research would be difficult but might be accomplished by devising rough indices of status which would allow an observer to develop some measure of the size of the status differential between members and officers of different groups. Hypotheses about the relation of the product market to union structures could be similarly tested.

Another method that could be used is analogous to the clinical procedure employed in the biological sciences, in which prognoses are made on the basis of a theoretical analysis. One could make predictions about the behavior of organizations in future critical situations that will require changes. One optimum situation for such research, the succession crisis, has an additional advantage for study since it is a repetitive event. There have been literally thousands of cases of succession in the labor movement, as leaders have died or retired. Studies of variations in the consequences of succession would permit the testing of hypotheses dealing with factors that operate to stimulate or repress internal conflict within organizations.

A third possible solution to the methodological difficulty is the analysis of *deviant cases*—in the labor movement, specifically those organizations which are characterized by a high level of democratic procedure, membership participation, or both. If one knows that a given behavior pattern, like oligarchy, is common to almost all large unions, then the repeated study of oligarchic groups will yield few new insights into the possible variations which may affect internal political structures.[23] Paul Lazarsfeld has pointed out that "deviant

[23] See Joseph Goldstein, *The Government of British Trade Unions* (London: Allen and Unwin, 1952), for an excellent description of oligarchic control in a British union. This study, however, adds little except more facts to Michels' classic analysis.

case analysis can and should play a *positive* role in empirical research, rather than being merely the 'tidying-up' process through which exceptions to the empirical rule are given some plausibility and thus disposed of." The existence of a deviant case (for example, the highly democratic political system of the International Typographical Union) always implies that the theoretical structure—in this case, the theory subsumed in Michels' "iron law of oligarchy"—is oversimplified and suggests "the need for incorporating further variables into . . . [the] predictive scheme."[24]

[24] See Patricia Kendall and Katherine M. Wolf, "The Analysis of Deviant Cases in Communications Research," in Paul F. Lazarsfeld and Frank Stanton, eds., *Communications Research, 1948–1949* (New York: Harper & Bros., 1949), pp. 153–54. The approach to the I.T.U. as a deviant case was central to the study *Union Democracy*, already cited.

A PERSONAL POSTSCRIPT

CHAPTER 13

The End of Ideology?[1]

A BASIC premise of this book is that democracy is not only or even primarily a means through which different groups can attain their ends or seek the good society; it is the good society itself in operation. Only the give-and-take of a free society's internal struggles offers some guarantee that the products of the society will not accumulate in the hands of a few power-holders, and that men may develop and bring up their children without fear of persecution. And, as we have seen, democracy requires institutions which support conflict and disagreement as well as those which sustain legitimacy and consensus. In recent years, however, democracy in the Western world has been undergoing some important changes as serious intellectual conflicts among groups representing different values have declined sharply.

The consequences of this change can perhaps be best illustrated by describing what happened at a world congress of intellectuals on "The Future of Freedom" held in Milan,

[1] I have taken the chapter heading from the title of Edward Shils' excellent report on a conference on "The Future of Freedom" held in Milan, Italy, in September 1955, under the auspices of the Congress for Cultural Freedom. See his "The End of Ideology?" *Encounter*, 5 (November 1955), pp. 52–58; for perceptive analyses of the nature and sources of the decline of ideology see Herbert Tingsten, "Stability and Vitality in Swedish Democracy," *The Political Quarterly*, 2 (1955), pp. 140–51; and Otto Brunner, "Der Zeitalter der Ideologien," in *Neue Wege der Sozialgeschichte* (Göttingen: Van den Hoeck and Ruprecht, 1956), pp. 194–219. For a prediction that the "age of ideology" is ending see Lewis S. Feuer, "Beyond Ideology," *Psychoanalysis and Ethics* (Springfield: Charles C. Thomas, 1955), pp. 126–30. Many of these topics are discussed in detail by Daniel Bell in *The End of Ideology* (Glencoe: The

Italy, in September 1955. The conference[2] was attended by 150 intellectuals and politicians from many democratic countries, and included men ranging in opinions from socialists to right-wing conservatives. Among the delegates from Great Britain, for example, were Hugh Gaitskell and Richard Crossman, socialists, and Michael Polanyi and Colin Clark, conservatives. From the United States came Sidney Hook, then the vice-chairman of the Union for Democratic Socialism, Arthur Schlesinger, Jr., of Americans for Democratic Action, and Friedrich A. Hayek, the arch-conservative economist. The French representatives included André Philip, a left-socialist leader, Raymond Aron, once active in the Gaullist movement, and Bertrand de Jouvenal, the conservative philosopher. Similar divergencies in political outlook were apparent among the delegates from Scandinavia, Germany, Italy, and other countries.

One would have thought that a conference in which so many important political and intellectual leaders of socialism, liberalism, and conservatism were represented would have stimulated intense political debate. In fact, nothing of the sort occurred. The only occasions in which debate grew warm were when someone served as a "surrogate Communist" by saying something which could be defined as being too favorable to Russia.

On the last day of the week-long conference, an interesting event occurred. Professor Hayek, in a closing speech, attacked the delegates for preparing to bury freedom instead of saving it. He alone was disturbed by the general temper. What bothered him was the general agreement among the delegates, regardless of political belief, that the traditional issues separating the left and right had declined to comparative insignificance. In effect, all agreed that the increase in state control

Free Press, 1960) and by Ralf Dahrendorf in *Class and Class Conflict* (Stanford: Stanford University Press, 1959).

[2] My original report on this conference which I attended was published as "The State of Democratic Politics," *Canadian Forum*, 35 (November 1955), pp. 170–71. It is interesting to note the similarities of the observations in it and the report by Edward Shils, *op. cit.*

which had taken place in various countries would not result in a decline in democratic freedom. The socialists no longer advocated socialism; they were as concerned as the conservatives with the danger of an all-powerful state. The ideological issues dividing left and right had been reduced to a little more or a little less government ownership and economic planning. No one seemed to believe that it really made much difference which political party controlled the domestic policies of individual nations. Hayek, honestly believing that state intervention is bad and inherently totalitarian, found himself in a small minority of those who still took the cleavages within the democratic camp seriously.

A leading left-wing British intellectual, Richard Crossman, has stated that socialism is now consciously viewed by most European socialist leaders as a "Utopian myth . . . often remote from the realities of day-to-day politics."[3] Few socialist parties still want to nationalize more industry. This objective has been largely given up by the socialist parties of the more industrialized states like Scandinavia, Britain, and Germany. The Labor party premier of the Australian state of Queensland, defending the retention of socialization as an objective at the party's 1950 convention, clearly acknowledged that its significance was largely ritualistic when he said:

"I point out that there are serious implications in any way altering our platform and objectives. In the first place it is a bad thing to break ground in attack if we can avoid it, and I think we should not duck around corners and pretend we do not want socialization of industry. It is a long term objective in the Labor movement, exactly in the same way that there is a long term objective in the Christian movement. The people who espouse Christianity have been struggling for over 2,000 years and have not arrived at it."[4]

[3] Richard Crossman, "On Political Neurosis," *Encounter*, 3 (May 1954), p. 66.
[4] Cited in T. C. Truman, *The Pressure Groups, Parties and Politics of the Australian Labor Movement* (unpublished M.A. thesis, Department of Political Science, University of Queensland, 1953), Chap. II, p. 82.

The rationale for retaining long-term objectives, even those which may not be accomplished in 2,000 years, was well stated by Richard Crossman:

> A democratic party can very rarely be persuaded to give up one of its central principles, and *can never afford to scrap its central myth*. Conservatives must defend free enterprise even when they are actually introducing state planning. A Labour Government must defend as true Socialism policies which have very little to do with it. The job of party leaders is often to persuade their followers that the traditional policy is still being carried out, even when this is demonstrably not true.[5]

The fact that the differences between the left and the right in the Western democracies are no longer profound does not mean that there is no room for party controversy. But as the editor of one of the leading Swedish newspapers once said to me, "Politics is now boring. The only issues are whether the metal workers should get a nickel more an hour, the price of milk should be raised, or old-age pensions extended." These are important matters, the very stuff of the internal struggle within stable democracies, but they are hardly matters to excite intellectuals or stimulate young people who seek in politics a way to express their dreams.

This change in Western political life reflects the fact that the fundamental political problems of the industrial revolution have been solved: the workers have achieved industrial and political citizenship; the conservatives have accepted the

[5] Richard Crossman, *op. cit.*, p. 67. (My emphasis.) And in Sweden, Herbert Tingsten reports: "The great controversies have thus been liquidated in all instances. As a result the symbolic words and the stereotypes have changed or disappeared. . . . Liberalism in the old sense is dead, both among the Conservatives and in the Liberal party; . . . and the label of socialism on a specific proposal or a specific reform has hardly any other meaning than the fact that the proposal or reform in question is regarded as attractive. The actual words 'socialism' or 'liberalism' are tending to become mere honorifics, useful in connection with elections and political festivities." Tingsten, *op. cit.*, p. 145.

welfare state; and the democratic left has recognized that an increase in over-all state power carries with it more dangers to freedom than solutions for economic problems. This very triumph of the democratic social revolution in the West ends domestic politics for those intellectuals who must have ideologies or utopias to motivate them to political action.

Within Western democracy, this decline in the sources of serious political controversy has even led some to raise the question as to whether the conflicts that are so necessary to democracy will continue. Barrington Moore, Jr., a Harvard sociologist, has asked whether

> . . . as we reduce economic inequalities and privileges, we may also eliminate the sources of contrast and discontent that put drive into genuine political alternatives. In the United States today, with the exception of the Negro, it is difficult to perceive any section of the population that has a vested material interest on behalf of freedom. . . . There is, I think, more than a dialectical flourish in the assertion that liberty requires the existence of an oppressed group in order to grow vigorously. Perhaps that is the tragedy as well as the glory of liberty. Once the ideal has been achieved, or is even close to realization, the driving force of discontent disappears, and a society settles down for a time to a stolid acceptance of things as they are. Something of the sort seems to have happened to the United States.[6]

And David Riesman has suggested that "the general increase of wealth and the concomitant loss of rigid distinctions make it difficult to maintain the Madisonian [economic] bases for political diversity, or to recruit politicians who speak for the residual oppressed strata."[7] The thesis that partisan conflict based on class differences and left-right issues is ending is based on the assumption that "the economic class system is

[6] Barrington Moore, Jr., *Political Power and Social Theory* (Cambridge: Harvard University Press, 1958), p. 183.

[7] David Riesman, "Introduction," to Stimson Bullitt, *To Be a Politician* (New York: Doubleday & Co., Inc., 1959), p. 20.

disappearing . . . that redistribution of wealth and income
. . . has ended economic inequality's political significance."[8]

Yet one wonders whether these intellectuals are not mis-
taking the decline of ideology in the domestic politics of
Western society with the ending of the class conflict which
has sustained democratic controversy. As the abundant evidence on voting patterns in the United States and other countries indicates, the electorate as a whole does not see the end
of the domestic class struggle envisioned by so many intellectuals. A large number of surveys of the American population
made from the 1930s to the 1950s report that most people
believe that the Republicans do more for the wealthy and
for business and professional people and the Democrats do
more for the poor and for skilled and unskilled workers.[9] Similar findings have been reported for Great Britain.

These opinions do not simply represent the arguments of
partisans, since supporters of both the left and the right agree
on the classes each party basically represents—which does not
mean the acceptance of a bitter class struggle but rather an
agreement on the representation functions of the political
parties similar to the general agreement that trade-unions
represent workers, and the Chamber of Commerce, businessmen. Continued class cleavage does not imply any destructive
consequences for the system; as I indicated in an early chapter, a stable democracy requires consensus on the nature of
the political struggle, and this includes the assumption that
different groups are best served by different parties.

The predictions of the end of class politics in the "affluent
society" ignore the relative character of any class system. The
decline of objective deprivation—low income, insecurity, malnutrition—does reduce the potential tension level of a society,
as we have seen. But as long as some men are rewarded more
than others by the prestige or status structure of society,

[8] S. Bullitt, *ibid.*, p. 177.
[9] See Harold Orlans, *Opinion Polls on National Leaders* (Philadelphia: Institute for Research in Human Relations, 1953), pp.
70–73. This monograph contains a detailed report on various surveys
conducted by the different American polling agencies from 1935–53.

men will feel *relatively* deprived. The United States is the wealthiest country in the world, and its working class lives on a scale to which most of the middle classes in the rest of the world aspire; yet a detailed report on the findings of various American opinion surveys states: "The dominant opinion on polls before, during, and after the war is that the salaries of corporation executives are too high and should be limited by the government." And this sentiment, prevalent even among prosperous people, finds increasing support as one moves down the economic ladder.[10]

The democratic class struggle will continue, but it will be a fight without ideologies, without red flags, without May Day parades. This naturally upsets many intellectuals who can participate only as ideologists or major critics of the *status quo*. The British socialist weekly, *The New Statesman*, published a series of comments through 1958–59 under the general heading "Shall We Help Mr. Gaitskell?" As the title suggests, this series was written by various British intellectuals who are troubled by the fact that the Labor party is no longer ideologically radical but simply the interest organization of the workers and the trade-unions.

The decline of political ideology in America has affected many intellectuals who, as I pointed out in Chapter 10, must function as critics of the society to fulfill their self-image. And since domestic politics, even liberal and socialist politics, can no longer serve as the arena for serious criticism from the left, many intellectuals have turned from a basic concern with the political and economic systems to criticism of other sections of the basic culture of American society, particularly of elements which cannot be dealt with politically. They point to the seeming growth of a concern with status ("keeping up with the Joneses"), to the related increase in the influence of advertisers and mass media as the arbiters of mass taste, to the evidence that Americans are overconformist—another side of keeping up with the Joneses. Thus the

[10] *Ibid.*, p. 149. The one exception is among the very poor who are somewhat less intolerant of high executive salaries than those immediately above them.

critical works about American society in the past decades which have received the most attention have been sociological rather than political, such books as David Riesman's *The Lonely Crowd*, William H. Whyte's *The Organization Man*, Max Lerner's *America as a Civilization*, and Vance Packard's *The Status Seekers*.

Yet many of the disagreeable aspects of American society which are now regarded as the results of an affluent and bureaucratic society may be recurring elements inherent in an equalitarian and democratic society. Those aspects of both American and socialist ideology which have always been most thoroughly expressed in the United States make a concern with status and conformity constant features of the society.

The patterns of status distinction which Lloyd Warner, Vance Packard, and others have documented have been prevalent throughout America's history, as the reports of various nineteenth-century foreign travelers plainly show. These visitors generally believed that Americans were *more* status-conscious than Europeans, that it was easier for a *nouveau riche* individual to be accepted in nineteenth-century England than in nineteenth-century America; and they explained the greater snobbery in this country by suggesting that the very emphasis on democracy and equalitarianism in America, the lack of a well-defined deference structure, in which there is no question about social rankings, make well-to-do Americans place more emphasis on status background and symbolism than do Europeans.

It may seem a paradox to observe that a millionaire has a better and easier social career open to him in England than in America. . . . In America, if his private character be bad, if he be mean or openly immoral, or personally vulgar, or dishonest, the best society may keep its doors closed against him. In England great wealth, skillfully employed, will more readily force these doors to open. For in England great wealth can, by using the appropriate methods, practically buy rank from those

who bestow it. . . . The existence of a system of artificial rank enables a stamp to be given to base metal in
Europe which cannot be given in a thoroughly republican
country.[11]

The great concern with family background (which generation made the money?) that many observers, from Harriet
Martineau (one of the most sophisticated British commenters
on American life in the 1820s) to the contemporary American
sociologist Lloyd Warner, have shown to be characteristic
of large parts of American society may be a reaction to the
feelings of uncertainty about social position engendered in
a society whose basic values deny anyone the inherent right
to claim higher status than his neighbor. As the sociologist
Howard Brotz has pointed out in comparing the status systems of Britain and the United States:

In a democracy snobbishness can be far more vicious
than in an aristocracy. Lacking that natural confirmation
of superiority which political authority alone can give,
the rich and particularly the new rich, feel threatened
by mere contact with their inferiors. This tendency
perhaps reached its apogee in the late nineteenth century
in Tuxedo Park, a select residential community composed of wealthy New York businessmen, which, not
content merely to surround itself with a wire fence,
posted a sentry at the gate to keep nonmembers out.
Nothing could be more fantastic than this to an English
lord living in the country in the midst, not of other peers,
but of his tenants. His position is such that he is at ease
in the presence of members of the lower classes and in
associating with them in recreation. For example, farmers

11 James Bryce, *The American Commonwealth*, Vol. II (New
York: Macmillan, 1910), p. 815. Cf. D. W. Brogan, *U.S.A.* (London: Oxford University Press, 1941), pp. 116 ff.; see Robert W.
Smuts, *European Impressions of the American Worker* (New York:
King's Crown Press, 1953), for a summary of comments by many
visitors in the 1900s and the 1950s who reported that "social and
economic democracy in America, far from mitigating competition
for social status, intensified it" (p. 13).

[that is, tenants] ride to the hounds in the hunts. It is this "democratic" attitude which, in the first instance, makes for an openness to social relations with Jews. One cannot be declassed, so to speak, by play activities.[12]

The problem of conformity which so troubles many Americans today has been noted as a major aspect of American culture from Tocqueville in the 1830s to Riesman in the 1950s. Analysts have repeatedly stressed the extent to which Americans (as compared to other peoples) are sensitive to the judgments of others. Never secure in their own status, they are concerned with "public opinion" in a way that elites in a more aristocratic and status-bound society do not have to be. As early as the nineteenth century foreign observers were struck by the "other-directedness" of Americans and accounted for it by the nature of the class system. This image of the American as "other-directed" can, as Riesman notes, be found in the writing of "Tocqueville and other curious and astonished visitors from Europe."[13] Harriet Martineau almost seems to be paraphrasing Riesman's own description of today's "other-directed" man in her picture of the early nineteenth-century American:

> Americans may travel over the world, and find no society but their own which will submit [as much] to the restraint of perpetual caution, and reference to the opinions of others. They may travel over the whole world, and find no country but their own where the very children beware of getting into scrapes, and talk of the effect of actions on people's minds; where the youth of society determines in silence what opinions they shall bring forward, and what avow only in the family circle; where women write miserable letters, al-

[12] Howard Brotz, "The Position of the Jews in English Society," *The Jewish Journal of Sociology*, 1 (1959), p. 97.
[13] David Riesman, *et al.*, *The Lonely Crowd: A Study of the Changing American Character* (New Haven: Yale University Press, 1950), pp. 19–20.

most universally, because it is a settled matter that it is unsafe to commit oneself on paper; and where elderly people seem to lack almost universally that faith in principles which inspires a free expression of them at any time, and under all circumstances.[14]

It may be argued that in an open democratic society in which people are encouraged to struggle upward, but where there are no clearly defined reference points to mark their arrival, and where their success in achieving status is determined by the good opinion of others, the kind of caution and intense study of other people's opinions described by Martineau is natural. Like Riesman today, she notes that this "other-directed" type is found most commonly in urban centers in the middle and upper classes, where people live in "perpetual caution." Nowhere does there exist "so much heart-eating care [about others' judgments], so much nervous anxiety, as among the dwellers in the towns of the northern states of America."[15] Similarly, Max Weber, who visited the United States in the early 1900s, noted the high degree of "submission to fashion in America, to a degree unknown in Germany," and explained it as a natural attribute of a democratic society without inherited class status.[16]

A society which emphasizes achievement, which denies status based on ancestry or even long-past personal achievements, must necessarily be a society in which men are sensitively oriented toward others, in which, to use Riesman's analogy, they employ a radar to keep their social equilibrium. And precisely as we become more equalitarian, as the lower strata attain citizenship, as more people are able to take part in the status race, to that extent do we, and other peoples as well, become more concerned with the opinions of others, and therefore more democratic and more American in the Tocquevillian sense.

[14] Harriet Martineau, *Society in America*, Vol. II (New York: Saunders and Otley, 1837), pp. 158–59.

[15] *Ibid.*, pp. 160–61.

[16] Max Weber, *Essays in Sociology* (New York: Oxford University Press, 1946), p. 188.

The politics of democracy are to some extent necessarily the politics of conformity for the elite of the society. As soon as the masses have access to the society's elite, as soon as they must consider mass reaction in determining their own actions, the freedom of the elite (whether political or artistic) is limited. As Tocqueville pointed out, the "most serious reproach which can be addressed" to democratic republics is that they "extend the practice of currying favor with the many and introduce it into all classes at once," and he attributed "the small number of distinguished men in political life to the ever increasing despotism of the majority in the United States."[17]

The same point has been made in Chapter 10 in regard to much of the discussion about the negative consequences of mass culture. Increased access by the mass of the population to the culture market necessarily means a limitation in cultural taste as compared to a time or a country in which culture is limited to the well to do and the well educated.

The current debates on education reflect the same dilemma—that many who believe in democracy and equalitarianism would also like to preserve some of the attributes of an elitist society. In England, where the integrated "comprehensive" school is seen as a progressive reform, the argument for it is based on the assumption that the health of the society is best served by what is best for the largest number. This argument was used in this country when liberal educators urged that special treatment for the gifted child served to perpetuate inequality and that it rewarded those from

[17] Alexis de Tocqueville, *Democracy in America*, Vol. I (New York: Vintage Books, 1954), pp. 276, 277. Of course, Plato made the same points 2500 years ago when he argued that in a democracy, the father "accustoms himself to become like his child and to fear his sons, and the son in his desire for freedom becomes like his father and has no fear or reverence for his parent. . . . The school master fears and flatters his pupils . . . while the old men condescend to the young and become triumphs of versatility. . . . The main result of all these things, taken together, is that it makes the souls of the citizens . . . sensitive." *The Republic of Plato*, ed. by Ernest Rhys (London: J. M. Dent and Co., 1935), pp. 200–26.

better home and class environments at the expense of those from poorer backgrounds. Educators in Britain today argue strongly that separate schools for brighter children (the so-called "grammar schools") are a source of psychic punishment for the less gifted. Many of us have forgotten that liberals in this country shared similar sentiments not too long ago; that, for example, Fiorello La Guardia, as Mayor of New York, abolished Townsend Harris High School, a special school for gifted boys in which four years of school work were completed in three, on the ground that the very existence of such a school was undemocratic, that it gave special privileges to a minority.

What I am saying is simply that we cannot have our cake and eat it too. We cannot have the advantages of an aristocratic *and* a democratic society; we cannot have segregated elite schools in a society which stresses equality; we cannot have a cultural elite which produces without regard to mass taste in a society which emphasizes the value of popular judgment. By the same token we cannot have a low divorce rate and end differentiation in sex roles, and we cannot expect to have secure adolescents in a culture which offers no definitive path from adolescence to adulthood.

I do not mean to suggest that a democratic society can do nothing about reducing conformity or increasing creativity. There is considerable evidence to suggest that higher education, greater economic security, and higher standards of living strengthen the level of culture and democratic freedom. The market for good books, good paintings, and good music is at a high point in American history.[18] There is evidence that tolerance for ethnic minorities too is greater than in the past. More people are receiving a good education in America today than ever before, and regardless of the many weaknesses of that education, it is still true that the more of it one has,

[18] See Daniel Bell, "The Theory of Mass Society," *Commentary*, 22 (1956), p. 82 and Clyde Kluckhohn, "Shifts in American Values," *World Politics*, 11 (1959), pp. 250–61, for evidence concerning the growth rather than the decline of "genuine individuality in the United States."

the better one's values and consumption patterns from the point of view of the liberal and culturally concerned intellectual.

There is a further point about the presumed growth of conformity and the decline in ideology which has been made by various analysts who rightly fear the inherent conformist aspects of populist democracy. They suggest that the growth of large bureaucratic organizations, an endemic aspect of modern industrial society, whether capitalist or socialist, is reducing the scope of individual freedom because "organization men" must conform to succeed. This point is sometimes linked to the decline in the intensity of political conflict, because politics is seen as changing into administration as the manager and expert take over in government as well as in business. From James Burnham's *Managerial Revolution* to more recent restatements of this thesis by Peter Drucker and others, this trend has been sometimes welcomed, but more often in recent years deplored.

The growth of large organizations may, however, actually have the more important consequences of providing new sources of continued freedom and more opportunity to innovate. Bureaucratization means (among other things) a decline of the arbitrary power of those in authority. By establishing norms of fair and equal treatment, and by reducing the unlimited power possessed by the leaders of many non-bureaucratic organizations, bureaucracy may mean less rather than greater need to conform to superiors. In spite of the emergence of security tests, I think that there is little doubt that men are much less likely to be fired from their jobs for their opinions and behavior today than they were fifty or even twenty-five years ago. Anyone who compares the position of a worker or an executive in a family-owned corporation like the Ford Motor Company when its founder was running it to that of comparably placed people in General Motors or today's Ford Motor Company can hardly argue that bureaucratization has meant greater pressure to conform on any level of industry. Trade-unions accurately reflect their members' desires when they move in the direction of greater bureaucratization by winning, for example, seniority rules in hiring, firing, and promotion, or a stable three-year contract with detailed provisions for grievance procedures. Unionization, of both manual and white-collar workers, increases under conditions of large-scale organization and serves to free the worker or employee from subjection to relatively uncontrolled power. Those who fear the subjection of the workers to the organizational power of unionism ignore for the most part the alternative of arbitrary management power. In many ways the employee of a large corporation who is the subject of controversy between two giant organizations—the company and the union—has a much higher degree of freedom than one not in a large organization.

Although the pressures toward conformity within democratic and bureaucratic society are an appropriate source of serious concern for Western intellectuals, my reading of the historical evidence suggests that the problem is less acute or threatening today than it has been in the past, if we limit our analysis to domestic threats to the system. There is reason to expect that stable democratic institutions in which individual political freedom is great and even increasing (as it is, say, in Britain or Sweden) will continue to characterize the mature industrialized Western societies.

The controversies about cultural creativity and conformity reflect the general trend discussed at the beginning of the chapter—the shift away from ideology towards sociology. The very growth of sociology as an intellectual force outside the academy in many Western nations is a tribute, not primarily to the power of sociological analysis but to the loss of interest in political inquiry. It may seem curious, therefore, for a sociologist to end on a note of concern about this trend. But I believe that there is still a real need for political analysis, ideology, and controversy within the world community, if not within the Western democracies. In a larger sense, the domestic controversies within the advanced democratic countries have become comparable to struggles within American party primary elections. Like all nomination contests, they are fought to determine who will lead the party, in this case the democratic camp, in the larger political struggle in the world as a whole with its marginal constituencies, the underdeveloped states. The horizon of intellectual political concerns must turn from the new version of local elections—those which determine who will run national administrations—to this larger contest.

This larger fight makes politics much more complex in the various underdeveloped countries than it appears within Western democracies. In these states there is still a need for intense political controversy and ideology. The problems of industrialization, of the place of religion, of the character of political institutions are still unsettled, and the arguments about them have become intertwined with the international struggle. The past political relations between former colonial countries and the West, between colored and white peoples, make the task even more difficult. It is necessary for us to recognize that our allies in the underdeveloped countries must be radicals, probably socialists, because only parties which promise to improve the situation of the masses through widespread reform, and which are transvaluational and equalitarian, can hope to compete with the Communists. Asian and African socialist movements, even where they are committed to political democracy (and unfortunately not all of them are, or can be even if they want to), must often express hostility to many of the economic, political, and religious institutions of the West.

Where radicals are in power—in India, Ghana, Ceylon, Burma, and other countries—they must take responsibility for the economic development of the country, and hence must suffer the brunt of the resentments caused by industrialization, rapid urbanization, bad housing, and extreme poverty. The democratic leftist leader must find a scapegoat to blame for these ills—domestic capitalists, foreign investors, or the machinations of the departed imperialists. If he does not, he will lose his hold on the masses who need the hope implicit in revolutionary chiliastic doctrine—a hope the Communists are ready to supply. The socialist in power in an underdeveloped country must continue, therefore, to lead a revolutionary struggle against capitalism, the western imperialists, and, increasingly, against Christianity as the dominant remaining foreign institution. If he accepts the arguments of Western socialists that the West has changed, that complete socialism is dangerous, that Marxism is an outmoded doctrine, he becomes a conservative within his own society, a role he cannot play and still retain a popular following.

The leftist intellectual, the trade-union leader, and the socialist politician in the West have an important role to play in this political struggle. By virtue of the fact that they still represent the tradition of socialism and equalitarianism within their own countries, they can find an audience among the leaders of the non-Communist left in those nations where socialism and trade-unionism cannot be conservative or even gradualist. To demand that such leaders adapt their politics to Western images of responsible behavior is to forget that many Western unions, socialist parties, and intellectuals were similarly "irresponsible and demagogic" in the early stages of their development. Today Western leaders must communicate and work with non-Communist revolutionaries in the Orient and Africa at the same time that they accept the fact that serious ideological controversies have ended at home.

This book's concern with making explicit the conditions of the democratic order reflects my perhaps overrationalistic belief that a fuller understanding of the various conditions under which democracy has existed may help men to develop it where it does not now exist. Although we have concluded that Aristotle's basic hypothesis of the relationship of democracy to a class structure bulging toward the middle (discussed initially in Chapter 2) is still valid, this does not encourage political optimism, since it implies that political activity should be directed primarily toward assuring economic development. Yet we must not be unduly pessimistic. Democracy has existed in a variety of circumstances, even if it is most commonly sustained by a limited set of conditions. It cannot be achieved by acts of will alone, of course, but men's wills expressed in action can shape institutions and events in directions that reduce or increase the chances for democracy's development and survival. Ideology and passion may no longer be necessary to sustain the class struggle within stable and affluent democracies, but they are clearly needed in the international effort to develop free political and economic institutions in the rest of the world. It is only the ideological class struggle within the West which is ending. Ideological conflicts linked to levels and problems of economic development and of appropriate political institutions among different nations will last far beyond our lifetime, and men committed to democracy can abstain from them only at their peril. To aid men's actions in furthering democracy in then absolutist Europe was in some measure Tocqueville's purpose in studying the operation of American society in 1830. To clarify the operation of Western democracy in the mid-twentieth century may contribute to the political battle in Asia and Africa.

NAME INDEX

SUBJECT INDEX

ANCHOR BOOKS

SOCIOLOGY

ANCHOR BOOKS

GOVERNMENT AND POLITICAL SCIENCE

ANCHOR BOOKS

PSYCHOLOGY

ANCHOR BOOKS

PHILOSOPHY AND RELIGION